ONE HUNDRED PERCENT AMERICAN

The Rebirth and Decline of the Ku Klux Klan in the 1920s

Thomas R. Pegram

IVAN R. DEE
CHICAGO

Published by Ivan R. Dee
An imprint of The Rowman & Littlefield Publishing Group, Inc.
4501 Forbes Boulevard, Suite 200, Lanham, Maryland 20706
http://www.rowmanlittlefield.com

Estover Road, Plymouth PL6 7PY, United Kingdom

Distributed by National Book Network

www.ivanrdee.com

Library of Congress Cataloging-in-Publication Data:

Pegram, Thomas R., 1955–
   One hundred percent American : the rebirth and decline of the Ku Klux Klan in the
1920s / Thomas Pegram.
      p. cm.
   Includes bibliographical references and index.
   ISBN 978-1-56663-711-4 (cloth : alk. paper) — ISBN 978-1-56663-922-4 (electronic)
   1. Ku Klux Klan (1915–) 2. Racism—United States—History—20th century.
   3. United States—Social conditions—1918–1932. I. Title.
HS2330.K63P46 2011
322.4'20973—dc22   2011008672

To the Pegrams and the Ingrams:
from the 1920s to today

Contents

Preface

To most contemporary Americans, the Ku Klux Klan of the 1920s is a curious artifact from a bygone age. The pointed hoods, nonsensical terminology, and bigoted ideology of the Invisible Empire appeared anachronistic even in the 1920s as the United States absorbed immigrants from around the globe and began the slow process of reconciling American democracy with racial, ethnic, and cultural pluralism. Today, in a nation presided over by a president from a mixed-race background, the preoccupations of the Klan seem even more remote. The sharp racial and ethnic divisions that in the Klan's worldview determined fitness for citizenship and separated authentic American identity from alien allegiances contrast markedly with a more diverse and open public culture. Contemporary Klansmen are despised as violent troublemakers skulking on the margins of society. Yet even from our vantage point in the early twenty-first century, the Klan phenomenon of the New Era—as Americans called the years after World War I—has relevance.

The American profile is now broader than the native-born Protestant characteristics defended by the Invisible Empire, but disagreement over the nature of American identity persists into our time. Distracted opponents of President Barack Obama insist that he is not a true American eligible to hold the nation's highest office. Others strain to curtail unregulated immigration, complaining that the flow of undocumented newcomers undermines the rule of law and endangers the economic interests and cultural rights of Americans. Catholics and Jews, the special targets of the New Era Klan, now reside comfortably within the American mainstream, but a substantial number of Americans consider another religious tradition, Islam, to be incompatible with the social and political institutions of the nation. All these contemporary issues are contested, but so too were the disputes of the 1920s in which the Invisible Empire engaged.

The 1920s Klan also invites our attention because it was a massive social movement that helped to shape our collective past. Between 1920 and 1925 it attracted several million members and exercised substantial influence in many American communities. As I researched this book, I discovered the degree to which the Klan movement had prospered in the familiar places of my life. I was born in Indiana, the hotbed of the Northern Klan movement. The family of my paternal grandparents, southern Indiana Baptists, conceivably could have included Klan members. Among my descendants on the maternal side was a German Lutheran saloon keeper of the type often targeted by prohibitionist Klansmen. After living in Ohio, close to the Klan meeting grounds at Buckeye Lake, I resided in a Pennsylvania community next to Carnegie, the site of a major anti-Klan riot in 1923. My family later moved to California and established a home in Brea, a small oil town dominated by a Ku Klux government in the 1920s. Even as I pursued graduate studies in Massachusetts, meadows on which Klansmen and their antagonists battled in 1924 and 1925 lay within thirty miles. Each of these communities seemed quite ordinary, but all had been touched by the turbulent Klan phenomenon. Understanding the history of the hooded organization therefore became one way of comprehending my own—and America's—historical lineage.

Scholarly opinion of the New Era Klan has shifted considerably over the last generation. Beginning in the 1980s and accelerating in the 1990s, historians reconsidered the image of the 1920s Invisible Empire as a violent, racially oppressive fringe movement populated by the rootless and defeated stragglers left behind by the nation's march to modernity. Building on earlier insights from Charles C. Alexander and Kenneth Jackson, scholars such as Leonard Moore and Shawn Lay deemphasized the national Klan organization and instead paid close attention to local manifestations of the Klan movement, often in Midwestern or Pacific Coast communities. A series of Klan community studies revealed the degree to which the Invisible Empire flourished at the grassroots level, reflecting a sense of American identity and civic engagement that was shared by many white Protestant Americans in the aftermath of World War I. Fraternal fellowship, community-building, reform of local government, and close attention to public schools, law enforcement, and proper moral comportment distinguished these Klansmen from the night-riding Ku Kluxers of earlier historiography.

The proponents of this populist or civic interpretation of the New Era Klan presented vigilantism as a minor theme in the grassroots Klan movement, confined chiefly to violence-prone regions of the South and Southwest. The unmistakable hooded emphasis on white supremacy, anti-Catholicism, and Protestant cultural chauvinism approximated broader patterns of intolerance that beset the United States in the 1920s. In short, the new interpretation of the Klan stressed how representative and mainstream were the attributes of the hooded order. In this view, the Klan phenomenon also was most authentic and vigorous as a social movement at the klavern, or local club, level. The national Klan's drive for political influence and mainstream acceptance, spearheaded by Imperial Wizard Hiram W. Evans, vainly sought to reproduce the civic accomplishments of local Klans on state and federal levels.

The last generation of Klan studies has clarified the interior life of local Klans and the civic activism that motivated many knights. But taken as a whole, the new Klan literature is incomplete. The violence and exclusionary politics that compelled attention to the Invisible Empire seem at odds with the citizen Klansmen highlighted in recent local studies. No general history of the 1920s Klan phenomenon reflects the new research and perspectives on the Klan movement. Nor is there an updated analysis of the movement that brings the fullness of the Klan experience from that period into balance. Ties of belief and a commitment to bold action linked the moral vigilantism of Southwestern knights with the school board politics and voluntary prohibition enforcement that occupied Midwestern Klansman. *One Hundred Percent American* is a new, comprehensive portrait of the New Era Invisible Empire that recognizes the diversity of the Klan movement while charting the shared patterns that determined the organization's rise and fall. The book situates the Klan within mainstream developments in American postwar life but also explains why the Klan failed to achieve mainstream status in the 1920s.

I have tried to rethink the history of the 1920s Klan by drawing on the rich inventory of theses, dissertations, articles, and focused studies of local or state Klans that have accumulated since the revival of Klan scholarship. The recent unpublished literature, which has been underused by historians, has been an especially important resource in this study. I have also sought to contextualize the New Era Klan movement in the light of new studies of race, ethnicity, political culture, social reform, and governance that have enriched the historical understanding of the post–World War I United States. Revisiting the documentary record of the Klan and the contemporary analysis of the movement provided by insightful New Era journalists helps connect the scattered Klan community studies into a more comprehensive examination of the hooded order's expansion, operations, and collapse. I have tried to supply more thorough analyses of community formation among Klansmen, the power of racial identity and anti-Catholicism in the hooded movement, and such topics as education reform, prohibition enforcement, violence, and political organization than are now available. Close attention to these issues also illuminates the tension between local Klans and the national organization that provoked the sudden and rapid decline of the Invisible Empire at mid-decade.

I hope this book will also advance discussion of the Klan movement's flirtation with the American mainstream of the New Era. The hooded empire clearly was not an anomalous development in the 1920s. It shared many of the same patterns and influences that distinguished American society in the wake of World War I. The collective weight of the new Klan community studies further emphasizes the representative qualities of 1920s Klansmen. Yet the Klan movement only approached the American mainstream of the 1920s, which was increasingly pluralistic if still not fully participatory.

Ku Kluxers never comfortably occupied the mainstream because the Invisible Empire aroused bitter contemporary opposition and denunciation. Anti-Klan sentiment extended beyond the groups specifically targeted by the Invisible Empire to the white Protestant establishment itself. Immediate and sustained criticism of the organization's secrecy, masks, and vigilantism was evident throughout the New Era. Several states took action to banish the Klan or passed anti-mask laws to break up its public events. Even in an age when assumptions of white supremacy, unembarrassed ethnic chauvinism, and religious intolerance toward Catholics and Jews were commonplace, the Klan's expression of these themes was deemed incendiary and objectionable. Nor were the Klan's public policy positions accepted as uncomplicated contributions to public life. Its civic stances in support of public schools and law enforcement were clearly tainted with anti-Catholicism and suspicion of immigrants. Local Klans frequently incorporated into their school reform proposals the demand that Catholic teachers and administrators be fired from public schools.

To consider the Klan a mainstream interest group defending beleaguered Protestant social and cultural standards, therefore, is to drain the contemporary controversy from the Invisible Empire. The new Klan historians have done a service in placing the revived Klan squarely at the center of the social, cultural, and political turbulence of what the historian David J. Goldberg has termed the discontented America of the 1920s.[1] In its assertion of what it saw as embattled American values, the hooded order incorporated reform themes from the populist and progressive traditions, as well as patterns of bigotry and repression that had deep roots in American society. And in areas with thin minority populations, such as Indiana and Oklahoma, where white Protestant domination was assured, the Klan was more likely to be regarded, at least temporarily, as a legitimate participant in civic discourse.

But it is an overstatement to characterize the second Klan as a mainstream proponent of culturally based reform. The 1920s Klan interacted with the mainstream and attracted the short-term loyalty of many ordinary Americans, but it was not, even when judged by its own intention to wield stealthy influence, a mainstream organization. One historian of the Klan, David A. Horowitz, has reflected the ambiguous position of the Invisible Empire in 1920s society by describing "the normality of extremism" evident in the "widespread legitimacy and pervasive appeal" of a masked, secret society that nevertheless lost members nearly as quickly as it recruited them.[2] In the end, however, Ku Klux extremism overwhelmed the community-based features of hooded fellowship, white Protestant identity, and local activism that had attracted many knights to the organization. Persistent violence committed by and against Klansmen, the arrogance and misbehavior of hooded leaders, and an ill-considered grab at political power drove disaffected knights out of the organization halfway through the 1920s. But it is an indication of the Klan's significance as a social movement and of the discordant cultural negotiations of the postwar period that so many average citizens were compelled to articulate their understanding of Americanism through such an extraordinary and flawed instrument.

Acknowledgments

WRITING A BOOK is a solitary and somewhat selfish enterprise, but, as with much else in life, the process fundamentally depends on the goodwill and talents of others. Once again I have been superbly assisted in my labors. Ivan Dee encouraged me to undertake a study of the 1920s Klan. As the book neared completion, he piloted me through the turbulent changes in the publishing industry. After I finished the manuscript, he edited the book with dispatch and uncommon acumen. It is a source of pride for me that this book will carry the Ivan R. Dee imprint.

My history department colleagues at Loyola University Maryland have listened for years to my Klan stories and inspired me with their scholarly commitment and accomplishments. I presented the first chapter to a department works-in-progress seminar and profited from their insightful remarks, particularly those of Chuck Cheape, Jack Breihan, Keith Schoppa, and Steve Hughes. Annual presentations of my unfolding research in the history methods course taught by Betsy Schmidt, Katherine Brennan, and Angela Leonard helped me sharpen my approach to the material. Conversations with Matt Mulcahy touching on the challenges of balancing scholarship and teaching helped keep me going as I conducted research and then tried to write during summer breaks and stolen moments in busy semesters. I am profoundly indebted to Chuck Cheape. He read and commented on every chapter of the book, listened to early-morning and late-afternoon ramblings, and served as an exemplary model of discipline, analytical precision, and personal modesty. It is both an advantage and a challenge to work next door to such a figure, but, most of all, it has been a pleasure.

Time, money, and materials have come from a variety of sources. Timothy Law Snyder, Loyola's vice president for academic affairs, deserves my thanks for a summer research grant that helped me draft several chapters. There would be no book without the swift and efficient work of Peggy Feild and the Inter-Library Loan office at the Loyola–Notre Dame Library. Archivists and librarians at the Indiana Historical Society, the Indiana State Library, the Ohio Historical Society, the University of Oregon Libraries, the University of Maryland Libraries, and the DePauw University Library helped me acquire important manuscript material. Alan Lessoff generously permitted me to reuse material originally published in "Hoodwinked: The Anti-Saloon League and the Ku Klux Klan in 1920s Prohibition Enforcement," which appeared in the *Journal of the Gilded Age and Progressive Era* 7 (January 2008): 89–119. Mark P. Richard sent me several useful citations uncovered in his research on the New England Klan. As a relative newcomer to the serious historical study of the 1920s Klan, I received helpful comments over the years from Shawn Lay and Len Moore, which allowed me to get my bearings in the field. Their pivotal studies of the Klan movement, in combination with the work of Charles C. Alexander, helped shape my perspective on the 1920s Klan. The notes attest to my reliance on the fine scholarship, much of it unpublished, of historians who have studied local outposts of the Invisible Empire.

Life with my family nourished me as I worked, though the book was more of a complication than a contribution to family affairs. My sons, Tavish and Rafferty, were starting elementary school when I published my last book. Today they are virtually adults and quite capable of puncturing any academic affectation on my part ("Wasn't that book manuscript due two years ago?" one or the other would ask). They should know that their character and accomplishments are a ceaseless source of joy to their parents. Patty Ingram read and commented less on this book than she has on other projects, but her impact is just as powerful on this work. Her intelligence, passion, and commitment are essential elements of our entwined lives. The dedication is a reminder that our bond extends back to the 1920s—our parents' generation.

T. R. P.
Baltimore, Maryland
March 2011

ONE HUNDRED PERCENT AMERICAN

1

The Klan in 1920s Society

O N A FEBRUARY NIGHT IN 1925, three blocks from the District of Columbia line and within walking distance of the Catholic University of America, several hooded figures from Klan No. 51 of Mt. Rainier, Maryland, ignited the fiery trademark of their order, a flaming cross, next to the public school.[1] After the revival of the Ku Klux Klan in 1915, and especially after local Klan movements erupted across the United States from 1921 on, drawing two to four million men, women, and children into various Klan associations, the burning cross had come to symbolize the complicated, contradictory energy of the Invisible Empire. Cross burnings were the Klan's most spectacular and entertaining public displays, accompaniments to the outdoor "naturalization" ceremonies that inducted initiates into the order, reinforced the fraternal bonds among Klansmen, and, according to eyewitness testimony, thrilled the often large crowds of onlookers attending the events.

On the other hand, the flame and the silent, hooded figures grouped around it in the darkness conveyed an equally apparent message of intolerance, intimidation, even malevolence toward those outside the fraternity of white Protestant values and behavior. The Klan had, after all, taken it upon itself to enforce the legal, moral, and cultural standards of its own community as guidelines for proper "Americanism." Catholics; bootleggers and other prohibition law violators; unfaithful husbands; sexually adventurous women; indiscreet, successful, or assertive blacks, Jews, or immigrants; even corrupt or unresponsive public officials—all found themselves targeted by organized, often extralegal, Klan activism. The fiery cross of the 1920s was a threat as well as a beacon.

The activities of Klan No. 51 over the preceding two years had reflected the peculiar mixture of fraternal benevolence, political engagement, religious intolerance, and moral policing that marked the Klan movement throughout the United States. As was common in any lodge, Mt. Rainier Klansmen collected money for Christmas donations and needy families, visited sick fellow knights, and decorated the graves and comforted the survivors of those who had died. Charitable work, however, was but part of a larger commitment to moral regulation. The Mt. Rainier klavern also helped fund a mother's legal effort to regain custody of her children, thus restoring proper family relations in the Klan's idealized Protestant commonwealth.[2] Klansmen themselves were expected to meet their fraternal and family obligations. A wayward knight from Klan No. 51 was formally banished from the order for "nonpayment of dues and desertion of family."[3] Other aspects of the group's moral stewardship edged toward vigilantism. Although there is no evidence that Mt. Rainier Klansmen followed the brutal example of Southwestern knights and beat abusive husbands, the klavern excitedly moved to investigate requests for intervention against men who were reportedly "misusing" their wives, some of the members emphasizing that it "was the duty of a Klansman" to act in such cases.[4] Grateful relatives of the distressed women became vocal supporters of Klan No. 51.

The politics of law enforcement and public schools, key elements of Klan concern nationwide, also dominated the attention of Mt. Rainier's klavern. Its political committees emphasized races for state's attorney and attorney general, both responsible for prosecuting crimes, and the membership commended the mayor for "his loyal stand on law and order."[5] As with moral regulation, the Mt. Rainier Klansmen advocated direct intervention into politics. Counseled by its political committees to "endorse their men for public offices,"[6] position knights "at the polls to talk them up," and vote "as a unit,"[7] Klan No. 51 advanced its members as candidates for mayor, school board trustee, and superintendent of school repairs.

Bigotry and hints of extralegal pressure combined with public spirit in motivating the Klan's participation in the politics of schools and crime. A Klan investigator warned that a candidate for attorney general initially supported by the local klavern was "a Fourth degree 'Casey,'" a member of the reviled Catholic fraternal order the Knights of Columbus.[8] Similarly, Klan interest in the school offices was sparked by a report that an objectionable candidate, probably a non-Protestant, would be named head of the repair department.[9] Even though this position involved little contact with children or control over public school policy, Mt. Rainier Klansmen authorized a representative to confront a "surprised" school official about it.[10] The hooded delegate revealed his identity as a Klansman and personally presented the klavern's case against the favored candidate. The Klan's obsession with race and ethnicity even led to extreme measures against its own members. An applicant for naturalization in Klan No. 51, soon to be an active Klansman, was not welcomed into fraternal embrace until the kligrapp, or secretary, of the klavern made an official inquiry to the Pennsylvania Bureau of Statistics "to ascertain if [the candidate] is Gentile or Jew."[11]

Thus the Klansmen who gathered a few miles from the capitol in February 1925 represented a complicated social movement of great force. On this particular night, however, the cross-burning ritual was not an expression of the Klan's swift rise to prominence and power but rather a reflection of its equally rapid collapse at mid-decade. The Mt. Rainier Klan had recently suffered from sporadic attendance at meetings, even among officers, and frequent nonpayment of dues. The flaming cross set up next to the public schoolhouse was part of an effort to restore the sagging energy of the local Klan movement.[12]

What transpired next, however, did not inspire hope. The Mt. Rainier Fire Department drove up to the assembled Klansmen, reported the sober minutes of the next klonklave, and "several of the fire company went up and cut the guide wires of the cross and put it out with the chemical truck." Where once there had been flames, excitement, and threatening postures, there were only cinders, frustrated Klansmen, and "gos[s]ip[ping]" neighbors.[13] Within a year, critics of the Klan across the nation joined Kansan William Allen White in deriding the "nightshirt"-wearing "hate factory and bigotorium now laughed into a busted community."[14] By 1925 the community of the Klan was fatally damaged, but the critical blows had not come from the enemies of the hooded order, despite the energy and determination of their work against the Klan. Instead, rank-and-file Klansmen abandoned the Invisible Empire when local political failures, moral and financial scandals involving prominent Klan officers nationwide, and corrosive disputes within klaverns or between local Klans and the national headquarters in Atlanta—over finances, policy, and jurisdiction—destroyed the cohesiveness of the movement and its effectiveness as an instrument of moral regulation.

A New Klan in a New Era

The 1920s Klan induced both fear and ridicule during its short, convulsive career, but it was anchored in the social context and everyday circumstances of the New Era. The workmanlike manner in which the firefighters extinguished the blazing cross suggests another quality of the 1920s Klan movement that has complicated the historical interpretation of the hooded order: its ordinariness. On the one hand, the 1920s Klan was clearly and, to some extent, deliberately exotic. The masks and robes, the elaborate ritual, the pompous and complex nomenclature that even many Klan officials failed to master, even the baroque compendium of threats to American values that Klansmen recited—all these identified the Klan movement as unusual and mysterious. Beyond appearances, the compulsive secrecy of the order, its taste for vigilantism, and well-publicized cases of Klan violence in the 1920s marked the Ku Klux Klan as sinister and extremist.

Yet for a short span of time there was an ordinary, everyday quality to the Klan's presence in the still-dominant white Protestant America of the 1920s.[15] While secret, Klan membership in many communities was nonetheless an open secret and included public officials, Protestant ministers, and ordinary and prominent citizens alike. During the three years in which the Klan flourished in the small city of Monticello, Arkansas, its roster included the mayor, the city marshal, half the city council, the sheriff, the county school superintendent, the county clerk, the treasurer, the tax assessor, the coroner, and eleven of the fifteen male teachers and administrators at the local agricultural college.[16] The Invisible Empire in Indiana was so tightly interwoven into the fabric of society that newspapers regularly advertised Klan events. Klan members there felt comfortable marching in public without masks, and many former participants expressed the view that "everyone was in the Klan."[17]

Many joined the Klan for fraternal and social reasons or to pursue local political issues. Even the racism, religious bigotry, and ethnic chauvinism that pervaded the rhetoric and policies of the Invisible Empire could be found, in more muted form, in the common white Protestant prejudices of the era. Indeed, most recent examinations of the 1920s Klan in specific communities have treated the Klan phenomenon less as an underground movement of alienated and sometimes violent dissenters from the patterns of modern America and more as an intensified expression of widely shared civic and moral values that many concerned local citizens judged to be threatened by dramatic cultural change in the aftermath of World War I.

The second Ku Klux Klan was both a product and a reflection of the distinctive patterns of postwar America. Even though the name, the air of secrecy, the devotion to white supremacy, and the robed and hooded regalia of the 1920s Klan was borrowed from the original Reconstruction-era Klan, there were few direct ties between the national popular movement of the 1920s and its regionally restricted, night-riding predecessor. "The old Klan was liquidated when its work was finished," Hiram W. Evans, the second imperial wizard of the 1920s, assured a reporter. "The new Klan has no essential connection with it."[18] The first Klan arose from political and social circumstances in the immediate aftermath of the Civil War.[19] Organized in Tennessee by disgruntled former Confederate soldiers, the Klan, in addition to some ritualistic and cultural elements, was an explicitly political terrorist organization committed to driving Republican policies and newly enfranchised blacks from the public life of the South. Klan violence and intimidation escalated until Congress passed anti-Klan legislation, which by 1872 allowed prosecutors and federal troops to suppress the hooded order forcibly even though the Klansmen's goal of returning white, conservative rule to the Southern states was realized during that decade.

The second Klan, reorganized nearly forty-five years later, also portrayed itself as a cleansing force in politics. But in contrast to the first incarnation of the Invisible Empire, the Klan revival built upon twentieth-century developments such as mass entertainment and leisure, patriotic voluntary associations, advertising and the go-go economic style of the 1920s. Moreover, the cultural balkanization of the urban, industrialized, pluralistic United States into a racialized, religious tribalism, to use the historian John Higham's term, produced a greater range of potential enemies for the new Klan to confront.[20]

The second Klan was born in 1915, yet it did not prosper until 1921. Its founder, Alabaman William J. Simmons, claimed to be the son of an original Klansman, but his vision for the renewal of the hooded order was primarily fraternal.[21] A middle-class itinerant of grand gestures, dissolute habits, and only mild career success as a soldier, farmer, history teacher, Methodist minister, and fraternal lodge organizer for the Woodmen of the World (from whom he gained the title colonel), Simmons reveled in the intricacies of fraternal ritual. While rehabilitating from a serious automobile accident, he developed the elaborate catalogue of titles, rules, and procedures for the Klan, then moved to organize the lodge when D. W. Griffith's landmark film *The Birth of a Nation*, which presented a heroic image of the Reconstruction Klan as the defender of white womanhood and Christian civilization, sparked new interest in the Invisible Empire. A monument to the inspirational power— and propaganda value—of the new art of cinema, *The Birth of a Nation*, when revived in theaters or special showings, eventually played a significant role in the organization of a nationwide Klan in 1921. Yet in 1915, after the dramatic inauguration of the second Klan on Stone Mountain outside Atlanta, the new lodge stagnated. During World War I, Simmons offered the services of his secret knights to the hyperpatriotic American Protective League, a self-appointed "band of amateur sleuths and loyalty enforcers"[22] who by extralegal surveillance and occasional use of roughhouse methods intimidated slackers, strikers, and suspected subversives. These wartime adventures[23] ingrained the tendency toward suspicion and vigilantism in the Klan, but the Ku Kluxers were active only in a handful of Georgia and Alabama cities and mustered fewer than two thousand members.[24]

The Invisible Empire became a national phenomenon only after Simmons in 1920 hired the Southern Publicity Association, a partnership of two professional marketing agents, Elizabeth Tyler and Edward Young Clarke, who previously had raised money for charities and political interest groups, to promote the Klan.[25] By targeting existing men's lodges and Protestant churches as likely sources for recruiting, or kluxing, fresh Klansmen in an age of eager, yet racially and religiously exclusive, camaraderie; by extolling the new order as a benevolent and patriotic men's organization at a moment of labor unrest, racial tension, and anti-radical sentiment; and by hiring professional salesmen, called kleagles, to sign up new members in return for four dollars from every ten-dollar initiation fee, the Southern Publicity Association used modern marketing and mass mobilization techniques to build a movement committed to the defense of tradition but rooted in the social context of the 1920s. The Klan not only arranged for screenings of *The Birth of a Nation* to attract members but it also produced and distributed its own propaganda films, such as *The Toll of Justice* and *The Traitor Within*.[26] As a marketing gambit, Clarke, who became the public face of the recruiting drive, offered Protestant ministers free membership in the hooded order. Often by prearrangement, a small group of hooded Klansmen would appear at a Sunday service, make a donation to the church, and thereby announce the local presence of the Invisible Empire. Similarly, armed with the knowledge that American fraternalists, much like Simmons himself, sought fellowship through simultaneous membership in several lodges, kleagles glad-handed their way through the meeting halls of the Masons, Elks, Odd Fellows, Red Men, and other fraternal clubs to draw attention to the Klan.

Even though the major Protestant denominations officially maintained a frosty distance from the Klan, and fraternal bodies, especially the Masons, mounted anti-Klan movements within their lodges, at a popular level the boosterism of Clarke and his kleagles was successful.[27] By 1924 the Klan claimed thirty thousand Protestant ministers had taken the hood as members of the Invisible Empire.[28] A Klan lecturer two years earlier boasted that 75 percent of Klansmen were recruited from the Masons.[29] The numbers may have been inflated, but the patterns were not. Despite controversy and some genuinely heroic opposition against its presence, the Klan became influential in the pulpits and congregations of many Methodist, Baptist, United Brethren, and Disciples of Christ churches, often by tapping deep wells of suspicion toward Roman Catholicism that remained beneath the landscape of early twentieth-century American Protestant culture. Likewise, under a Klan hierarchy that celebrated its ties to the Southern branch of Scottish Rite Freemasonry, the Invisible Empire ignored its fraternal critics and presented itself as "the 'fighting brother' of masonry."[30]

Part of the Klan's appeal was that the Invisible Empire was more broadly Protestant than any particular denomination and more intensely and chauvinistically Protestant than any fraternal order. Evidence from Indiana indicates that evangelicals, nonevangelicals, and self-identifying Protestants without a church affiliation all joined the Klan.[31] This last group of unchurched "cultural Protestants" composed from a third to roughly half the membership of many Western and Midwestern klaverns. A Denver Klan official (and Protestant minister) applauded the fact that the hooded order "includes more Protestants who are without the church than it does those that are within it," thus "gathering together the great arm of Protestantism into a single unit and counteracting the great tragedy of Protestantism, namely its division."[32] Within the often contentious confines of the klavern, doctrinal differences and rivalries between Protestant sects nevertheless were deemphasized in favor of a united front of Protestant political activism against the perception of Catholic influence in public life.

Militant Protestants usually found the Klan preferable to fraternal lodges as a vehicle of Protestant nationalism.[33] Despite their often overwhelmingly Protestant character and membership, fraternal bodies retained less restrictive religious, racial, and ethnic membership policies than did the Klan, tended to be more circumspect in their anti-Catholicism, and often voiced what was at least a rhetorical commitment to tolerance. "The Invisible Empire of the Knights of the Ku Klux Klan is the only 100 per cent American organization I know of in the whole world," enthused one initiate. "All the other organizations, political parties, schools and colleges, churches and lodges, states and nations, admit in one way or another, all nationalities, races and religions."[34] In its firm racial and ethnic exclusivity and its overt anti-Catholicism, the 1920s Ku Klux Klan acted as a sort of superlodge for white Anglo-Saxon Protestants who sought to institutionalize their cultural practices as public policy.

The startling growth of the Ku Klux Klan was also aided by mechanisms of publicity beyond the control of Clarke and Tyler. Newspapers and magazines, which would later contribute to the Klan's fall from prominence, unwittingly assisted the expansion of the Invisible Empire beyond the South. According to a contemporary account, a photographer, after being rebuffed by Clarke and Simmons, paid twenty black men in Atlanta to pose in Klan outfits he had patterned after the costumes worn in *The Birth of a Nation*, then sold the pictures to the press, which distributed them across the country. More sensationally, after reports of Klan violence and misdeeds aroused interest, the *New York World* in 1921 published a series of articles attacking the Invisible Empire, which were syndicated to major newspapers across the nation.[35] Reactions to the articles helped prompt a congressional hearing on the Klan, and

Colonel Simmons was summoned to Washington. Easily distracted and unsystematic as a manager, Simmons was nevertheless a forceful and charismatic
orator, and the imperial wizard turned his testimony into an impassioned
advertisement for the Klan.[36] Denying all charges of violence, prejudice, or
financial opportunism against his creation, Simmons dramatically collapsed
in exhaustion as he called upon God "to forgive those who have persecuted
the Klan."[37] In some confusion, the House Rules Committee shut down its
inquiry.[38]

Instead of disabling the Klan, journalistic and political opponents of the
hooded order buttressed the salesmanship of the kleagles. The *World*'s anti-
Klan publicity campaign of 1921 generated new applications to the Invisible
Empire, with many prospective knights mailing in membership blanks cut
from the pages of the paper's exposé.[39] By the end of the year the Klan had
established a concentrated Southwestern presence in Texas, Oklahoma, Arkansas, and Louisiana, and it then spread to Colorado (a Klan stronghold),
Kansas, and Missouri. Powerful chapters on the West Coast developed in
California and Oregon. The second Klan, under the vigorous kluxing of a
onetime coal dealer named David C. Stephenson, had become especially influential in Indiana, Ohio, and, to a lesser extent, Illinois. The order also was
making inroads from Pennsylvania and New York into New Jersey and pockets of the Northeast and the upper Midwest. Even where it was not dominant,
the Invisible Empire occupied footholds in many other states.

❖

Contested as well as shared themes of the 1920s nourished the Klan movement. "The Klan, indeed, is the concretion, sublimate, and gratification of
the passions in play since the coming of the Great War," exclaimed Horace
Kallen, a pioneering advocate of cultural pluralism and critic of the Invisible
Empire, in 1924.[40] Despite the image of the early 1920s as a self-indulgent,
ephemeral jazz age, the period was marked by a series of interlocking and
historically important confrontations and adjustments that shaped twentieth-
century American institutions, beliefs, and behavior.[41] In international affairs
the United States confronted the consequences of the great-power status its
economic strength and its 1917 intervention in World War I had thrust upon
it. The Klan's loud insistence on 100 percent Americanism (also voiced by
the American Legion and other 1920s associations) and its bitter resistance
to American participation in the League of Nations and the World Court
reflected in exaggerated fashion more widespread concerns that international
engagement could threaten the nation's autonomy. Indeed, the Klan's extravagant charge that the World Court was a "Vatican . . . tool for Romanizing

America"[42] shared an alarmist perspective with Senator James Reed, a Missouri Democrat and a fierce opponent of the hooded order, who nevertheless declared Senate supporters of the international tribunal to be "disloyal."[43]

The debate over international involvement, often conducted as if it were a referendum on the inviolability of American institutions, had its domestic analogue in the quest for home-front loyalty. As American society ended its irresolution over the European war and, following Woodrow Wilson's lead, reimagined the squalid imperial conflict of 1916 as the democratic crusade of 1917, issues of uneven wealth, corporate monopoly, urban infrastructure, and political corruption that had energized the Progressive Era gave way to a heightened concern with "hyphenated" Americans, slackers, and other dissenters from national unity.[44] As the perceptive Kallen put it, "what this war did was to turn the anxiety about property into one about people."[45] The robust patriotism of the war years generated a lingering postwar suspicion of labor unionists, political radicals, recent immigrants, Southern black migrants, and other Americans then considered marginal. In the estimation of the eminent black intellectual W. E. B. DuBois, the revived Klan became the literal representation of the "Shape of Fear" produced by the "great catastrophe" of war.[46] The Red Scare, open-shop labor campaigns, and race riots that accompanied the end of the war exemplified the tumultuous social and cultural atmosphere in which the new Klan's hypersensitive attention to safeguarding an idealized American identity took form.

After the war, Americans continued to struggle with the reality of ethnic and religious pluralism. As a resource-rich and labor-poor nation, the United States had encouraged immigration throughout its period of industrial development from the nineteenth into the early twentieth centuries. During that time the largely English, German, Irish, and African character of the American population became much more ethnically diverse. Moreover, the political and cultural domination exercised by white Protestants was increasingly challenged as Eastern and Southern European immigrants, blacks, Catholics, and Jews carved out pockets of political influence and cultural autonomy in public institutions such as political parties and in privately created communities of neighborhoods, clubs, and associations. The Klan was a created community of its own, celebrating white native-born Protestant civilization within a fraternal framework, but it was also an aggressive counterforce to cultural pluralism.

The Klan argued that white, Protestant values were the standard for true Americanism and demanded that public institutions, especially schools and government, uphold those standards as normative. Hiram W. Evans, Simmons's successor as imperial wizard and the chief architect of the Klan's political program, made explicit the patriotic necessity of the hooded order's opposition to Catholic schools and its battle to prohibit the application of Catholic teachings and the influence of the Holy See from American political discourse. "The Roman Church," he charged in print, "is, fundamentally and irredeemably, in its leadership, in politics, in thought, and largely in membership, actually and actively alien, un-American and usually anti-American."[47] Simmons himself had remarked that the multicultural product of open immigration was not a melting pot but "a garbage can."[48]

Once again, the Invisible Empire's expression of these themes was extreme, but it elaborated upon mainstream concerns. While praising the hooded order's efforts to oust Catholic politicians from city governments, a Fort Worth Baptist minister called his fellow Protestants "the real white folks."[49] One respected journal, in an editorial that criticized the Klan, nevertheless warned that the "alien ideas" of some immigrants represented "disintegrating forces . . . organized to destroy the institutions on which the present strength and freedom of America rest."[50] Another analysis of the Klan accepted the notion of Anglo-Saxon "race suicide" and, without irony, mourned "our vanishing Americans,"[51] clearly identified as white Protestants, even as the population of the United States surged to more than one hundred million. A third journalistic investigation of the Klan expressed sympathy with the proposition "that native-born citizens, trained in the National schools, sons and heirs of the men who built up the Nation, are on the whole better interpreters of National thought and purposes, and hence more fitted to rule the country, than are people of alien blood, tradition, and training."[52] The immigration restrictions contained in the 1924 National Origins Act, which ended the period of free entry into the United States, were the clearest formal manifestation of this confrontation over pluralism, but episodes from the celebrated prosecutions of the Italian anarchists Sacco and Vanzetti to the race riot in 1919 Chicago and the obliteration of black Tulsa neighborhoods in 1921 at the hands of a white mob testified to its power in the postwar years.

The early 1920s also exhibited tensions over structures of governance and behavior that collided in the public and private realms. A generation of progressive state building at the state and federal levels had constructed government agencies dedicated to the protection and welfare of children, mothers, factory workers, farmers, and consumers. This growing commitment to public regulation contrasted with the long, slow ebb of Victorian cultural practices that had emphasized individual responsibility and the firm separation of public regulation from private life. Yet, as the experience of the second Klan demonstrates, state authority and private belief after World War I interacted in complex patterns that blended modern regulatory initiatives with traditional cultural values. Although several historians have identified the 1920s Ku Klux Klan as a reactionary defender of Victorianism, Klansmen were willing to employ state power when the internal gyroscope of Victorian morality failed to set a proper course for American society.[53] Thus the Invisible Empire advocated the creation of a federal Department of Education both to improve public schools and to counterbalance the influence of Catholic education. Klan sentiment in much of the country supported the enfranchisement of women with the expectation that white Protestant women would vote in defense of their social values. Most notably, Klansmen committed their movement to the enforcement of national prohibition.

Yet many Americans, still invested in the individualistic, self-policing, family-centered assumptions of Victorian social relations, were profoundly uncomfortable with government authority that touched on matters of personal choice or family autonomy. "The remorseless urge of centralization, the insatiable maw of bureaucracy," complained Republican senator William Borah of Idaho in this vein in 1925, "are depriving more and more the people of all voice, all rights touching home and hearthstone, of family and neighbor."[54] Defenders of distinctive ethnic patterns of family organization and belief offered similar objections to expanded state powers that appeared to challenge communal or parental rights. "The best kindergarten is the family," insisted late nineteenth-century German immigrants when faced with Midwestern compulsory school laws.[55] American political traditions of local control—for democratic or repressive purposes—and limited government further complicated the transition to modern patterns of public responsibility.

The boldest assertion of state responsibility over individual behavior in the postwar period was the implementation in 1920, after ratification of the Eighteenth Amendment in 1919, of national prohibition of beverage alcohol. Prohibition required amending the Constitution, and the expansion of government personnel and authority necessary to enforce the dry reform would have been unprecedented in peacetime—had they been enacted. But the experience of prohibition also emphatically established the limitations of government regulation of personal behavior. Many Americans, most of them from the same Protestant denominations—Methodists, Baptists, United Brethren, Disciples of Christ—that supplied members to the Klan, enthusiastically favored prohibition as an essential reform that justified the commitment of substantial public resources; yet national and state governments withheld adequate means to enforce it in the face of vigorous opposition from urban, ethnic, and conservative strongholds in the Northeast, on the Pacific Coast, and in other enclaves scattered across the country. In response, the Invisible Empire, which had backed expanded government authority to protect traditional white Protestant behavioral standards, now undertook extralegal steps to regulate behavior when government action proved inadequate.[56] In perhaps the most widely shared collective action of the second

Klan, klaverns throughout the nation organized private raiding parties or joined with sympathetic local lawmen as voluntary deputies to crack down on prohibition violators. Vigilantism in support of law enforcement is a logical contradiction, but to Klansmen who believed they served a higher, or more fundamental, code of Americanism, extralegal methods employed to enforce a law unjustly neglected by established legal authorities was not lawlessness at all but rather the defense of order.

The Klan was also motivated by another confrontation hastened by the fading dictates of Victorian comportment in the 1920s—new patterns of heterosocial leisure and entertainment, sexual behavior, and family life, especially on the part of women. Patriarchy, sexual restraint, and traditional gender norms still prevailed in the 1920s, but the era was more candid and analytical toward marriage, more open in its embrace of an emancipated style of dress and leisure, and afforded the New Woman, in the historian Nancy MacLean's phrase, greater "sexual self-determination."[57] Moreover, the speakeasy society of the prohibition years encouraged a new mixed-gender atmosphere of drinking and sociability that, beyond its defiance of the law, unsettled traditional moralists who still associated public drinking with a coarse masculine culture that was unsuitable for respectable women.[58] The Klan's public pronouncements in support of the family and its anxious moral policing, which extended from masked visitations to unfaithful or irresponsible spouses to patrols of lovers' lanes, suggest a sense of moral crisis motivating the Invisible Empire. MacLean contends that the Klan's moral emphasis aimed to reassert patriarchal control over women, tighten parental authority, and restore family discipline in a context of impending social disorder.[59] These themes are evident in the Klan movement, but as with society in general in the 1920s, repression commingled with assertions of independence among women in Klan auxiliaries, whose vision of white Protestant supremacy included a commitment to women's rights and what normally would be identified as progressive positions.[60]

Rank-and-file Klansmen, who enlisted in the Invisible Empire by the hundreds of thousands each year between 1921 and 1924, thus found a kind of solidarity, comfort, and purpose in the Klan movement that fit their experience in the postwar period. Within the restricted sphere of religious, racial, and often gender exclusivity, the Klan provided meaningful community and sociability for its members. The ritualized brotherhood of ceremonies in the klavern, the secret handclasps, codes, and campaigns encouraging commercial relationships with fellow Klansmen were one aspect of the self-selecting community of the Invisible Empire. But there was an additional public expression of Klan sociability, especially in the Midwestern realms, in the form of picnics (some of them gigantic affairs featuring hot-air balloon rides, displays of horsemanship, athletic contests, and speeches), parades, and concerts which provided entertainment as well as identity. Thrill-seeking Iowa knights livened up cross burnings by setting off dynamite.[61] Demands for proper law enforcement (potently symbolized by prohibition) and responsive government, defense of the public schools as white Protestants wished them to be, patriotic display and an identification of Americanism that corresponded with one's own religious, racial, and ethnic background, and fidelity to an idealized family life and moral order—those were additional public manifestations of the shared beliefs and values of Klansmen that strengthened bonds within the hooded order.

Nonetheless, there were potential fractures in the Klan movement that left the Invisible Empire vulnerable to division and hastened its rapid dissolution at mid-decade. Preeminent among these weaknesses was the basic tension between the Ku Klux Klan as a hierarchical, national organization and the locally based, decentralized phenomenon of the Klan as a social movement. When Clarke and Tyler sent more than two hundred kleagles scouring the nation to form local klaverns, they created a popular Klan movement that was at odds with several of the principal features of the national organization that had set itself up in Atlanta.[62] Although there were charlatans and megalomaniacs present in many klaverns, most Klansman at the local level initially shared the belief, naive or blinkered though it may have been, that the Klan was indeed a morally upright, benevolent fellowship that would clean up local politics, enforce the law, save the public schools, and defend Americanism. Simmons probably felt something along the same lines, but the imperial wizard, drinking more than he should and tucked away in Klankrest (his official Klan residence in Atlanta), had surrendered practical control of the Klan to the Southern Publicity team in 1920.

For their part, Clarke and Tyler regarded the Klan as a commercial enterprise. The two had formed an odd yet effective team. Clarke was a nervous-looking, cigar-smoking former newspaper reporter with bushy hair and thin, tightly pressed lips. He craved success and, according to a dissenting observer, had "acquired a degree of flashy prominence as a press agent and 'booster.'"[63] In contrast to her excitable partner, the somewhat heavyset Tyler was refreshingly direct in manner and skilled as a businesswoman. While Tyler did much of the creative work in the background—partly to allay suspicions that the prominent men's organization the Klan had become was to some degree piloted by a woman—Clarke obtained from Simmons the contractual right to the office of imperial kleagle, the head Klan salesman ostensibly at the helm of the Propagation Department. The Klan's financial structure included regional sales supervisors, called grand goblins, and king kleagles at the state, or realm, level, who directed the kleagles harvesting the fields of nativist fraternalism. For every ten-dollar initiation fee, or klecto-ken, submitted by a naturalized knight of the order, four dollars remained with the local kleagle, one dollar went to the king kleagle, fifty cents became the grand goblin's cut, and $2.50 fortified Clarke and Tyler's Propagation Department. Imperial Wizard Simmons pocketed the remaining two dollars. A 1924 revision of the formula granted $2.50 to the grand dragon, the chief Klansman in each realm, and correspondingly reduced the amount paid to the national office. Imperial and realm officers nevertheless still raked in money from mandatory robe purchases, membership fees, and annual taxes. A recent economic analysis estimated that the Klan took in at least $25 million in 1924; D. C. Stephenson, the charismatic grand dragon of Indiana and the most powerful Klan figure in the Midwest, outearned Babe Ruth by a factor of four. This study concluded that the 1920s Klan was chiefly notable as "a wildly successful pyramid scheme."[64] The Knights of the Ku Klux Klan was more than simply a moneymaking venture. Still, ordinary Klansmen often resented what one disgruntled Hoosier exalted cyclops, or lodge president, called "the hollering for money all the time . . . and not using the principles which our men was sold upon."[65] Many klaverns refused to remit annual taxes to the national office, and bitter relations over money developed between Atlanta and the grassroots of Klandom.

In addition to financial tensions, power relations and matters of moral integrity provoked rifts between Klan leaders and the rank and file. At the local level the Klan movement usually was an expression of popular will. During the great organizing drive, kleagles had customized their appeals to fit local concerns. In some communities Klans were organized to enforce prohibition laws and eradicate vice; elsewhere elite resistance to road construction or upgrades to public schools became the issues around which klaverns took shape. Some coalesced against the looming shadow of Rome while others stressed business or social connections. Local Klans elected the exalted cyclops and other officers of the klavern. Many grassroots knights had only a dim perception of the national body. "We knew that the Klan came out of Georgia, but we never thought of them being at the head of it," reminisced one western Colorado Klansman. "As far as we were concerned, Denver was the head of it."[66] But outside the klavern, the Invisible Empire was structured so as to maximize the power of the imperial wizard and, in more restricted settings, that of the grand dragons. The imperial wizard had the authority to appoint or dismiss all national officers, banish those who displeased him, and extend or revoke local Klan charters. Some grand dragons, most notably Stephenson, the self-styled "Old Man" of the Indiana realm, operated like hooded sultans. Inevitably, conflicts arose between the local movements and the stifling hierarchy.

Misbehavior by Klan leaders particularly disrupted unity within the hooded order. Intrigue, scandal, and brusque displays of power at imperial headquarters brought into question the commitment to fraternity and moral regeneration that had attracted many Klansmen into the Invisible Empire. Special concern focused on Clarke and Tyler, who were exercising more power over the Klan than many members felt was appropriate. During the 1921 congressional hearings, word emerged that in 1919 Clarke had been charged with desertion by his wife and had been found tipsy, half-dressed, and in compromising company with the widowed Tyler. The pair's arrest for disorderly conduct led some Klan officials to demand their resignation. Simmons defended his assistants and banished their most vocal critics. Tyler soon retired from the Klan and remarried. But Clarke, who despite his bold actions was a fretful man, accumulated more power and further notoriety. In May 1922, Simmons took an ill-advised leave of six months while Clarke acted as de facto head of the Klan. That September Clarke was arrested for possession of liquor in Indiana after a speaking engagement dedicated to strict law enforcement. A cabal of exasperated and power-hungry Klan officers, led by Hiram W. Evans, an amiable-seeming but opportunistic former dentist who had ably led the Dallas Klan, moved to push aside Simmons and Clarke. In an extraordinary 3 a.m. confrontation at Klankrest, hours before the opening of a national Klan convention, or klonvocation, called by Simmons to reinforce his position as imperial wizard, the conspirators manipulated the credulous Simmons into accepting the honorary position of emperor while Evans slipped into office as imperial wizard.[67]

The transfer in leadership also marked a change in the character and direction of the Klan. Simmons's nostalgic vision of hooded fraternalism was reinforced by his antique personal appearance. Favoring stiff collars, frock coats, and pince-nez eyeglasses that were falling out of fashion in the 1920s, the colonel was a walking embodiment of an outdated era.[68] His florid features and ornate rhetorical style lent to the founder of the second Klan an overall impression of distinguished late Victorian irrelevance. Evans, on the other hand, was a New Era man on the make. He lacked the imposing physical presence of his predecessor. Of middling height, soft-featured, and, as the journalist Stanley Frost put it, "tending to put on flesh," Evans was not a striking figure. He described himself as "the most average man in America," an appropriate representative of the ordinary patriots who, he claimed, filled the ranks of the Invisible Empire.[69] But Evans was unusually ambitious. His eyes were large, restless, and sometimes took on a hard, pitiless quality. The Klan had offered him a path to prominence beyond where his small-time dental practice could take him, and he embraced it. He rose through the ranks of the Texas Klan and then contributed capable assistance to Simmons in the national office. But when the opportunity came, Evans cast Simmons aside without sentiment or hesitation. Alternating soft-spoken smoothness with curt assertions of authority, Evans looked to put his personal stamp on the Klan movement.

For the next fifteen months, during which time Simmons's personal attorney was murdered by the handpicked press agent of Imperial Wizard Evans,[70] the rival Klan leaders sued and countersued one another for possession of Klan property, titles, and copyrights. In the end, Evans dismissed Clarke, paid off and eventually banished Simmons, and consolidated his own power over the Klan.[71] He then reformed Klan finances, put some kleagles on salary, announced that he would restrain violence in the order, and pushed the Invisible Empire more firmly into politics and anti-Catholicism—but he continued to act peremptorily and to feud with powerful rivals like Stephenson. By 1925, Stephenson, now banished from the Klan by Evans, was himself imprisoned for murder, and the impressive Indiana realm he had organized crumbled around him. State and local Klan organizations were pulled into and split apart by the elite power struggles in the Invisible Empire while ordinary Klansmen by the hundreds of thousands were alienated by the tawdry display of high-level Klankraft in action. Splinter movements, appropriating the Klan name, seceded from the beleaguered national body. Dissension pervaded local klaverns as well, so much so that by 1924 one Iowa knight positioned himself near the door at meetings to escape more easily when conflict escalated.[72] Given the poor quality of leadership and the constant and debilitating struggles within the Klan, the wonder was not that the hooded order collapsed in the late 1920s but that it grew and flourished for a good part of the decade.

The 1920s Klan movement was most dynamic and varied at the local level, where the grassroots concerns that energized the Invisible Empire retained vitality longer. But even away from the battle over power and profits that engulfed the national Klan, local movements failed to come to terms with violence and political action, the two most noted public manifestations of the second Klan. Shocking incidents of murder at Mer Rouge, Louisiana, and sensationalized accounts of hooded vigilantes whipping, branding, or applying hot tar and feathers to hapless transgressors of local moral norms established a firm and vivid impression in the early 1920s of the Klan as fundamentally violent, dangerous, and aberrant. Most Klan violence was, in fact, restricted to the South and Southwest, areas with strong vigilante traditions and a high incidence of violence in general. In the Midwest, where the 1920s Klan phenomenon was strongest, overt violence by Klansmen was rare. Yet many of the brutal incidents featured in the news were real, not fabricated, and even in more peaceful realms, an undercurrent of violence, often unbidden, ran through the Klan movement. The Klan's rhetoric, both in public and within the klavern, was frequently acrid, confrontational, and by its very excess suggested the possibility of violence, as did the masks, hidden membership lists, and obsessive air of secrecy that pervaded the order. Vigilante action, a favorite and highly publicized method of Klansmen to enforce prohibition and control moral behavior, by its extralegal nature included the potential for unrestrained physical force. Thus Colorado's grand dragon, John Galen Locke, a charismatic homeopathic physician not known for religious intolerance or violent inclinations, nevertheless threatened a teenaged Klansman with castration unless he married the woman he had impregnated, an action that helped shatter the Klan movement in Denver.[73] Finally, in the North the Klan often attracted violence in the form of reprisals and anti-Klan riots against parading Klansmen by ethnic clubs and crowds of outraged foes of the hooded order. Gunplay between Klansmen, police, bootleggers, and anti-Klan vigilantes was not restricted to the back roads of Louisiana and Oklahoma. Such incidents occurred in Los Angeles, Buffalo, Pittsburgh, and scattered locations from the southern Illinois coalfields to the meeting grounds of the Invisible Empire in Massachusetts. Even where local Klansmen did not advocate violence or act provocatively, the stain of violence left by a national Klan lecturer's tactless remarks or brutal actions by distant knights befouled the Klan movement. Neither Evans, whose commitment to eradicating all forms of Klan violence invited skepticism, nor civic-minded local members who resisted appeals to violence escaped its scarring presence. The controversy over Klan violence, in combination with the Invisible Empire's internal disorder, clearly influenced the decline of the hooded order.

Dissatisfaction with state and local governance and the effectiveness of the Klan as a force in electoral politics were primary factors in the rise of the Invisible Empire in many communities. Driven by the politics of public schools, law enforcement, and morality, Klansmen organized politically to elect like-minded public officials. In Indiana, Oklahoma, Texas, Colorado, and Oregon, the Invisible Empire elected slates of candidates committed to Klan issues and became a force in public life. A Klan-dominated coalition of interest groups helped enact a mandatory public school attendance bill in Oregon. Klan-friendly officials appointed members of the hooded order to public posts in many communities. But this success concealed disharmony over political involvement among rank-and-file Klansmen. While the highly disciplined "military machine" developed in Indiana elicited worried admiration from the press, ordinary Indiana Klansmen grumbled that the political ambitions of the leadership had derailed the original fraternal purposes of the order.[74] This uncertainty was matched by the division introduced by the Klan's entry into national politics. The 1924 Democratic convention failed to muster enough votes to condemn the Klan by name, thus revealing some support for the secret order, yet only enough to deadlock the convention and hamstring the party. Ku Kluxers had a paralytic rather than propulsive effect on national party politics.

On the state level the promise of the Klan as an agent to restore white Protestant cultural values in public life was quickly tarnished by the rough and tumble of practical politics. Once in office, many Klansmen and their allies proved themselves to be incompetent amateurs easily outmaneuvered by veteran politicians. Moreover, Klan-backed candidates were no more trustworthy or upstanding as officeholders than their predecessors had been. They misbehaved, compromised on legislation, and ignored the demands of their constituents. Most Klan-supported legislative programs failed to pass, even in Indiana where the Invisible Empire supposedly terrorized and dominated the political parties. Most of the notable achievements of Klan-based coalitions, like the Oregon education law, were quickly invalidated. On both the national and local levels, prohibition proved unsalvageable as public policy. By 1925 the Invisible Empire's political adventure, critical though it was to the formation of the Klan movement, ultimately discouraged and alienated rank-and-file knights.[75]

A minor revival of Klan political interest was generated by opposition to the presidential campaign of Al Smith, the wet, Catholic governor of New York who, in nativist circles, was irredeemably associated with the foreign-flavored "sidewalks of New York."[76] But even this flicker of enthusiasm failed to sustain involvement in the Klan. By 1930, according to some accounts, membership had dropped from the high point of several million to as few as thirty-seven thousand.[77] In 1936 the Catholic Church bought the Klan's imperial palace in Atlanta and on the site of the erstwhile headquarters of Klandom constructed the Cathedral of Christ the King, mother church of the Atlanta diocese.[78] Three years later an exhausted Evans, who with grim fortitude attended the dedication of the cathedral, ended his seventeen years as imperial wizard. In 1944 federal tax obligations forced the hooded order formally to dissolve, to be replaced in a new postwar period by a loose combination of Klans that were more clearly subversive, violent, and outside the shifting mainstream of American belief and behavior than had been the experience of the vast, troubled, and evanescent popular movement of the 1920s.

2

Building a White Protestant Community

IN LATE NOVEMBER 1924, Ernest H. Cherrington of Westerville, Ohio, received an anonymous invitation to attend a meeting at the local high school auditorium. The program would feature the singing of the Snyder Brothers Quartette and "the facts regarding our movement." Cherrington, a leading official of the Anti-Saloon League of America, a well-known publicist, and a prominent Methodist layman, was being recruited by the Ku Klux Klan. "Your eligibility to become a part of the Nation-wide movement to organize American Protestants within the folds of one great organization has been certified to by your friends within our ranks," the note confided, adding that the bearer should bring the letter to secure admission to the meeting.[1] Despite his identification with prohibition and Protestantism, Cherrington's belief in outreach to wet ethnic groups and his internationalist inclinations led him to reject the entreaties of the Invisible Empire.

The recruiting letter nevertheless identifies some of the principal components of kluxing, as the Klan's recruiting efforts of the 1920s came to be called. Klan insiders would identify likely prospects, emphasize shared interests between the Klan and the potential member, then woo the recruit with promises of fellowship, recreation, the thrill of secrecy and exclusivity, and an appealingly vague purposefulness. Personal contact and 1920s techniques of salesmanship were especially prominent in the Klan's great membership drive of 1921–1922. While on a business trip in east Tennessee, Henry P. Fry was recruited into the hooded order by a kleagle whom Fry took to be a traveling salesman. The kleagle noted Fry's Masonic pin and established rapport with the prospective knight by emphasizing their mutual involvement in fraternal societies. Fry became a Klansman within a day, and before the month was out he also was a commissioned kleagle, guiding additional converts into the Invisible Empire.[2]

Klan instructions for kluxing frankly encouraged deception and subterfuge. They also acknowledged the variety of motivations that led men to join the hooded order. Pat Emmons, exalted cyclops of a northern Indiana klavern, was trained by his Klan superiors to pose as an interested outsider when sounding out potential initiates. Emmons had the broad, sympathetic face characteristic of his former trade—bartending. Converted years before to evangelical work, he was attracted to the Klan as a fellowship for like-minded men, perhaps finding in the klavern a replacement for the lost conviviality of the barroom. Whatever his motivations, Emmons applied his easygoing manner and light conversational touch to the task of winning over fellow Hoosiers to the Invisible Empire. Working from Protestant church records, Hoosier Klan recruiters identified native-born white Protestant men; then, according to Emmons, an undercover Klansman gingerly introduced the topic of the Invisible Empire and outlined its general principles, avoiding overtly bigoted or political statements. Once the unknowing recruit revealed his own attitudes, the recruiter steered the conversation accordingly. "You can't sell two men alike," Emmons related. "If you see that this is a religious fellow, or a minister, talk to him on the tenets of the Christian religion, and bring up this subject of white supremacy, in this way—not anti-negro, but to keep the black man black and the white man white." If the recruit responded to a mildly anti-Catholic remark, "then you can ram in a little anti-Catholic talk. . . . If it was a laboring man I should talk to him to sell him as a laboring man. If it was a doctor, talk to him from a business standpoint—show him how much business you could throw to him. . . . Sell them the thing they want." Only after the recruit had agreed to join the Invisible Empire would the secret Klansman reveal his affiliation and sponsorship to the initiate. "Naturalized" knights alone would be exposed to the harshest Klan sentiments uttered within the restricted space of closed meetings, or klonklaves. "Then is when your anti-Catholic and anti-Jew and anti-negro talk came in—and your politics," Emmons said.[3]

For many new Klansmen, then, the hooded order initially was attractive for a variety of reasons beyond its intolerant attitudes and political ambitions. Within native-born Protestant circles from which the Invisible Empire recruited in the early 1920s, endorsements of native white Protestant rule often were perceived not as narrow-minded bigotry but as simple expressions of patriotism. As the historian Lynn Dumenil found in her study of Masons in the 1920s, "Protestantism was equated with Americanism—it was inseparable from the American political and cultural tradition."[4] It was not considered by its partisans to be parochial or exclusionary, even when its application to public policy clearly was discriminatory. Imperial Wizard Hiram W. Evans framed his efforts to block Catholics from positions of authority in American public life with a similar appeal to a cultural understanding of U.S. citizenship that many Protestants had come to accept as normative. "The unity between Protestantism and Americanism is no accident," he claimed, knowing that many American Protestants would not disagree. "The two spring from the same racial qualities, and each is a part of our group mind. . . . Americanism provides politically the freedom and independence [that] Protestantism requires in the religious field."[5] This secular, politicized, even tribal sense of Protestantism, in which piety and formal religious practice were secondary to cultural identity, was a central feature of the 1920s Klan. The language of Klan recruiting, by which an "alien" was "naturalized" into "citizenship" in the Invisible Empire, used the terminology of democracy to suggest that devotion to white Protestant ascendancy produced a purer, more authentic Americanism.

The Klan's forms and application papers promoted this blurring of patriotism and brotherhood with native-born white Protestant identity. Bearing the legend *Non Silba Sed Anthar,* a nonsense phrase that KKK founder William J. Simmons claimed to have assembled from Latin and Saxon and that he translated to mean "Not for Self But for Others,"[6] the standard Klan recruiting card promised potential members entry into "the most powerful secret, non-political organization in existence." Any native-born, community-spirited, independent-minded American who endorsed "Christian religion," white supremacy, justice, liberty, the Constitution, states' rights, separation of church and state, and freedom of speech, and who sought "a closer relationship between Capital and American Labor," the prevention of "mob violence and lynchings" and "unwarranted strikes by foreign labor agitators," the pursuit of "local reforms," "Law and Order," and "the limitation of foreign immigration," was eligible to join the hooded knights.[7] Anti-Catholicism was implicit in some of these positions, and nativism was explicit; however, the thrust of the advertisement was more fraternal than political. Serious aspirants to membership in the Invisible Empire encountered more pointed questions about race, religion, and fraternal interest in the Klan's formal petition for "citizenship" in the secret order. "Are you a Gentile or a Jew?" the form inquired, following that up with equally blunt questions concerning political and religious affiliation, membership in other fraternal orders, devotion to white supremacy and "pure Americanism," and disavowals of allegiance "to any foreign nation, government, institution, sect, people, ruler or person."[8]

Potential Klansmen thus were well aware of the racial and religious exclusivity and militant Protestant sectarianism of the Invisible Empire. But the final stage of initiation into the hooded brotherhood—the naturalization ceremony—reinforced the secret, fraternal, and sociable components of Klan identity that remained foremost in the perception of many rank-and-file knights. During the ceremony the new "citizens" of the Klan learned the special handclasps and coded phrases that identified Klansmen to one another as fellow members of a secret brotherhood. They swore to guard the secrets of the order and to protect its interests.[9]

Most important, the oath emphasized the principle of Klannishness—that is, the obligation of Klansmen to support and protect fellow knights. Initiates pledged to "be faithful in defending and protecting the home, reputation, and physical and business interest of a Klansman and that of a Klansman's family." The secret ties of fraternity were meant to have a practical—and public—application by fostering business patronage, community formation, and sociability. The importance of public expressions of the supposedly secret world of the Klan was underscored by the frequency with which the secret obligations of naturalization were carried out in public outdoor ceremonies. In addition to publicity-attracting cross burnings, Klansmen conducted parades, orchestrated Klan days at state fairs, and organized other public events partly to express the power of their movement but also to entertain themselves and build community. "Oh, it was fun" to burn a cross, recalled a woman from Indiana's female Klan auxiliary. "The way they wrapped it in gunny sacks and soaked it in oil and then those guys went up and lit it, it was just a fun thing to do." Other Klansmen remembered Klan equestrian parades as more exciting than the traveling lecturers and entertainers of the Chautauqua circuit, county fairs, and the roster of mainstream community amusements that competed with Klan events.[10]

Community activism was another public expression of the Klan movement and an important element of its popularity in the early 1920s. The first gathering of the Invisible Empire in Denver called itself the Doers Club, a self-confident name that reflected the civic boosterism of the decade.[11] Profiles of Klan members reveal a greater involvement in community groups than among non-Klansmen.[12] Klan charity, often delivered in person by hooded emissaries of the Invisible Empire, was a simultaneous exercise in intimidation and community involvement. For instance, Klansmen regularly made small cash donations to African American churches, musical groups, and other social organizations, but usually with a hooded show of force. Voicing their desire "to encourage Protestant Christianity among negroes," a group of Klansmen interrupted services at a black church in Trenton, New Jersey, in 1924 to donate fifty dollars to the congregation's building fund. Their appearance sparked "alarm and indignation" among the worshipers.[13] A year earlier, seventy Texas knights "in full regalia" broke into a performance at the state legislature by a chorus from an African American orphanage, handed "a purse of money" to the chorus director, and then presented a statement of Klan principles to the astonished audience.[14] Klansmen in Oneida, New York, paid off the $850 mortgage due on an African Methodist Episcopal Church in late 1924 but almost certainly overwhelmed the congregation by filling the church with three hundred knights, though only six of them were robed and hooded.[15]

Financial support for activities that represented, in the paternalistic viewpoint of the hooded knights, proper outlets for African American cultural expression also reinforced white domination and communicated the Klan's insistence on monitoring the behavior of the black community. Still, the interest of many local klaverns in community projects, especially those that would further Protestant solidarity or Klannishness, was undeniable. Klansmen and African Americans marched together in the 1925 parade of Protestant churches of Jersey City.[16] Grandiose, usually unrealized, proposals for "100% American" institutions speckled the record of local klaverns: a Klan-sponsored orphanage in Dallas, which was actually constructed;[17] a Ku Klux country club near Youngstown, Ohio;[18] and a Klan-owned college in Indiana.[19]

Drawn by the variegated elements of the Klan program and the promises of its boosters, white Protestant men poured into the Invisible Empire between 1921 and 1924. Klan recruiters, eager to gather in as many members as possible, sometimes employed few filters beyond racial and religious profiles to screen those crowding for a place in the klavern. As Emmons jocularly put it, the Klan welcomed all "white, gentile, Protestant, native-born Americans with $10."[20] Kleagles earned commissions on every new recruit they brought into the hooded ranks, but ordinary knights also had a stake in proselytizing for the Invisible Empire. In order to advance in the Klan ritual to the second degree of membership, a level known as Knights of the Kamelia, a Klansman was required to attract one new member who paid the ten-dollar klectoken to join the secret brotherhood. "You never get the second degree unless you bring a man in," Emmons related. "A 'cash customer,' he is called."[21] On the other hand, evidence from some klaverns reveals more careful investigation of candidates and denial of membership to a small number of applicants. An eastern Oregon klavern suspended the naturalization of one prospective Klansman in the face of reports "that he was seen in the company of a Klansman's wife and in an intoxicated condition," thus subverting Klannishness as well as violating the hooded order's moral code.[22]

The true number of Klan members naturalized during the boom of the early 1920s is difficult to determine. Not only are reliable records scarce but there was also considerable fluidity in membership. Many knights entered the klavern expecting one promised feature of the Klan to predominate, whether it was business contacts, moral activism, fraternal fellowship, or even organized bigotry. Some of these Klansmen quit when their local Klan took on a character that differed from their expectations. Others failed to pay their dues or annual taxes and fell into a delinquent status.[23] Some of these were restored to full membership, some were banished, and others drifted along for months or even years as shadow members.

Reasonable estimates of Klan membership range from about two million members to four or even five million Klansmen at the peak of the movement. The largest realms, each attracting a membership in the hundreds of thousands, were Indiana, Ohio, Texas, and Pennsylvania. Illinois, Oklahoma, and New York were close behind, with many smaller states such as Oregon and Colorado supporting a relatively large Klan movement in relation to overall population. Some understanding of the problems inherent in estimating membership in the 1920s Klan can be gained by examining the various figures suggested for Indiana, perhaps the best-documented realm in Klandom. In formal testimony, Emmons, an officer in the Hoosier Klan, claimed on one occasion a maximum state membership of 400,000; yet in another deposition two years later, he reported a significantly different figure, just over 178,000.[24] Leonard Moore, the most thorough historian of the Indiana Klan, estimated a peak membership of fewer than 166,000.[25] More than two decades earlier, Kenneth Jackson arrived at a figure of 240,000 Hoosier Klansmen, including women initiated into the auxiliary Women of the Ku Klux Klan, during the entire range of the second Klan's existence from 1915 to 1944.[26]

Other complications arise. In addition to the Women of the Klan, several Southwestern states supported the Kamelia, a rival women's Klan organization founded by the deposed imperial wizard William J. Simmons. Other splinter Klans broke off from the Atlanta men's organization. Foreign-born white Protestants, not eligible for mainstream Klan membership, were organized in Klan affiliates called the Krusaders or, in the West, the Royal Riders of the Red Robe. Finally, it was rumored that Imperial Wizard Evans maintained an elite "imperial Klan" for politicians and other high-profile knights who wished to conceal their affiliation with the Invisible Empire, even from other Klansmen.[27]

Precise enumeration of the full extent of the Klan movement in the 1920s is impossible, but both contemporaries and historians recognized its size, its energy and short-term flair, and its uncanny appeal to several million ordinary white Protestant Americans. At least in this sense the Klan achieved for a brief time its purpose of establishing an invisible, influential community of white Protestant nationalism within the shifting American ethnic and religious mosaic of the early twentieth century. Political anxieties and ambitions, racial and ethnic intolerance, and a white Protestant demand for cultural dominance suffused the Klan movement and determined much of its public career, but the hooded order also promised fellowship, commercial ties, sociability, and community to its restricted membership. This chapter documents these latter elements—the attractions of Klan membership, especially those that reflected the prevailing ethos of the New Era.

Masked Spectacle and Entertainment

The business of the Klan may have been formulated within the shuttered klavern, but much of the life of the 1920s Ku Klux Klan, especially at the grassroots level, took place in public. As part of what Kathleen Blee has aptly termed "the totality of Klan culture,"[28] the Invisible Empire was in plain sight as a sponsor of community activities that ranged from lavish public events to Klan-themed family recreation and Klan recognition of personal milestones in the lives of rank-and-file knights. Just as the purposes of the Klan's public ceremonies encompassed the recruiting of new members, community formation among white Protestants, and intimidation of the religious, racial, and ethnic opponents of the hooded order, so too did participation in Klan events variously involve the knights themselves, their families, and ultimately the broader community of native white Protestants. "With the myriad of Klan weddings, baby christenings, teenaged auxiliaries, family picnics, athletic contests, parades, spelling bees, beauty contests, rodeos, and circuses," Blee notes, "it is perhaps little wonder that the 1920s Klan is recalled by former members as an ordinary, normal, taken-for-granted part of the life of the white Protestant majority."[29] Moreover, as Lynn Dumenil recognized, "it was fun to be a Klansman."[30] Klan extravaganzas were meant to be stimulating, entertaining, and, for the Klan constituency, welcoming.

In a new locality the Klan's theatrical displays began with the introduction of the secret order. After some furtive recruiting, a core group of robed and hooded Klansmen would announce their presence with a dramatic nighttime cross burning, usually located on a hillside for maximum visibility. Dynamite blasts or small bombs sometimes added color to the event and drew people onto the streets to witness the fiery display.[31] In one small Indiana town, three hundred spectators watched as the Klan burned a thirty-foot-high cross. According to a Klan press account, the secret order's ceremony left the town "agog with intense excitement," a reaction magnified by the hooded order's employment of "a high-powered motor car with a fire alarm whistle attachment sounding its shrill warning" that drove through town as the cross was ignited.[32]

The Klan's public appearances often seemed to parallel the elaborate marketing campaigns of the 1920s that advertisers contrived to thrust products into the consciousness of consumers. According to the pattern of public performances by newly formed klaverns, groups of mysteriously costumed Klansmen also made seemingly spontaneous, but usually prearranged, visits to Protestant churches, timed to coincide with the excitement generated by cross burnings. With an air of solemnity intended to underscore the mystery and high purpose of the Invisible Empire, a silent delegation of Klansmen would enter the sanctuary and hand a note to the minister—often, but not always a Klan sympathizer—who would then read the local Klan's manifesto aloud to the attentive congregation. A small group of hooded knights delivered the following message to four different Protestant churches in Helena, Arkansas: "We who stand thus silently before you are more than a million strong; we are friends of this minister, this church, and this congregation; we stand for the Christian religion, for the protection of womanhood and for the everlasting supremacy of the white race. As such we most earnestly ask your friendship and your prayers."[33]

Sometimes, as a reflection of the priorities of the local Klan movement, the church letter would sound a more political note. Declaring its "militant" Protestant intentions, the Pueblo, Colorado, Klan denied any prejudice on its part ("We are not Anti-Catholic, Anti-Jew, Anti-Negro, or Anti-anything") and pledged its efforts in support of law enforcement, political reform ("elimination of graft in public offices"), and defense of "strictly American" institutions.[34] Usually the Klansmen would present a cash donation to the minister and silently glide out of the church, sometimes to be followed by a pro-Klan sermon from the sympathetic clergyman.

Beyond the cross burnings and church appearances, the third common element of a new klavern's public inauguration was a parade of Klansmen in full regalia, preferably with a mounted contingent or its modern equivalent. Klansmen introduced their order to a crowd of onlookers in Monticello, Arkansas, with a parade of Model T Fords. It carried their hooded occupants down the main street and around the courthouse before departing for a Klan barbecue and watermelon picnic and an outdoor naturalization ceremony.[35] At larger gatherings, such as the 1924 naturalization extravaganza in Clanton, Alabama, Klan organizers employed elaborate pyrotechnics, including, in this case, "a rocket which spiraled upward toward the North Star, and released a parachute to which was attached a silken American flag" to underscore the thrill of membership in the white-robed ranks.[36]

Spectacle was a device for establishing the Klan as a mysterious presence and for winning converts to the Invisible Empire, but it was also a continuing tool for community-building among white Protestants. The internal world of the klavern, restricted to men naturalized into the order, was of critical importance to the 1920s Klan, but the public celebrations, events, and huge gatherings that local and regional Klans regularly organized entwined the values of Klannishness in the lives of the wives, children, and neighbors of Klansmen. "Open to everyone," claimed a newspaper advertisement for a regional Klan rally in Sturgis, South Dakota. "Come and bring your wife and kiddies with you."[37] Most large Klan outdoor festivities formally welcomed all comers. Even though the clear intent of Klan festivities was to form ties of fellowship within the white Protestant community, some of the spectacular displays attracted "alien" revelers. The band music, floats, torches, and excitement of uniformed marchers was so compelling to one Jewish man from Muncie, Indiana, that he took his son to watch Klan parades for their entertainment value.[38] Idaho Klansmen in one small settlement included the town's only Jewish family in their celebrations.[39] But the fellowship in "open" Klan events was almost exclusively of the "100% American" variety. A journalist considered that the country families at large Klan events "would have seemed perfectly at home eleven years ago in a Progressive party rally—bronzed, homely, good-natured persons who might have been selected at random from the farming populations of Indiana, Ohio, Illinois, Kansas, or Nebraska."[40]

Picnics, barbecues, music, and speeches of the type that traditionally accompanied political rallies in the United States were staples of Klan festivities. In keeping with the technological boom of the 1920s, however, the recreational options of the Invisible Empire were often more up to date. A Texas "Dance for Klansmen and Their Ladies" featured a full orchestra.[41] Airplane overflights were popular at regional gatherings.[42] The Denver Klan sponsored an automobile race that was not restricted to "100%" drivers since a Catholic racer won the competition.[43] Most notable, especially given the Invisible Empire's oft-stated criticism of modern popular culture's moral laxity, was the Klan's embrace of such contemporary cultural forms as radio, recorded music, and especially film. The enterprising Denver Klan broadcast events over the radio to the broader community.[44] An amateur, hooded Tin Pan Alley rearranged popular tunes into Klan-themed songs while professionals produced sheet music and records that blared from phonographs at gatherings of the hooded order.[45]

The Invisible Empire's enthusiasm for the movies extended beyond the popularity in Klan circles of D. W. Griffith's pro-Klan masterpiece, *The Birth of a Nation*. As with much of New Era popular culture, the hooded order offered a mixed response to the cinema.[46] On the one hand, Klan publications shrilly denounced Jewish and Catholic influence in the commercial film industry, and local Klans carried out scattered boycotts of particular movies.[47] Charlie Chaplin's *The Pilgrim* (1923) offended Klansmen with its irreverent treatment of the Protestant clergy. The sexually provocative *Bella Donna* (1923) crossed the forbidden color line by dramatizing the romantic attraction between a white woman and "an Egyptian Negro." So "coarse, degrading and insulting" was *Bella Donna* to hooded sensibilities that the Indiana Klan considered its release sufficient provocation to call for the resignation of fellow Hoosier Will Hays from his position monitoring the motion picture industry.[48] An official Ku Klux guidebook in 1925 asserted that "lascivious scenes upon the white sheet" should "shock . . . parents into protest and open war on the picture trade in general."[49] Yet officials of the hooded order recognized the value of film in attracting white Protestants to the Klan community. A Klan lecturer "did not urge Klansmen to stay away from the motion picture houses" but rather to support those films that reinforced native white Protestant values. The Invisible Empire endorsed patriotic films such as *The Face at Your Window*, which featured the 100 percent American convictions of the American Legion, and screened them at Klan gatherings.[50]

As a recruiting device, and no doubt as an alternative to the unsanctioned products of Hollywood, Klan auteurs also made and distributed their own films. Two short-lived Klan production companies were active in the Midwest and released two films, *The Traitor Within* and *The Toll of Justice*. Although shown at a handful of commercial theaters, the Klan films were usually screened before select audiences in churches, schools, and rented rooms. A Klan recruiting lecture in Oregon, for instance, was paired with a Ku Klux double feature promising "Eight Reels of Thrilling Pictures with a Message of Warning to American Manhood and Womanhood."[51] As cinematic equivalents to klavern meetings, picnics, or musical gatherings, the screenings of Klan films were intended to reinforce a self-sustaining hooded community that provided its members entertainment as well as inspiration and fellowship.

In pursuit of an entertaining introduction to the Invisible Empire, one Klan film, *The Toll of Justice*, aped the lurid conventions of contemporary Hollywood. The Ohio-made feature, which claimed to have used twenty-five thousand Klansmen in the cast along with a "picked squad of the [Klan friendly] Columbus Police Force," offered a positive portrayal of the 1920s Ku Klux Klan as a patriotic crusader against vice.[52] The screenplay featured action footage and a love story. A ring of drug smugglers provoked a strike, murdered one upright Klansman and framed another, and imperiled the hooded knight's all-American "sweetheart." Hooded Klansmen pursued the criminal gang, resulting in spectacular airplane maneuvers and a car chase that concluded with dramatic, crowd-pleasing crashes. Advertisements for the film, which claimed to have "the endorsement of the Ku Klux Klan," promised vivid entertainment and offered sensual suggestions, indicating that "100%" audiences had absorbed as much as they had shunned the tempting products of popular culture. Promoting the film as "a Sensational, Amazing, Unique Drama of the Dope Ring, an American Girl and the Ku-Klux-Klan," one overheated advertisement promised "daring that thrills, action that's tense, deeds that inspire, love that throbs, suspense that grips."[53] Evidently, even though some Klan publications advocated "the abolition of vile and degrading movies," the Invisible Empire exploited the most dramatic elements of popular culture, including the suspect medium of film, to maximize its appeal to the community of native white Protestants.[54]

The largest Klan-sponsored events were spectacular affairs that attracted thousands of amusement seekers and offered a mixture of familiar community pastimes and unusual diversions. The renowned July 4, 1923, "klonklave at Kokomo," made legendary by D. C. Stephenson's dramatic arrival in a small airplane,[55] entertained at least fifty thousand people with boxing matches, pie-eating contests, a beautiful baby competition, a parade featuring Klansmen towering on twelve-foot stilts, and everywhere the extravagant display of American flags. The outdoor dinner consumed "six tons of beef, hundreds of pounds of hamburger and hot dogs, five thousand cases of pop and near-beer, two hundred fifty pounds of coffee, and thousands of pies."[56] A massive gathering at Valparaiso in the same year advertised "20 brass bands, High, Tight Wire Walking, 100 Feet in the Air—Wild Bronco-Busting—Outlaw Horses— Imported Texas Cowboys."[57] Luther Dennis, "a 100% [American] balloonist," offered his services for "ascensions" at Klan celebrations in Indiana, using a hot-air balloon emblazoned with a "fiery cross" emblem.[58] Another Indiana Klan gathering resembled "the coming of a big circus to a small city," with twelve tents, "talking machines . . . playing Klan songs, . . . brass bands," and a "Klan quartet" singing "I Belong to the Ku Klux Klan."[59]

The Denver Klan sought to raise its profile by sponsoring a boxing and wrestling tournament that ran for nine days.[60] In 1923, Klan No. 66 in Dallas, Texas, arranged for Klan Day at the Texas State Fair. Nearly 150,000 people enjoyed Klan-themed rodeo events and Klan speeches in addition to the fair's usual rides and displays.[61] Fully outfitted Klansmen also rode ferris wheels in Colorado[62] and, in more casual attire, Ku Kluxers placed their children on merry-go-rounds and thrill rides at a Klan Karnival in Indiana,[63] enjoyed magic acts at a "Kollosal Karnival and Indoor Circus" in Texas,[64] attended Klan days at county fairs across the country, and participated in open-air Klan singalongs.[65]

The depth to which Klan social events reinforced a sense of an all-inclusive community of Protestant solidarity and sociability may be glimpsed in the program for the 1927 Klan "Field Day and Baseball Game" organized by several klaverns from Maryland and the District of Columbia. The contest pitted a Klan nine against a team from the Junior Order of United American Mechanics, a belligerently Protestant fraternal group often associated with the Invisible Empire. The event was a fund-raiser to support the Junior Order's

Orphans' Home in Tiffin, Ohio, and the Klan Haven Home, a state-supported institution established by the Invisible Empire in Harrisburg, Pennsylvania, to care for displaced and impoverished children, most of them from Klan backgrounds. Fifteen pages of advertisements from 100 percent businesses expressed community support for this exercise in Protestant philanthropy. Sponsors ranged from two housing development companies to the Dixie Pig Barbecue Sandwich Shoppe, the Pierce Mill Tea House in Washington's Rock Creek Park, and numerous gas stations, grocers, hardware and repair shops, coal dealers, plumbers, undertakers, and car dealers. Several of the advertisements sported the letters T.W.A.K., the Invisible Empire's trademark of commercial Klannishness, encouraging fellow knights to "trade with a Klansman." Figures representing Uncle Sam and the Goddess of Liberty led a parade before the game that boasted three bands, among them the Eagle Court Clown Band, and drill teams from Job's Daughters (the Masonic auxiliary for girls), the Klan's own Tri-K Girls club, and the Klaveleers, another Ku Klux–sponsored group. For the merrymakers at the game, the Klan and its allies seemed capable of providing a comprehensive network of charitable services, fellowship, recreation, and commerce within an exclusively white native-born Protestant framework.[66] The historian Leonard Moore goes so far as to argue that, unlike business or service clubs that maintained elite membership standards or rival fraternal groups, "the Klan represented the community as a whole."[67]

The Boundaries of Community

Despite the festive and community-building side of Klan extravaganzas the intolerant and repressive qualities inherent in the Klan's elevation of native-born white Protestant culture above all others took vivid form in the Klan's public spectacle. Observers noted that the evident "social grievances" among the participants at huge Klan celebrations represented "a parade of Americanism gone a little sour."[68] In brutal juxtaposition to its overall air of family-centered recreation, Klan Day at the Texas State Fair was the setting for one of Imperial Wizard Hiram Evans's most notable public articulations of bigotry against African Americans, Jews, Catholics, and immigrants. Ten thousand fairgoers listened to Evans demean the "low mentality of savage ancestors" and a "jungle environment" that left blacks incapable of "attain[ing] the Anglo-Saxon level"; impugn Jews as "absolutely unblendable," "alien," and "money mad"; and attack Catholics as posing "the gravest danger to our institutions" through their loyalty to a power-seeking church that "thrives upon ignorance."[69]

Even at the community level, the neighborhood displays that delighted Klansmen and their families delivered chilling messages to others. A sign placed in front of a burning cross in Seymour, Indiana, bore the incongruous legend: "In Honor of Our Savior Who Died to Save the World. Bootleggers, Gamblers, Law Violators, Beware. The Eyes of the Klan are Watching You!"[70] In another Indiana town, Klansmen placed a fiery cross menacingly next to a Catholic nunnery. A ten-year-old Catholic boy took no pleasure from an "eerie and threatening" Klan parade that featured a float depicting a public school. To the upset child, the salute to the "Little Red Schoolhouse . . . left no doubt as to what was being targeted: our parochial school!"[71]

Even among white Protestants, the boundaries of the Klan's self-defined community were uncertain and subject to local variation. In some locales a more pluralistic version of native white Protestantism buoyed the Klan movement. German Lutherans, who identified strongly with their ethnic heritage, were welcome and influential members of the Midwestern realms. Many Lutherans among Hoosier Klansmen, according to Moore, had at least one immigrant parent.[72] The German presence in the hooded order extended to the Northeast, where up to 40 percent of Buffalo Klansmen had German roots.[73] There was even a strong Klan movement among the Pennsylvania Dutch, fortified by "sauerkraut dinners and goat roasts," more exotic fare than was usually to be found on Klan tables.[74] Nevertheless, the independent-minded "Dutch" klaverns in the Keystone State participated in the familiar round of excursions, comic storytelling, illusionist performances, and orations that generally characterized sociability in the Invisible Empire. In the Western realms a sprinkling of Mormons, most but not all of them "inactive" saints, found membership in the Klan.[75] This despite the fact that the church hierarchy had officially denounced the Invisible Empire and Klansmen considered the Mormon faith to be outside the Protestant fold. "A good Mormon cannot be a Klansman for first he owes his allegiance to his church," admitted a hooded scribe from an Oregon klavern. But the opportunity for fraternal fellowship was nevertheless tendered. "If he can live up to our oath," the Klansman reasoned, "he is accepted by this organization."[76]

The limits of the inclusive approach to Klannishness were to be found in Louisiana, where Klan rosters in the southwestern parishes reportedly included two (most likely anti-clerical) Catholics and a knight of Jewish descent,[77] and Utah, where the klavern in a single small town boasted a foreign-born Protestant as exalted cyclops, welcomed the Catholic proprietor of Burke's Smoke Shop as a full member, and performed Klan funerary rites for another local Catholic.[78]

On the other hand, the Klan movement failed to attract the support of some white Protestant institutions, most notably churches that rebuffed the

Klan's ritual overtures. Most denominational bodies condemned the secret order or withheld their approval. At the community level, where ministers and church members frequently supported the Klan, many churches remained hostile to the Invisible Empire's proffered embrace. Several congregations barred entry to the Klan's hooded delegations. Ministers refused donations from the hooded order or soon returned them. Few of these rejections matched the performance in a Pittsburgh Methodist church when Klansmen chose to visit on Easter Sunday in 1923. The minister asked the unwelcome intruders to depart as an usher, who also was an attorney, attempted to seize and arrest one of the sixteen Klansmen. The hooded emissaries broke for the door, pursued by the congregation. Six of the interlopers were detained and unmasked before they could reach three waiting cars. As the Klan autos loaded their frantic passengers, another congregant copied down the license plate numbers, which church members announced they would forward to the police for prosecution of the holiday disruption.[79]

Local circumstances also determined the relationship of white Protestant labor unionists to the Klan community. The national leadership of the Invisible Empire made opposition to strikes and "labor agitators" core elements of the order's principles. In the early years of organizing during World War I, Klan vigilantes had acted against "slackers" whose job actions they felt would disrupt the war effort.[80] For their part, central labor organizations were reliable critics of the Ku Kluxers throughout the 1920s. But during the heyday of the local Klan phenomenon in the early years of the decade, when the American labor movement was especially weak, some local Klans identified with white Protestant workers. Striking railroad workers in eastern Oregon and Kansas were strongly supported by the Klan movements there. In La Grande, Oregon, where the repair and maintenance facilities of the Union Pacific Railroad employed 850 workers, almost 37 percent of the local klavern's membership (whose occupations could be traced) worked for the railroad. When most of them went on strike in support of a national railroad walkout, the local Klan backed the striking workers. Articulating its support for labor in the familiar Klan language of ethnic and racial intolerance, the La Grande Klan emphasized the presence of Asian and African American strikebreakers and the persecution of Klansmen railroad employees by their Catholic supervisors.[81] The Kansas Klan was more clearly opportunistic in its support for labor, recruiting alienated white workers whose jobs had been taken over by imported black strikebreakers.[82]

Despite hostility from the Klan movement, some white Protestant unionists were attracted to the racially and religiously exclusive community offered in the Invisible Empire. Ignoring the clear enmity of their state federation of labor to the hooded order, sufficient numbers of Colorado unionists belonged to the Klan to merit the formation among the Ku Kluxers of an even tighter band of hooded labor men, a "circle within the circle." [83] Recognizing the labor contingent in its midst, the Colorado Klan's political organization judged candidates on their labor positions in addition to the usual catalogue of concerns. Nancy MacLean, who has examined the class elements of the Klan movement more thoroughly than other scholars, argues that craft workers, smarting from union reverses, anxious to maintain their privileged place in the labor aristocracy against black and ethnic workers, and antagonistic toward strikebreakers from minority groups, found membership in the Klan a comfortable expression of their conservative labor outlook. For the smaller group of unskilled Georgia millworkers enticed into the Invisible Empire despite the Klan's commitment to middle-class standards and individualistic striving, she points to the incomplete development of class formation among the migrants from the Georgia countryside as an explanation. Tied more to the family, religious, and social institutions of their communities, these workers, as was the case with many of their fellows in the "lean years" of the 1920s union era, perhaps felt the pull of their class interests less than the more familiar tugs of racial, religious, and rural community identity.[84]

But as with other elements of the 1920s Klan, there was significant local variation in Klan actions toward organized labor. In the Arkansas Ozarks a bitter strike against the Missouri and North Arkansas Railroad by "sober and industrious local men, Masons and Christians," met the unrelenting opposition of the local Klan, whose members supported town business interests against the desperate violence of the strikers. Along with other townspeople organized into a community protective league, Klansmen intimidated strikers, boycotted the businesses of strike supporters, and eventually joined in violent vigilante acts that broke the strike. The strikers' identity as fellow white Protestant community members in this case was not enough to overcome features of the conflict that antagonized local Klansmen. Embittered workers had carried out acts of sabotage against the railroad, mainly by burning railroad bridges, which cut off the isolated towns along the track and alienated their residents. Because the railroad did not import strikebreakers from immigrant or minority groups, there was no pressure for ethnic and racial solidarity with the strikers. The few ineffective scabs who were hired were local white Protestant men like the strikers themselves. Finally, the strike imperiled the livelihood of most local Klansmen. The great majority of hooded knights in northwest Arkansas lived or worked in the small towns that relied on the railroad for economic survival. Unlike the situations in Kansas or Oregon in which white Protestant workers were beset by outside forces, in Arkansas the strike itself was seen by Klansmen as a threat to community stability.[85]

A Private/Public Presence: Charitable Activities

Recent historians of the Klan have emphasized the civic activism of the hooded order. The Invisible Empire's imprint on such public questions as school policy, prohibition enforcement, regulation of morality and vice, and governance was substantial and will be treated at length in later chapters. But as a device that linked the closed fraternal activities of the klavern with the Klan's public desire to build a place for the hooded order in local civic affairs, charitable giving deserves treatment here as an essential component of Klan community formation.

Central to the fraternal relationship of Klansmen was the obligation of Klannishness. Klansmen were required to attend to the needs of one another. It was standard in klavern meetings for the secretary to ask, "Does any Klansman know of a Klansman or a Klansman's family who is in need of financial assistance?"[86] The knights would immediately pass the hat to assist a fellow Klansman in financial distress or one who had suffered a misfortune. Upon learning that the child of a local kleagle had died, a Maryland klavern literally "placed [a hat] on the altar and a sum of $22.40 was donated by the Klansmen."[87] Sometimes more substantial sums were raised. Pennsylvania knights donated more than $34,000 to pay legal expenses and family support for Klansmen arrested in a 1923 shooting affray in the town of Lilly.[88] The national headquarters claimed more than $10,000 had been raised to help the family of another hooded Pennsylvanian fatally injured at Carnegie, though the ultimate disposition of the funds was unclear.[89] Committees to visit the sick and attend to the funeral rites of those within the extended Klan family were also active.

Expectations of Klannishness extended beyond emergency assistance, however. As a sign of fellowship and, by word of mouth, a promised benefit of Klan membership to entrepreneurial Protestants, Klansmen were directed to patronize the businesses of fellow knights and to avoid (or actively boycott) the establishments of their non-Klan competitors. "A Klansman was supposed to trade with nobody but someone who was in the Klan," a California knight remembered, "and you could tell who was a member of the Klan because they had the American flag hung way back in a certain place." Hooded officials took note of the membership's patronage of local businesses. "The first time you're caught trading in a store that's not a Klansman's store, you'd be warned," recalled the former knight. "The second time you'd be fined, and the third time, God help you!"[90] Threats of formal sanctions notwithstanding, officers of the Invisible Empire often struggled to channel hooded fellowship into desired action.

Despite the difficulty encountered by local klaverns in enforcing commercial Klannishness (klavern minutes contain oft-repeated admonitions to "trade with Klansmen" or to observe boycotts against popular Catholic or Jewish vendors[91]), the practice was important, and not simply for building cohesion within the hooded order. Like the easily detected code words of recognition between Klansmen, Klannishness represented another element of Klan secrecy that was meant to be carried, half-disguised yet visible, into public life. Part of the thrill of Klan membership lay in meeting a fellow Klansman in public and exchanging fraternal signs. When secret political members of the order used the Klan handshake or ended correspondence with the letters I.T.S.U.B. ("In the sacred and unchanging bond"), Klansmen knew that they had encountered an ally and fellow knight.[92] Still, most of the Klan code phrases—*ayak* ("Are you a Klansman?"), *akia* ("A Klansman I am"), *san bog* ("Strangers are near, be on guard")—while not necessarily intelligible to outsiders, clearly identified their users as members of the Ku Klux Klan.[93] Indeed, one Oregon chapter printed the "secret" phrase *kotop* ("Klansmen obey their oath persistently") on stickers to be displayed on members' automobiles.[94] These phrases were advertisements of the Klan's presence and public stature. So too were the T.W.A.K. and "100%" signs placed on the windows of Klansmen's shops. They announced the extent to which the Invisible Empire was entrenched in the local community.

The Klan's charitable efforts shared this private and public function, on the one hand strengthening solidarity within the order but also expanding its visibility and legitimacy in the larger community. Many of the beneficiaries of Klan benevolence were not members of the hooded order. An impoverished farmer "who was about to lose his cow due to the lack of feed" received "a ton of alfalfa hay" from an Oregon klavern.[95] Klansmen near Houston paid $250 to redeem a widow's lumber bill.[96] It was commonplace for Klansmen to distribute food baskets to needy families on holidays or during organizing campaigns.[97] In 1922 the powerful Indianapolis Klan contributed twelve truckfuls of food and clothing at Christmas.[98] Local Klans also paid rent and mortgage interest for families in danger of losing their homes. A band of Oklahoma knights presented a "worthy widow" with a $2,000 bungalow.[99] Klanswomen in Muskogee, Oklahoma, underscored both the traditional service roles expected of women in the Invisible Empire's construction of social relations and the hooded order's desire to establish itself as a respectable community presence by operating a "day nursery," fixing chicken dinners for patients at the local veterans' hospital, and contributing furnishings for the community indigent home.[100] Even modest donations, such as the sponsorship of two Kentucky boys "to become members of the Junior Pig Club of West Liberty," enhanced the standing of the hooded order in small settlements.[101]

Charitable initiatives varied according to the particular interests of individual Klans. Pat Emmons remembered no special philanthropic programs in his northern Indiana klavern.[102] Yet most Ku Kluxers stood to gain from community involvement. Part of the motivation for charitable giving by Klansmen was, as with other lodges and service clubs, a genuine sense of community obligation. But Klan benevolence also gave legitimacy to the Invisible Empire as an extralegal force, which suited its political and cultural aims. In Georgia, the historian Edward Akin found, "the Klan earned the right to police morality in some communities by serving as an ad hoc social welfare agency, doling out charity to widows, abandoned wives and others it considered the deserving poor."[103] Applicants for financial assistance—and those seeking extralegal intervention in family disputes, lawbreaking, or violations of community mores—contacted the Klan directly, thus increasing the standing of the hooded order as a quasi-public authority.

On occasion even Klan vigilantism took an unexpected philanthropic turn. Such was the case in 1923 when Klansmen and police on a prohibition enforcement raid in Mishawaka, Indiana, discovered "a golden-haired girl yet in her teens" among the three female "habitués" at the Bird's Nest Inn. Dubbed a "Modern Magdalene" by the hooded press, the young prostitute reportedly had entered the sex trade to support her baby, whom she otherwise would have had to surrender to the local orphans' home. The hooded vigilantes, no doubt acting in response to the young woman's Anglo-Saxon racial profile as well as her desperate situation, "interested their wives in the girl's misfortune." The Klan women found employment for the mother and her child in a private home, whereupon the Invisible Empire's report declared "her past a closed book."[104] Such gallantry highlighted the informal network of white Protestant solidarity directed by the Klan. When contextualized as a cooperative venture with local police, the entire enterprise reinforced the Ku Kluxers' self-image as engaged community reformers.

Some klaverns took care to establish the Klan as a respected actor in public benevolence. The La Grande, Oregon, Klan tried to place itself within the structure of private and public social welfare mechanisms in its community. After a needy widow had written to a klavern member seeking the Invisible Empire's assistance, an investigating committee concluded "that just at present she was in no dire needs as the Elks Comm[ittee] had not forgotten her." The Klan, however, promised to act on her behalf if other charitable bodies failed to provide adequate help.[105] In another case of family neglect on the part of a local man, the klavern determined that this "particular case should come under the jurisdiction of the county health nurse."[106]

In his pioneering study of the Pennsylvania Klan, Emerson Loucks argued that the benevolence of the hooded order was unsystematic and that Klansmen, seeking maximum credit for their good deeds, made their donations to individuals rather than to the organized charities of their communities, such as "Boy Scouts, Red Cross, Community Chests, City Charity boards, or temperance societies."[107] Much of the Klan's giving was indeed haphazard and self-serving, but a multitude of evidence indicates that in its effort to legitimize its credentials as a quasi-public organization, many klaverns did contribute to key charitable institutions in local communities. Upon its appearance in El Paso, Texas, Frontier Klan No. 100 made donations ranging from fifty to two hundred dollars to the local Young Men's Christian Association (YMCA), the Salvation Army, and the Associated Charities.[108] Houston knights contributed five hundred dollars to the YWCA, financed the building of a watchtower for the local Boy Scouts, and contributed ninety dollars to a Parent-Teacher Association for needed school improvements.[109] Missouri Boy Scouts received one thousand dollars from the Jefferson City Klan.[110] Macon, Georgia, Klansmen in full regalia presented money to the city's Community Chest at a luncheon meeting of the charity,[111] while Charleston knights manned committees during the local YMCA membership drive.[112]

Protestant-directed social welfare agencies, such as the YMCA and the Salvation Army, were especially favored by philanthropic Klansmen. These semi-public but culturally sectarian institutions fit the Klan's vision of a community and public culture that, in their provision of services, were open and participatory yet remained discernibly Protestant. Texas klaverns in several cities made gifts of more than a thousand dollars to local YMCAs and private Protestant hospital funds.[113] Denver Klansmen opened their major organizing drive in 1922 with an ostentatious gift to the Mile High City's YMCA,[114] while, on the western side of the Continental Divide, Grand Junction Klansmen provided one hundred dollars to allow youngsters without means to enjoy the Y's programs and its distinctly Protestant fellowship.[115] Eastern Oregon knights donated fifty dollars to the Red Cross, provided the Salvation Army with leftover food from Klan events, and proposed to install a Salvation Army donation kettle in the klavern itself.[116] St. Louis knights constructed a vacation "hut" at a Salvation Army camp.[117]

Klansmen also sought to raise the community profile of the Invisible Empire by contributing to national and regional patriotic displays. American flags, along with Bibles, were among the most common Klan gifts to churches, schools, and community groups.[118] Klansmen gave an American Legion post in Houston money to purchase eight bugles.[119] In Southern realms, local Klans enthusiastically took part in celebrations of the Confederacy. Twenty hooded knights marched in Macon's 1922 Confederate Memorial Day parade.[120] El Paso Klansmen did them one better by financing the costs of eight aging local rebels to attend the national convention of the United Confederate Veterans.[121]

Just as in churches and politics, however, the Klan's efforts to enter the mainstream of community involvement provoked controversy and division.

The Associated Charities of El Paso rejected the Klan's donation, prompting indignant protests from the hooded order and close scrutiny of those charities that did accept money from the Invisible Empire.[122] Discord rippled through the local Salvation Army and American Legion post as to the propriety of accepting Klan support. The purchase of bugles with money donated by the Klan led to resignations by the commander and nine of the twelve top officers of the Houston American Legion post favored by the patriotic generosity of the Invisible Empire. Even the Boy Scouts drew criticism for accepting tainted Klan money.[123]

Controversy dogged the community activism of the Klan because, even in its charitable endeavors, the restrictive nature of the Invisible Empire's self-defined native white Protestant community was clearly evident. The boldest institutional initiatives of Ku Klux philanthropy—the handful of hospitals, orphanages, and children's homes that the Invisible Empire built and funded—were often identified as "100%" alternatives to the existing social welfare infrastructure, even when they were nominally public institutions or cooperated with government agencies.[124] The strong desire to construct white Protestant charitable institutions was demonstrated in 1923 by Shreveport Klan No. 1. Working undercover, a hooded minister from that klavern investigated reports that a local female bootlegger hired her daughters out as prostitutes. Upon confirming the story, the Klansman turned the information over to local authorities, who placed the girls in the only available institution for abused young women: the Catholic Home of the Good Shepherd. Stirred into action by the thought of Protestant girls harbored in a Catholic refuge, the Louisiana knights pledged to raise money for a Protestant girls' home that would be administered by state authorities.[125] Similar hooded efforts to construct medical or child welfare institutions were launched in Oregon, Arkansas, Kansas, and Texas.[126]

As with the proposals to create a "Klan university," most of the scattered campaigns by local Klans to sponsor new hospitals failed to materialize, but not in Indiana. According to Leonard Moore's account, in a remarkable display of civic dedication Hoosier Klansmen (and the women of the WKKK) in Howard County spearheaded a two-year fund-raising campaign to construct a public hospital for the county. The massive rally in Kokomo was part of the undertaking, though skeptics in the press questioned whether the fifty thousand dollars raised at the event found its way into the hospital fund. Still, the hospital construction effort attracted the support of the local school superintendent and minority voices in the community. Other problems threatened to undermine the project, however. A Klan-backed bank in Kokomo, in which the hospital fund had been deposited, collapsed in 1927, costing its depositors 60 percent of their money and leaving its Klansman president under indictment for financial misappropriation. Moreover, the funds raised by the hooded order covered only the initial phase of construction, which had to be completed in late 1926 by the county. Nevertheless, the Invisible Empire had proven itself an essential partner in a valuable public project.[127]

Behind the public spirit of the enterprise, the new institution would offer local Protestants an alternative to the county's existing Catholic hospital. Moore argued with some justification that "beneath the anti-Catholic sentiment lay a genuine interest in civic improvement" on the part of Klan activists. But it remained true that intrinsic to the groundswell of Klan-directed "populist insurgency" against unresponsive community elites, as represented by the hospital project, the Klan bank, and other Klan efforts at institution building, was a vision of community that was both adversarial and severely restrictive on the basis of race, religion, and ethnicity.[128] The finished public medical center, perhaps appropriately, was known as the "Klan hospital." Ironically, it closed during the Depression and was purchased in 1935 by its erstwhile rival, the Sisters of St. Joseph.[129] Even the enthusiastic Kokomo Klan failed to sustain an alternative institutional structure in the Invisible Empire's most powerful realm.

Hope Cottage, the foundling home funded by the Dallas Klan, while draped in the robes of the hooded order, was a genuine philanthropic enterprise. Founded in 1918 as a nursery and adoption center for abandoned babies, the home had become destitute when Klan No. 66 intervened. Zeke Marvin, one of the most dynamic figures in the Texas realm, was the guiding force in the Invisible Empire's takeover of the beleaguered home. Marvin combined his dedication to Klan principles with a notable zeal for philanthropy. He forged ties between Dallas Klan No. 66 and the Dallas Welfare Council, and engineered a fund drive for the infants' home that raised eighty-five thousand dollars from local Klansmen. The Klan presented the restored Hope Cottage to the Dallas community on Klan Day in 1923 at the Texas State Fair. In step with Klanswomen elsewhere who helped expedite the adoption of unwanted babies, the Dallas Klan's effort to place infants in established families conformed with the secret order's interest in moral regulation and stable patriarchy. Klan sponsorship of Hope Cottage was also an exercise in image crafting, diverting public attention from a damaging series of violent incidents that had tarnished the Southwestern Klan movement and the public standing of Dallas Klan No. 66 in particular. As with other Klan institutions, the Invisible Empire was unable to manage Hope Cottage for more than a few years, and the home eventually was turned over to the city. Hope Cottage is still in operation, though its Klan roots are little known.[130]

Klan Haven, the children's home in Harrisburg, was not simply the project of Pennsylvania Klansmen but, as the baseball fund-raiser on its behalf in

Washington, D.C., indicated, it was a mainstay for Klan philanthropy over a much larger area. As a successful charitable enterprise, Klan Haven advanced both the Klan community and the recognition of the Invisible Empire's place within the structure of public institutions in Pennsylvania. Originated by the state's women's Klan organization, both men's and women's klaverns supported the home, creating an image of unity as well as benevolence within the hooded order. Annual fund-raisers and competitions between klaverns to raise money for Klan Haven became part of the yearly cycle of hooded celebrations in Pennsylvania, as was an annual pilgrimage to Harrisburg to visit and entertain the young wards of the home. Even though most of the children cared for at Klan Haven were from Klan families, the hooded order took care to have them placed in the home by court order, thus ensuring state support and interest in the institution. Still, its clients and its reputation were firmly bound to the Invisible Empire. Once again, community involvement by the Klan attempted to embody a mixed public/private character while remaining committed to a restricted vision of community.[131]

The Klan Community Compromised

As much as Klan Haven reflected the ideals of Klan unity and public service, the sad struggle for control of the institution foreshadowed the internal disputes that uprooted community-building within the Invisible Empire and devastated the Klan movement by mid-decade. A destructive fire in 1926 that necessitated the rebuilding of Klan Haven became the occasion for a nasty fight between men's and women's Klan organizations in Pennsylvania to control the home. Women in the Klan, as elsewhere in 1920s America, were more active participants in charitable enterprises than were the men of the Invisible Empire. But the visibility and public stature of Klan Haven made it a tempting prize for Klansmen, and the hooded order asserted its claim to manage the institution. As Pennsylvania Klanswomen found themselves edged out of the direction of their major benevolent enterprise, powerful national Klan officials, who supported the men's takeover of Klan Haven, also replaced the leaders of the Pennsylvania WKKK. These maladroit displays of power fractured Klan unity in Pennsylvania and led the large Philadelphia and Chester women's klaverns to secede from the order. Similar disarray and division confounded the men's movement in Pennsylvania.[132]

This discord, embedded as it was in one of the major community-building efforts of the Klan, symbolized the oddly shallow roots of the Klan community. On the one hand, Klansmen and even, to some extent and in some locales, their neighbors, embraced the spectacles, celebrations, and charitable efforts of the Invisible Empire, forming an intense Klan community in the early 1920s. But, just as with the "movement culture" of the 1890s populists, the binding quality of that community was conditional, evanescent, and dependent upon political success and organizational probity. As the Klan dissolved amid political setbacks and personal scandals involving its leading figures, ordinary Klansmen transferred their recreational allegiance to other communities: churches, lodges, neighborhood groups, and families.[133]

The Klan's attempt, through its charitable enterprises as well as its political thrusts, to establish itself within the public sector displayed similar weaknesses. At bottom the Klan's charitable and institutional efforts, though they produced some significant achievements, were not truly public enterprises in the fullest, most inclusive, and most permanent sense of that term. They were, instead, as was the Ku Klux Klan itself, quasi-public initiatives that claimed to represent the community as a whole but were widely recognized by non-Klansmen as self-interested and narrowly conceived, even if beneficial to some.

The authentic yet attenuated nature of the Klan community in the 1920s can also be traced in the commercial relationships among Klansmen encouraged by the Invisible Empire's official doctrine of Klannishness. To some extent the practice of selling and purchasing within a 100 percent American network was imperfectly imposed upon the hooded rank and file by the hierarchy of the Klan. Nowhere was this more apparent than in the mandatory patronage of the Gates City Manufacturing Company, owned by top Klan officials, for the purchase of robes required for Klan ceremonies. Each robe cost two dollars to produce, but was sold to the membership for $6.50 apiece, with the profits going to Atlanta.[134] This was not Klannishness so much as it was price gouging. But even here, glimmers of grassroots Klan economic fraternalism appeared. La Grande, Oregon, Klansmen were steered to local tailor Rube Zweifel, a fellow hooded knight, to purchase their robes.[135]

Klan commerce followed this two-tier track throughout the life of the second Klan. On the one hand, large enterprises sanctioned by the national headquarters and seeking to profit from the loyalty of the hooded brotherhood continuously sprang up in the early 1920s. These companies ranged from the Empire Mutual Life Insurance Company, which promised to write policies for "none but native born, White, Gentile, American Citizens," to an abortive candy concern that attempted to market "100%" confections.[136] None of these businesses achieved anything beyond temporary and regional success, and most of them failed utterly. Indeed, the perception that such Klan companies were solely intended to fleece the membership worsened the tension between local klaverns and the national leadership of the Invisible Empire. For instance, agents from the headquarters of the Invisible Empire, working under the auspices of the Klan-operated National Service Company, gathered names of Ku Klux businessmen for a proposed nationwide Klan business directory and collected money from hooded knights in Pat Emmons's northern Indiana klavern to participate in the publication. But the proposed directory never materialized. When asked what his men received for their thirty-five dollars, Emmons replied with resignation, "They got a tin plate."[137]

Underneath the cynical surface of Klan commerce, a more authentic exchange of goods and services was carried out by local Klansmen. Even as the planned national Klan business directory failed, Emmons's Klansmen successfully produced a South Bend community guide to Klan-owned businesses.[138] Official bulletins from the Indiana realm included postings of job opportunities, products, or skilled Klansmen in search of work. They functioned as a sort of "100%" bulletin board, a manifestation of the vibrant yet limited nature of the Klan's self-created community. Thus Klansmen in Fowler, Indiana, advertised for "a 100% physician" because the community's two doctors, one "too old to be called upon nights and the other . . . a Catholic just moved in," were considered inadequate.[139] Hooded representatives from a medium-sized town of eleven thousand requested the services of "a 100% brick contractor" as well as "a 100% architect."[140] Searches for veterinarians and meat cutters, both of the "100%" variety, were pursued through the bulletins of the Indiana realm. Similarly, job seekers, such as the "100% instructor in Science and Athletics," and Klannish manufacturers of cigars and cigarettes relied on official Klan correspondence to make connections for themselves within a trusted community.[141]

Nonetheless, as with other elements of the hooded enthusiasm of the 1920s, the self-sustaining network of Klan business patronage proved short-lived. The One Hundred Per Cent American department store in Indianapolis fell into receivership within six months, as did several Klan-themed restaurants and small repair shops.[142] Even in the well-organized La Grande, Oregon, klavern, support by fellow knights of Gar Holm, a grocer who catered the local events of the Invisible Empire, faltered. After Holm's business nearly failed, contrite knights noted that "our Klannishness toward Klansman Holm has been very lax." Despite their prejudices and their fraternal vows, many of Holm's fellow Klansmen had been buying their food from his rivals, including a popular Catholic tradesman. Two months later Holm noted that "the newly made Klansmen are giving him their entire support but that the original Klansmen are still catering to the Pope."[143] Even among active knights, Klannishness was not an airtight doctrine. Similarly, the Klan community as an enterprise ultimately failed to replace other forms of identity and familiar interaction in the lives of its hooded adherents. Although compelling and exciting for many native white Protestants, especially during the boom years of the early 1920s, neither the public nor the secret, insular manifestations of the Ku Klux Klan community won the permanent loyalty of the hooded multitudes it had attracted into its ranks.

❖

Given the sharp rise to prominence of the 1920s Klan and its precipitous collapse at mid-decade, it would be tempting to compare the Klan movement of the New Era to the wispy fads and fleeting enthusiasms that have framed popular images of Jazz Age America. But just as the real-estate boom and bust and stock market speculation of the 1920s pointed to deep structural issues in the economy, so too did the Klan's flawed effort to build and sustain a white Protestant community reflect important shifts in twentieth-century American society. The historian Lynn Dumenil has insightfully argued that 1920s America reflected the "modern temper," as Americans struggled to reconcile assertions of community with the centrifugal influences of ethnic pluralism, bureaucratization of power, fragmentation of identity, and a shifting cultural landscape.[144] Klan attempts at community formation embodied that struggle. Efforts to build a Klan community employed elements of the modern consumer culture such as film, radio, and sporting events as well as such traditional pastimes as picnics, parades, and bonfires. Similarly, Klansmen applied the modern commercial tools of advertising and boosterism along with the attractions of traditional fraternalism to create a united community of native-born white Protestants.

But the Klan community drive ran against the grain of the modern temper of the 1920s in one critical respect: most of its tools were most effective when applied to the preservation of distinctive ethnic, racial, or religious identities within a broader American orientation. Immigrants from Eastern Europe, black Southern migrants, Catholics, and Jews might reinforce their particular communal ties through fraternal organizations, business patronage, athletic leagues, and civic engagement. But their participation in other aspects of mass culture underlined their shared identity as Americans. They developed a dual but self-reinforcing identity as Italian Americans or American Catholics. The Klan's sense of Americanism, on the other hand, demanded a community that was not only separate, exclusive, and autonomous like the others but also normative—the dominant, defining culture. It was not enough for Klansmen to identify themselves as Protestant Americans within a larger collection of pluralistic countrymen and women. The logic of Klan beliefs dictated that native Protestant Americans were the *only* authentic Americans. Community formation on that premise was unsustainable in the fragmented, pluralistic 1920s.

3

Defining Americanism:
White Supremacy and Anti-Catholicism

A S MUCH AS KLANSMEN WERE DRAWN into the Invisible Empire by promises
of fraternal bonhomie and a vibrant community life, the bedrock of
the 1920s Klan movement remained its commitment to the continuation of
native-born white Protestant hegemony in American culture and governance.
The journalist Stanley Frost, a keen and somewhat sympathetic observer of
the hooded order, identified the Invisible Empire's claim to the "exclusive
Americanism of 'native, white, Protestant' supremacy" as the "really distinctive thing about the Klan."[1] The order's national leadership repeatedly
emphasized this restrictive definition. Dismissing ethnic pluralism as an
undesirable model for American democracy, Imperial Wizard Hiram W.
Evans boldly asserted in 1925 that Klansmen's status as the descendants of
the pioneers reserved for the Invisible Empire and the white Protestants it
claimed to represent "a prior right to control America" over the interests of
other social groups.[2]

Evans demanded more than pride of place for native-born white Protestants in determining national policy. Pluralism, he declared, was antithetical to American institutions and should be excluded from public influence.
American democracy, in his view, took the form of "Protestantism translated
into government,"[3] a mixture of individualism, equality within a select community of believers, and a militant posture toward outside hierarchies and
rival systems of law and belief. Antithetical religious traditions, especially
Roman Catholicism, ethnic customs and loyalties derived from foreign cultures, and nonwhite racial identity, which Evans collectively characterized as
"alienism," could not be made compatible with this vision of governance and

culture. From the Klan's perspective, the "melting pot" model of assimilation had failed to produce real Americans. Indeed, Evans liked to point out, "the very phrase was coined by an alien!"[4] Only by explicitly and thoroughly renouncing one's cultural and religious heritage could an ethnic American hope to become worthy of authentic American citizenship in the Klan's eyes. "The test of fitness of an alien for Americanism," the imperial wizard intoned, "is how much of his old loyalties he can abandon."[5] For nonwhites, the barrier of race remained immutable. Despite their largely American nativity, their overwhelmingly Protestant confessional orientation, and the constitutional guarantee of citizenship explicitly given to them, blacks in the view of the Klan hierarchy were excluded as "a special case" from the opportunity to meet the Klan's "standard of Americanism."[6]

By denying immigrants, African Americans, Jews, and Catholics the authority to define Americanism on their own terms, as an adaptive or syncretic identity, the Klan's ideology thus branded pluralistic understandings of Americanism as antagonistic, "un-American" doctrines that threatened the integrity of American culture and democracy. A Klan lecturer extolling the Invisible Empire's role as "Protestantism's Ally" on public questions articulated this belief in a 1925 article. "Americanism does not mean that men can come here with their race instincts, culture, customs and religion . . . to set up their own ideals of democracy," he asserted. American democracy must rebuff alien ways. "America must not only be saved for Americans," the Klan lecturer stressed, "but by Americans."[7] The notion that only a shrinking band of "true" Americans maintained a legitimate national identity against a welter of alien and corrupted beliefs underlay the public activism of the Klan movement in the 1920s. The Klan's attempts to promote and control public schools, to enforce prohibition laws, to influence legislatures and political parties, and to police private behavior all stemmed from the Invisible Empire's sense of the importance and the current vulnerability of American principles grounded in native-born white Protestant beliefs.

The Klan's devotion to a restrictive, purified American identity was a formula for a *Kulturkampf* in the 1920s, but not for the ultimate success of the hooded enterprise. Decades of immigration (most of it drawing from regions other than the "Nordic" lands favored in Klan mythology), expanding American engagement with the rest of the world, and the development during the Progressive Era of a liberal commitment to a more culturally expansive understanding of American identity—all contributed to what the historian Morton Keller called "the fact of American pluralism" in the early twentieth century.[8] Most Klansmen recognized that fact. Their resentment of it, in many cases, most likely had spurred their entry into the hooded order. For many ordinary Klansmen, the klavern and the native-born white Protestant community that it celebrated provided a buffer between their idealized America and the reality of an increasingly pluralistic society in the 1920s. Until mid-decade, many rank-and-file Klansmen probably hoped that the political initiatives championed by national Klan leaders might indeed prompt the state to enforce the Klan's version of cultural nationalism. Yet the commitment of the hooded membership to that end rarely matched the intensity demanded by the leadership of the Invisible Empire.

Klankraft may have provided a ritualized community of model Americanism satisfactory to average Klansmen, but the public struggle to construct a system of law and governance that reflected the restrictive sense of Americanism envisioned by Evans and the Klan hierarchy faltered within a few years. Its temporary success was rooted in mainstream assumptions of behavioral norms and power relations that reflected a tradition of white Protestant political authority and cultural dominance in the United States. The enactment of immigration restriction, anti-Catholic theatrics in politics, and the persistence of the color barrier in the 1920s all attest to the general strength of native-born white Protestant identification in America. The growth of the Klan and the degree of respect shown toward it in the early 1920s mirrored, even if in exaggerated outline, long-standing patterns of racism, anti-Catholicism, and nativism in American private belief and public institutions. But the controversy that dogged the Klan and the eventual repudiation of the hooded order later in the decade reflect the distance between the national Klan leadership's commitment to codifying Americanism in public life and the rank and file's greater willingness to slip into a mostly cultural—that is, a more pluralistic—expression of American identity

Shades of Whiteness

In the context of the early twentieth century, there was no more basic tenet of Ku Klux Klan ideology than the assumption of the naturalness and suitability of white supremacy. Betraying defensiveness on some issues of Klan doctrine, Evans was straightforward and untroubled in his assertion of white racial privilege. It was an "undebatable" proposition, he wrote, that "the white race must be supreme, not only in America but in the world."[9] Nonwhite critics of the Klan publicly challenged assumptions of white superiority. James W. Johnson, secretary of the National Association for the Advancement of Colored People, for instance, mocked the "wholly mythical pioneer" undergirding Evans's claim for native white Protestant hegemony and curtly dismissed the imperial wizard's attention to racial purity with the tart observation that "all races are mixed."[10] Few white Americans in the early 1920s, however, even those made uneasy by the blunt declarations of the Invisible Empire, questioned their own sense of racial superiority. One embittered former Klansman prefaced his critique of the hooded order's racist propaganda with the disclaimer, "I believe that the United States is a white man's country."[11] From the court system that left the Fourteenth Amendment a dead letter and accepted disfranchisement in the South, to the redlining realtors and angry mobs that gathered to prevent African American settlement into previously all-white neighborhoods in Chicago, Detroit, and other Northern cities, the United States as a society stood firmly behind the racial line of division it had drawn at the end of the nineteenth century. "We Americans all deny equality to ten millions of our own [African American] citizens," Evans accurately observed in support of the Invisible Empire's doctrine of inherent inequality.[12]

Assertions of white supremacy that took the form of political domination by the white majority of European descent, along with social separation between whites and blacks, were relatively uncontroversial in 1920s America, even if violent acts and pronouncements in pursuit of these aims did foment disagreement. But the Klan's notion of white supremacy drew upon an expanded, if unsystematic, conception of racial identity. It pushed beyond the binary color line to encompass notions of racial difference that tested the boundaries of mainstream New Era racism. Too much of a patchwork to be considered an ideological system, the assertions of Evans and other nationally prominent Klansmen nevertheless articulated several features of racial identity and differentiation that distinguished the Klan's notion of Americanism from the competing model of pluralism.

Ideology and behavior as well as biology were central to the Klan hierarchy's notion of race. On several occasions Evans expressed the belief that "the races and stocks of men are as distinct as breeds of animals," with corresponding characteristics and behavior that could be preserved only by careful husbandry. Thus the "American race" to which Evans was devoted was not only "Nordic" in appearance but also peculiarly fitted for democracy through selective breeding, Protestant religious training, and a cultural legacy of individualism. The admixture of "closely related stocks" could improve the race, as Evans claimed had been done in the early years of the republic by intermarriage among "English, Dutch, German, Hu[e]genot, Irish and Scotch" strains.[13] Conversely, improper race mixing threatened to dilute the characteristics of the "American race." Citing "both biology and anthropology," Evans in his noted Texas State Fair address declared blacks racially incapable of civilization at the "Anglo-Saxon level."[14] Enforcing this racial vision, Klan vigilantes throughout the 1920s punished couples engaged in interracial sexual liaisons, and the hooded order formally advocated the passage of miscegenation laws that would bar interracial marriage "in every state of the Union."[15]

To the ideologues of the Klan, the threat posed by "mongrelizing . . . the citizenship of the United States" was religious and political as well as biological.[16] Open European immigration was therefore a danger to American "racial integrity."[17] A 1922 publication that reflected Klan priorities stated the issue plainly: "a republic is possible only to men of homogenous race."[18] This essentialist notion of race incorporated a belief that specific cultural roots such as Protestant religious traditions and Western European lineage bred an aptitude for patriotism and democracy. Thus the pluralistic framework for American identification, by which immigrants retained portions of their home cultures while assimilating to American structures of governance and public life, was inadequate in Klansmen's eyes. Authentic American citizenship to Evans involved a "racial understanding of Americanism."[19] It could not simply be acquired by residency in the United States. Each "race," or, in later terminology, ethnic or cultural group, he explained, had the facility for certain social and political traits, but not others. The vote, therefore, was not a tool for creating Americans out of the heterogeneous ranks of immigrants, as assimilationists proposed. To the contrary, the Klan's racial doctrine taught that universal suffrage was a weapon mistakenly placed in the hands of strangers who held no reverence for American institutions and who were likely to inflict fatal injury to the republic. Returning to his animal husbandry analogy, Evans reasoned that just as it was fruitless to "train a bulldog to herd sheep," so would it be unreasonable to trust American democracy to foreign "races" whose religious dispositions and political traditions rendered them incapable of exercising freedom responsibly.[20]

To an extent, this vision of the breakdown of Americanism incorporated the fluid dimensions of racial identity in the late nineteenth and early twentieth centuries that went beyond cultural markers of color and physiognomy. As historians of whiteness have argued, into at least the 1920s, the cultural assignment of white racial identity in the United States was provisional and variegated. Although Greeks, Italians, Poles, Czechs, Slavs, and Eastern European Jews were recognized as white by the standards of American naturalization law (which after 1875 admitted "free white persons" and those of African nativity or descent to citizenship but excluded Asians[21]), during the great wave of immigration from the 1880s until the 1920s immigrants from Southern and Eastern Europe were nevertheless deemed racially distinctive from and inferior to Americans of Anglo-Saxon ancestry. The determinants of racial distinctiveness were assembled from physical characteristics such as skin tone and hair color;[22] generalized "national" qualities such as Jewish "clannishness" and "materialism" or a Latin propensity for excitability and violence; relative degrees of "civilization" or "barbarism" as measured by family organization, educational attainment, and economic development; and the imprint of religious and political traditions, especially those considered autocratic by Americans.[23] Matthew Frye Jacobson has argued that the behavior and associations of immigrants in America sometimes influenced racial status in such a way as to establish local variations of racial categorization. For instance, late nineteenth-century Italian immigrants in Louisiana who interacted with black Southerners and performed similar types of labor occupied a racial category closer to black than white in the estimation of other local whites.[24] In the hardscrabble mining and railroad towns of Utah, local white Mormons called Southern European immigrants "blacks" and objected to the marriage of a Greek immigrant to a white Mormon woman as a serious breach of racial boundaries.[25] Elsewhere immigrant communities that sharply distinguished themselves from their African American neighbors or assimilated to dominant Anglo-Saxon norms moved more quickly to white racial status.

Much of the Klan's racial sensibility reflected widespread American patterns of belief from the Gilded Age on. In step with European imperialism and economic expansion, old-stock Americans celebrated their subjugation of the continent and its native peoples as proof of the superiority of white, Western civilization. Neglecting the contributions of African, Asian, and Arab civilization over the centuries and brushing aside the protests of some cultural anthropologists, Western racial chauvinists casually misapplied Darwinian categories of natural selection to construct a racial hierarchy of human capability, with Anglo-Saxons at the pinnacle and other European-based racial/ national groups clustered some distance below.

But the second Klan's strong sense of racial threat from inferior European strains as well as from restive nonwhite races was more specifically informed by American racial alarmists and eugenics advocates of the early twentieth century.[26] Warnings that diseased, disorderly, and backward Eastern European races might outbreed and overwhelm old-stock Americans of Anglo-Saxon blood propelled the immigration debate. It culminated in legislation (in 1921 and in stronger form in 1924) imposing a quota system intended to reduce entry into the United States and redirect the smaller immigrant stream in favor of Western European national sources. American amateur racial theorists, endorsed by Theodore Roosevelt and other respectable voices, worried that the smaller families of old-stock American households presented the possibility of "race suicide" in the face of the immigrant demographic onslaught. As the second Klan took form and began to organize, two popular exemplars of what may be termed academic racism, Madison Grant's *The Passing of the Great Race* (1916) and Lothrop Stoddard's *The Rising Tide of Color against White World Supremacy* (1920), presented a systematic and, to white supremacists, more troubling framework of white decline under the weight of global racial competition.

Grant and Stoddard were influential in shaping the 1920s Klan's sense of imminent racial crisis. Their books sold well for scientific titles (both were reprinted several times, and *Passing* went through four editions) and attracted significant attention from prominent figures, including Marcus Garvey and W. E. B. DuBois. Moreover, the arguments of Grant and Stoddard seeped into the political and literary culture of the New Era. President Warren Harding once publicly endorsed Stoddard's work and F. Scott Fitzgerald dropped a reference to the two men's racial theories into *The Great Gatsby*.[27] Unlike nineteenth-century white racial chauvinists, Grant and Stoddard, working as European civilization shuddered and its colonial empires contracted during World War I, did not stress Anglo-Saxon superiority so much as the dire threats facing the purity of white racial lines and the perpetuation of white hegemony in a sharply altered world. Imperial Wizard Evans borrowed substantially from both authors in crafting the Klan's racial positions. Evans aligned the Invisible Empire with Stoddard's assertion that "the imperious urge of superior heredity" was fundamental to civilization.[28] Evans argued that the Klan was a natural expression in American terms of the biological imperative of white control. He furthermore appealed to Grant to underscore the necessity of the Klan's strict adherence to a Nordic definition of whiteness and corresponding commitment to a white supremacy of the narrowest type.[29] "The dangerous foreign races," Evans warned in an extended quotation from Grant, "will in time drive us out of our own land by the mere force of breeding," unless those "still of American blood . . . recognize and meet this danger."[30]

The Protestant and Nordic qualities of white racial identification were paramount in shaping the anti-Semitism of the Klan. On the one hand, the Invisible Empire shared in and drew upon the intensified hostility toward Jews evident in both Europe and the United States in the aftermath of World War I and the Bolshevik Revolution. In the bigoted imaginations of Henry Ford, Tom Watson, and other influential twentieth-century American anti-Semites, the traditional caricatures of the stateless wandering Jew and the materialistic Shylock fused with the more recent radical image of Leon Trotsky to produce a unique threat to Americanism—"an international enemy," in the apt description of John Higham, that was "half banker and half Bolshevik."[31] Klansmen boycotted local Jewish merchants or protested the works of Jewish film producers, often repeating these common tropes of the 1920s.

Klan ideologues, on the other hand, while clearly hostile to the Jewish presence in the United States, placed greater emphasis on what they defined as the racial bar of separation between Jews and authentic—that is, Nordic and Protestant—Americans. Hiram Evans expressed admiration for Jewish solidarity, racial purity, and a commitment to communal welfare, which he

described as "Klannishness."[32] Yet the distinctiveness and non-Christian identity of Jews, a quality that Evans called "racial rather than religious," barred
them from true fellowship as Americans.[33] Seeking to cast Jewish "otherness"
in plainer ethnic terms, Evans at one point insisted that the Eastern European
Jews who dominated the new immigration were "not true Jews" at all, "but
only Judaized Mongols."[34] In short, unlike the nineteenth-century European-
ized Jews who carried the prospect of assimilation as they immigrated to the
United States, the majority of American Jews in the 1920s were indisputably
alien. Thus the Klan accepted the blunt analysis of Madison Grant that "the
cross between any of the three European races [including Nordics and the
lesser white strains] and a Jew is a Jew," and never a white American.[35]

The Klan's commitment to white supremacy was derived from the cultural currents of racialist thinking in the early twentieth century. Yet during
the 1920s, at least in terms of attitudes toward European ethnic populations
within the United States, American society began to relax racial divisions
along the spectrum of whiteness. As Jacobson framed it, the "Anglo-Saxon
exclusivity" of the long nineteenth century slowly gave way to "a pattern of
Caucasian unity . . . in the 1920s and after."[36] The theoretical sources of the
Klan's racial taxonomy unevenly reflected this shift. Stoddard, sobered by
the possibility of "colored" civilizations offering serious challenges to white
hegemony, deemphasized the degrees of racial differentiation among European strains in favor of a broader "white" solidarity against a rising nonwhite
world.[37] Grant, by comparison, was more fixated on the debilitating consequences to American society posed by the absorption, or even toleration, of
weaker Eastern European racial characteristics. Evans, and the formal Klan
movement, steadfastly held to Grant's restrictive conception of Nordic white
Americanism, amplified by the Klan's unyielding anti-Catholic animosity
against the Irish. The historian Matthew Guterl suggests that Stoddard and
New England Klan official A. J. Padon Jr. brought entirely different racial
sensibilities to a celebrated 1922 joint appearance near Boston: the Klansman
refracted Stoddard's fame as a white supremacist to irritate the Irish in their
Massachusetts stronghold while the racial theorist viewed the meeting as a
gesture of white solidarity, which embraced the white Irish, against "the threat
posed by a deeply racialized and color-coded 'under-man.'"[38]

By fiercely advocating a fading standard of racial distinction among white
Americans—bound up as it was with religious intolerance and a severely attenuated definition of Americanism sure to insult those whom it excluded—
the Invisible Empire courted notoriety and controversy, and not solely from
white ethnics or racial liberals. "The classification of the white Catholic and
Jew with the negro is a stupid blunder," argued an estranged former Klansman. "It is splitting the white race into factions at a time when it should stand

together."[39] Methodist bishop Edwin Hughes denounced the Klan at a 1926 church conference in language that inadvertently paralleled Stoddard's call for white unity in the face of global racial competition. "If we keep on with our silly [Klan] movement," he fulminated, "we will cause the black, yellow, and brown races to combine against Caucasians, and then God help the white peoples of the world."[40] Discord also stemmed from Imperial Wizard Evans's declaration that racial difference invariably required a contest for power, an outlook clearly grounded in the arguments of Stoddard and Grant. "Maudlin theories of cosmopolitanism," he asserted, could not hide the brutal fact that "each race must fight for its life, must conquer, accept slavery or die."[41] Many white Americans in the 1920s, no doubt including many rank-and-file Klansmen, were comfortable with the concept of racial hierarchy yet distressed by the prospect of inevitable and unending race war.

Inconsistencies and contradictions marred what the Klan hierarchy claimed was its straightforward and natural ordering of the racial attributes of Americanism and "alienism." Racial definitions, especially involving Jews and immigrant Catholics, broke down into their religious and cultural components. At times Evans suggested that such religious and cultural barriers to full assimilation were permeable and that immigrants could become fully American. He once speculated that Jewish distinctiveness would disappear if Jews would heed the Klan, "boast of being . . . American" instead of embracing a separate identity, and allow themselves to be overwhelmed by the majority culture of Christian Americanism.[42] Three months later the imperial wizard declared that Jews were an "absolutely unblendable element" that would "not in a thousand years of continuous residence . . . form basic attachments" to American society and institutions.[43] One of the chief objections to Jews, as articulated by Evans, was their ban on intermarriage, a position that the Klan paradoxically endorsed as part of its own racial prophylaxis.[44] That complaint also contrasted with the stock image, promoted by the Klan, of Jewish men's interest in seducing white Protestant women.[45] Demography, in the inconsistent ideology of Klan leaders, either threatened the Invisible Empire's ideal white supremacist democracy with a debilitating "mongrelization" or held out the possibility of promoting Americanism through reproduction.

Considerable confusion also attended the placement of Catholicism within the Klan's framework of racial determinism. Evans and other hooded spokesmen routinely asserted that the Klan made no protest against the strictly religious practices of Catholicism. The hooded order objected only to the church's intrusion into politics and its curtailment of American loyalties and attitudes among its communicants. Catholicism, to that extent, was not a component of racial categorization. Yet the Invisible Empire also insisted that the Catholic Church, as an institution and a cultural force, was willfully alien; indeed, as Evans described it, "the Roman Church today [is] the chief leader of alienism, and the most dangerous alien power with a foothold inside our boundaries."[46] In the Klan's racial cosmology, alienism was the product of both blood and tradition, a deeply embedded cultural code that went beyond heritage in its power to predispose minds and influence behavior. "The alien in the vast majority of cases," Evans charged, "is unalterably fixed in his instincts, character, thought and interests by centuries of racial selection and development . . . [so] he thinks first for his own people, works only with and for them, cares entirely for their interests, considers himself always one of them, and never an American."[47]

By the strange chemistry of the Klan's racial principles, not only was the Catholic Church perceived as an institutional threat to American liberty and democracy but Catholic identity also functioned as a primary marker of racial incompatibility between the alien and American temperament. Thus despite the "nearly American . . . tone"[48] of New York governor Alfred E. Smith's personal articulation of his "creed as an American Catholic"[49] (offered in a 1927 exchange with Protestant attorney Charles C. Marshall), in the judgment of the imperial wizard the genetic stain of Catholic identity invalidated the Happy Warrior's suitability for high public office. Hinting that a force beyond human volition was at work, Evans conceded that a Catholic politician who broke free from "the evils in his Church's position" might be considered a true American, "but we fear this exception is theoretical rather than real, for we have found no Roman Catholics who meet that test."[50] The intellectual precariousness of this hybrid doctrine in a nation that was sufficiently pluralistic in 1928 to award Smith the Democratic nomination for president (and the majority of Southern votes in the general election) reveals the intrinsic weakness of the Klan movement's hyperbolic conception of race.

Beyond contradictions in doctrine, there is evidence that local Klans often neglected the racial priorities of the national order. As we have seen, many Northern and Western klaverns, while indulging in the bigoted wordplay that accompanied assumptions of white Protestant superiority, nevertheless devoted more attention to fraternal and community-building concerns than to the activities of minority communities.[51] In the Northern realms the most searing racist sentiments were uttered by traveling Klan lecturers rather than by local officials or rank-and-file knights. During the kluxing of western New York, Buffalo knights heard a national Klan lecturer from Texas excoriate blacks as "menacing figure[s], threatening the heart of America"; claim that Catholic assassins had murdered Lincoln and McKinley; and intimate that Jewish entertainment moguls sought to "destroy the morals of the world."[52] These sentiments, and those of the national Klan hierarchy, appeared radical in comparison to the explanation of Klan principles outlined by New

York's main hooded recruiter. "Klansmen don't doubt the loyalty, integrity and bravery of Catholics, Jews, negroes and foreign born persons," the king kleagle stressed, pitching his appeal to fit the sentiments of the state's Klansmen. "These classes proved themselves good and brave Americans during the recent war and we are not against them."[53]

The contrast between the casual assumption of white supremacy at a local klavern and the urgent advocacy of repressive action by agents of the Klan was also evident in an escalating series of encounters between northwest Indiana Klansmen and visiting national speakers. Representatives of the Atlanta headquarters advised the unreceptive locals to tar and feather neighborhood Catholics, distribute anti-Catholic pamphlets, boycott Jewish and Catholic businesses, and, in a final appeal from the Indiana grand dragon, "pull off a midnight parade, and run [job-seeking] negroes out of town."[54] Although this group of Klansmen eagerly blamed Catholics for prohibition violations and celebrated white Protestant culture, they were unwilling to aggressively confront those whom the Klan hierarchy defined as enemies of Americanism. "Our men wouldn't stick for that kind of stuff," the exalted cyclops responded in rebuffing the proposed intimidation of blacks.[55]

Even in the racially charged Southwest, local klaverns were selective and elastic in their application of Klan racial proscriptions. These themes were clearly expressed in the Texas realm. Dallas Klansmen engaged in a curious wooing of the local Jewish community in political campaigns, even as Klan officials rained vitriol on Jews and masked vigilantes assaulted a local Jewish man. A group of Klansmen approached one Jewish merchant in the hope that he would become their kleagle and went away disappointed when it became clear that he was ineligible for membership in the Invisible Empire. A Klan statement on public schools objected to Catholic teachers and school board members yet signaled acceptance of Jewish participation.[56] While Texans offered thunderous applause when Evans detailed black inferiority in his state fair address, they responded lukewarmly to the imperial wizard's strident attacks on immigrant Catholics and Jews.[57] In the tension evident here between the eagerness of the national Klan leadership to tutor the rank and file in targeted bigotry, and the tendency of local klaverns to emphasize their own divergent concerns, one can detect fissures in the Klan movement. They soon expanded into unmanageable ruptures between the Ku Klux hierarchy, state and regional hooded officers, and disaffected ordinary Klansmen.

Regional and even local variations, and a distinction between rhetoric and action, complicate any evaluation of the Klan's interactions with its self-defined "alien" enemies. Each section of the Invisible Empire identified regionally specific threats to white Protestant hegemony that subtly altered the dynamics of Klan activism. "The Klan," a *New Republic* reporter pointed out in 1923, "adapts itself to each community it enters. In the South, it uses the Negro as a stalking horse. In California, it is anti-Japanese. Along the Atlantic seaboard, where anti-Semitism is found, it attacks the Jew; and in the northern part of the Middle West the Catholic church is its foe."[58] In 1923 the grand dragon of Oregon singled out "the rapid growth of the Japanese population and the great influx of foreign laborers, mostly Greeks" as the distinctive challenge to "American institutions" in the Northwest. Oregon Klansmen, acting in concert with a broader nativist coalition, thus added agitation for a law barring alien land ownership to the standard array of hooded concerns.[59] Klan officials endorsed California nativists' demand for total exclusion of Japanese immigration to their state.[60]

But the correlation between local and national hooded preoccupations was even more complex than the *New Republic* model suggested. Hooded hostility to seasonal Mexican workers and immigrants, for example, was noticeable in south Texas[61] and in Colorado sugar beet towns.[62] When Evans joined in by identifying Mexican migrants as dangerous carriers of both Catholicism and communism,[63] who were "waiting a chance to cross the Rio Grande"[64] and infect America, it appeared that the Invisible Empire was about to promote a serious anti-Mexican campaign. Ku Kluxers in other centers of Mexican American settlement, however, remained silent. According to Shawn Lay, the large Catholic and Mexican presence in El Paso restrained rather than promoted the influence of the Klan in that border city.[65] Southern California Klansmen, reflecting the dominant perception of the region's Anglos in the 1920s, tolerated the (segregated) presence of Catholic Mexicans as a necessary and mobile workforce that did not disrupt existing power relations.[66] Yet local Catholics from European backgrounds drew the ire of the Invisible Empire because they were legitimate rivals in matters of governance and public authority. And even though the Oregon Klan identified regionally particular threats to Americanism by decrying Japanese land ownership, its most prominent public campaign was against Catholic private education, a reflection of national patterns within the Invisible Empire.

The relative scarcity or concentration of Jews and Catholics in Klan hotbeds, even in the South, did not diminish the nearly universal presence of anti-Semitic and anti-Catholic rhetoric among Klansmen. Acrid denunciations of Jews and Catholics, often recycled from nativist zealots such as Georgia's Tom Watson (who maintained cordial relations with the national Klan hierarchy), sometimes found reflection in Klan boycotts of Jewish merchants and concrete attempts to purge Catholic teachers and administrators from public schools.[67] On the other hand, Charles Alexander concluded that Southwestern Klansmen refrained from mounting challenges against prominent Jewish families and political figures in the region.[68] The papal toadies and Jewish moneylenders of Klan lore grew faint in some hooded strongholds as Klansmen busied themselves correcting the moral errors of fellow white Protestants. Yet racially based presumptions of white Protestant supremacy, sometimes bordering on mainstream white beliefs and sometimes moving beyond them, remained formative in the Klan's definition of Americanism. Among these intolerant sentiments, the assumption of black inferiority was a constant of Klan conviction.

Regulating the Color Line

Mainstream white American racial prejudice against African Americans was more compatible with the anti-black principles of the Invisible Empire than with other elements of Klan racial doctrine. The formalization of Jim Crow and the unquestioned assumption of white political dominance accommo-dated the outlook, if not specifically the vigilante methods, of the hooded knights. In light of that congruence, the Klan movement of the 1920s was not obsessively concerned with electoral threats to white supremacy from African Americans, with the significant exception of some Southern realms where a hair-trigger sensitivity to the political implications of racial identification at times produced explosively violent repression of black Southerners. But even in the South and Southwest, the willingness of whites to assemble in extralegal mobs and use violent means to ensure white domination was not restricted to the membership of the Klan.

Racist action against blacks was a minor theme of the 1920s Klan, not be-cause the Invisible Empire entertained egalitarian notions but because white willingness to suppress African Americans in the New Era made extraordinary efforts by Klansmen unnecessary. Racial intimidation and frightening epi-sodes of organized violence aimed at controlling black behavior and main-taining racial subjugation were widespread in the World War I era. Anger at black competition with whites for jobs, bitter opposition to black residential mobility and economic aspirations, political conflict, and prickly encounters in public spaces fueled a destructive wave of racial rioting. Chiefly provoked by white mobs, from the turn of the century into the early 1920s such riots spilled blood in Wilmington, North Carolina; Atlanta; and, in an escalating pattern of violence, the Illinois cities of Springfield, East St. Louis, and Chi-cago. In 1921 armed white mobs entered the black section of Tulsa, Okla-homa, and obliterated the Greenwood neighborhood, resulting in more than fifty deaths and the forcible internment of nearly half the African American residents of the city.[69] Although these events reflected the social and cultural turbulence in which the Klan movement of the 1920s appeared, the Invisible

Empire did not provoke or take part in these spectacular episodes of racially targeted violence. Indeed, one of the major instigators of the 1919 Chicago riot, the Irish athletic club Ragen Colts, became an avowed enemy of the revived Klan.[70]

Nor did Klansmen dominate the grisly ritual of lynching, though historians have identified Klan involvement in specific incidents.[71] Hooded knights in two racially tense north Georgia counties were the most likely culprits in the murders of a handful of black men in the winter of 1921–1922.[72] In a more spectacular event in Aiken, South Carolina, in 1926, a suspicious raid on the household of the Lowman family resulted in the shooting death of the sheriff leading the operation, a prominent Klansman, and the mother of the assaulted family. When the murder trial of three of the surviving Lowman sons and daughters took an unexpected turn toward acquittal, hooded colleagues of the fallen sheriff abducted the black siblings from jail and shot them in the woods.[73]

But Klan lynch mobs were rare, even in the violent South. Although Southern Klansmen enforced white supremacy through brutal measures, the violent work usually was shrouded in secrecy and performed by a small band of masked assailants under cover of darkness. Lynching as an instrument of white collective violence—in most but not all cases—remained a public spectacle, a horrifying expression of community will in allegiance to an unbending and ruthless racial hierarchy. Masks were unnecessary, even antithetical, to such an enterprise. "The naked truth," argued a black Savannah newspaper, "is that when a band of lynchers set out to kill a negro they do not take the trouble to mask. They do not think it necessary to join a secret society, pay initiation fees and buy regalia when negroes are the quarry." In company with other white Southerners, Klansmen may have approved of lynchings and even, unmasked, participated in them. But the Klan's moral vigilantism, exercised against wayward whites as well as blacks, took other forms. "Ku Klux methods are employed in the South against white men," continued the *Savannah Tribune*, "because the victims may have friends who would cause arrests or otherwise 'fight back.'"[74] A Texas Klan official claimed in 1923 that knights there, serving as guardians of the legal process, actually prevented a lynching.[75] Whatever their motivations, Klansmen in regalia tended not to lead or participate in lynch mobs. From 1922 to 1924, the most influential and active years of the second Klan, the national lynching toll actually declined.[76]

In the taut, racially sensitive atmosphere of the postwar years, anti-black violence by the Klan did not exceed that committed by white society in general. In a similar vein, the Klan's commitment in the 1920s to maintain the separation and subordination of African Americans in a white-controlled society blended with popular white sentiments in racially contested neighborhoods and institutions across the country. In the most volatile expression of this trend, Detroit Klansmen encouraged the formation of white neighborhood associations to block the movement of black home seekers into white sections of the city.[77] A coalition of whites, including some Catholics hostile to the hooded order, organized to defend residential segregation, leading to a series of mob actions against black households that reached a flashpoint when friends of a beleaguered African American physician fired into a crowd of white attackers, killing one.[78] The Klan, though it stirred up the campaign, was but one part of a polyglot expression of white racial hostility to black residential expansion. Nor could the Invisible Empire take comfort in the unusual denouement of the affair, when attorney Clarence Darrow and the National Association for the Advancement of Colored People (NAACP) managed to block a furious effort by local prosecutors to convict Dr. Ossian Sweet and his brother of murder in the death of the white rioter.[79] Indianapolis Klansmen more smoothly aided white neighborhood groups resisting black homeowners.[80] Klansmen on the city council passed an ordinance empowering white neighbors to block home purchases by African Americans. An NAACP challenge invalidated the ordinance.[81]

Both for the Klan and the broader white community, racial separation was a critical component of white supremacy.[82] The familiarity that accompanied social interaction could lead to transgressions across the more sensitive sexual color line, which in turn could undo racial integrity, a central aspect of white supremacy to the Klan. Interracial cooperation of any sort, one frantic Klan sympathizer from Georgia maintained, would expose "our PRICELESS white girls" to the disastrous possibility of racial pollution.[83] Southern Klansmen therefore firmly maintained the importance of the Jim Crow system of segregation that was already in place by World War I. Klaverns outside the South sought to minimize social contact across racial lines, even while accepting black suffrage and the small political influence that came with it. The Denver Klan threatened the local NAACP head after the organization put its influence behind a movement by black Denverites to integrate theaters and public facilities. But even here the Klan was not always the most radical voice among white institutions. After black youngsters joined an exclusively white school dance, the local PTA suggested the need for segregated schools. Betraying its overwhelming interest in the social manifestations of the color line, the Denver Klan suggested that segregated schools were not required but that social events should be strictly separated by race.[84]

Still, racial boundaries of sexuality and social familiarity between whites and blacks were linked with the essentials of political control, sometimes in harshly worded pronouncements, by Klan officials. Colonel William Simmons, the founder of the second Klan, made a number of such crude appeals to Southern audiences as part of his promotion of the revived order. On one occasion he reportedly laid a collection of weapons before him and dramatically dared "the Niggers, Catholics, Jews" and other enemies of the Klan to "come on."[85] In the spring of 1922, as recounted in the Klan press, Simmons employed raw language connecting black political aspirations to the dangers of social mixing as twin forces challenging white supremacy. "I am informed," he announced with demagogic theatricality, "that every buck nigger in Atlanta who attains the age of twenty-one years has gotten the money to pay his poll tax and register, and that 6,000 of them are now ready to vote, and that these apes are going to line up at the polls, mixed up there with white men and white women." Simmons then made explicit his suggestion that public mingling would promote private intimacy. "Keep the Negro and the other fellow where he belongs," he advised. "They have got no part in our political or social life. If in one, he will get into the other."[86] In a bid to make the Invisible Empire appealing to white racist sentiment that feared the possibility of public and private racial amalgamation, William Y. Clarke, the original salesman of the 1920s Klan, briefly advocated the sterilization of male black children.[87]

Although he used a calmer tone than his Klan predecessors, Evans nonetheless maintained that white supremacy ultimately rested on the retention of white political power over blacks. "America owes it to the Negro to give him every privilege and protection and every opportunity consistent with our National safety," he averred, "but dare not risk the destruction of our civilization that might come if its control should ever fall into his hands."[88] In portions of the South, Klansmen violently truncated black political activity. This theme was most widespread in Florida, where, according to one historian, "practically all Klan activity in local politics was channeled into preventing the Negroes from exercising the franchise."[89] Klan parades, distribution of circulars, and intimidating demonstrations of force specifically aimed at minimizing African American voting took place in Orlando, Jacksonville, and Miami.[90] But even these repressive acts occurred against a backdrop of collective white violence in 1920s Florida that, by most accounts of the spectacular destruction of black settlements in Ocoee and Rosewood, operated independently of the Klan.[91] An isolated but disturbing incident in Oklahoma punished both political and racial infractions. A team of masked Klansmen abducted a black Tulsa activist, charged him with registering black voters and addressing a white woman impertinently, then beat and whipped him, cut off his ear, and urged him to leave the state, which he refused to do.[92]

"Warning out," another traditional instrument of white racial hegemony in the South, was adopted by Klansmen in some localities to discourage black economic competition with whites or to cow collective action by black workers that challenged racial subordination.[93] Klan activity in some overwhelmingly white up-country Georgia counties aimed to drive out black job seekers drawn to the area by elite white employers,[94] but elsewhere in the South the desire to retain black agricultural workers and laborers during the Great Migration northward produced different tactics. Texas knights, for instance, issued threats that broke up a strike by African American cotton harvesters.[95] Unemployed blacks were warned out by Klansmen in one Oklahoma town.[96] In other Oklahoma communities the established practice of driving out black residents with violent threats was redirected by the Klan at bootleggers and other violators of moral norms, both black and white. Some of the African American victims of the practice, however, were also business owners, and the language of intimidation was sometimes racially specific, as in the case of an Enid feed dealer who was reminded by Klansmen of the destruction of black Tulsa. "What do you want us to do," the hooded vigilantes wrote, "burn that [black] end of town?"[97]

Politically based terrorism in many forms was present in the 1920s Klan movement, but the primary focus of the Klan's attention toward blacks remained the tight regulation of personal race relations. In much of the nation, as the highly visible presentations of money by hooded Klansmen to African American churches and cultural groups were intended to emphasize, Ku Kluxers took it upon themselves to steer African American associational life into acceptable channels. According to an official of the Tuskegee movement, Southern knights offset accusations of violence with charitable acts that also served to draw the color line forcefully. Klan contributions to segregated black institutions—a hospital in North Carolina, a rest home in Mississippi, a modest trade school in Georgia—were exercises in racial control as much as acts of philanthropy.[98] Klan officials went so far as to salute the racial separatism of the black nationalist Marcus Garvey as a wise and responsible doctrine. "Garvey is out fighting for the negro on right lines," argued a Texas Klan newspaper, "and the negro will go a long way if he hews to a line of demarcation."[99] Determined "to keep the black man black and the white man white," the 1920s Klan asserted that interracial familiarity was not only inappropriate but also genetically dangerous. Because the integrity of white bloodlines was essential in retaining the American aptitude for democracy and safeguarding the civilizing qualities of Anglo-Saxon culture, Klansmen acted to police the sexual and social boundaries of the color line.

Within the Klan movement, speakers periodically aired vivid and exaggerated rumors of imminent threats to white racial purity. New Jersey's grand dragon claimed in 1923, without documentation, that in the preceding year "87,000 white girls were living with negroes and members of the yellow race."[100] Charges that black men acquired white brides as an assertion of status and racial equality enlivened the 1925 presentation of a Klan lecturer.

"Scores of the most fashionable and elite Negro clubs and societies in America demand that each applicant must first have a white wife," he charged, adding that the Invisible Empire was the necessary "organization . . . to guard and protect our race."[101] The national Ku Klux leadership stepped in to give direction to the outrage their lieutenants had stirred up. "The Negro is America's problem," Evans emphasized, and proper regulation of that "problem" required a vigilant insistence "that intermarriage and social equality are impossible."[102]

The imperial wizard's determination was, in this case, echoed by many in the hooded rank and file. A local Klan official in Marion County, Ohio, affirmed to a reporter his conviction that "when a mixture of the races occurred Providence intervenes" by producing sterile children. Untroubled by any blacks residing near his rural home, this Ohio Klansman nevertheless counseled "relentless firmness" in preventing African Americans "from intermarrying with whites."[103] Even a group of white Texas educators who presented themselves as racial moderates endorsed the Texas Klan's "determination to prevent cohabitation and promiscuous intimacy between whites and blacks."[104]

Despite the inflated rhetoric of the Klan's defense of white racial integrity, its hostility to interracial relationships tapped into a cultural reservoir of white supremacist conviction so deep that it rarely required examination. The hooded order's public remedy to sexual pollution, so-called miscegenation laws—which in their various embodiments outlawed marriage (and in extreme versions, sexual contact) between blacks and whites as well as whites and Asians or other "nonwhite" groups—were not an innovation in the 1920s. Laws barring interracial marriage or sexuality had been present in America since colonial times and had accelerated in the late nineteenth century and in the racially constrictive Progressive Era. In 1913, two years before the founding of the second Klan, twenty-nine states already had miscegenation statutes, and eleven others were proposing passage of their own bans. The entire South and nearly all the Western states had enacted miscegenation laws before the 1920s.

The Klan's New Era initiative thus placed the secret order within a broad white racial consensus rather than in the radical vanguard of racist regulation, especially in preventing black amalgamation with whites. Nevertheless, the Invisible Empire worked to expand the barriers to interracial marriage into the Midwest and Northeast, regions that had resisted formal strictures against mixed unions. Klansmen, sometimes in competition with other supporters of white supremacy, pushed miscegenation bills in Indiana, Ohio, and Michigan in 1925 and helped introduce eight more in 1927, penetrating into New England.

The Klan's advocacy of miscegenation laws did not guide the legislative expression of mainstream white supremacist convictions in the early twentieth century. The Invisible Empire was checked in its attempts to exclude mixed marriage by the NAACP, which, in combination with its victory in the Sweet case and its successful challenge of Indianapolis residential segregation, expressed the increasingly pluralistic institutional structure of 1920s America that hindered the Klan movement. The historian Peggy Pascoe has documented the extent to which NAACP lawyers and lobbyists turned back the 1920s wave of Klan-backed miscegenation bills. All of the 1927 initiatives died in state legislatures. Any assessment of the Klan as the bellwether Negrophobic force in the 1920s cannot rest on the Invisible Empire's legislative achievements. But the Klan's vigilantism, even in defense of widely shared racial prejudices, displayed the power to shock Americans.[105]

While in public the Klan vigorously advocated legislative remedies to the perceived danger of miscegenation, the strong desire to blot out interracial sexuality prompted direct action by local knights. Historians of the Klan have clearly established that the order's moral vigilantism was not exercised solely, or even chiefly, against African Americans. The overwhelming majority of victims subjected to Klan beatings, whippings, and more serious violence were white. Still, much of the vigilantism that occurred outside the South and Southwest, aside from quasi-legal prohibition raids, and most of the rare violent actions and threats issued by Western and Midwestern Klansmen involved punishment of interracial sexual transgressions. "Indiscretions" with a white woman led to a mock hanging and beating of a black Pennsylvanian at the hands of Klansmen.[106] Complaints from "a white prostitute" spurred the state's grand dragon to order the beating of another black man, an act later repudiated by the disaffected rank and file.[107] Allegations of "abusive language" and "intimate relations with white women" by a black Denver custodian prompted the local Klan to mail the offender a letter promising to abuse his "hide" unless he left town immediately.[108] The journalist Robert Duffus reported that hooded knights in Muncie, Indiana, "seized a Negro boy accused of flirting with white girls, carried him to the woods, warned him, and turned him loose."[109] Pennsylvania Ku Kluxers boasted that hooded intimidation had scared away from their communities a collection of black prostitutes and a "nigger living with [a] white widow-woman."[110] Even the relatively mild-mannered Wisconsin Klan intervened to stop a proposed marriage between a white Milwaukee man and a black woman, though the wedding eventually took place.[111]

Warnings alone were not sufficient for the Klans of the violent Southwest, especially during their tumultuous formative years of 1921–1922. Masked Klansmen in Texarkana delivered a beating as well as a caution to a young black man to cease "fooling about a white woman."[112] Hiram Evans himself, while head of Dallas Klan No. 66, reputedly led a party of Klansmen that seized a black hotel bellman suspected of pandering and other sexual improprieties involving white women; they branded the letters KKK on his forehead with acid.[113] Houston Klansmen in 1921 outdid their fellow Texas knights in their brutal enforcement of the racial code against an African American dentist who had been fined in court for having sexual relations with a white woman. Brushing aside the legal sanction, armed Klansmen kidnapped and castrated their victim, then arranged for an ambulance to bring him to a hospital.[114] Houston area Klansmen had violently abused white sexual offenders as well, even castrating one. But violations of the sexual color line seemed to provoke a particularly visceral response in the South and Southwest. Most of the whites severely punished by squads of Klansmen had accosted underage girls or engaged in reckless adultery; several blacks suffered as a result of consensual adult relationships.

Unlike the Klan's miscegenation proposals, vigilante action that escalated to mutilation offended mainstream Southern white sensibilities. Amid rumors of possible black retaliation, Houston's dominant institutions rebuked the Klan, some prominent voices even calling for its dismantling. White critics of Klan violence did not dissent from the hooded order's commitment to white supremacy, however, only to its masked and brutal expression. "White supremacy means white intelligence, white dealing and white methods," the *Houston Chronicle* declaimed in a revealing display of racial pride. "It is not to be found in this harking back to sheeted violence."[115] Public outcry led Texas Klan authorities to restrain night riding and vigilante violence in the realm and helped persuade Hiram Evans to emphasize political action over vigilantism as he ascended to national leadership as imperial wizard. Yet the Klan commitment to enforce white supremacy by regulating interracial familiarity and interaction continued, especially when the Invisible Empire's aims dovetailed with those of the larger white community.

Much of the Klan's rough policing of African Americans overlapped with other elements of the Klan's moral agenda. A Klan newspaper in 1924 reported that "white women and colored men danced and drank together" in a house located in the "red light district" of Evansville, Indiana.[116] Although race was not the most prominent factor in the Klan's campaign to suppress immoral behavior, the illicit atmosphere of forbidden amusements created opportunities for interracial mingling that threatened the white supremacist social order. Prohibition violations, gambling, and involvement in prostitution joined interracial sexuality in a perceived chain of misbehavior. Klansmen singled out for attention black men whose jobs in hotels, barbershops, and other public spaces placed them in a position to make contacts between the vice industry and weak-willed whites. A federal vice investigator in Tulsa in 1921 reported that "at the leading hotels and rooming houses the bell hops and porters are pimping for women, and also selling booze."[117] In Savannah, according to the Klan press, one could "go to a barber shop and the barber would ask if you wanted some liquor. The bootblacks were agents for the liquor rings, as well as bell boys in hotels."[118] Southern Oregon Klansmen, in an unusual mixture of frontier vigilantism and hooded night riding, subjected a bootlegging African American bootblack, as well as a white sexual libertine and a Mexican chicken thief, to a terrifying ordeal of near hanging. After the masked band raised the bound malefactors nearly off their feet, the ropes were lowered and the panicky victims ordered to leave the state.[119] A journalist chronicling Klan activity in the Southwest learned that local knights had warned "colored porters of disorderly houses in which both inmates and patrons were white . . . that they must get out of the disreputable business."[120] The hooded vigilantes who burned Alex Johnson, the Dallas bellhop, intended to punish his involvement in commercial vice as well as his flouting of the sexual color line. Similarly, Oklahoma Klansmen abducted and whipped a black Muskogee bellhop for selling illegal liquor as much as for his alleged sexual familiarity with white women.[121]

Violations of community moral standards attracted Klan attention whether committed by African Americans or, as in the overwhelming majority of cases, by whites. Although Klan publications noted a black propensity for illegal gambling and prohibition breaking, much greater emphasis was placed on the threats to American behavioral codes posed by "alien" immigrants, Catholic presence, and backsliding Protestant morality. According to one journalist, even in the most violent region of Klandom, the Southwestern states of Texas, Louisiana, Arkansas, and Oklahoma, black community leaders evaluated the local Klan as "mainly an anti-bootlegging, anti-home-breaking organization," which did not pose a special danger "as far as the security of their own people is concerned."[122] The brutal attacks on Alex Johnson and J. Lafayette Cockrell, the Houston dentist, were but two of fifty-two vigilante punishments doled out by the Texas Klan in a six-month period in 1921.[123] Virtually all the other assaults targeted whites.

Ku Kluxers, especially in the South and Southwest, often dealt harshly with whites who dared to ignore the sexual color line. In a notorious incident in Arkansas, two white men warned by local Klansmen to end their relationships with black women engaged in a shootout with hooded vigilantes that left one of the men dead.[124] Others sometimes found themselves on the wrong side of the Klan's definition of whiteness. Agitated Tampa Klansmen, employing the fluid racial categories of the 1920s Invisible Empire, whipped a local Greek man for "going out with white women."[125] The same fate befell a Greek native in Alabama who had married a local woman.[126] Hooded visitors scared away a Pennsylvania Greek accused of "messing around with [a] little girl."[127] A white Oklahoma woman was kidnapped by a group of Klansmen, bound, gagged, and splashed with acid because, they said, she "was engaged to a foreigner."[128]

But for several whites who received beatings or coats of tar and feathers from Southern Klans, undue familiarity with African Americans did not involve sexual encounters but rather professional assistance or social interaction that implied an equality of station. The first victim of the Klan's campaign of violence in Texas was a white attorney who worked for black clients and also defended "habitual lawbreakers."[129] Hooded Florida knights whipped and tarred a white Baptist minister to a black congregation in Miami because he allegedly preached "race equality" and belonged to a British veterans association.[130] Commercial relations between white tradespeople and African Americans occasionally led to hooded intervention. Klansmen in Birmingham, Alabama, brutalized a German grocer and his daughter because the shopkeeper overrode Klan complaints and allowed the young woman to serve black customers.[131] Other incidents linked economics and tensions over residential space. Atlanta Klansmen jammed the street with hooded protesters after a white grocer hired a black clerk in a racially contested neighborhood.[132]

In commerce as well as in social relations, hooded moral policing sometimes intersected with regulation of the color line, especially during the tumultuous growth of the Klan movement in the early 1920s. A white pool hall operator in Little Rock was whipped by Klansmen for welcoming black patrons as well as for his shady livelihood, which attracted gamblers, bootleggers, and a transient clientele.[133] A white sandwich seller's sales to blacks and his illicit relations with a female employee together spurred Atlanta knights to warn him. When he ignored the threats, four Klansmen tried to abduct him, and the incident took a fatal turn as the angry merchant stabbed one of the Klan vigilantes to death.[134]

❖

The Invisible Empire's commitment to white supremacy mandated the social separation of whites from blacks and the perpetuation of a secondary, inferior place for African Americans in public affairs. That position did not differ dramatically from mainstream white American attitudes in the 1920s, though the Klan's dedication to secrecy and its use of vigilante threats and nocturnal violence to enforce the color line, especially in sexual matters, exceeded accepted social norms of the period. Still, in the years after World War I, large aggregations of whites not involved in the Klan movement also turned to intimidation and violence to counter black assertiveness. Finally, the Klan movement generally outstripped most Americans in its eagerness to punish whites involved in cross-racial sexual and social interaction. Thus the Invisible Empire's doctrine of racialized Americanism, as it related to African Americans, was an exaggerated—and in its more violent expressions, an overtly offensive and repugnant—extension of well-established racial norms of the early twentieth century in the United States. The Klan's methods, rather than its convictions, were more often a source of controversy and so represented a theme of secondary importance in the Klan's challenge to the development of American pluralism in the 1920s. Steeped in American tradition, yet more transgressive in the context of the New Era, was the Invisible Empire's tenacious anti-Catholicism.

Catholicism as Anti-Americanism

Despite the 1920s Klan's rigorous commitment to protect white supremacy by maintaining the color line, a campaign that flared into violence in the South and Southwest, the most strikingly consistent feature of the revived Klan was its antipathy to Catholicism. This stance was usually framed as a necessary defense of the Protestant foundations of Americanism. With the simplicity one acquires from unexamined faith, Imperial Wizard Hiram Evans laid out the incompatibility between Protestant Americanism and the Catholic Church in America. Lauding Protestant Christianity as "the most perfect instrument of human progress," Evans attributed to the reformed faith the rise of "education for the peoples, freedom for inquiry into nature, science and all its fruits, free thought, free speech, free mental development for us all."[135] This legacy of Protestant freedom, the Klan insisted, reached its apogee in the creation of American democracy.

In contrast to the progress and individualism enshrined in American Protestant culture, Evans claimed that "Romanism denied every one" of the freedoms essential to civilization and cherished as a birthright by Americans. The Catholic Church was not only the foremost enemy of the hooded understanding of Americanism in the 1920s but also the faith of the great majority of new immigrants who, in the view of worried Klansmen, were flooding the country with alien folkways. In politics, religion, and culture, Klansmen came to regard the Catholic Church as a shorthand representation of all the alien, un-American threats against which the revived Klan had organized.

Anti-Catholicism was by far the most dominant force throughout Klandom in the New Era. An investigator exploring hooded bigotry in Indiana "heard little concerning the Jews and Negroes" from rank-and-file Klansmen. "I heard much concerning the Catholics," he added.[136] In a rural Iowa county that contained only one Catholic parish and a small mission, the letters of an ordinary Klansman revealed a preoccupation with the "fish church" and the threatening designs of the "fish-eaters" against expressions of Protestant culture such as public schools, prohibition enforcement, and the Klan itself.[137] Small Southern newspapers that constituted what one critic called "the shrieking Klan press" produced a stream of criticism directed at nuns, priests, Catholic schools, and rumored church plots to dominate America.[138] These attacks were so vitriolic that Imperial Wizard Evans, who presided over the Invisible Empire's war with Catholicism, was compelled to chide "vicious and ignorant anti-Catholic papers" that distracted attention from the Klan's important disputes with organized Catholicism.[139] The historian Mark Morris counted "at least 150" articles about Catholic topics in forty-five issues of the four-to-eight-page Klan newspaper, the *Texas 100 Per Cent American*, published in 1923 alone.[140]

Concern over the supposed Catholic conspiracy against American liberties at times nearly overcame other prejudices that motivated Klansmen. In 1924 a handful of hooded officials and allies of the Invisible Empire in Midwestern and Northeastern realms tentatively encouraged the formation of Klan-like auxiliaries for black Protestants, which bore such names as the Loyal Legion of Lincoln and the Ritualistic Benevolent Society for American Born Citizens of African Blood and Protestant Faith.[141] Although these exotic manifestations of the Klan movement failed to take root, the willingness of some knights to reach across the color line to build Protestant solidarity, severely limited and tenuous though such gestures remained, indicates the power of the anti-Catholic impulse in the Klan movement. Ideology as well as race sometimes gave way to the primacy of anti-Catholic activism. The centrality of anti-Catholicism in the 1920s Klan led large numbers of socialists into the hooded order in Milwaukee, the vigorous anti-clericalism of these radical knights overpowering the national Klan's pronounced hostility to socialism and its adherents.[142] Anti-Catholicism thus shaped the Klan movement as a pillar of American identity and, in strange corners of the hooded realms, reshaped the local manifestations of the Invisible Empire.

❖

The landscape of American demography and politics combined with an American Protestant tradition of hostility to Rome to raise anti-Catholicism into the central feature of the 1920s Klan movement. Among the roster of enemies identified by the Klan, only American Catholics posed a reasonable threat to the hooded order's idealized white Protestant commonwealth. African Americans were consigned by law, custom, and the assumptions of the majority white society to a separate, secondary status in American life. Black expressiveness was present in the arts, in intellectual matters, and, in some regions, in politics; but despite the hallucinated cries of "Negro domination" uttered by worried white supremacists, American public life in the 1920s remained the preserve of the white majority. The Jewish population was small, isolated, and, despite prominence in various fields of achievement, too negligible to draw much attention even from intolerant Klansmen.

By contrast, Catholics were numerous (more than eighteen million in the United States by 1922[143]) and, as the overwhelming majority of them were of white European lineage, they had access to levers of public influence as voters and officeholders. Catholic mayors, judges, state legislators, and congressmen helped determine public policy at national, state, and local levels, while Catholic civil servants, clerks, and police officers enforced the law alongside Protestant public officials. If, as suspicious Klansmen charged, Catholics were inclined to act in concert with the interests of their church, the Catholic presence in American public life and institutions allowed at least a foothold of influence.

Moreover, the church and its communicants' positions on several high-profile public questions clashed dramatically with the outlook of the Invisible Empire. In contrast to the Klan's fervent defense of American public education, Catholic parishes maintained an alternative network of Catholic schools. Many Catholic households considered them superior to the public educational system and an important resource in safeguarding the Catholic identity of their children and communities. As a Jesuit priest argued in print, "Catholics are not opposed to public schools because they are public, but because they are lacking in what Catholics hold to be essential to education."[144] This case for religious instruction was recast by Klansmen into a rebuke of the Americanizing influences of public schooling and a defense of undemocratic religious indoctrination. "The majority of the leaders and of the priests of the Roman Church are either foreign born, or of foreign parentage and training," Hiram Evans asserted. "They, like other aliens, are unable to teach Americanism if they wish, because both race and education prevent their understanding what it is."[145]

In a less formal vein, most American Catholics considered constitutional prohibition to be an unwarranted intrusion into the province of family life and individual behavior. The church, while encouraging personal temperance, reflected the viewpoint of its parishioners that the proscription of drink was not a proper matter for intrusive state authority. "A certain class of our people have erected Prohibition into a dogma," complained the same Jesuit critic of the Klan, "and anathematized everybody who does not agree with them in their interpretation of the way it should be carried into effect."[146] On the other hand, prominent Catholics' criticism of the dry reform as fanatical was "making 'Kluxers' out of everybody who does not agree" with that designation, fretted a Catholic supporter of prohibition.[147]

To Klansmen, prohibition was not only a test of whether Protestant moral standards should reign in public life but also of whether the law itself would be given due reverence. Catholic hesitation to support prohibition enforcement became, in hooded circles, evidence of patriotic shortcomings and criminal inclinations among Catholics. "People used to say that the saloon was a recruiting agency for crime," sneered a Klan newspaper. "But, as we look over the long list of crimes committed by the Pats and Mickeys, we are inclined to think that some religions are recruiting agencies for crime, too."[148]

Since immigrant communities were largely Catholic, the church also served as the shepherd and protector of these newest Americans, thus inevitably confronting the Klan's anti-alien posture and its specific support for restricting immigration. Evans maintained that the recent wave of "unassimilable and fundamentally un-American" Catholic immigration had "submerged" the remaining Catholics of "American stock" so that the Catholic presence in America had become a rank tidal pool of stagnant alien ideas. "The Roman Church seems to take pains to prevent the assimilation" of Catholic immigrants, Evans continued. "Its parochial schools, its foreign born priests, the obstacles it places in the way of marriage with Protestants unless the children are bound in advance to Romanism, its persistent use of the foreign languages in church and school, its habit of grouping aliens together and thus creating insoluble alien masses—all these things strongly impede Americanization."[149] By its very presence and function, most Klansmen believed, the Catholic Church in the United States was undermining American identity.

As with the racial doctrines of the Invisible Empire, its anti-Catholicism was deeply rooted in mainstream U.S. beliefs and practices. Sustaining the Klan's vivid sense of the Catholic threat to American institutions was a legacy of anti-Catholic folklore that had flourished in American Protestant culture and influenced American historical assumptions for more than a century. The basic elements of that legacy—buoyed by nativist riots in the 1840s, the political movement of Know-Nothingism in the 1850s, and the exclusionary demands of the American Protective Association in the 1890s—remained powerful in the public assertions of the Klan movement and, the evidence suggests, in the troubled imaginations of individual Klansmen. These can be quickly summarized: The hierarchical structure of the church, the power of priests and pope over subordinates and the laity, and the authority of church tradition in shaping theological positions crushed dissent and free inquiry among Catholics and required unconditional obedience from the faithful. The Roman church was a political organization as much as a religious body and, as such, directed the political actions of its communicants through the confessional and the homily. The supreme loyalty of American Catholics, therefore, was not to the United States but to a foreign pope and his agents among the bishops and priests in America. Corrupted by power and twisted by the unnatural demands of celibacy, priests and nuns engaged in shocking acts of immorality behind the walls of convents, monasteries, and other church property, requiring an even more pronounced commitment on the part of the church to secrecy and evasion, lest the terrible misdeeds of the clergy and religious become known. Unwilling to function within a climate of religious tolerance, the church plotted to undermine Protestantism and establish Catholic political control in the United States—subverting public schools, diverting public money to support Catholic institutions, and even preparing a palace in Washington in which the pontiff would take up residence to rule his American prize.

Long before the rise of the second Klan, public discourse in the United States routinely referred to the Roman church as the paradigm of illiberal hostility to democracy and enlightenment, a preeminent example of the immoral corruption that attended absolute authority. In the course of a stinging indictment of the depravity connected to the slave system, Massachusetts Republican senator Charles Sumner in 1860 likened isolated Southern plantations to "the irresponsible privacy of monastic life," which in sixteenth-century England had produced "vice and disorder in startling forms." Appealing to familiar Protestant tropes, the anti-slavery reformer repeated the stale medieval claim that "six thousand skulls of infants are said to have been taken from a single fish-pond near a nunnery" to make the point that the sexual appetites of unchecked slaveowners produced an equally startling toll in human commerce as the illicit slave children of masters were sold into bondage.[150]

The ubiquity of anti-Catholicism in nineteenth-century American culture, ranging from the popularity of *Fox's Book of Martyrs* in the libraries of respectable Protestant households to the crude slurs of the sensationalistic genre of convent "confessions" from the likes of Maria Monk and other dubious figures, was carried into the pluralistic twentieth century on the underside of formal Protestantism to influence the renewed Klan movement. Small but persistent and constantly alarmist rural anti-Catholic newspapers, such as *The Menace*, *Watson's Jeffersonian Weekly*, and the *Rail Splitter*, yipped and snarled at the heels of mainstream Protestant reform in the early years of the century.[151] In the 1920s their dyspeptic arsenal of anti-Catholic stories were reissued in such Klan journals as *The Searchlight*, *Colonel Mayfield's Weekly*, and the *Texas 100 Per Cent American*. Other holdovers from the marginal anti-Catholic press that blossomed during the heyday of the Invisible Empire were the professional "ex-nuns" and repentant priests who offered titillating insights into the allegedly lascivious worlds of the convent and cloister. Klavern minutes and Klan publications record steady engagements before hooded audiences for the reputed former nun Helen Jackson, passionately denounced as a charlatan by furious Catholics,[152] and "Sister" Mary Angel,[153] whose performance in Denver was characterized by a local Catholic newspaper as an exercise in "utter foulness,"[154] clearly intended to provoke Catholics and incite religious intolerance. The pornographic style of anti-Catholicism influenced at least some Klansmen to imagine links between Catholic depravity and public policy. "It does make my blood boil," one hooded commentator groused in denouncing a New York corruption probe involving Protestant support of prohibition, "to see Protestant activities subjected to the Roman Catholic investigations when [Catholics] defy every official to look behind the bolted iron doors of their convents where wickedness is carried on in its worst form against the young and unprotected girls just reaching the age of womanhood."[155]

A second stream of anti-Catholic conviction that flowed into the Klan movement came from Protestant fraternal organizations. The Junior Order of United American Mechanics had carefully tended the fires of anti-popery since the late nineteenth century and became a close ally of the second Klan.[156] Scottish Rite Masonry, a key source of recruits into the hooded empire in the early 1920s, was particularly keen to prevent Catholic influence over American public education. Scottish Rite Masons joined with Klansmen in Oregon to drive through the state legislature a short-lived statute that required Oregon children to attend public schools.[157] The *Fellowship Forum*, a Masonic journal, provided a platform for figures such as William H. Anderson, whose anti-Catholic obsession and encouragement of the Klan drove him from the mainstream of the Anti-Saloon League.[158] *Fellowship Forum* was so cordial in its coverage of the Invisible Empire that most observers regarded it as an unofficial Klan publication. Even though the hierarchy of Freemasonry denounced the Klan, officials of the hooded sect appealed to the anti-Catholic principles of the organization to strengthen the fraternal bond of militant Protestantism between Klansmen and Masons.[159] "You know," blurted the exalted cyclops of the Dallas Klan to a fellow Scottish Rite Mason who took up an anti-Klan position, "that Rome has never stopped at anything . . . to accomplish her purpose in controlling governmental affairs and the free institutions of this country. If you do not believe these things," he darkly warned, "then you do not believe the things that are taught by Masonry."[160]

Finally, even though most Protestant denominations had tempered their official hostility toward the Catholic Church by the 1920s, a collection of anti-Catholic firebrands among the ministry joined the Klan movement. They brought a zealous conviction that active Romanist plots to upend Protestant American values were afoot. Protestant ministers were sprinkled throughout the leadership of the Invisible Empire. And, among the thirty-nine known national lecturers for the Klan active between 1922 and 1928, twenty-six were Protestant ministers.[161] As Klan witnesses and klavern minutes make clear, the national lecturers were among the most unrestrained, insistent anti-Catholics in the hooded ranks. Some local Klan-affiliated ministers matched the anti-Catholic ardor and outspokenness of the national lecturers. W. A. Redburn, a Methodist pastor and Klan ideologue in Sacramento, California, intemperately appealed to hooded images of Catholic iniquity in 1922. "Nearly all the bawdy houses, bootleg joints, and other dives are owned or controlled by Romanists," he famously railed. "A member of the Catholic faith may go to Mass in the morning and lie drunk in the gutter all day, Sunday or any other day."[162]

❖

However they acquired their religious chauvinism, plentiful examples of credulous anti-Catholic assertions by hooded officials and rank-and-file Klansmen alike fill the documentary record of the 1920s. Most of the rumors popular among Klansmen purported to reveal evidence of Catholic plans to seize political control of the United States. Cards printed by Klan headquarters in the early 1920s asserted that "the pope is a political autocrat" who started World War I, maintained "one hundred and sixteen princes of his government . . . enthroned in our cities," oversaw "courts here enforcing the canon law . . . control[led] the daily and magazine press," and "denounce[d] popular government as inherently vicious."[163] The grand dragon of Pennsylvania distributed circulars claiming that Woodrow Wilson's administration had been overrun by Catholics, presumably because of the secret machinations of Joseph Tumulty, the Presbyterian president's Catholic secretary. Disdaining public records to the contrary, the breathless communication claimed that "over seventy per cent of all appointments made by President Wilson were Catholics," and that "62 per cent of all offices in the United States, both elective and appointive, were held by Roman Catholics."[164] Klan pamphlets spread elsewhere charged that in large cities, three-quarters of public school teachers and 90 percent of police officers were Catholics subservient to the demands of the Vatican.[165]

Anxious Klansmen in Buffalo and in the southern Colorado mining country tore the corners off dollar bills, intent on removing the secret markers of papal allegiance that Catholic engravers had supposedly inserted into the design of the Wilson-era currency.[166] The journalist Stanley Frost explained that the altered money "symbolizes the watchful eye which the Popes have had on America from the moment of its discovery, and their intention of dominating it." The skeptical reporter observed that "every good Klansman, when he gets one of these bills, tears off the corner with the 'Pope's picture.'"[167] Suspicion of the currency among Klansmen was amplified by the widely stated belief that land had already been purchased—at various spots in Washington, D.C., or across the Hudson River from West Point—and construction possibly begun on the American Vatican.[168] Another reporter was surprised to find, even in the overwhelmingly Protestant realms of the Southwest, "rather more anti-Catholic sentiment" than he had anticipated in 1922. "Southwestern Baptists, Methodists, and other Protestants," he related, "seem very generally to believe that there is a Roman Catholic menace to American institutions," a concern that "flares into acute expression in the new secret and masked order."[169]

Perhaps the most fantastic yet strangely durable legend was that Catholic churches maintained arsenals of weapons in their basements, awaiting the inevitable outbreak of open warfare against Protestant America. According to this tale, the birth of a son into each Catholic family became the occasion to add a weapon to the storehouse of the papal army. Versions of this rumor were repeated in all sections of Klandom, but with particular certainty in the Midwest and South. According to Frost, "men there may not be very good Protestants, but they are vigorously anti-Catholic. There is real fear in them. I know intelligent men, well educated, apparently sane in every other way, who were 'brought up to believe'—and are not yet emotionally convinced to the contrary—that the day will come when they or their sons will have to fight with weapons in hand as their forefathers did to escape Papal rule."[170] To break down the suspicion he detected among his acquaintances in the Indiana Klan, another journalist seriously proposed that Catholic officials welcome fact-finding commissions and even allow church inspections to disprove the rumors.[171] But even on the rare occasions when this advice was followed, candor failed to dampen hooded suspicions. An Illinois priest in 1924 opened his church to a Klan search party, conducted a tour of the building, and provided cigars for the Ku Kluxers. Despite the hospitality Klansmen later burned a cross on church property and fired shots at the priest when he investigated the fire.[172]

Unlike the wily Jesuit of classic anti-Catholic demonology, the principal antagonist of the 1920s Klan was a Catholic fraternal order—the Knights of Columbus. Encumbered with the same secret signs, rituals, and degrees that marked its Protestant fraternal counterparts (and, in some measure, the Klan itself), the Knights of Columbus embarked on an active, public defense of Catholicism during the Klan era. Stressing the patriotism of American Catholics, promoting Catholic contributions to the formation of American history and institutions, and displaying a willingness to answer anti-Catholic critics directly, the Columbians openly contradicted the Invisible Empire's claim to the Protestant character of American identity.[173] "At the foot of a flaming cross men are gambling away the seamless garment of our national happiness," a speaker told an annual convention of the Knights of Columbus. "In this land which Catholics discovered and made known they are treated as pariahs and looked on as outcasts."[174] Furthermore, the Knights of Columbus funded legal challenges and lobbying efforts against anti-Catholic legislation and public slurs. In communities across the nation, its 770,000 members disputed the doctrines and disrupted the activities of the Invisible Empire.

Derisively labeling them as "Caseys," the Klan sized up its rivals as the visible manifestation of Catholic militancy in the United States. The "oily knights of the Pope's militia,"[175] claimed excited Klansmen, maintained weapons and secretly drilled the armed agents of the Vatican, rewrote American history to wrongly insert Catholic prominence into the nation's patriotic narrative, insinuated themselves into positions of authority from which they weakened public schools and encircled governmental institutions with the yoke of Rome, and everywhere carried out the will of the pope, to whom they were slavishly devoted.[176] "To them the Pope is Christ," exclaimed one stricken Klansman.[177] Frost suggested that rank-and-file Klan hostility to Catholic assertions of power "does not run so strongly against the Church itself as against the Knights of Columbus."[178]

Fueling much of the hooded suspicion of the Columbians was an old and clearly fraudulent oath supposedly used in the Fourth Degree ritual of the fraternity. This counterfeit document allegedly bound the Catholic knights to "extirpate the heretical Protestant or Masonic doctrines . . . wage relentless war, secretly and openly, against all heretics . . . always vote for a K. of C. in preference to a Protestant," and "place Catholic girls in Protestant families" to spy on the heretics.[179] Despite legal maneuvers on the part of the Knights to suppress the bogus oath, thanks to the sponsorship of the Klan hierarchy it enjoyed wide distribution and influence among Klansmen. A Protestant opponent of the Klan accused the hooded order of "sending Boy Scouts and members of the Sunday school from house to house, circulating that false and bogus oath."[180] Even after an Iowa Columbian debunked it by reciting the lodge's actual obligation on the dare of a Klan-affiliated minister, the spurious document continued to circulate.[181] Six people were convicted of libel for distributing the oath during Al Smith's 1928 campaign,[182] including a Protestant minister involved "in Ku Klux Klan activities," who "printed the pamphlets on a press in the basement of his home."[183]

Even if they doubted the authenticity of the extravagant crimes attributed to the Catholic knights by hooded propaganda, Klansmen in many cases nevertheless took precautions. "All good K. C. carry a 32-automatic when they go out at night," eastern Oregon Klansmen were warned.[184] The Cañon

City, Colorado, Klan was shocked into civic activism on a variety of fronts by the simultaneous construction of a Benedictine abbey and the formation of a Knights of Columbus local in the town, which seemed to presage a Catholic assault on local Protestant control.[185] In a bid to discourage Catholic activism, hooded monitors maintained watchful vigils near Columbian gatherings. For instance, Klansmen set alight a cross "at an almost inaccessible spot" overlooking a New York state meeting of the Knights of Columbus.[186] Hooded watchfulness led to retaliation against Protestant public servants who edged too close to the Columbians. In the Southwest the Klan harried from office a public school principal who had accepted money from the Catholic knights to fund financially strapped evening courses for the benefit of the community.[187] Minneapolis Klansmen launched an unsuccessful challenge against a popular mayor who not only had blocked the Klan movement from local public institutions but had also employed a Catholic secretary and attended a Knights of Columbus dinner.[188] When even frank critics of the Klan such as John M. Mecklin nevertheless asserted that "the Catholic Church emphatically discourages the critical independence of thought so necessary to citizenship in a democracy,"[189] at the height of the hooded enthusiasm rank-and-file Klansmen and their Protestant sympathizers had difficulty recognizing Catholics as a legitimate interest group in a pluralistic society. Catholic influence, especially when exercised by the Knights of Columbus, was often understood to mean papal domination.

Kulturkampf on the Corner

In some locations, such as portions of the rural South, Catholic power was an abstract threat. Legislative sparring between the Klan, the Knights of Columbus, and Catholic officials usually took place in state capitals and in Washington. But most of the intensity of the conflict between Klansmen and Catholics stemmed from its local, familiar, and deeply personal character, especially in Midwestern and Western states where mixed populations were commonplace. Contesting the Catholic juggernaut at the klavern level meant firing Catholic public school teachers and closing parochial schools; turning Catholic sheriffs, town clerks, and councilmen out of office; boycotting main street merchants; and shadowing the faithful from the local parish. Klansmen and their Catholic antagonists were often neighbors, coworkers, and, in many cases, onetime friends.[190] The exalted cyclops of the La Grande, Oregon, klavern arranged for a post office box because his mailman was a Knight of Columbus who would be interested in the correspondence of the Klan official on his route.[191]

Intelligence gathering worked both ways. "If any of you Klansmen get invited to a K. C. party," hooded officers advised La Grande knights, "do not fail to go and keep your eyes open as the raising of funds to defeat the school bill is the social object centered in their behalf."[192] Catholic neighbors familiar with the physical characteristics of Protestant townsmen delighted in identifying masked and hooded Klansmen on parade. "Now, Frank," cried one Indiana Catholic woman, puncturing the intimidating anonymity of the Invisible Empire, "anybody would know you by your big feet."[193] Sometimes the discovery of familiar Klansmen was unnerving. Two Catholic Italian American women who slipped into an "open klan meeting" in a small Utah town recognized several hooded figures as members of their recreational card and dancing clubs.[194]

Although the organized violence that attended the moralistic vigilantism of Southwestern Klansmen between 1920 and 1921 was largely absent from the Invisible Empire's anti-Catholic campaign in the North and West, much ugliness and damage was inflicted as acquaintances turned on one another. Isolated violent episodes did occur. In 1922, Kansas knights abducted and flogged a Catholic small-town mayor who had refused meeting space to the Invisible Empire.[195] A group of Denver Klansmen seized and pistol-whipped a Knight of Columbus one year later.[196] A handful of Catholic churches caught fire under suspicious circumstances.[197] Talk of violence was plentiful. An agitated Buffalo Klansman proposed shooting "some of these d——n K. of C."[198] A fatal gunfight between a Klan investigator from North Carolina and a Catholic Buffalo policeman working undercover in the hooded order later took place, but it was not instigated by local Klansmen. After a national Klan lecturer stirred up a northwest Indiana klavern against the "great machine" assembled by the Knights of Columbus, an emotional hooded balloonist pledged to "go over Notre Dame University and blow it to pieces with . . . dynamite." Rather than encourage the rash act, the local exalted cyclops banished the airman from the Klan.[199]

Against Catholics, the gun, the tar bucket, and the whip gave way to political conflict, economic pressure, social ostracism, and instances of physical intimidation by Ku Kluxers that usually stopped short of outright violence but left internal scars. Klan election materials identified Catholic candidates and urged hooded voters to oppose them, especially in the case of school board members and law enforcement officials. Hooded pressure was applied to local government to sweep out Catholic employees and replace them with Klansmen or reliable Protestants. Indianapolis mayor John L. Duvall apparently signed a pledge to that effect.[200] In a case that was unusual only for its location outside the cultural battleground of Midwestern and Western communities, the election of a Klan-dominated school board in El Paso led to the dismissal of three of the city's four Catholic public school principals.[201] Klan-directed economic efforts to seal off Catholic influence moved beyond public life into the daily affairs of business. Klansmen from a small western Colorado community committed their efforts "to deprive every Catholic of employment, no matter how small or inconsiderate."[202] A Chicago Klansman withdrew the offer of a job upon learning that the newly hired man was a Knight of Columbus. One enterprising Ku Kluxer joined a Catholic-owned firm under a false Irish name, then used his position to fire Catholic workers and replace them with fellow Klansmen.[203]

The boycott was the most common and, as soon became apparent, riskiest tool of Klan economic warfare against Catholics, Jews, and corporations or individuals who opposed or criticized the Invisible Empire. Either officially sanctioned, as with the printed lists[204] of banned Catholic businesspeople handed out in Denver Klan meetings and published in Indiana Klan newspapers,[205] or informally spread by Klanswomen through a network of individual conversations known as "the poison squad of whispering women,"[206] instructions went out to Klansmen to withhold their patronage from specific restaurants, groceries, car repair shops, hotels, banks, and businesses of every kind that were operated by enemies of the hooded order. "People wouldn't go in [some stores], because the Klan would tell you not to," recalled a participant in a Midwestern boycott. "If you had an empty house . . . you were told not to rent it to a Catholic."[207] Most Klan historians stress the general ineffectiveness of Klan boycotts, which collapsed in such hooded strongholds as Texas, Oregon, Ohio, and Indiana. The point is accurate in a greater sense, as ordinary Klansmen often failed to buy exclusively from within the Invisible fellowship, had difficulty maintaining their boycotts of proscribed merchants, and frequently sacrificed Klannishness to the convenience, comfort, familiarity, and sometimes cordial personal relations that marked established commercial patterns.[208]

Yet in some communities, boycotts cut deeply into the livelihood of the Invisible Empire's targets. During the Denver boycott, one Catholic business suffered a 35 percent drop in trade.[209] Klan informants interviewed by Kathleen Blee "gave specific information about Jewish- or Catholic-owned stores that were driven into bankruptcy by the Klan."[210] Catholic and Jewish merchants in some Ohio towns with significant Klan activity shuttered their businesses and left the area.[211] Even non-Catholic establishments, such as the resorts near French Lick, Indiana, felt the impact of Klan demonstrations that drove away Catholic and Jewish vacationers.[212] Klan boycotts were not only economically damaging to Catholic and Jewish merchants but they also delivered devastating personal blows to shopkeepers who keenly felt the exclusion and cold hostility exhibited by former customers. "I blame the Klan indirectly for my father's death," the daughter of a Catholic grocer who did business directly beneath the headquarters of an Indiana klavern remembered decades later. "It just broke his heart to have people shun him, pass right in front of our grocery store door and go upstairs and not look at him."[213] Paper crosses applied by Klansmen as markers of Catholic shops became visible symbols of isolation from the community to a Catholic boy in Colorado. "Being a Catholic," he painfully recalled, "you were in a group all by yourself."[214]

Angry Catholics turned the weapon of the boycott back onto their hooded antagonists as a barely contained cultural conflict spread through communities across the Northeast, Midwest, and West. Sometimes aided by Jewish and African American groups, Catholics scoured the advertisements in Klan newspapers and then boycotted the firms supporting the Invisible Empire. A Columbus, Ohio, dairy that had advertised in a Klan newspaper to drum up business for a new product was instead driven to the wall by a retaliatory boycott. A driver for the defunct dairy confirmed that all but one of the Catholic and black customers on his route canceled their orders.[215] Catholic clergy and lay officials helped select hooded targets for counterboycotts. A Milwaukee Catholic newspaper reprinted the advertisement of a local insurance agent from the Klan newspaper. A wave of cancellations by Catholic policyholders followed. The East St. Louis Knights of Columbus hired detectives to tail likely Klansmen so as to confirm their membership in the Invisible Empire, after which Catholic officials encouraged boycotts of the exposed Kluxers' businesses.[216] A Catholic Ohio police chief used his office to reveal the identity of secret Klansmen and make possible economic retaliation against them. The chief ordered the arrest of seventy-two hooded knights at a funeral, obtained their identities during processing, then released their names to the public. Several firings and boycotts of Klan-owned establishments followed as the disgruntled targets of Klan hostility turned the tables on the hooded knights.[217]

The main actor in this Catholic counteroffensive was the Chicago-based newspaper *Tolerance*, operated by Catholic attorney Patrick Henry O'Donnell in the name of the Catholic-dominated American Unity League. *Tolerance* specialized in printing the names of Midwestern Klansmen taken from stolen Klan membership lists. From 1922 until limited circulation and high court costs forced O'Donnell to cease publication in 1925, the pages of *Tolerance* exposed the (occasionally erroneous) Klan connections of businesses as disparate as chili restaurants, lodging houses, and banks. Such controversial publicity compelled the anxious operators of those enterprises hurriedly to disavow connections to the Invisible Empire, dismiss the hooded officers that brought the unwanted attention, or hunker down to endure a boycott. Several businesses, including financial institutions, were forced to close due to the effects of

Tolerance-inspired boycotts.[218] Catholic bankers in one Indiana town adopted O'Donnell's tactics to employ a reverse boycott against hooded customers. The bankers obtained copies of a membership list of local Klansmen (secured by a safecracker hired to break into klavern records) and thereafter used the list to ensure that Ku Klux applicants for loans were briskly denied.[219]

The Midwestern pattern of boycotts and counterboycotts between hooded knights and Catholic foes of the secret order indicated a period of more sustained cultural tension and physical confrontations. By the mid-1920s they plagued communities wherever Catholics were numerous enough to challenge their hooded detractors. Even the patriotic rituals that onlookers hoped would unify disaffected Americans inflamed the growing conflict. A wreath-laying ceremony in 1924 meant to honor the three soldiers from Hicksville, New York, killed in the world war, all of them Catholics and Columbians, instead became the occasion for a disturbing scuffle when local Knights of Columbus discovered a Ku Klux Klan wreath surreptitiously laid before the monument. The previous Memorial Day, similar Klan garlands had disrupted solemn ceremonies and provoked recriminations in two other Long Island communities.[220] City officials in Portland, Maine, were forced to deny the Invisible Empire the use of the streets after the local Klan announced its intention to parade on Columbus Day, a direct challenge to the annual march of the Knights of Columbus.[221]

Compelled into action by the provocation of the Klan's stinging anti-Catholicism, Catholic opponents of the Invisible Empire took on their antagonists in a series of tense encounters that threatened to escalate into communal violence. Across the Midwest—as a survey of Catholic newspapers by the historian Michael Jacobs abundantly documents—and into New England, Catholic partisans, often members of the Knights of Columbus, spread tacks on the road to puncture the tires of Klansmen attending outdoor meetings and hurled rocks as the hooded knights marched or drove past. They interrupted Klan speeches with catcalls, barrages of rotten fruit, vegetables, and eggs, or by cutting the electricity; kicked over burning crosses and vandalized Klan automobiles and meeting places; harassed vendors hawking Klan newspapers; and sometimes, with the complicity of Catholic police or government officials, roughed up or even seriously beat individual Klansmen who fell into their hands.[222] For their part, Klansman at times disrupted Catholic gatherings and engaged in street skirmishes, occasionally even producing handguns when confronted by Catholic hecklers.[223] "I got a gun permit and a gun so if the fish start anything I can account for myself," confided an Iowa Klansman as he prepared to take part in a Klan parade.[224] Despite such bravado, the aggressive initiative more often came from the Klan's enemies.

The fistfights and handful of stabbings that occurred on the margins of the public scuffling between Klansmen and their organized, mostly Catholic, opponents deepened into more dangerous action as the intolerant religious expressions of the hooded order reaped a whirlwind of violent retribution. Bombs destroyed Klan printing presses, and bullets fired from concealment whizzed over the heads of hooded speakers.[225] Young, immigrant Catholic men, organized in athletic clubs and social organizations, coalesced into a shadowy group called the Knights of the Flaming Circle, which in its militancy and flair for direct action outpaced the restraint shown by the lawyers and politicians who made up the Knights of Columbus. With its own fiery symbols and nighttime rituals, the Knights of the Flaming Circle became a sort of counter Klan that aimed to terrify and, if necessary, brutalize the hooded knights into silence.[226]

Increasingly after 1923, masked and often armed Ku Kluxers marched into Catholic communities and suffered the consequences as well-prepared defenders set upon them. Gunfire and brickbats broke up a Klan procession in Pennsylvania, leaving a dead knight behind.[227] In 1924 trainloads of Klansmen from Chicago and beyond converged on South Bend, Indiana, intent on demonstrating their strength on the doorstep of Notre Dame, the nation's most prominent Catholic university. Notre Dame students instead seized the initiative and routed the Klansmen in an extended street fight that brought rebukes from the school administration but produced exhilaration among beleaguered Midwestern Catholics irritated by the taunts of the Klan.[228] Full-scale riots by anti-Klan Catholics broke out in northeastern Ohio and in Massachusetts. Throughout 1924 and 1925, outdoor Klan meetings in the Bay State attracted mobs of angry opponents armed with guns and stones who waded into the hooded ranks. Brawls became a standard accompaniment of large Klan meetings there.[229]

❖

Violent resistance to the Invisible Empire orchestrated by offended Catholics damaged the Klan movement in several ways. First, it drove away the moderate, fraternal-minded, or skittish Klansmen who had no stomach for the vituperative anti-Catholicism promoted by traveling Klan lecturers, or no desire to absorb bruises or social disfavor in its pursuit. While militant Protestant rhetoric was nearly universal in klaverns, as with other elements of Klan belief and practices, the depth of commitment to anti-Catholicism varied between and within local Ku Klux assemblies. After firsthand observation of Pennsylvania Klans, Emerson Loucks noted that "practically every Klavern had its quota of 'young bloods' who wished to secure fire-eating 'ex-priests' to lecture at open meetings, to burn crosses on the front lawn of some Catholic priest . . . or parade masked and heavily armed through Catholic communities where violent opposition had been aroused."[230] But these were seldom in the majority and they faced resistance from "conservative" knights who "opposed the use of strong-arm methods." Indeed, one of the formal complaints made by rebellious Pennsylvania Klansmen in 1927 against the arrogant, dispiriting leadership of Grand Dragon Herbert Shaw was his penchant for "ranting and inflammatory speeches against Catholics and Negroes."[231]

Even some hooded officials harbored reservations about the bigoted logic of white Protestant nationalism. Clyde Osborne, the Ohio grand dragon who used the Klan movement to fulfill political and personal ambitions, "frankly admitted to confidants that he had little interest in the Klan's program, especially its anti-Catholic and anti-Negro principles."[232] In 1927, Imperial Wizard Evans tried to force North Carolina Klan officials to place bills before the state legislature invalidating "prenuptial agreements regarding education of children" in mixed Catholic-Protestant marriages and outlawing member-ship in the Catholic Church and the Knights of Columbus. Tarheel Klans-men rebelled against the directive, and some cut their ties with the national organization. Grand Dragon Henry A. Grady denounced "the silly, unseemly and unconstitutional measures which [the Atlanta hierarchy] are attempting to foist upon the people of a liberty-loving state," and resigned his office. Sixty-six of the eighty-six Klan chapters in the state reportedly followed suit and renounced their charters, though only a small number of North Carolina klaverns made a formal break with the national Klan.[233]

Elsewhere, Klansmen who firmly espoused Protestant solidarity never-theless disagreed on the utility of a vigorous anti-Catholic agenda. In the Youngstown, Ohio, Klan a collection of moderate leaders minimized the hooded order's attention to Catholics and immigrants and presided over a period of local political influence for the Invisible Empire. They were replaced by a coterie of militant anti-Catholics who led the Klan into the disastrous riot that punished hooded marchers in Niles, Ohio.[234] Sometimes the progression ran in the opposite direction, toward greater toleration. An El Paso Presbyte-rian minister, openly sympathetic to the Klan, declared in 1921 that, unlike free, patriotic Protestants, "Romanists are bound" by church discipline and gave their loyalty to "the Church of Rome first, last and all the time." But within a year he suggested "there should be a bigger place in America for a real Catholic Christian than for a half-hearted Protestant."[235]

Personal encounters with Catholics in several instances revealed the super-ficiality of anti-Catholic convictions among some Klansmen. An Arkansas Klan organizer lured into a Long Island Knights of Columbus assembly, which he took to be a Klan meeting, was compelled to listen as Catholic orators pointed out the "un-Christian and un-American" nature of Klan intolerance. The next day the erstwhile Klan organizer admitted "that his belief in that organization had been shaken by the Knights of Columbus."[236] A Colorado Klansman was charmed by the ecumenical outlook and prohibitionist convictions of Patrick H. Callahan, despite Callahan's profound loyalty to Catholicism and his leading position in the Knights of Columbus. "I have been strongly opposed to your church," the Ku Kluxer confessed, "but your tolerant attitude toward things Protestant and your stand on Prohibition have given me a more kindly feeling toward Catholics than any influence I have ever encountered."[237] The seemingly improbable conclusion reached by this Klansman—but one reflected in other hints that hooded knights retained friendships and working relationships with familiar Catholics—was that "I can still adhere to my principles as a Klansman and live in peace and harmony among my Catholic neighbors."

Open Catholic resistance to the Klan and the perils associated with it played upon each of these weaknesses in the Klan's white Protestant Americanism project. It encouraged those hooded knights who harbored doubts about the wisdom or efficacy of provocative displays of religious intolerance to drift away from their allegiance to the Invisible Empire. Along with the disaffection from unmet political promises and the web of moral scandals and power disputes that gripped the leadership of the Invisible Empire at mid-decade, second thoughts of hesitant Klansmen about the connections between militant Protestant activism and violent retribution contributed to the loss of energy that beset the Klan movement.

The second blow to the movement touched off by anti-Klan riots was the renewed public association of the Invisible Empire with distressing and unpopular violence. The organizing drive of 1921 and 1922 had resulted in an unwanted harvest of violent images that tarnished the Klan movement. The public revulsion from stories of whipping squads and vigilante brutality, magnified by the unsavory revelations of Klan-driven murders in Louisiana, pushed Imperial Wizard Evans to dampen Klan violence and redirect the hooded order's activities into political reform and the robust defense of Protestantism. Now a second wave of violence associated with the Klan had crashed down on Americans. It did not really matter that in 1924 and 1925 Klansmen were more often the victims. Their belligerence had provoked Catholics and other infuriated citizens to assault hooded assemblies. Violence seemed to be the constant companion of the Klan movement, a perception that was debilitating to its health.

Finally, in pushing back against the Klan's aggressive assertion of an exclusively white Protestant definition of Americanism, Catholics and other opponents of the Invisible Empire refined an alternative, pluralistic vision of American identity in the 1920s. Over time it revised accepted notions of authentic Americanism. Among Catholics, the threat posed by the Klan helped overcome ethnic divisions that had beset American Catholicism. Italian, Polish, and German Catholic communities historically had remained separate from the dominant Irish wing of the American church. Even Klansmen occasionally made similar distinctions. Buffalo knights, according to Shawn Lay, concentrated their enmity on a German Catholic mayor and the Irish Knights of Columbus, yet they ignored the city's large Polish and Italian Catholic populations.[238] But Klan persecution and hostility drew American Catholics closer together. The Catholic mobs that assaulted open-air Klan meetings in Massachusetts were multi-ethnic in composition. French, German, Irish, and Polish Catholics from four different parishes in Marinette, Wisconsin, had little to do with one another until a Klan speech insulting a neighborhood priest spurred a united rush to shut down the offensive meeting. As they banded together in defense against Ku Klux attacks on their culture and faith, disparate immigrant Catholic communities began to forge a more assertive American Catholic identity.[239] This process unfolded unevenly. French Canadians, for instance, maintained a tight ethnic identity apart from other Catholics as they battled the Invisible Empire in Maine.[240]

Still, the church itself encouraged the development of an American Catholic identity during the tumultuous Klan era. The Knights of Columbus represented one dimension of that effort with their celebration of Catholic contributions to American freedoms. Catholic critics of the Klan emphasized the un-American nature of hooded intolerance and framed their defense against charges of foreign affiliations with appeals to the fundamental American commitment to liberty of conscience and association. But Catholic officials took special pains to assert the Americanism of the church under the pressure of Klan abuse. "We might be a little more demonstratively patriotic," advised an officer of the Loyola College of Law. "A few dollars spent for flags in school yards will save us hundreds we'll have to use to fight such measures as the Oregon [compulsory public education] bill."[241] Indeed, a Catholic school in Youngstown, Ohio, accepted the gift of an American flag purchased by Klan-backed members of the public school board.[242] But the Americanization effort within U.S. Catholicism in the 1920s went beyond patriotic bunting. Thousands of American Catholics had died fighting for the United States in World War I, and millions more had established lives and connections in American communities. Wartime service, assimilation, and the hostility of the Klan all helped produce a deeper American identity that folded ethnic ties and Catholic identification into a firmer sense of pluralistic American nationalism.[243]

The Klan's bid to maintain an exclusionary Americanism advanced the development of pluralism by driving together, into anti-Klan coalitions, American cultural groups that had previously exhibited separate and even hostile relations. African Americans, Jews, some working-class groups, and isolated liberal white Protestants joined Catholics in demonstrations against the Klan. In 1923 "a crowd of negroes and whites," urged on by two local bankers who were officers in the Knights of Columbus, invaded a Ku Klux Klan meeting in Perth Amboy, New Jersey.[244] In the Klan stronghold of Indianapolis, the American Unity League affiliate included African Americans, Jews, and Germans along with Irish Catholics. Italian musicians played "Wearin' o' the Green" in the 1923 St. Patrick's Day parade there.[245] These temporary alliances did not dispel the tensions and animosities that had hampered relations between ethnic Catholics, blacks, Jews, and white Protestants into the 1920s, nor did they produce a fully functional multi-ethnic democracy. The Irish Catholic publisher of *Tolerance*, for example, lamented the "counting house instincts" of Jews while orchestrating united ethnic opposition to the Invisible Empire.[246] But under the pressure of hooded provocation, the targets of Klan hostility were more likely to accept the common Americanism, if not the equality, of other ethnic, racial, and religious communities that had been singled out by the Klan as threats to American culture and institutions.

Even the press, redolent as it was with assumptions of white Protestant supremacy as a cultural norm, patiently consulted African American, Jewish, and Catholic authorities for commentary on the Klan.[247] Some prominent Protestant foes of the hooded order, most notably Kansas governor Henry J. Allen, entertained lingering suspicions of Catholics.[248] Most Anglo-Saxon critics of the Klan, however, implicitly acknowledged the American bona fides of Jews, Catholics, and blacks in order to explain the threat to democratic institutions posed by the Klan's attempts to restrict American national identity.[249] As the acerbic William Allen White put it, "to make a case against a birthplace, a religion, or a race is wickedly un-American."[250]

❖

In the end, the Klan's definition of Americanism, while capable of attracting initial support among many white Protestants, could not sustain public policy or popular affirmation. It defined whiteness too narrowly, failed to establish legitimate African American threats to white supremacy that required measures beyond existing Jim Crow restrictions, and overplayed the xenophobic suspicion of American Catholics. The Invisible Empire's claim that without white-sheeted intervention, American culture stood in peril of becoming, as one Louisiana Klan officer put it, "Catholicized, mongrelized, and circumcised"[251] was recognized by mid-decade as extremist rhetoric rather than realistic prognosis.

With the possible exception of immigration restrictions that fell short of the sweeping exclusion favored by the Klan, the hooded order failed to codify its version of white Protestant Americanism into law. Instead, assertions of white Protestant solidarity began to retreat to the klavern itself. They became expressions of cultural preference and fellowship within the fraternal walls of the Klan's shrinking empire. Some Klansmen preferred it that way from the outset; others accepted it as a tactical retreat. But the evidence of such Klan excess only slowly became apparent in the postwar period. The hooded assembly still managed to influence public life and cultural attitudes before 1925. It also harnessed real reform together with intolerant excess in its campaigns to improve public schools and sustain national prohibition.

4

Learning Americanism:
The Klan and Public Schools

AMONG THE MORE CONSPICUOUS ITEMS in the storehouse of 1920s Ku Klux Klan iconography was the little red schoolhouse. Hooded parades and public ceremonies frequently showcased this symbol of public education as a comforting representation of shared community values, a token of the national devotion to progress and enlightenment, and an invitation to patriotic nostalgia. A Tennessee klavern constructed a model one-room schoolhouse that could "easily be fitted on a Ford truck" for use as a decorative float in parades.[1] The Klansman urged other Klan organizations to borrow their "little school house" for their own public displays.

Yet the iconic schoolhouse that Klansmen fondly cherished also symbolized cultural conflict, anti-Catholic intolerance, and a restrictive, illiberal definition of community. Celebrated by the American Protective Association nativists of the late nineteenth century as a defiant signal of native white Protestant supremacy, the little red schoolhouse in the 1920s communicated the Invisible Empire's intention to guard white Protestant hegemony against pluralistic influences and, especially, Catholic cultural assertiveness. "Visit our Public Free School," read a tribute in the Klan press, "run by the free and untrammeled powers of Protestants."[2]

So it was with the Klan's self-styled defense of public schools in the New Era. On the one hand, the Invisible Empire demonstrated a commitment to certain elements of the progressive educational agenda and at times worked in coalition with liberal educators and interest groups such as the National Education Association. Ku Klux officials and rank-and-file knights alike acted to implement better funding for public schools, including vocal support for local taxation and bond measures; agitated for physical improvements of public school buildings; supported better compensation for teachers; demanded more equitable distribution of school funding across lines of class and community size; advocated compulsory school attendance laws in jurisdictions that had resisted state educational development; and, in some communities, pressed for free textbooks. In contrast to conservative farmers and small-town Americans, the Invisible Empire advocated increased state authority in support of public education, including the establishment of a cabinet-level Department of Education and a willingness to supplement state and local school funding with federal money—just as it welcomed a stronger government profile in prohibition enforcement and the adoption of stern laws to curtail free immigration into the United States.

Although the Klan program in support of public schools paralleled efforts of educational reformers, the hooded commitment to improve the performance and influence of public education was steeped in the intolerant worldview of the Invisible Empire. Klan leaders envisioned public schools as guarantors of native white Protestant cultural control over diverse ethnic folkways and Catholic institutional challenges. Imperial Wizard Hiram Evans, who in 1923 made public school reform a priority of the national order, frankly acknowledged the importance of what he termed "democratic education" as the "one unfailing defense against every kind of alienism in America."[3] Just as the Klan movement sponsored children's organizations, such as the Junior KKK for boys and the Tri-K Klub for girls,[4] in order to surround young white Protestants with the cultural milieu of 100 percent Americanism, so too did it intend to employ common schools as "the training school" for "responsible citizenship" that would expunge un-American allegiances from the national life.[5]

Evans stressed that "the two remedies"—"a free public school system" and "rigidly enforced immigration" restrictions—would "go together" in the hooded campaign to defend Americanism.[6] Even when some Klan officers articulated the hope that public schooling would be the agent "for the fusing of our newer racial elements into our national life,"[7] Evans, in his major statements on education, downplayed assimilation in favor of exclusion. "In order to be genuine Americans men and women must be born in America," he reiterated. Therefore "you must base your hopes for the future on native born white citizens."[8] Immigrant children might learn to submit to American ways in the model public schools of the Klan's aspirations, but the critical lessons of governance and control, like the racially restrictive progressive reforms in the American South, were for white Protestants only.

Most of all, the Klan's hopes for strengthening American public schools were intended to check what the Invisible Empire contended was the Vatican's bid to extend its temporal authority to the United States. From the imperial palace in Atlanta to the curtained voting booth in local school board elections, Klansmen expressed the conviction that American Catholics were hostile to the democratic sensibilities of American public schools. Even more stridently, the Klan contended that the alternative system of private Catholic education threatened to corrupt and even disable American democracy. Evans, who appeared capable of discussing some educational issues with equanimity and insight, shifted into demagoguery when touching upon Catholic educational convictions. "The public school, in its every phase, aspect and result," he railed, "is repugnant to the Pope and all his priesthood."[9]

Time and again, Klan publications charged that Catholic officials were the chief opponents of American public education. They stood between deteriorating public schools and patriotic intentions to repair and improve them. "The head and source" of the "Un-American Influences" that worked to subvert American democratic education, claimed one Klan journalist, "is in Rome."[10] The Catholic hierarchy, echoed Evans, was "the only organized force . . . that is opposing the American public school system." Elsewhere in the same address, the imperial wizard asserted that "*the Roman Catholic hierarchy is the one influence that is successfully obstructing adequate public school education in America.*"[11]

The grassroots of Klandom widely, though not uniformly, reflected the national leadership's suspicion of Catholic intrigue against public education. In the early 1920s, local klaverns exhibited a special sensitivity to what they considered Catholic attempts to insinuate Roman loyalists into the public schools as teachers and administrators with the intention of undermining patriotic Protestant values in favor of Catholic propaganda. A state senator warned eastern Oregon knights of an alarming increase of "Old Black Crows," or Catholic nuns, teaching in the state's public schools.[12] Two weeks earlier the same klavern buzzed with reports of a local Catholic public school teacher's refusal to accept student essays saluting the Invisible Empire. "If You Don't Like the Hand That's Feeding You Then Go Back to Ireland Where You Belong," suggested the insulted Ku Kluxers.[13] In the small eastern Kansas community of Mulberry, the local Klan's attempt to unseat the Catholic superintendent of public schools escalated to the point where the beleaguered official pulled a gun on his hooded antagonists.[14] Fears of Catholic infection so distressed Paterson, New Jersey, Klansmen that they unsuccessfully petitioned to reverse the mayor's decision, made at the request of an interfaith delegation, to close the city's public schools during the funeral of an esteemed Catholic prelate and community activist.[15]

By 1922 the Invisible Empire had moved beyond defense of the public schools against Catholic encroachment to an active campaign to suppress

Catholic parochial schools. The slogan adopted by the Klan during the campaign for a mandatory public education requirement in Oregon, "One Flag—One School—One Language," rejected any educational alternatives to the pure Americanism that the Klan hoped to cement into the public school curriculum.[16] According to Klan authorities, Catholic schools were a tool of the church hierarchy, meant to indoctrinate American Catholics in blind loyalty to church officials and to suppress the free and open inquiry that characterized public schooling. They were therefore hostile to democratic practices and incompatible with the patriotic values espoused by Protestant American culture. "It is their practice," Evans claimed of educators in the Catholic schools, "to teach *what to think*." By contrast, the imperial wizard declared that Klansmen and other Protestant nationalists "desire that the young be taught *how to think*" and thereby to become fit for creative and progressive-minded citizenship.[17] However sincere Evans may have been in criticizing the doctrinal constraints of Catholic instruction, the freedoms of public education that he celebrated were not intended to produce independent or diverse outlooks but rather to reinforce white Protestant American orthodoxy. That same year he expressed the hope that public schooling "will build a homogeneous people; ... grind[ing] out Americans just like meat out of a grinder."[18]

Hooded logic argued that the separation of church and state in education required the removal of all Catholic signs, symbols, and teachings from public schools and the institutionalization of a nondenominational, culturally Protestant nationalism in the schools as the baseline of patriotic instruction in practical citizenship. Since Klansmen and like-minded old-stock Americans considered Protestant religious principles uniquely expressive of American political and governmental forms, they perceived no sectarian intrusion into the schools from this reformed outlook on public education.[19] As one Protestant enthusiast reasoned, "it is *not* the clergy, but the *government*, which holds the Bell-Rope" in the public schools.[20] What had become in reality a sectarian position in the pluralistic culture of 1920s America was defended by the hooded order as an uncomplicated public assertion of essential American convictions. As with other aspects of the Klan movement, there was an inherent contradiction in the Invisible Empire's demand that the tightest form of racial, religious, and cultural conformity was necessary to empower democratic institutions.

The practical application of the Klan's educational beliefs thus blended genuine attempts at community formation and interest in educational advancement with an outdated (yet still potent) Protestant chauvinism in public affairs, and a propensity for crude intolerance and open bullying of dissenting voices. Themes of reform and coercion characterized Evans's 1924 indictment of the state of American public education. "Our schools are in every way inadequate," he charged. "They have not the institutional standing to which they are entitled; they do not prevent illiteracy, nor always promote patriotism; too often they teach a divided allegiance."[21] Hooded activists suggested the need for immediate and drastic redress. In numerous communities, Klansmen insisted that Bible verses be read in public schools, sometimes in compliance with existing statutes whose enforcement had lapsed. Catholic versions of the Bible were to be excluded, and local campaigns were waged to expel Catholic teachers and administrators from positions in public schools. These goals often stimulated the formation of Klan tickets in local school board elections, resulting in more overt hooded direction of public education in some communities. Klansmen championed state-level statutes to bar or restrict Catholic nuns, brothers, and priests from employment as teachers in public schools, usually in the guise of bans on religious garb, though such bills allowed unemployed Protestant ministers to take up the chalk and pointer. In several states the Invisible Empire allied with other militant Protestant groups to advocate laws requiring all children in specified grades to attend public school, thereby closing down private and parochial rivals to the state-run system. Even the campaign to establish a federal Department of Education became a weapon with which the Invisible Empire scourged parochial schools since Catholic educators opposed the reform as a troubling centralization of school administration.

Progressives of a Sort

A mixture of administrative reform and patriotic coercion typified the educational position of the Invisible Empire in the 1920s. The harsh unity of American society enforced during World War I did not extinguish the progressive drive to build public institutions that were both efficient and humane. One area of progressive persistence in the postwar years was the effort by educational professionals, especially the "administrative progressives" represented by the National Education Association (NEA), to construct a more effective network of public schools throughout the United States, staffed by competent teachers and trained administrators.[22] Extraordinary unevenness characterized the state of public schools at the outset of the New Era. Although individual examples of functional, well-ordered public schools could be found in every region of the country, and public education had been improved since the turn of the century, urban schools in the North were still frequently overcrowded and disorderly. Underfunded, isolated rural schools, serving at most a few dozen students, lagged behind in teacher training and struggled with aging and limited facilities. Most Southern public school systems had emerged only since Reconstruction and suffered from inadequate resources and neglect by taxpayers and public officials alike.

Despite nationalistic boasts that American accomplishments were anchored in the common school system, recent evidence derived from census data and the testing of World War I soldiers revealed alarming rates of illiteracy, nearly 25 percent among draftees. Almost 4.5 million American children of school age did not attend any educational institution.[23] Klan officials as well as leading school experts highlighted these educational shortcomings to illustrate the need for a greater expenditure of resources and expertise to meet the heretofore unrealized promise of American public schools as a bulwark of national strength and cultural uniformity. Thus the imperial wizard cited the observations of a professor from the Harvard School of Education that "our large foreign population constitutes a serious problem for education and for society, that most country children do not have anything like a fair opportunity for education, that in many sections of the country short school terms make effective education all but impossible, that a large part of our teachers lack proper education, training and experience."[24] A subdivision of the NEA, respectfully described by the *New York Times* as "the most powerful and forward-looking body of public schoolmen in America," acknowledged the same problems and in 1923 suggested serious remedies. These included "the creation of larger units of taxation and administration" to support stronger rural schools, and the introduction of federal aid and leadership "for the purpose of stimulating the several States to remove illiteracy, Americanize the foreign-born, prepare teachers, develop adequate programs of physical education and 'equalize educational opportunity.'"[25] In one of the odd juxtapositions of interest that characterized the modernizing impulse of 1920s America, educational progressives and hooded Klansmen found themselves jointly recommending the expansion of state authority in pursuit of cultural unity.

The efforts of administrative progressives at the state and national levels to improve and standardize the public schools embroiled educational professionals and their political allies in sometimes highly charged conflict with communities and parental groups that cherished local control of the schools as a hallmark of democracy and family rights. Initiatives by reformers to consolidate small, often one-room, rural schools into centralized district schools sparked determined resistance in Northern rural communities. "Individuality will be lost" with the surrender of neighborhood rural schools to the district schools fancied by professional educators, complained an upstate New York mother. "The pride taken in 'our' school and 'our' teacher [will be] gone and in a few years the country schools will be run by one or two man power." So widespread was the resistance to public school consolidation that by 1928 less than 10 percent of rural schools in the Northeast and Midwest had more than a single room.[26] Rural Southerners also considered school consolidation a blow to democratic control and community pride. Parents in one North Carolina community depicted school consolidation as the action of hostile outsiders "defrauding us out of our school."[27] Southerners, especially in the countryside, also defied the imposition of compulsory school attendance laws of the type that had been enacted in Midwestern and Western states two decades earlier, and they aggressively acted on their perceived right to ignore school procedures and directly manage the classroom conduct of teachers, even firing unpopular instructors.[28]

On these issues, despite its invocation of the one-room schoolhouse as the embodiment of American identity, the Invisible Empire was as likely to side with educational modernizers as with clusters of native white Protestant parents and taxpayers resisting further government authority over the direction of public schools. "Our Children [are] the Chief Asset of the State," Evans argued, and therefore government support, funding, and direction of public education were justified and essential.[29] In western Pennsylvania the Klan supported the consolidation of rural public schools into larger district schools in several instances.[30]

As with the educational progressivism of the Klan in general, many of these specific cases apparently also reflected the intense anti-Catholicism of the Invisible Empire. Pennsylvania Klansmen were more likely to endorse school consolidation if that became the means to absorb pockets of concentrated Catholic population into a larger Protestant district, thereby eliminating Catholic domination of certain public schools and ensuring a Protestant majority at the district level. According to the contemporary research of Emerson Loucks, Klan sentiment sometimes opposed school consolidation when it would create a majority Catholic district. Bigotry as well as bureaucratic reform advanced together as the Klan sought to build "Schools to Save the Country" from what they perceived as un-American influences.[31] In this enterprise, the hooded order was not alone.

Immigration and the shock of World War I also spurred popular demands to engage the public schools as instruments to remake a nation. In the estimation of some Americans, the country had become dangerously fragmented by competing ethnic nationalisms, racial strife, and, with the Bolshevik Revolution and the Red Scare that capped the wartime crisis, the introduction of radical socialist and Communist ideologies. The fervent calls of Klansmen to reinforce Americanism through patriotic lessons and ceremonies in the formative years of schooling were by the 1920s only the latest in a stream of such urgent requests following the upsurge in European immigration of the late nineteenth century. "There were more than eight times as many laws dealing with what should be taught or what should not be taught in 1924 than there were twenty years before," estimated one expert educator.[32] In 1885 only nine states had required that lessons be presented in English, and just eleven had included mandatory instruction in American history or citizenship. Sharp increases in these and other patriotic requirements occurred at the turn of the century and then accelerated in the era of the Great War. Veterans' organizations such as the Grand Army of the Republic and the post–World War I American Legion joined professional bodies such as the American Bar Association and ad hoc patriotic groups to encourage the formal study of American history and the Constitution. A prominent Mason and university trustee urged in 1923 that the private sector be compelled to join in the Americanization effort. "All persons, firms and corporations employing persons not educated in or who do not speak English," urged Elmer D. Brothers, "should be required to provide approved schools for teaching the English language, the rudiments of an education therein and the history of our common country, including the origin and development of our constitution and our political liberty."[33]

A succession of military interventions from 1898 through World War I, and the intense suspicion of alien cultures and ideologies that characterized American society during the world conflict, brought added emphasis to the ceremonial reinforcements of patriotic national culture: displays of the flag, patriotic songs, and a greater insistence on English-language instruction as an acculturating agent and marker of shared American identity. As a 1919 magazine article put it, the national trend was to "Mak[e] Teaching Efficient and Patriotic."[34] By 1913 more than one-third of the states mandated English-only instruction, and nearly two-thirds provided for the display of the flag. In 1923, at the height of the Klan movement, the addition of the Invisible Empire to the established nationalistic lobbies resulted in the widespread adoption of patriotic lessons and rituals in the public schools: thirty-five states offered English-only instruction, thirty-nine required the display of the flag while the same number made provisions for citizenship education (only one state had done so in 1913), and forty-three states mandated the teaching of American history.

Beyond the curriculum, some states required public school teachers to swear loyalty to the United States and to certify by means of examination their fitness to teach American history and the Constitution. Professional school administrators in the NEA protested against some repressive features of the patriotic agenda for the schools or offered more inclusive understandings of American institutions, but, as the historian David Tyack has concluded, the educational establishment endorsed the thrust of the Americanizing educational project.[35] The Invisible Empire was provocative and extreme in its demands that the public schools inculcate Protestant values as part of American national culture in the 1920s, but its patriotic assertiveness built upon a popular groundswell of more than twenty years' duration.

❖

The national Klan's interest in improving public schools was not only more derivative than original but also self-serving. It formed a part of Evans's strategy to escape the Invisible Empire's association with vigilante brutality and to redirect its energies into legitimate public channels. Still, the evidence indicates that Klansmen authentically and energetically took up the cause of public school reform. During the New Era, as Morton Keller has noted, the "dramatic expansion of the American educational system coexisted with deep antitax attitudes."[36] When even reform governor Al Smith of New York tempered his support for educational modernization in the mid-1920s with vetoes of proposed salary increases for New York City teachers, the Invisible Empire's consistent demand for increased public school funding placed the Ku Kluxers firmly within the progressive educational coalition. National Klan publications strongly endorsed higher taxes and other financial support for improving school facilities, recruiting skilled teachers, and renovating country schools. "We must look beyond the personal and selfish limitations," the mouthpiece of the imperial wizard counseled, and "be willing to pay a sufficient tax to maintain our schools at the highest standard."[37] Another statement from the Atlanta headquarters maintained that "better salaries must be paid" by "voters and taxpayers" to attract "the best talent as teachers." Economy in this case had to give way to the public interest. "We pay without protest for services from members of other professions," reasoned the hooded journalist, "and teachers should receive the same consideration."[38]

Rank-and-file Klansmen in numerous communities supplied real dollars to back up these imperial pronouncements. An ordinary knight in rural Iowa communicated his intention to vote for a bond issue that would allow for the construction of a new school and "expressed great surprise that some people—particularly people with children—might be opposed to the issue."[39] The Indianapolis Klan intervened in 1923 in a complex dispute over school construction and improvements that pitted reformers against the formidable opposition of the city's chamber of commerce, the state taxpayers' lobby, and a major city newspaper. The knights publicized the dilapidated state of city public school buildings and joined a popular coalition that passed a second bond issue to fund school construction. Two years later Klansmen helped engineer the election of a Klan-supported school board that completed work on three new high schools.[40]

Overcrowded conditions in public schools and the apparent indifference of the town's political and business leaders to the problem stirred Cañon City, Colorado, Klansmen in 1924 to join the campaign to pass a bond issue for the construction of an elementary and a high school. After the bond issue passed, the local Klan marched to the high school and burned a cross on the football field.[41] Similarly, Klansmen in Greensburg, Pennsylvania, gave vital support to another faltering bond issue to fund high school construction.[42] In Chicago the Invisible Empire, under fire in 1923 from vociferous critics, rallied to help pass a school bond measure.[43] Klansmen in a small Arkansas community purchased a park adjacent to a public school and donated the green space to the local school board for the use of children and the general public.[44] After a state appropriation for a new high school fell short of construction costs, hooded knights on Virginia's eastern shore raised an additional $4,000 to cover the remainder of the expenses. When the cornerstone was laid, a national Klan representative gave the celebratory address.[45]

A commitment to adequate school facilities, the acknowledgment of physical education as a critical element of children's development, and recognition of the need for high schools were among the chief attributes of public school reform in postwar America. The involvement of hooded volunteers in bringing new buildings, recreational space, and high schools to these communities was for many local people as concrete an expression of educational progressivism as they were likely to encounter.

Sometimes local Klans demonstrated a commitment to free public schools through cost savings rather than higher taxes. Such was the case in Anaheim, California, where a hooded school board member bypassed local lumber firms and awarded the building materials portion of a school construction contract to an outside bidder at a 13 percent savings. The Klansman also turned down the services of a local architect who proposed to design the school building for a fee of $4,000 and instead obtained plans for a mere $247. The hooded school official explained that the snubbed local businesses were favorites of Anaheim's government, which Klan activists had accused of extravagant public spending, and had expected to profit unjustifiably from their close connection to a corrupt, spendthrift city administration. The bypassed firms were also prominent local enemies of the Invisible Empire, an indication of the partisan design of the public interest that also characterized hooded civics in many communities. In any case, the Klan member of the school board boasted that the $50,000 price tag for a necessary school addition "contrasts favorably with the expert figures of our city council's public improvements."[46]

In some locales, public school improvement became the signature issue of the Klan movement. Stunted by a limited tax base, El Paso public schools were roundly condemned as inadequate by angry parents. Students in one city district, the local Parent-Teacher Association charged, "study on the stairs, many lower grade pupils are shifted about the building three times a day before finding a roosting place," and the local junior high school had "only one desk for each three students." One frustrated parent erupted, "This is the sort of thing that makes Bolsheviks." El Paso's Frontier Klan No. 100 gained a foothold on the school board, where Klansman Charles Ward expressed the need to raise the tax rate to save the schools from collapse. The city's business and political establishment, however, blocked school board requests for additional funds for the strapped community school system. Denouncing the "political machine" that contravened the community desire for strong public schools, and dismissing the prominent business leaders who ran for the school board as the favored candidates of the city administration, the Klan in 1922 moved to prominence as part of a good-government coalition intent on securing control of the El Paso school board. Supporters of the Klan ticket rejected the wealthy administration candidates, saying it was "the common people who must educate their children in the public schools, who are the most vitally interested in the school system." When three Klansmen gained seats on the school board, the Invisible Empire took control of city school policy. The Klan-led board won an appropriation of nearly $750,000 for El Paso public schools and began construction on several new schools.[47]

In step with the New Era's school professionals, the Invisible Empire's expressed concern for public education extended beyond city and town schools to address the deficiencies of rural schooling. The language used in Klan statements on country schools at times appeared to be ripped directly from the pages of education journals. "Statistics show that one-half of the rural teachers of the United States have never finished a four-year high school course," read one hooded lesson. "Ten percent have never studied beyond the grade they teach. Only two out of one hundred graduated from a normal school or college." Improvement of rural schools also required reform outside the classroom. The need for professional administrative standards and freedom from local political interference was manifest. "In only twelve states," Klansmen were informed, "is provision made for a professional prepared supervision for rural schools. In more than one-half of the states the county Superintendent[s] of Education—those in charge of rural schools—are chosen on the basis of their political affiliation."[48] The hooded order welcomed federal aid to education to raise the standards of teachers, administrators, and facilities in country schools. It was not a matter of bureaucracy, argued the Klan's official publication, but a vital question of democracy. "In a land where, theoretically at least, democracy reigns supreme, should not equal privileges of acquiring an education obtain everywhere?" inquired the Klan hierarchy.[49]

The Invisible Empire's educational stance was especially provocative in Southern realms where the public school movement had advanced only tentatively and sensitivity to centralization and government direction of local affairs was especially pronounced. Compulsory schooling laws that set minimum days of instruction were notably slack in Southern states. Tax support for public schools, though far higher for white children than for blacks, nonetheless trailed the rest of the nation. Hoping to reverse this situation, the Invisible Empire gave vocal support to a 1924 federal measure that proposed to inject $50 million of federal funds into state school systems, to be dispensed by the individual states, on the condition that participating states require "all children between the ages of seven and fourteen to attend some school for twenty-four weeks each year" with English as "the basic language of instruction in all schools, public and private."[50] The Klan movement's endorsement of higher school taxes, federal aid to education, improved teacher salaries and training, and tighter attendance requirements, to say nothing of the national organization's 1924 announcement that "Klansmen who have the interest of their children at heart . . . are anxious to see that Child Labor Laws, that will withstand the attack of the big corporation lawyer are passed by the individual states," all cut against the grain of popular Southern opinion on the proper relationship between individuals, families, and the state. "The illiteracy of Protestant America is not so astounding after a careful study of the school system without a compulsory education or child labor law," Klan rhetoricians asserted in defense of heightened regulation of Southern school-age children.[51]

Even when justified in this way by native Protestant white supremacist arguments, the Invisible Empire's appeal to the public interest and the state challenged conventional outlooks in the region and conservative, pro-business sentiment nationwide. "Child labor regulation goes hand in hand with school expansion," one observer noted in sizing up anti-regulatory fears that perceived looming national power behind every public measure to protect children. "School expansion means federal taxes; and federal taxation is a nightmare to the great corporations whose business bestrides state boundaries."[52] Rejecting such anti-government scenarios, Alabama Klansmen pushed for state legislation requiring school attendance for children aged seven to sixteen. Compulsory school laws in the Klan era were usually intended to disrupt or destroy competing Catholic schools, but in the Southern context they had a stronger reform cast, forcing white Protestant children who had been laboring on farms or in shops and mills into the classroom. The Alabama Klan also endorsed merit pay for teachers. Tuscaloosa knights "took to the stump" to help pass a half-million-dollar school bond measure. When Birmingham authorities threatened to close city public schools in 1925 because of money shortages, the Invisible Empire arranged concerts and appeals that raised sufficient funds to pay teachers for the remaining five weeks of the term.[53]

Klansmen in Atlanta applied progressive methodologies along with the South's anti-elitist populist traditions to improve the city's struggling public schools. Hooded school board members collaborated with reformers to commission the Strayer-Engelhardt Report, an exhaustive survey of public schools and neighborhoods that documented the imbalance between the better-supported public schools of the city's wealthier north side and the substandard schools in the white working-class and black residential districts of the south side. According to the historian Edward Akin, "a startling number of white children attended poorly lit and ventilated schools in areas where teachers had to struggle to be heard over the din of railroads and factories." Armed with the progressive tool of statistical analysis, the Atlanta Klan pushed for the equal distribution of resources among white schools. Working with a mayor who was both a Klansman and a veteran of the Klan contingent on the school board, a coalition of hooded knights, public-spirited reformers, and Protestant zealots from the Junior Order of United American Mechanics overcame financial obstacles and freed up $3.5 million in public money to improve city schools. Klansmen also attempted to reform the cozy relationship between local business interests and the school system, purging an ineffective superintendent and publicizing alleged sweetheart deals between politicians and realty firms and textbook companies that sold property and materials to the school system. Resuscitating an issue from Georgia's turbulent populist period, the state Klan championed the provision of free textbooks to students in all public schools, to be dispensed, assured Nathan B. Forrest III, grand dragon of the Georgia realm, "regardless of race, creed or color."[54]

Education Restriction

The Klan's demand that well-funded and efficient public schools inculcate patriotism, American identity, citizenship, and orderliness encompassed important themes of educational progressivism in the 1920s. But in its pursuit of a narrow and superficial Americanism, the hooded order applied reform methods that far surpassed the mainstream white Protestant biases that influenced some professional educators. The full portfolio of education reform undertaken by Atlanta Klansmen, for instance, included insistent and sectarian demands for daily Bible readings in the schools, a vigilant though largely unsuccessful effort to root out and dismiss Catholic public school teachers, a resolute determination to purge allegedly unpatriotic and pro-Catholic textbooks from the classroom, and the shepherding of resources exclusively for white schools while public schools for blacks remained ignored and mostly unimproved.[55]

Sometimes even standard reform methods were jettisoned. The Klan majority on the Akron, Ohio, school board met secretly to arrange votes before formal board meetings, pressured reluctant colleagues to dismiss Catholic teachers, and drove the board's anti-Klan minority to resign in protest. They then named as school superintendent a known Klansman who, in his previous service as school chief in Springfield, Ohio, had engineered the segregation of black students and alienated local citizens by ignoring restraints on spending. In Akron the new Klan superintendent provoked further outrage by filling public school posts with hooded cronies.[56]

Although the open misbehavior of the Akron Klan was unusual, the Invisible Empire's record of religious and cultural intolerance in public education was much the same elsewhere. Florida Klansmen bemoaned the state's educational shortcomings yet intimidated supporters of an African American school and agitated for the ouster of a Catholic priest who had organized a drama club at the University of Florida.[57] The public school building campaign of the Indianapolis Klan had been urged on by frequent rumors in the Klan press of Catholic designs to subvert patriotic public schools, and included the construction of new segregated facilities.[58] El Paso Klansmen, once they gained control of the school board, refused to renew the contracts of three of the city's four Catholic public school principals, cut the salaries of half the Catholics teaching in high schools, and fired seven of the city's thirty Catholic teachers working in public elementary schools. New construction and repairs lagged behind in the public schools serving El Paso's Mexican immigrants, so that the overcrowded conditions that motivated the Klan school campaign persisted outside the Anglo districts.[59] In Birmingham the Klan organizations that had worked heroically to keep the public schools open in 1925 also bullied a popular Jewish principal out of a city high school.[60]

Allied with progressives in its desire to strengthen public schooling in a pluralistic society, the Klan's hypernationalism and insistence on white Protestant ascendancy shifted its school program sharply away from other elements of educational progressivism. Hooded knights were generous in funding schools, but their visions of curricular content were decidedly limited. Beyond a commitment to developing basic literacy, Klansmen indicated that the public school's primary duty was to drill students in the glories of a Protestant-inflected Americanism. A close investigation of hooded involvement in Pennsylvania public schools concluded that most Klansmen were undisturbed by short terms, slim budgets, underachieving teachers, and inadequate facilities if the schools were resolute in sponsoring daily Bible readings, displaying the flag, and removing Catholic teachers and "any recognized symbols of Catholic or foreign origin in the equipment or activities of the school."[61]

In some communities, despite the national promotion of public school protection as a defining issue of the Invisible Empire, klaverns demonstrated no special alertness to public education as a vital question. Absorbed by conflict with a Catholic mayor over prohibition enforcement, Buffalo knights mostly withheld comment on school issues.[62] Although the minutes of the La Grande, Oregon, and Mt. Rainier, Maryland, klaverns document avid attention to public school policy and personnel, Klan records from St. Joseph County, Indiana, and Monticello, Arkansas, betray no such interest. Uniformity, even on this basic issue, eluded the Klan movement.

Even in locations where the Klan's educational involvement was keen, hooded advocates of public schooling made clear their preference for moral and patriotic education over purely academic subjects. "We need something more than grammars and fractions and geographies to prepare our youths and maidens for good citizenship," reasoned one hooded argument for mandatory scripture reading in public schools. "The great curse of the whole world today is the educated villain."[63] Instruction in Americanism was the ultimate goal of public schooling for the Klan movement. Appearing before the Second Imperial Klonvocation, a Protestant minister affirmed his conviction that "our school system must be the very best"—but he then complained that "our schools have become a training ground of intellect and not a training ground of patriotism and character."[64] The preferred educational innovation for the hooded order was in Protestant character formation rather than in scholarly pursuits. To Klan ideologues, reinforcing cultural Protestantism as normative and thereby safeguarding traditional American democracy determined the success of public education. One such hooded schoolmaster pointed out that Protestant population concentrations served by public schools had lower rates of illiteracy than Catholic districts. But culture mattered more than academic rigor. "A parochial school or any separate school which is educationally equal, or even superior to a public school," he maintained, "is its hopeless inferior as a democratic school."[65]

Despite its aggressive campaign on behalf of public schools, the Klan's activism at the schoolhouse level tended to favor practical lessons and familiar procedures over new approaches to learning. In his national statement, Evans denounced the vocational track and limited educational opportunity that he claimed prevailed in Catholic Italy. "*We demand that the advantages of education be universal,*" he asserted, and school systems not try to predict "the capacity and career of any boy." The path to "high and higher education" must remain clear.[66] Yet Klan editorialists in Georgia noted that "already we have too many professional men" and encouraged schools to "teach the girl how to make a home, and the boy how to make [a] living and be honest and clean."[67]

Not only were the aims of education traditional for many Klansmen, so too were their favored methods. The chief Klan ally on the Atlanta school board discouraged the adoption of newer reading methods and advocated instead the retention of letter and sound-based reading instruction that had been practiced since the nineteenth century. In a more brutal demonstration of the same approach, a Klansman on the Athens, Georgia, school board rejected his colleagues' attempt to end corporal punishment in the schools with an appeal to the Old Testament. "King Solomon says beat the devil out of them," the hooded knight rejoined, with a firmness that banished the doctrines of John Dewey and administrative progressives alike to the outer darkness.[68]

Klansmen were also cool to the teaching of evolution. In print, Evans admitted that God "could create a man in a single moment, or He could as easily create a single cell and, from it, man, by the process of evolution." But the imperial wizard went on to characterize the question as "non-essential" except to a small group of scientists.[69] The organ of the national Klan movement dismissed evolutionary theory on ideological grounds. "The men who founded our great institutions, wrote the Declaration of Independence, and firmly set this continent upon the solid rock of political government of the people and by the people," argued the representative of the hooded order, "believed that man is the product of Infinite Mind rather than the outcome of an inanimate fish."[70] The teaching of evolutionary theory, from this perspective, was not intellectually incorrect so much as it was inappropriate and unhelpful in building a reverence for American institutions that the Klan understood as the central purpose of public education. How else could the beliefs of the Enlightenment-era Founders matter in questions of contemporary scientific debate? Occasionally, influential knights such as Leon Myers (the exalted cyclops of the Anaheim, California, Klan) indicated a desire to suppress public school instruction in evolution on the grounds that its implicit challenge to Christian dogma contaminated morals. Myers, who was also the pastor of Anaheim's First Christian Church, suggested in 1924 that one of the "opportunities" for action by the local hooded order was "the removal of the teaching of evolution and Biology as now taught from our high school curriculum."[71] Despite local outbursts of this type, the Invisible Empire did not play a significant role in the popular movement to ban the teaching of evolution in public schools, which during the course of the 1920s reached twenty-one state legislatures.[72] But neither did Klansmen step forward to protect trained teachers or administrators from interference at the hands of outraged Christians and patriots.

On the contrary, Klansmen were as intrusive in the classroom as any up-country farmer or Southern mountaineer whose harassment of teachers had drawn rebukes from educational reformers. "In a quiet way," New Jersey knights helped force a "popular and . . . competent" black teacher out of her assignment teaching white students and, instead, into a classroom "of backward negro pupils."[73] The Invisible Empire's anti-Catholic obsession was the most pronounced cause of intervention. In Ohio, Klan zealots warned that the "Roman Octopus [was] Crushing Ohio Public Schools." The author of that alarming charge, a school board member who moonlighted as editor of a Ku Klux newspaper, spread stories that Catholic teachers decorated classrooms with Catholic religious art, forced their young public school charges to make the sign of the cross, and, with the connivance of lax school officials, welcomed priests and nuns into the schools as "substitute" teachers, thus opening public schools in one district to Catholic proselytizing.[74] Acting on similar concerns, eleven knights in full Klan regalia invaded a school board meeting in another Ohio district to demand that "only real Americans" be permitted to work in public schools.[75] Committees of concerned Pennsylvania knights visited the classes of teachers rumored to skip the daily Bible verses or, worse, to convey them in Catholic or unapproved versions of the Holy Book.[76] Hooded "watchdog committees" in Atlanta monitored the personal, patriotic, and professional qualities of teachers and scanned textbooks for "anti-American or anti-Protestant propaganda."[77]

Particularly vexing for educational professionals was the insistence of Klansmen in many realms that classroom history books criticized American heroes and lauded the achievements of Catholic civilization. Echoing a widespread complaint that resonated in numerous Klan rallies, a Long Island knight grumbled that "American high schools and colleges were not teaching historical facts."[78] In 1923, Indiana Klansmen petitioned the state board of education to remove two histories of ancient and medieval Europe from the classroom because of their alleged pro-Catholic biases. The next year Indiana Klan officials leafleted all state officers and klaverns to communicate the urgent need "to cleanse our school system and to extract from the school books the flood of Roman Catholic doctrine,"[79] purported to include "800 pages of Roman Catholic history in our school books."[80] Four pro-Klan members of the Atlanta school board turned the panel into an inquisition of the printed page, questioning the suitability of any early European history texts that covered the actions of the papacy or the then-universal church without condemnation. Julia O'Keefe Nelson, the most implacable foe of Rome in the group, even objected to an illustration in the very book she had recommended, and the local Klan had endorsed, as a proper substitute for an allegedly pro-Catholic text. Frustrated by the "ravings of ignorance" displayed by Nelson and her Klan associates in their insistence that histories of Catholic Europe expunge the agency of the Catholic Church, the majority on the school board finally outvoted the Klan members and ended the schoolbook imbroglio.[81]

Hooded interference in such basic elements of public education as the hiring of teachers, curriculum formation, and textbook selection was disruptive, offensive, and clearly unprogressive, but it was not unique in the New Era. As the wider controversy over American history textbooks in the 1920s documents, the Klan's prejudices as well as its progressivism reflected in exaggerated but recognizable form the convulsive cultural debates of America's pluralistic postwar society. Competing patriotic visions demanded representation in American history textbooks of the postwar period. Led by the Knights of Columbus and the National Catholic Welfare Council, a product of cultural mobilization during World War I, organized Catholicism in the United States was alert to educational and intellectual trends that affected American Catholics and their faith.[82] Not only did Catholic cultural advocates oppose the Nordic Protestant exclusivism of the Invisible Empire's reading of American history, but they also supplied their own patriotic counternarrative that championed immigrant and Catholic involvement in the development of the nation. Representatives of Irish, German, Jewish, African American, and Native American groups called for the inclusion of their contributions in the patriotic story. So unsettled was one old-stock American by the prospects of a pluralistic patriotism that he argued the necessity to "put none but Americans on guard when we make up our histories or . . . they will have George Washington either an Irishman or a German."

Professional historians too were caught up in the controversy. The New History championed by Charles and Mary Beard, David S. Muzzey, and other scholars elevated economic and social forces over the heroic actions of individuals. Some studies of the Revolutionary generation were critical in their treatment of the motives and actions of the Founders and appeared to be more evenhanded than before in analyzing British policies. Frustrated by the methodological exclusion of their representative figures from a broadened patriotic narrative, some proponents of ethnic and Catholic history linked the New Historians with the Klan in perpetrating an Anglo-Saxon whitewash of the past. "*Americans, Wake up!*" declared a pamphlet from the Knights of Columbus. "*Our History is being distorted and polluted and our children thereby de-Americanized . . . to the glory of England.*" Thus, as the historian Jonathan Zimmerman has observed, not only did the Invisible Empire, the American Legion, and the Veterans of Foreign Wars demand patriotic revisions of history textbooks, so too did the Knights of Columbus, the Steuben Society, and the Jewish Alliance. By 1923 twenty-one state legislatures had contemplated measures to oversee the content of history textbooks. "Boastful, intolerant nationalism," as one of the denounced historians put it, was not the exclusive province of the Klan in educational matters. Even as the Invisible Empire sought to restrict Americanism to its native white Protestant subset, it unintentionally shared in the patterns of a multi-ethnic nationalism.[83]

Coercion and the Classroom

The Klan movement's dedication to an idealized conception of public education was joined by exaggerated concern that public schools would be corrupted by Catholic intrigue and secular inattention to the moral and religious roots of citizenship. Furthermore, parochial schools could undermine the necessary training for true Americanism that public schools provided. These perceived dangers led Klansmen to turn to state authority as a means to safeguard the Americanizing functions of education. Tentative hooded attempts to influence universities or to develop Klan-controlled institutions of higher learning faltered. The Invisible Empire instead applied its political influence to purifying primary and secondary education. Three major initiatives marked the Klan's public policy agenda for the schools: the uniform adoption of Bible readings in public schools, the elimination of Catholic schools and suspect doctrine in public education through compulsory public school attendance laws and strictures on teacher selection, and the creation of a federal Department of Education and the expansion of federal support of public schools.

The Klan established only a limited presence at the large public universities, though clusters of knights were to be found on several campuses among faculty and students. Hooded influence over university affairs was quite rare and usually restricted to the hobbling of Catholic organizations on campus. The small Klan contingent at the University of Oregon included the exalted cyclops of the Eugene klavern, who chaired the Latin department, and the school's football coach, but not even these influential figures made the Invisible Empire a significant factor in university affairs. The academic Klansmen at Oregon, for instance, were unable to drive the Catholic Newman Club from campus.[84] At the University of Colorado the Invisible Empire sought greater influence, but in this case the initiative came from the hooded governor of the state, Clarence Morley, rather than from Klansmen at the university. Morley tried to use the power of appropriation to force the university to fire its Jewish and Catholic faculty members. Klansmen in the state legislature did cut appropriations to the university, but the targeted professors kept their jobs and the state's Klan administration was pilloried as "the worst failure ever inflicted upon the people."[85]

The most notable innovation of the Klan movement in higher education did not involve gaining control of public universities but rather establishing Klan-run private schools that would provide a guaranteed "100% American" education to a self-selecting community of students.[86] Although the press mocked these "Ku Klux Kolleges,"[87] the founding imperial wizard of the second Klan, William J. Simmons, spent $150,000 in 1921 to purchase Lanier University, a struggling Atlanta institution at which Simmons had once offered courses in Southern history. With Georgia grand dragon Nathan Bedford Forrest III as business manager and a board of trustees sprinkled with prominent Klan leaders, Simmons and Forrest announced grandiose plans for Lanier, including a million-dollar building program and the construction of a related "Hall of Invisibles" that would be "devoted to instructions in the ideals and principles of Ku Kluxism."[88] Coeducational classes in subjects from music to pharmacology were proposed, but the distinctive feature of Lanier was to be its emphasis on "the inculcation and practice of the tenets of the Christian religion" through an introduction to "Biblical literature" and "the teaching and application of the principles of purest American citizenship," based on required study of the Constitution and the Declaration of Independence.[89]

The Klan sponsors made it clear that Lanier was intended as a corrective to the irreligious and radical trends they perceived in current higher education. "Many of the textbooks and much of the teaching of the present in our schools are tainted with false science and unwholesome humanitarianism," declared the promotional material for the new college, "leading ultimately to a corrupt and degenerate citizenship."[90] Forrest was more direct. "Most of our large universities now are turning out Socialists, cynics, and atheists," he asserted. Lanier would appeal to "all real Americans who desire that their children shall receive instructions in the true history of their country in an institution where Americanism and the teaching of patriotism and loyalty to home and country are the predominant features."[91] Fellowships funded by Klan sources would enable white Protestants of modest means to attend Lanier. "Here was to be trained the future leadership of America," Simmons told an interviewer.[92] The hopes for Lanier reflected the confidence of the expanding Klan in the community of native white Protestants and their willingness to sustain such an enterprise. But the need for such a school also betrayed anxiety over the state of existing public education—which should have been one of the glories of America, according to Klan propaganda.

The promise of Lanier University collapsed in the face of meager enrollments and the insupportable costs of the enterprise. The school went bankrupt in 1922, and its main academic building, a copy of Robert E. Lee's mansion in Arlington, Virginia, later became the site of Atlanta's chief synagogue.[93] Hiram Evans's 1923 seizure of the national Klan leadership from Simmons further dampened the Invisible Empire's interest in higher education. That same year a more promising acquisition was pursued by David C. Stephenson, the charismatic Klan empire builder of the Midwest and grand dragon of the powerful Indiana realm. Stephenson acted to purchase Valparaiso University, an established Indiana college that had made a reputation as an open-access institution before it fell into financial difficulties. But Stephenson was more a rival than a subordinate to Evans, and the prospect of a dynamic Klan university in the former's Hoosier stronghold gave pause to the wary imperial wizard. When legal roadblocks to the acquisition of Valparaiso appeared, the national Klan leadership backed out of the deal. Instead, Evans steered the educational energy of the hooded order toward the protection of public schools and encouraged brazen anti-Catholicism in pursuit of that aim.[94]

❖

The Klan's drive to reinforce a normative cultural Protestantism through public education reignited debate over the use of the Bible in public schools. In the 1880s as many as 75 to 80 percent of American public schools allowed Bible reading as part of the curriculum, but only Massachusetts had required the practice throughout the state.[95] Deference to community preferences and the disruptive political conflicts that arose when Catholic, Jewish, or free-thinking parents discovered that their children in the public schools were tutored under the auspices of the King James Bible persuaded state governments into the twentieth century to allow local regulation of Bible reading in the schools. Still, many educational authorities throughout the period, reflecting the opinion of Horace Mann, the founder of the public school movement in the United States, considered the daily reading by teachers, without commentary, of several Bible verses to be a useful tool for moral and civic education, not evidence of a sectarian strain in public education. Elements of that civic Protestant outlook informed Evans's 1924 assertion that educational reform naturally should include "imbibing the lessons of patriotism from [the] properly taught history of Christianity from the great source-book of our faith, the Bible."[96]

Yet it was clear by the 1920s that conflict rather than comity accompanied the Bible into the public schools. The nondenominational Protestant nationalism reflected in the use of the King James Bible for patriotic instruction was challenged in the twentieth century by alternative traditions brought on by immigration and assertions of Catholic, Orthodox, and other ethno-religious forms of American nationalism. This cultural conflict was further fanned by the patriotic excesses of World War I. Commentary from Klan sources on the necessity of Bible reading in public schools took on the desperate features of a struggle for civilization. "Without the doctrines of Jesus Christ the white race would degenerate to the level of the mongrel races of the world," John Galen Locke, the grand dragon of the Colorado realm, asserted in a national Klan meeting. "It is our obligation to God," he urged, "that we place the Open Bible in the Public Schools of America."[97] Hoping to check pluralistic influences that could possibly compromise authentic American values as they understood them, various Protestant cultural groups, including the Invisible Empire, acted to employ state power to require the use of the Bible in the public classroom in the years surrounding World War I. Between 1913 and 1930, eleven states and the District of Columbia passed such statutes, with six of them appearing at the height of the revived Klan movement.[98] Several other states explicitly empowered local communities to adopt Bible use in the free schools.

As in other examples of its political activism, the Klan was part of a larger cultural movement in its battle to make Bible reading a required component of the public school curriculum. Efforts to expand Bible reading in the Atlanta and Indianapolis public schools, for instance, predated the Klan's period of dominance on the school boards of those cities.[99] Alongside church people, fraternalists, members of Protestant patriotic associations, and other cultural representatives of reformed confessions, Klansmen attended rallies asserting that "the Christian protestant religion should be [America's] guiding light" in education as in politics.[100] They packed galleries in statehouses from Trenton to Columbus in support of laws to expand the use of the Bible as an educational aid. And where state laws failed to pass, Klansmen pressured local school boards into adopting daily readings or launched political coalitions to elect new school boards that would implement the classroom use of scripture.

Sometimes the Invisible Empire's justification for such measures reflected the widely shared goal of Americanizing immigrants. In this vein, one hooded argument for the use of the Bible in the schools extolled the good book as a doubly effective instrument of both language instruction and citizenship training for new arrivals. "The principles of the Bible are interwoven and entwined with our whole social and national life," explained an article reprinted in the Klan press, "and the reading of it for the sake of learning English, will make for good citizenship as well as develop noble Christian character."[101]

Moreover, the Klan's Protestant activism fit within a more general effort in the 1920s to find a place for religious instruction in public education. Concerned observers from diverse religious traditions argued that the lack of moral or religious education in the schools contributed to lawlessness and other social pathologies. Jews and Catholics joined the conversation in Indiana. Insufficient religious instruction, according to a Jewish publication, was "harmful to the child." The headline of an Indiana Catholic newspaper blared, "Godless Education Causes Increase of Crime." School boards and legislatures throughout the decade, in addition to the Bible-reading demands, also entertained proposals to incorporate into the school day release periods for religious instruction, to be held in adjacent buildings off school grounds, or to allow students to receive credit for after-hours religious schooling in their own confessions. Mainstream Protestant bodies often were in the forefront of such initiatives, but cautious Lutherans, Catholics, and Jews who feared the imposition of state control over religious instruction nevertheless encouraged these attempts to accommodate their faith traditions within the framework of public schooling.[102]

The Klan's endorsement of a public interest in religious education shared elements of this wider viewpoint. The Indiana Klan unsuccessfully sponsored a release-time bill to allow public school students two hours weekly for religious instruction.[103] Youngstown, Ohio, knights endorsed an ecumenical proposal for a religion course in the public school curriculum.[104] Even though Klansmen gave pride of place in religious instruction to the Bible, the hooded order's worry that "over eight hundred thousand children in New York City hear no Bible reading and . . . more than fifty percent of the population grows up without any knowledge whatever of the Scriptures" was broadly consonant with the social positions of other religious bodies.[105]

Once again, however, the Invisible Empire cannot be characterized as mainstream in its insistent campaign to insert the Bible into the public schools. Its aggressive actions and apocalyptic pronouncements placed the hooded order on the extremes of an already-controversial movement in the increasingly pluralistic society of 1920s America. However open Catholics, Jews, and some Protestant denominations were to moral instruction in the schools, the use of one religion's sacred text to impart public lessons in citizenship was intolerable to many Americans whose children were enrolled in public schools.[106] Many professional school administrators also considered the issue intrusive. Hooded intimidation to force the Bible onto the public agenda in mixed communities only worsened divisions. Klansmen in Michigan burned three crosses on the public schoolhouse lawn after Catholic parents brawled with a substitute teacher (and Methodist minister) who had introduced Bible readings into the school day. Authorities had to close the school over the resulting controversy.[107] In Seymour, Indiana, according to the Klan press, "a bitter fight" attended the "moral pressure" applied by local knights to enforce compulsory Bible readings in Jackson County free schools.[108] Unguarded comments such as the assertion of the king kleagle of Maine that "this is not an Italian nation, this is not an Irish nation, and this is not a Catholic nation, it always has been and always will be a Protestant nation,"[109] formed an unmistakable backdrop of intolerance and hostility that overwhelmed occasional Klan protests that its Bible-reading proposals were intended as nonsectarian patriotic lessons.

Despite the upsurge in public school use of the Bible in the New Era, many mainstream politicians learned to avoid Bible-reading initiatives. A 1925 Ohio bill mandating use of the King James Bible in public schools produced a filibuster that choked off state business until opponents of the proposal consented to pass it, whereupon the governor vetoed the bill. No bill requiring use of the Bible in Ohio public schools passed the state legislature thereafter, but the issue remained to unsettle stomachs and complicate political business for several additional legislative sessions.[110] Lawmakers in Indiana, Michigan, and New Jersey, states with active and powerful Klan movements, rejected similar proposals without suffering effective reprisals from unhappy knights.[111]

Struggling to place Protestant religious themes uniformly into public education, activist Klan movements also boldly worked to remove Catholic participation from the public schools and even to outlaw Catholic schools altogether. In common with some Protestant fraternalists and watchful journalists, Klansmen in many realms regarded the network of Catholic parochial schools as a rebuke of public education and a rejection of the democratic principles that underlay it. The popular newspaper columnist Arthur Brisbane asserted that critics of public education, including Catholics who placed their children in parochial schools, did "not believe in the American principle upon which the public school is founded."[112] But suspicion also fell onto Catholics who attended or worked in public schools. Parents who questioned Protestant-themed instruction in public schools, lay Catholic public school teachers, and especially the small number of nuns and other Catholic religious employed in public education attracted keen attention from Klansmen alert to signs of papal mischief. In some states in which clusters of Catholic religious taught in public school systems, 1920s Klansmen proposed formal corrective action. Along Maine's border with New Brunswick, the heavily French Canadian population employed some nuns in the public schools. Detecting sinister intent in that fact along with a related Catholic proposal to apply public taxes to the support of parochial schools, Down East knights suspected a Catholic takeover of public education. They endorsed the gubernatorial ambitions of a state senator who proclaimed the need to draw sharp distinctions between public and parochial schools and to offer public tax support only to the former.[113] In Indiana and in Oregon, where nuns also taught public school in a few scattered counties, Klansmen and their anti-Catholic allies pushed for state laws barring teachers who wore religious garb from the public schools. The Oregon bill, sponsored by the chief of the Portland school board, was enacted into law.[114]

The high tide of the Klan movement, especially in the Midwest, coincided with focused campaigns to remove lay Catholics from teaching positions in public schools. Writing from the hooded stronghold of Akron, one worried correspondent suggested in 1923 that "with the Klan victorious in the November election there is an immediate danger that many teachers who cannot measure up to the Klan's idea of what is pure Americanism will be discharged at the earliest possible moment."[115] According to the historian Douglas Slawson, a placement service for parochial school teachers maintained by the National Catholic Welfare Conference (formerly Council) in 1924 experienced an upsurge of complaints from Catholic teachers who had been denied jobs in the public schools of Iowa, Kansas, Minnesota, Missouri, Illinois, Indiana, Kentucky, and Oklahoma, all states in which local klaverns, sometimes in concert with other chauvinistic Protestants, harassed public school officials to purge Catholics from the teaching force. Vulnerable to local opinion, many school boards wilted under the hooded assault. "Your qualifications make you the very teacher we want," the Kansas Department of Education confided to an Irish Catholic aspirant. "But I am sorry, for my board are averse to hiring a Catholic as a teacher in our schools."[116]

In addition to the local and informal pressure Klansmen applied to school boards to fire Catholic teachers on staff, in Ohio, Oregon, and Indiana hooded lobbyists steered bills onto the legislative agenda that restricted public school teaching jobs to the graduates of public schools, thus filtering out the supposedly unreliable products of parochial education.[117] According to Ohio's grand dragon, Klansmen there wanted "100 percent American teachers to instruct the 100 percent Americans of tomorrow."[118] These bills revived a practice of the Detroit school board, which had arisen from the nativist demands of the American Protective Association in 1892.[119] Few such measures became law in the 1920s, and in some locations, such as New Jersey, public officials barred school boards from applying religious tests when hiring or retaining public school teachers.[120] Occasionally even the hooded advocates of laws intended to screen Catholic influence from public schools seemed to become indifferent to their passage. Embroiled in a factional struggle to control the Invisible Empire in Indiana, the expelled grand dragon D. C. Stephenson directed his legislative lieutenants to smother the Klan's 1925 package of education bills and thereby damage his hooded rivals. At bottom, according to one scholar, Stephenson "was far more interested in acquiring influence than in keeping the nuns out of public schools."[121]

As with other elements of the Invisible Empire's Protestant cultural nationalism, hooded proposals to purify public education found common purpose with a residual strain of popular Protestant chauvinism in 1920s American culture. But formal efforts to have the state enforce an exclusively Protestant regime in public education achieved only limited success. Intimidated school boards in communities with a substantial Klan presence often sought to avoid controversy by transferring Catholic teachers to majority-Catholic districts or denying them employment altogether. But most states, and even many local boards, balked at formal proscriptions against Catholic teachers. Even the radically anti-Catholic Atlanta school board managed to fire only a single Catholic public school teacher, a woman who carried the additional baggage of union activism and a quarrelsome relationship with the board.[122]

More flamboyant was the movement, largely directed by Klansmen but involving other Protestant associations, to pass state compulsory public school attendance laws. Aimed at primary school students, the legislation was meant to eradicate Catholic and other private schools. The bellwether campaign in this movement, the 1922 Oregon initiative to compel all children in the state aged eight to sixteen to attend public schools through the eighth grade, drew on the mixed traditions of progressivism, white Protestant fraternal regard for the democratizing role of public schools, and anti-Catholic paranoia to construct the nation's boldest attempt at educational conformity in the New Era. The original design for a campaign to use the initiative procedure, Oregon's progressive instrument for popular democracy, to make public schooling compulsory did not derive from the Invisible Empire but rather from the Southern Jurisdiction of Scottish Rite Masons. Despite the deep mistrust of the Catholic Church that marked this branch of Masonry, Oregon Masons downplayed anti-Catholicism in the public campaign for the public school proposal, concentrating instead on the unifying democratic qualities of public education.[123] Handbills favoring the initiative declared that "there is no religious question involved in the Public School bill—it is entirely educational." Extolling public schools as "power houses of citizenship," the Masonic literature aimed to empower public education to act as "the only sure foundation for the perpetuation and preservation of our free institutions."[124] It was nevertheless clear that private and religious schools would be eliminated by the proposed law.

Oregon's Invisible Empire quickly assumed prominence in the initiative campaign. Some historians argue that Klan infiltration of the Masons amounted to the hooded order manipulating the fraternal organization as a front to mask Klan sponsorship of the proposal. The Klan's open embrace of the initiative makes such deception seem unnecessary. (In Michigan the Invisible Empire took over a similar initiative that had been pioneered in 1920, before the Klan movement organized in the state, by James Hamilton, an iconoclastic nativist and anti-Catholic activist.[125]) Although the hooded order probably did not introduce the Oregon compulsory school initiative, it came to define it, especially its anti-Catholic component. After the *New York*

Times linked the measure to the Klan, the paper charged that "one purpose, perhaps the main purpose, was to destroy schools maintained by or under the auspices of the Catholic Church."[126] Klansmen worked for the successful passage of the initiative (often by sponsoring prominent anti-Catholic speakers); Klan officials gave updates on the campaign within the fraternal walls of klaverns; and when the initiative succeeded in 1922, Oregon Klansmen took credit for the victory. While awaiting court tests of the law, which would not take effect until 1926, Oregon knights continued to associate their order with the law. During a 1923 election campaign, eastern Oregon Klansmen placed "under every door in town a copy of the school bill and a 100 Percent American ticket."[127]

Elsewhere the Invisible Empire demanded the passage of similar laws. "We must begin the compulsory education of *every child in America* in public schools, at the earliest possible moment," declared the Klan's national headquarters.[128] With varying degrees of intensity, between 1922 and 1924 Klan-backed initiatives, constitutional amendments, and legislative bills to force students into public schools appeared across the nation.[129] The 1924 Michigan initiative to add mandatory public schooling to the state constitution attracted Imperial Wizard Hiram Evans to the state to speak in support of the proposal.[130] Knights and Masons together promoted a mandatory public schooling bill in California. Oregon Klansmen crossed the border into Washington and attempted to re-create the Oregon initiative drive. In Arkansas, Indiana, and Ohio, bills to compel attendance in the public schools appeared in state legislatures. Missouri voters entertained an initiative to establish compulsory public school attendance, and the Mississippi legislature debated a constitutional amendment along the same lines. A milder bill which measured private school accomplishments against the standard of the public schools was introduced into the Texas legislature. Efforts by Oklahoma knights to bar parochial schools from the Sooner State failed to take legislative form.[131] The wave of such proposals spoke to the vitality of the public school issue in the New Era and the persistence into the twentieth century of anti-Catholicism as an American social ferment.

Still, the larger lesson of the Klan-backed initiatives was their failure to win majority support. Aside from the Oregon initiative, none of the compulsory public school attendance proposals was adopted. Moreover, opposition to them, and especially to the Klan's vituperative anti-Catholicism, was widespread and diverse. Despite their own anti-Catholic beliefs, Michigan Lutherans felt the threat of the Klan-backed public school initiative to their own schools and cooperated with Catholic groups in opposing it.[132] They were joined in opposition by Seventh-Day Adventists, Dutch Reformed Protestants, and representatives of private academies. In defending the right of churches to establish their own schools, one Dutch Reformed minister laid aside the anti-Catholic militancy of his own tradition to challenge the very basis of the Invisible Empire's hostility to Catholicism. "Have the Catholics ever tried in any point *actually* to establish the supremacy of the Pope over the American government?" he asked.[133] The president of the Jewish Theological Seminary, who also sat on the Philadelphia school board, declared that the Klan's compulsory public school demands "threaten[ed] the welfare of the country."[134] Other occasional allies of the Invisible Empire objected to the hooded proposals to outlaw parochial schools. The National Education Association, which tolerated the Klan's endorsement of its federal public education program, nevertheless declared the Michigan proposal unwarranted. "Citizens have the right to educate their children in either public or private schools, when the educational standards of both are approved by the State educational authorities," the school reform body announced in 1924. Even Masonic groups in Michigan and New York denounced the Klan proposals and upheld the American right to private schooling.[135]

The Klan's effort to ensure Protestant ascendancy through mandatory public schooling clearly outran mainstream sentiment, even amid the contested cultural and religious landscape of the 1920s. Confirmation of that arrived when the federal district court overturned the Oregon school bill in 1924, arguing that the law exceeded the limits of state power.[136] A U.S. Supreme Court decision the following year affirmed the judgment of the federal district court. In this as in many other areas of state authority, the revived Klan movement was able to force its views into the public arena and even influence public policy at the local level, but it could not grasp the controls of state power so as to make public policy in the pluralistic America of the 1920s conform to its vision of white Protestant national identity.

❖

Nevertheless, the Klan movement also reflected of the mixture of centralizing and localistic outlooks and policies that distinguished the public life of the New Era. The Invisible Empire's involvement in the NEA's unsuccessful push for national direction and funding of public education revealed deeply divisive contests over the proper function of state authority that involved a complex web of overlapping and incongruous interests. As with many aspects of educational policy in the New Era, the NEA's attempt to create a federal Department of Education that would dispense aid to state school systems and bring order to the nation's disjointed structure of public education, first introduced in Congress in 1919, predated the Invisible Empire's strong interest in school uniformity and reform. A surprising array of forces and viewpoints

marked the early 1920s debate on the measure. Distinguished proponents
ranged from the educational professionals of the NEA, the American Federation of Labor, numerous local chambers of commerce, and commercial societies to the General Federation of Women's Clubs. But the bill also attracted
the backing of Protestant nationalists such as the Southern Jurisdiction of
Scottish Rite Masons and the Daughters of the American Revolution. Reform and cultural nationalism blended together in the bid to strengthen and
rationalize American public schools. The public school movement, in turn,
became to some supporters of the federal bill a surrogate for Americanism
itself. Hugh Magill of the NEA, in a meeting sponsored by New York Masons,
declared himself "sick of this business of attacking the Federal Government.
. . . It is our Government, and its flag is our flag." Opponents of the NEA's
measure included business conservatives in the U.S. Chamber of Commerce,
states' rights advocates, and Catholics who saw bigoted Protestant fraternalism behind the NEA's professional veneer and feared for the independence
of parochial schools. But criticism of federal education control also came
from within the educational establishment. Several prominent university
presidents detected a centralizing, undemocratic, "Prussian" uniformity in
the proposal.[137]

Columbia's Nicholas Murray Butler, who also opposed the expansion of
federal authority inherent in constitutional prohibition, foresaw in the school
bill "a bureaucracy worse than that of Czarist Russia."[138] Catholic critics of the
NEA bill tugged at this theme when the proposal was revived in 1924. "The
philosophy behind this idea is that the child does not belong to the parents,"
James Ryan of the National Catholic Welfare Conference stressed, "but to the
State." Because the bill was endorsed by the Scottish Rite Masons and, by that
time, the Klan, Catholic interests understood federal supervision of education
to be one with the ongoing efforts of Masons and Klansmen to destabilize and
even destroy parochial schools. But Ryan's objection struck the broader vein
of local resistance to modern state formation in the 1920s. "We don't want
nationalized children," he continued, "who will develop into machine men as
the result of standardized education."[139]

The Klan's engagement in the issue also exhibited contradictory themes
of narrow bigotry combined with openness to an expanded system of state-
supported welfare. As its publications from the onset of Klan support for
a federal Department of Education bill in 1923 clearly attest, the Invisible
Empire envisioned the NEA's proposal as part of its legislative assault on parochial schools and its commitment to frustrate Catholicism's alleged designs
on public education.[140] Laying opposition to educational reform at the feet
of "the Roman Catholic Hierarchy in the United States," the Klan stridently
proclaimed public education to be "the only workable means" to counteract

the "dangerous disintegrating tendencies" of the nation's pluralistic population.[141]

Yet in its strange unity with educational progressives (certainly embarrassing for them), the hooded order also struck out at the disabling limitations
of American localism and hostility to the use of state power for the public
good. Ku Klux journalists condemned "a number of Southern Congressmen
who see in the [NEA] bill a menace to their beloved states rights theory. In
the Towner-Sterling bill, they profess to see federal control of their country
schools, and to prevent that they are willing to sacrifice the education of the
youth of America. States rights must be preserved, they seem to argue, if the
country goes to hell."[142] Thus the Invisible Empire embodied the dilemma
of bureaucratic modernization in the New Era. Despite its cultural chauvinism and religious intolerance, the Klan was a circumstantial partner in the
construction of modern state responsibility. Yet its fulsome contention that
"the slightest opposition to this program of unifying into a common national
thought and feeling is un-American"[143] marked the Invisible Empire as irre-
trievably outside the mainstream of political compromise and national con-
ciliation. On educational matters the Ku Klux Klan both reflected the national
school debate of the 1920s and removed itself from any realistic chance of
resolving it in a pluralistic nation.

5

Dry Americanism:
Prohibition, Law, and Culture

IN THE SUMMER OF 1923 a party of seventeen men struggled through dense vegetation to reach two illegal stills hidden in a rugged section of Fayette County in east central Indiana. Although the local police chief and four deputies led the raid, the bulk of the squad was made up of citizen volunteers from the Fayette County Horse Thief Detective Association (HTDA). The Horse Thieves, as they were popularly known, were a collection of part-time lawmen deputized under the provisions of an old constabulary law, which at the behest of the Indiana Ku Klux Klan had been revived to assist undermanned federal and state authorities in prohibition enforcement. Since nearly 10 percent of the Fayette County population belonged to the hooded order, it is likely that most if not all of the HTDA constables deputized for this raid were Klansmen.[1] Most of them also carried weapons. The four surprised bootleggers, an unusual company including two women and a deaf-mute man, defended their stills, prompting what a Klan journalist called "a running gunfight." Almost seventy-five shots were exchanged and one deputized citizen (identified in a later document as the klaliff, or vice president, of the Fayette County Klan) was wounded before the bootleggers were subdued. The raiders seized ten gallons of the rough whiskey that local people called white mule, a car used to distribute the illegal liquor, and 250 gallons of mash meant to produce more alcohol for the thirsty underground market. Deepening the imprint of the Invisible Empire on this episode was the hooded reporter's assertion that the successful raid had been initiated by "information furnished by the Ku Klux Klan."[2]

Crisscrossing the border separating vigilantism from quasi-legal action, hooded knights from other realms joined their Indiana compatriots in rallying to grassroots defense of the Eighteenth Amendment. Sometimes Klansmen acted in cooperation with beleaguered law enforcement officials, at other times they operated in the face of official refusal to pursue violators of federal and state prohibition laws, but in nearly every case an earnest sense of community law enforcement that superseded formal legal authority pervaded the populistic behavior of the dry, hooded bands. Thirteen months after the Fayette County raid, thirty deputized citizens from Poplar Bluff, Missouri, working under the supervision of a "private detective of St. Louis," purchased illegal liquor and then arrested the sellers as part of a community "Booze Clean-Up." Klan press reports crowed that "every one of the thirty men taking part in the drive as deputized officers were members of the Ku Klux Klan, and each one was sworn in with power to make arrests and serve warrants," all of which "were sworn out on evidence obtained by local Klansmen." Government authorities played a subsidiary role in the campaign. Four federal prohibition agents issued warrants for the Klan undercover operatives while the Poplar Bluff police melted into the background.[3] The following October a Klan posse led by a volunteer "constable" in a western Pennsylvania town near Pittsburgh was halted by the unsympathetic chief of police in the midst of a raid on "moonshine dens." Chief Reider even arrested one of the Klan raiders, leading a local Methodist minister to charge that the police protected bootleggers and that "the only steps toward enforcement of" the state dry law "that were taken in the community were started by Klansmen."[4]

Prohibition and Pluralism

In the early 1920s the Invisible Empire clearly seized significant responsibility for enforcing national prohibition at the local level, engaging in a series of community struggles that hooded sources characterized as elemental "strife between the bootleggers and Americans."[5] In the simplified rhetoric of dry Klansmen, the fate of prohibition would determine whether the Constitution, patriotic respect for the law, and the cultural preeminence of Protestant Americanism would endure or be washed away in a flood tide of alien defiance and governmental neglect. As with most aspects of the Klan movement, the hooded order's perception of decisive cultural conflict reflected important pluralistic struggles in 1920s American society; yet the Ku Kluxers' exclusionary and confrontational posturing blunted their ability to influence the ultimate outcome of events. Constitutional prohibition, in defense of which the hooded order rallied in the 1920s, was the product of more than a century of agitation, disagreement, and reform commitment among Americans. Buoyed by religious perfectionism, secular reform enthusiasm, and evidence drawn from medical and sociological studies as well as racial, class, and ethnic prejudice and chauvinism, the movement to regulate and then eliminate beverage alcohol was complex, multidimensional, and among the most divisive public policy questions since the end of American slavery. Integrated into the structure of governance by decades of local, state, and national regulation, the liquor issue by the twentieth century also had become enmeshed in debates surrounding modern American state formation. Hooded engagement in prohibition enforcement derived from the dry movement's complicated legacy of progressivism, ameliorative state interventionism, and repressive nativism—but it was nativism that dominated the Klan's dry convictions and polarized the prohibition coalition in the 1920s.

Although the Invisible Empire played no role in the passage of national prohibition, chronology and common roots linked these two powerful expressions of 1920s cultural conflict. Prohibition built on state dry laws, a wartime restriction on liquor and beer production, and the implementation of a ban on the manufacture, sale, and transportation of beverage alcohol as a constitutional requirement in 1920. It paralleled the second Klan's formation in 1915, its patriotic assertiveness during the war, and its rise to prominence as a social and political force beginning in 1921. Prohibition reform and the hooded order also drew support from similar constituencies of hopeful, anxious Americans who struggled to impose a culturally contested vision of order and progress on a pluralistic citizenry. "With prohibition came the bootlegger," one skeptical observer of the Klan movement commented, "and many anxious parents, seeing their sons and daughters going in for 'petting parties,' all-night automobile escapades and bad gin, sincerely thought the foundations of society were being undermined by the vicious elements identified in their minds with the illegitimate traffic in liquor. In town after town, all over the country, the first act of the newly formed Klan was to horsewhip the proprietor of the most notorious local speak-easy."[6] For both Klansmen and many prohibitionists, enforcement of the dry ban after 1920 became a concrete as well as a symbolic test of the integrity of the legal structure and a battle to determine national standards of behavior.

As a public issue, prohibition encapsulated the Klan's commitment to establish native white Protestant values as normative. Even more than the defense of public schools, which generated greater attention from the hooded order's national leadership, prohibition enforcement motivated Klansmen at the community level. Leonard Moore, one of the most influential recent historians of the 1920s Klan movement, maintains that the commitment to prohibition enforcement was "the single most important bond between

Klansmen throughout the nation. The crisis created in communities through-out the United States by the ban on alcohol provided the greatest catalyst for the Klan movement," he continued, "and during the early 1920s, the Klan became the most popular means of expressing support for the Noble Ex-periment."[7] No other public policy issue engaged as many Klansmen in direct action, combined the reform and coercive aspects of the Klan movement, or better highlighted the contradictions between moral language and repressive behavior by hooded knights than did the Invisible Empire's determination to enforce prohibition.

While the dry reform institutionalized the social and cultural values of Prot-estant abstainers and reformers against the more favorable attitudes toward alcohol use still practiced by many immigrants, the alcohol ban contained built-in vulnerabilities that encouraged community division over enforce-ment. First, the Volstead Act, which put into detailed operation the principles of the Eighteenth Amendment, established an alcohol content of one-half of 1 percent as the baseline for banned intoxicating beverages, a surprisingly strict standard that deflated hopes for access to low-alcohol beers and light wines under the prohibition regime. Second, the enforcement mechanism charged with policing this stringent and in many areas unpopular standard was deeply flawed. In deference to dry Southerners' suspicion of invasive federal power, the Eighteenth Amendment called for "concurrent" enforce-ment of the alcohol ban, thus splitting responsibility for prohibition between federal and state authorities. Congress and the advocates of prohibition, who were interested in downplaying the costs of the reform, furthermore created a minimal federal enforcement body in the Prohibition Bureau, which from 1921 to 1926 operated on cut-rate budgets of between six and ten million dollars.[8] These allotments were sufficient to field only an ill-trained and un-derpaid force of some three thousand federal prohibition agents, who quickly established a reputation for corruptibility, incompetence, and poor gun dis-cipline (one dry agent shot an overly curious U.S. senator in a Washington alley).[9] According to a 1927 government review, "seven years of chaos" distin-guished the record of the Prohibition Bureau.[10]

Inadequate federal power left a substantial enforcement responsibility with the individual states. But many state governments underfunded or even ignored their end of the concurrent enforcement bargain. Along the Eastern seaboard, drys faced a solid wall of wet resistance from Maryland to Mas-sachusetts. Industrial centers in the Midwest and on the Pacific Coast also harbored large populations resistant to prohibition. Several states enacted statutes that were stricter than the Volstead Act, but Maryland refused to pass an enforcement act; New York repealed its enforcement measure in 1923, followed by three more states by 1929; and twenty-eight states budgeted no money for enforcement in 1927.[11] Local enforcement lagged even in the dry heartland: "90% of our local officers of the law are entirely willing that 'George' should [enforce the law]—only in this case 'George' is Uncle Sam," fretted a Tennessee prohibitionist in 1924.[12] The failure of national prohibition strategists to construct a workable scheme of enforcement invited hooded and other vigilantes to intervene in defense of the Constitution, often by crashing into the homes and recreational spaces of their immigrant and Catholic neighbors.

❖

Individual knights differed in their drinking habits, but the Invisible Empire as a whole quickly aligned itself with the Protestant outlook of the prohibition movement and embraced the need for rigid enforcement once constitutional prohibition became a formal component of American law and governance. The chief organized advocates of the dry reform, the Anti-Saloon League of America (ASL) and the Woman's Christian Temperance Union (WCTU), were disproportionately Protestant in membership and vision. Like the Invisible Empire, the Anti-Saloon League, considered the principal force behind the passage of national prohibition, sought to direct the influence of Protestant clergymen against alcohol and advertised itself as the (Protestant) "Church in action against the saloon."[13] Virtually all the officials of the league were Protestant ministers or active laymen. In 1903 the league had rearranged its state affiliates into church federations, whereby participating denominations elected representatives to the board of trustees of each state ASL, solidifying the alliance between organized Protestantism and anti-liquor reform. Methodists, Baptists, and, in some locations, United Brethren congregations, all of whom also supplied members and ministerial support to the Invisible Empire, were among the more enthusiastic allies of the ASL. In spite of missionary efforts by coalition-seeking league officials, Catholics, Episcopalians, and the more liturgical Lutheran confessions remained cool or actively antagonistic to the ASL and the dry enterprise, as well as to the Klan.

On the other side, native white Protestant opponents of prohibition, such as Columbia University president Nicholas Murray Butler and New York senator James Wadsworth, were vocal in their criticism of the dry measure, and moonshiners and drinkers who could trace their ancestry to Cromwell's England abounded. Nevertheless, popular opposition to prohibition and outright resistance against the Eighteenth Amendment clustered in the same social groups and settings vilified by the Klan: among Catholics and representatives of the church itself; in immigrant enclaves and large cities; and amid nightclubs, gambling dives, and red light districts. In immigrant and Catholic neighborhoods, resistance to prohibition enforcement was framed by the broader and more tolerant aspirations of a pluralistic American identity that celebrated freedom and diversity over the restrictive practices advocated by native-born Protestant nationalists. Thus, with an assertiveness sure to prick the sensibilities of Klansmen and other guardians of old-stock hegemony, ethnic New Yorkers in 1921 celebrated wet defiance with patriotic displays that ranged from a pro-beer rally led by a Lower East Side resident in cowboy attire to a formal Fifth Avenue parade featuring, according to the historian Michael Lerner, "Irish hansom cab drivers, members of the Sons of Italy and Garibaldi Association, representatives from German societies, and a division of African-American marchers, all carrying American flags and signs with slogans like 'We're American Citizens, Not Inmates,' and 'We Prefer Brewers of Beer to Brewers of Bigotry.'"[14] Even in an Ohio hamlet, a bootlegger arrested in 1923 by a "vigilance body" composed of the community's self-described "real Americans" appealed to the privileges of ethnic Americanism. "All Slavishmen have a right to have a little liquor in their homes for private consumption," he argued, buttressing his case with "a Slavic newspaper, published in Cleveland, which appeared to bear out his contention."[15] By appropriating American patriotic symbols and civil protections, ethnic opponents of prohibition challenged the restrictive definition of American customs and comportment favored by the Invisible Empire and many prominent advocates of dry reform.

Catholic resistance to prohibition was also notable and stirred resentment in dry ranks, even among opponents of the Klan. Patrick Callahan, a top official of the Knights of Columbus and one of the most prominent American Catholic prohibitionists, regretted that Catholics seemed to dismiss prohibition as a distinctively Protestant enthusiasm. "For the last five years," he reflected in 1929, he regularly had observed "orators, Catholic as well as non-Catholic, and Catholic politicians and Catholic priests . . . denounce the Eighteenth Amendment and the Volstead Act, practically preaching defiance of the law, before Holy Name Society gatherings and Communion breakfasts and banquets of the Knights of Columbus."[16] Such sentiments, he worried, inflamed anti-Catholic predispositions among drys, as when a WCTU field-worker testily reported that a belligerent wet, Catholic Wisconsin school superintendent had blocked her from speaking in the school auditorium— though later investigation determined that the official was not Catholic and was faithfully enforcing school board policy prohibiting "religious or political meetings" in school facilities.[17] Absorbing the themes of the popular anti-Catholicism of the 1920s, elements of the dry movement edged closer to the intolerant outlook of the Invisible Empire.

Certain leading drys also framed disputes over prohibition enforcement in the nativist terms familiar to the Klan's social analysis. James Cannon

Jr., the combative Virginia Methodist bishop and national ASL lobbyist, was not a Klansman, yet he appraised the Northeastern urban centers of anti-prohibition resistance in language similar to that employed by hooded authorities. In one concentrated outburst he denounced "the un-American liquor-controlled nullifying attitude of the foreign populated city called New York,"[18] which mocked the values of old-stock Americans and threatened to derail the supremacy of the law. To Cannon, who habitually engaged in billingsgate with Catholic and immigrant wets, Catholic political critics of prohibition were "intolerant bigots."[19] Their supporters, "the Italians, the Sicilians, the Poles, and the Russian Jew . . . the kind of people that you find today on the sidewalks of New York," Cannon exclaimed in remarks that drew immediate condemnation, could not be assimilated and gave the "good citizens in this land . . . a stomach-ache."[20] The bishop's dyspepsia was not eased by the patriotic claims of a pluralistic version of American identity. Instead, the growing ethnic understanding of American identity indicated the possibility that "these strangers" may "gradually overcome us."[21] Most prohibitionists were more temperate in speech than Cannon, and majority opinion among organized drys favored outreach to ethnic and religious wets. But a general sense pervaded dry ranks that effective enforcement of prohibition was hampered by an alliance of wet politicians, the Roman hierarchy, and immigrants unwilling to relinquish alien customs. Again the frustrations encountered by the mainstream prohibition movement produced attitudes that conformed to the worldview of most hooded supporters of the dry reform.

The prohibition divide cast other antagonists of the Invisible Empire into the wet camp. Even though many African Americans supported temperance, and Jews, as a class, were not considered disruptive drinkers, popular attitudes identified both groups as enemies of prohibition. Bootleggers frequently set up shop in the black sections of Midwestern towns and, despite the dry encouragement of African American elites, many middle-class blacks did not allow prohibition to disrupt their use of alcohol. In one telling incident, police seized 250 liquor bottles from a party of picnickers on an outing from Harlem's most prominent African Methodist Episcopal church.[22] Jewish distillers and grocers often were familiar public faces of the liquor trade, and Jewish bootleggers were prominent in the illegal commerce carried out in violation of the national alcohol ban. In common with Catholics and liturgical Protestants, Jews also enjoyed a sacramental exemption from the Volstead Act that produced a small but steady diversion of sacramental wine into the bootlegging stream. Chauvinistic drys characterized this trade as evidence that religious observance was merely a screen to camouflage cynical and destructive indifference to authentic American laws and customs. Thus a Texas Klan newspaper linked the threats posed by "the Homebrew and the Hebrew."[23]

Given the themes of cultural conflict that coursed through the mainstream of the prohibition cause, Klan representatives found it possible to reshape the complexities of the ban to fit the Invisible Empire's straightforward narrative of national crisis. Defined by local Klan raiders with an ambiguous relationship to legal authority, the grassroots enactment of prohibition reform became a concrete, daily contest between American identity and alien proclivities. Hooded activism promoted an understanding of the controversial dry reform that downplayed community discussion of the limits to government authority over private behavior. Instead, the Klan refocused the issue as a measurement of collective reverence for the law and national institutions versus local wet unwillingness to conform to American standards and practices that betrayed a fundamental disloyalty to the nation and its founding people. Finally, the widespread inaction of official authorities energized the Klan to challenge ineffective political institutions and, in their stead if need be, to press enforcement of the law as an act of populist democracy. Thus a Ku Klux editorial adjusted a speech by the amiable but ineffective national prohibition director, Ohio's Roy Haynes, to cast the conundrum of enforcement into nativist terms. "To scan the names of bootleggers arrested each day in all of our large cities," the Klan press paraphrased Haynes, "one immediately realizes that the bootlegging industry is receiving its greatest impetus from persons who are not Americans." Political resistance to national prohibition centered in "foreign societies and lodges," the report continued. Alienism, in this perspective, was the primary force impeding the success of prohibition. "Without the influence created by persons who can not, in a strict sense of the word be called Americans, the continued upheaval arising from the passage of the Volstead act would be practically negligible."[24] Framed in this manner, the patriotic duty of hooded Americans was clear and compelling.

Yet despite similarities with some aspects of the mainstream prohibition movement, the Klan's unbending religious and ethnic intolerance pushed the Invisible Empire toward the radical and ultimately disruptive fringe of the dry effort. To Imperial Wizard Hiram Evans, the particulars of prohibition did not matter as much as the degree to which widespread violations of the dry laws contributed to an alien-driven crime wave that, in Evans's typical language of crisis, threatened "our existence as a nation." The scale of the criminal challenge to Americanism rendered it "folly to argue about the exact amount of liquor that is drunk, or to quibble over the number of convictions." Basic corrective action by the Invisible Empire was required. According to Evans, the Klan movement had formed in response to white Protestant perceptions that the strength and integrity of familiar American institutions had been weakened by a postwar surge of pluralistic influences that were transforming cultural practices in the United States. Now the dignity of the law and, most critically, the supremacy of the Constitution had been undermined by a rush of lawlessness that the imperial wizard attributed to "the influx of unassimilated, unfit, un-Americanized and unsafe aliens." Despite its masks, secret ceremonies, and clandestine operations, the Invisible Empire claimed its special task was to support, uphold, and preserve the law and to retain the nation's legal structure as a necessary guarantor of Protestant-inspired values that were at the heart of American identity. Thus crime and, especially for Evans, "alien" crime became a primary target of Klan activism.

Evans's catalogue of "alien" assaults on American mores included an array of misdeeds far more extensive than violations of the Volstead Act, but he perceived a distinctive threat inherent in wet defiance. The first danger lay in the clear cultural challenge to native white Protestant control posed by the persistence of alien folkways in the face of laws that required their suppression. Extracting data from government hearings in 1926, the hooded ideologue recited a doleful record of persistent immigrant and ethnic refusal to abide by American law: "In Arizona 85 per cent of the bootleggers were aliens; in Connecticut, 90 per cent of arrests were of aliens; in California 85 per cent, mostly Italians and Greeks; in Colorado 52 per cent; Maryland 75; Illinois 90." Widespread violation of the law also corroded American institutions. Police and judges refused to support the law or took bribes to withhold enforcement, thereby spreading a culture of official corruption that undermined public rectitude. By turns outraged, cynical, and indifferent, citizens lost faith in the efficacy of a maladroit or untrustworthy justice system. Facing the disintegration of public authority, Evans reasoned, the Klan needed to uphold law enforcement by providing its knights as supplementary agents to help make prohibition functional. Moreover, Evans maintained that the Invisible Empire "must also create public sentiment in favor of obedience by others; create public disapproval of any lawlessness."[25] Thus besides acting as a shadowy constabulary, local Klans were urged by the hooded body's top official to monitor and direct public opinion by means of extralegal advocacy. Such a bold display of public authority by a private, secret, racially and religiously exclusive body invited controversy. Both the motives cited and the methods adopted by the hooded order to sustain prohibition tarnished the dry cause and drove the Klan out of the mainstream of the prohibition effort.

Hooded Deputies

Evidence of disorder and the demonstrated inability of established authorities to act against unlawful behavior was one of the most powerful inducements to the organization of local Klans in the early 1920s and perhaps the major theme in the grassroots Klan movement. For many communities, open violation of prohibition laws provided the catalyst for Klan recruiting and shaped the moral vigilantism that distinguished the early phase of the Klan's drive to prominence. As with most issues that concerned the Invisible Empire, however, the degree of hooded commitment to prohibition varied among top officials and local organizations. D. C. Stephenson, the dominant hooded personality of the Midwest, betrayed an opportunistic take on the dry reform. Before he joined the Klan movement, Stephenson had unsuccessfully run for Congress as a wet Democrat. Despite his profligate use of liquor, he recognized the appeal of prohibition to Indiana Klansmen and acted accordingly, but without personal conviction.[26] Joseph Huffington, the brutal Klan strongman of southern Indiana, who in 1925 allegedly boasted that "it took a lot of whiskey and a lot of money" to win a decisive municipal election, supplied both dry speakers and alcoholic inducements to voters in practical pursuit of Klan power. Zeke Marvin, the Texas grand dragon who helped construct the influential realm in that state, suffered from internal Klan charges that he had dispensed illegal liquor from the chain of drugstores he operated in Dallas. Imperial Wizard Evans was another latecomer to prohibition. Never as enthusiastic as the rank and file on dry matters—perhaps because he saw the Anti-Saloon League as a rival for Protestant loyalty—Evans framed prohibition within his anti-alien obsession and primarily stressed wet criminality while trying to thwart the presidential ambitions of Al Smith, the celebrated anti-prohibition governor of New York.

On the other hand, clear evidence indicates that many Klan leaders and the majority of ordinary knights fervently believed in the dry cause. Charles J. Orbison, the legal counsel of the Indiana Klan, had been an officer in the Indiana Anti-Saloon League in the first decade of the century and in 1920 served as Indiana's federal prohibition supervisor. Hugh "Pat" Emmons, the talkative exalted cyclops of the St. Joseph County Klan, was a reformed bartender who had evangelized for temperance in the years before the Invisible Empire expanded to Indiana. The hooded volunteers who made up the citizens' committees that participated in innumerable liquor raids showed determination as well as a longing for action and adventure.[27]

In klaverns across the country, local manifestations of the Klan movement were not uniformly bone dry, yet the grassroots of the Invisible Empire maintained a strong connection to prohibition as an issue. One Western example illustrates the complexity of the hooded ties to prohibition. Colorado Klansmen responded unevenly to the dry regime. Prohibition violations contributed to the perceived crisis in law enforcement that spurred the growth of the hooded order in the state. One of the few instances of Klan violence in Colorado involved Denver knights beating a Jewish attorney who defended bootleggers. Yet in some areas of the state the Invisible Empire exhibited a restrained outlook on dry activism. The chief Klan figure in Grand Junction was a civic booster who downplayed charges of wet lawlessness in his community. The local klavern even served beer at its meetings. In other communities, Klansmen expressed satisfaction with official enforcement of the dry laws (often because fellow knights served as sheriffs, police officers, and judges) and showed little inclination to pursue extralegal action. On the other hand, Pueblo knights conducted a series of high-profile liquor raids while elsewhere in southern Colorado prohibition enforcement was a vibrant issue in Klan circles. Finally, dry vigilantism played an ironic role in the collapse of Klan momentum in Colorado. In 1925, Clarence Morley, the newly elected Klansman governor, appointed a collection of fellow knights to patronage posts as state prohibition agents. Unexpectedly, the hooded agents launched a series of rough, controversial raids and used their authority to bully critics of the Invisible Empire. Angry public reaction indicated that, in a reversal of its origins, the Klan had now become the symbol of an arrogant, unresponsive government. Chastened, the governor was forced to revoke the commissions.[28]

Elsewhere, as with many Americans, Klansmen mixed support for prohibition enforcement with occasional violations of the law. Groups claiming Klan allegiance lined up on both sides of the question in South Carolina. In 1922 a white-robed group urged a bootlegging state lawman to enforce the dry law more vigorously; two years later, an unidentified band of hooded men ordered a state marshal to ease up on prohibition enforcement to protect their illegal trade in ginger, a key ingredient in recipes for homemade liquor.[29] In Indiana, Emmons once suggested that Klan political canvassers might win over Protestant voters with "a little home-brew party," but his overall commitment to prohibition enforcement did not flag.[30] Rumors circulated among detractors of the Invisible Empire that local klaverns harbored bootleggers and even offered protection to moonshiners. An anti-Klan journalist in the Texas panhandle charged that hooded jurors refused to convict certain criminals and added that area Klans recruited bootleggers into the hooded fellowship.[31] Colorado Springs's police chief rebuffed Ku Klux offers to supply aid in law enforcement with the opinion that "thieves and crooks join the Klan to secure the protection of Klan police officers."[32] Dallas critics complained that drugstore owners, whose authority to dispense medicinal alcohol often masked bootlegging operations, flocked to the Klan in order to eliminate rivals in the illegal liquor business. One reporter heard that "90 per cent of the bootleggers" in Dallas had become Klansmen.[33] Corruption also periodically infected the ranks of the hooded constabulary. Several special deputies among the hundreds of hooded agents appointed by the Ku Klux sheriff near the Klan center of Akron were arrested in 1925 after 130 gallons of confiscated white mule went missing.[34]

Klaverns routinely banished Klansmen who turned up drunk or who engaged in bootlegging. The Akron Klan purged several confirmed bootleggers.[35] Two such miscreants were dismissed from the dry Monticello, Arkansas, Klan.[36] "We have two Klansmen in this order by the name of Smith Bros. who are bootleggers," reported the minutes of the La Grande, Oregon, Klan, "and if this is true we are going to get rid of them as fast as the mail can carry the notification." Although this Northwestern klavern did not engage in vigilante raids and occasionally acknowledged the arrest of a member for prohibition violations, its close attention to the law documents the significance that most Klansmen attached to orderly obedience to dry requirements. The klavern's minutes detail avid, extended attention to local liquor cases of note, recording demands that a druggist charged under wartime prohibition restrictions not be allowed to escape punishment and that a prominent local bootlegger be sentenced properly. In the latter case the Klan dispatched a delegation to the jail to confirm that the "King of Bootleggers" was indeed incarcerated. News of boisterous downtown drinking generated a petition to the city council requesting corrective action; on another occasion, hooded colleagues were admonished not to provide bail for arrested bootleggers.[37] In the end, few hooded public policy issues aroused as much clear and honest grassroots enthusiasm as did prohibition enforcement. From Long Island to the Pacific Coast, Klansmen rallied in favor of prohibition, demanded strict enforcement of the law from local governments, questioned the patriotism and American identity of wet resisters, and, in many cases, took to the streets to enforce the law on their own authority.

Without doubt, popular mobilization against the constellation of vices that accompanied defiance of prohibition spurred the growth of the Klan movement in the early 1920s. The development of oil and gas fields in southern Arkansas, northern Louisiana, eastern Oklahoma, and east Texas, for instance, produced hard-bitten boomtowns such as Smackover, Arkansas, which attracted bootleggers, illegal saloons, gambling, prostitution, and raucous assemblies of carousing roughnecks. In the absence of effective police or officeholders, klaverns arose from citizens' movements determined to stamp out "open vice."[38] Influential Klan concentrations in small towns such as El Dorado, Arkansas, and regional centers such as Shreveport, grew from these efforts. Some local citizens not only tolerated but also encouraged the vigilante organization and violent threats of these early Southwestern Klans. One Oklahoman saluted the necessity and effectiveness of hooded intimidation. "In the oil towns . . . where no school girl is safe from this rough and tumble bootleg element, one 'visit' and the town is almost a 'Sunday-School class,'" he assured congressional investigators. "I have not seen a case, not a single one," he continued, "that all the leading good people of town have not said, 'It's a good thing.'" The Klan, he argued, had functioned as a people's police in the absence of effective official lawmen. "The delay in our laws is a great protection to the criminal class, and the people, taxed to the limit, are taking this method to put a stop to this cost on the town and country."[39]

Prohibition enforcement made up a prominent part of the violent wave of hooded moral regulation that convulsed the Southwest from 1920 to 1923. Distinctions between violations of the law and of customary moral codes blurred as hooded night riders meted out punishment to bootleggers, adulterers, and misbehaving spouses alike. But bootlegging, unlike individual moral failings, prompted larger-scale struggles for community control. In 1921, when some 150 Oklahoma knights raided a local bootlegger, a gunfight killed the bootlegger and two Klansmen. The next year about two hundred hooded vigilantes attacked Smackover's vice districts, routing some two thousand "undesirables" amid flaming nightspots, gunfire, whippings, and applications of tar and feathers.[40] In more divided communities, such methods led to violent outcomes that identified the Invisible Empire, and not wet reprobates, as lawless threats to order. A bungled raid in 1921 on a supposed bootlegger near Los Angeles led to an exchange of gunfire between a lawman and disguised Klansmen, killing one of the knights and wounding two others. Upon inspection, two of the hooded victims were identified as a deputy sheriff and a constable, thereby revealing the Invisible Empire's infiltration of local law enforcement and its continuing taste for extralegal activity despite its penetration of the formal structure of power. In a German settlement in Texas, where picnics featured free-flowing beer (the county agricultural society recorded the purchase of thirty-one kegs of illegal beer between 1921 and 1926 to lubricate its social events), simmering tensions in 1922 led to a downtown gunfight between Klansmen from neighboring towns and local Germans that killed four participants.[41] Finally, in Mer Rouge, Louisiana, site of the most infamous Klan murders of the 1920s, threats between local wets and nearby Klansmen over bootlegging in Mer Rouge formed the backdrop to the incident that established the popular image of the Klan as a band of violent killers.[42]

Despite clear evidence of vigilantism and outbursts of violence, dry Klansmen worked mostly in cooperation with legal authorities and with varying degrees of official sanction to inhibit prohibition violations. In some cases Klansmen argued for the exercise of moral authority when local law enforcement neglected to act, as we have seen in the lawless Southwest. But usually local Klans formed arrangements with sympathetic public officials. As the Southwestern Klans moved into politics, Klan-backed judges and lawmen aggressively enforced the dry laws. "We had a mighty crew of bootleggers and innumerable liquor dispensaries" in one section of Arkansas, recalled a Klan politician, but he and other drys "joined the Klan and . . . sat on juries and backed up the prosecuting attorneys and circuit judge until we cleaned up Lamar and Johnson County."[43] Although the Monticello, Arkansas, Klan formed in the hope of curbing prohibition violations, it did not undertake vigilante raids. Instead, the Klan's "Shock Committee" proposed to write letters to suspected bootleggers, threatening prosecution, and three times it paid fifty-dollar rewards to informants who contributed "to the arrest and conviction of anyone guilty of manufacturing or selling whiskey." When informed that the reward offer meant that hooded knights would be barred from juries, the Monticello Klan ceased its incentive, preferring to work within the Klan-infiltrated local judicial system.[44] In Chattanooga a Klan committee gathered the names of more than one hundred bootleggers, then supplied the information to established authorities for proper action.[45]

Elsewhere, especially in the Northeast and Midwest where substantial immigrant and Catholic populations were represented in government, law enforcement officials were often hostile toward the Invisible Empire and disinclined to enforce the unpopular dry regulations. In those locations, hooded bands identified dry sheriffs, district attorneys, or federal prohibition administrators and operated in informal partnership with them. Stymied by a wet mayor, a brewer who had been fined for violating the dry law, and a hostile police force and sheriff's office, Buffalo Klansmen gathered evidence of illegal drinking on their own and presented it to an enforcement-minded U.S. attorney, the war hero and future founding leader of the OSS "Wild Bill" Donovan. Armed with warrants from Donovan, who felt duty-bound to enforce prohibition despite his Catholicism and personal skepticism about the reform, Klansmen and dry agents executed a series of raids on illicit drinking spots through the spring and summer of 1924. One such mission surprised the sheriff with a beer in his hand, drinking with his deputies and municipal workers.[46] At mid-decade in eastern Kansas, A. H. Carl, a district attorney elected with hooded votes, relied on a shadowy group of Klansmen known as "Carl's Raiders" to follow him on operations against bootleggers. In a few months the district attorney and his extralegal posse seized "4,700 gallons of moonshine and thousands of gallons of 'wine, hootch, and other stuff,'" a haul that Klansmen said bested the performance of official law agencies.[47] A resident of an Italian district in Youngstown, Ohio, recalled that deputized Klansmen, armed with "John Doe" warrants (allowing general searches) issued by the mayor's court in a nearby Klan stronghold, routinely swept through his neighborhood in search of homemade wine and, local people claimed, opportunities to plant incriminating whiskey.[48]

Indiana Klansmen maneuvered around the opposition of city authorities in Fort Wayne, Gary, and South Bend to get legal backing for urban raids from the federal prohibition director or county authorities. The scale of the Fort Wayne operation, in which Klansmen claimed to find police involvement in illegal liquor sales, showed the depth of cooperation between the Invisible Empire and federal authorities. Local knights supplied federal agents with "affidavits involving eighty-three persons and a big quantity of liquor purchased as evidence, and furnished clerical help in compiling data and affidavits," with a stenographer supplied by the state Klan newspaper on call.[49] The divisiveness generated by the Klan's participation in dry crackdowns was evident in the aftermath of the 1923 Gary raid carried out by deputized Klansmen. The city's mayor claimed that he "welcomed the Federal prohibition agents to operate in Gary, but I wanted them to work with the police and not 'outsiders.'" A Klan editor replied that Gary's un-American population and weak law enforcement precluded a local solution to wet lawlessness. "The size of the foreign element in Gary is so large," he argued, "that . . . the county is looked to to provide the deficiency." But county authorities also faltered. "A sheriff, big enough to fight and who can deliver a squared fist at the jaw of the Gary foreign element, battering it to a recognition of the laws of the state and the nation, is wanted and wanted badly," the Klan press concluded.[50]

Despite such confrontational rhetoric and the extralegal circumstances of many Klan raiding parties, local knights insisted that their actions were lawful and just. Only when established authorities failed to act, hooded drys contended, did the Invisible Empire intervene. In a typical example, Klansmen in Lima, Ohio, monitored bootlegging and gambling activities for three months in the winter of 1923 but found that city police, though "in possession of the same information . . . failed to take action." The Ku Kluxers took their evidence to county officials and gained cooperation from the probate court and the sheriff, who planned raids on vice nests using "special deputies . . . furnished by the [Klan]."[51] By such methods, claimed Iowa knights who operated in conjunction with like-minded federal and local officeholders, the Invisible Empire demonstrated that it was "not the wild-eyed, law opposing organization that it is said to be, but rather works with the law in a co-operative attitude."[52]

Although promoted by the Indiana Klan to further its war on illegal liquor, the Horse Thief Detective Association enjoyed legal standing and support from formal law enforcement agencies. In April 1923 the sheriff of Marion County, the police chief of Indianapolis, and the Marion County highway superintendent met with the Klan-dominated HTDA to review legal procedures and request the organization's support in enforcing laws against bootlegging, transporting illegal liquor, drunk driving, and gambling—but also to curb speeding, illegal parking on highways, chicken stealing, and "liquor brawls in summer tourist camps."[53] Commissioned Horse Thief Detectives were deputized as assistant sheriffs and issued badges and firearms. Additional HTDA members without commissions, badges, or guns also participated in raids as lookouts and assistants. In South Bend nearly thirty knights carried commissions, and about one hundred others operated without commissions. As many as five hundred men held HTDA commissions in Indianapolis.[54]

The relationship between the Indiana Klan and the HTDA was extremely close. The St. Joseph County klavern devoted one meeting each month for a report on HTDA activities and participated in as many as fifty raids monthly. HTDA operatives used Klan funds to make the purchases of illegal liquor that often preceded raids. To solidify the alliance between the constabulary and the hooded order, the Indiana realm offered honorary memberships (with reduced dues) to commissioned Horse Thief Detectives, the same privilege that the Invisible Empire extended to Protestant ministers. Klan sources claimed that the HTDA "has been responsible for 60 per cent of the arrests in Indiana for violation of the liquor laws."[55] A similar collection of Ku Klux deputies regulated traffic and performed "impromptu liquor and vice-raids" around Akron, Ohio.[56]

Beyond arguing for the legal status of the hooded constabulary, some Klan sources reveal a genuine concern that prohibition violations would erode respect for the law and the Constitution. In a distressed tone, the Midwest's major Klan newspaper declared, "We insist—we must insist—upon active co-operation between courts and police . . . and all law-abiding citizens" in enforcing prohibition. "We must feel the necessity in our own hearts . . . to uphold our foundational laws. We insist that illegal distilleries, liquor-selling drug stores, hidden fruit-stand saloons, soft drink beer joints, back-alley bootlegger grog shops and 'speakeasies,' be hunted out and suppressed. . . . If the nation, as a whole, does not like the eighteenth amendment, let it take the necessary steps to repeal it. Until then it is a part of the law of the land and the law must be respected, feared, and obeyed."[57] Another statement that, in the context of typical hooded journalism, took on the tones of statecraft, conceded the unpopularity of constitutional prohibition but nonetheless appealed for the rule of law. "Even though an amendment may seem fanatical and unwholesome," the *Fiery Cross* offered, "even though we may feel personally that a certain amendment may be poor general policy in a broader sense—we should respect the principle of the law itself, and govern ourselves accordingly, until the will of the people as a whole sets aside that which the commonwealth may deem undesirable."[58]

Klan authorities went beyond counseling fidelity to the law, however, stressing that Klankraft demanded direct action against lawlessness. In 1923 a great titan from Texas asserted that a Klansman "not only pledges himself under oath to abide by the laws of his country, but that he will assist in the enforcement thereof through regular and constituted authorities." By way of illustration, the Texas official commended the action of a single Klansman who, upon his own initiative, gathered sufficient evidence to convict "a quasi respectable citizen" who had previously eluded authorities by manufacturing and selling whiskey "on his premises."[59] South Carolina's grand dragon instructed his entire realm to take up the work of prohibition enforcement. "The manufacture and sale of whiskey may not in themselves be the greatest crimes," he admitted, "but open and continued violation of the prohibition laws brings all the laws into contempt." Therefore he urged South Carolina knights "to join in making our organization a militant agency for the enforcement of the prohibition laws."[60]

Despite its appeal to the law, Klan vigilantism often existed in a tense relationship with legitimate authorities. Lawmen realized that raiding Klansmen welcomed the protection offered by legal sanction but felt unhindered by its limitations. As one scholar of Klan vigilantism has argued, "Vigilantism is often, but not necessarily, extralegal. It can be nonviolent, though the use of violence is always implied. Vigilantes may work in cooperation with public officials, have public officials among them, and enjoy a temporary legal status through special deputation, although they retain a private and voluntary character and act always on their own initiative."[61] Settling in the loose spaces of regulation, the Klan's agents of prohibition enforcement frequently irritated their official colleagues. Hooded knights from Pittsburgh Klan No. 1 in 1922 peremptorily notified the local federal prohibition agent "that he must raid a North side saloon named by the Klan, and that he should follow the same procedure with the saloons that will be named by the organization in the near future."[62] The agent indicated that legal directives rather than the extralegal advice of the Invisible Empire would dictate his actions. At the end of 1924, conflict erupted between various branches of municipal government in Madison, Wisconsin, when the mayor appointed a special squad of Klansmen to carry out prohibition raids without the approval of the police or the district attorney. Following an anti-liquor raid on the city's Little Italy section by Klansmen and several night-shift policemen acting on their own authority, a "civic row" ensued.[63] After a 1923 hooded raid in Muskegon, Michigan, landed eight bootleggers in jail, the local press offered no thanks to Ku Klux vigilantes. "Rather than to give the Klan credit," complained the hooded press, "newspaper articles were written so as to make it appear that the whole raid was a mistake, and played up a supposed fight between the Klan and certain officers of the law."[64]

At times the disputes generated by Klan raids involved hooded lawmen. In early 1926, Birmingham Klansmen acting on misdemeanor court warrants, and claiming to be accompanied by masked deputy sheriffs, raided three Chinese restaurants in a fruitless search for illegal liquor. In place of supportive comments, the chief deputy sheriff, a fellow knight, disavowed any participation from his office in the raid, tore up the warrant, and released the six suspects seized in the action. This was followed by public disagreement between the deputy sheriff and his hooded superior, who praised the raid. The resulting lawsuit from the case fractured the Birmingham Klan.[65] Similarly, the prosecution of hooded special deputies in Akron was carried out by a Klan public official as part of a power struggle with the Ku Klux sheriff.[66]

In locations hostile to prohibition and the Klan, raids by Ku Kluxers prompted official resistance and drew nativist ripostes from Klan representatives, furthering the cultural division over the enforcement of dry laws and associated moral regulations. Complaints against excessive and unsanctioned actions by the Horse Thief Detectives produced ill will and in Indiana's urban districts led local officeholders to initiate steps to break up the HTDA. One woman died after HTDA raiders ransacked her house, a raid that critics attributed to her husband's links to the vigorously anti-Klan American Unity League. Two years later another woman miscarried as a result of an HTDA incursion, after which the grieving couple sued the Horse Thief Detectives.[67] County commissioners near Terre Haute and Indianapolis attempted to revoke HTDA commissions after vigilantes tore up a private home in a fruitless search for liquor and posted guards at polling places during an election. Klansmen dismissed the ultimately unsuccessful effort to reduce HTDA authority as the partisan design of Marion County attorney Russell Ryan, a Catholic Democrat promptly dubbed "Roman Ryan" by the Klan press.[68]

Similar episodes unfolded across Indiana and neighboring states. Hooded raiders, "deputized by a constable from the court of a magistrate," broke up a gambling house in Jeffersonville, Indiana, but found no support from local authorities. At the behest of the Catholic, anti-Klan mayor, according to sources from the Invisible Empire, the surprised constables were instead "immediately arrested for carrying and pointing guns." The hooded order attributed this resistance to the un-American orientation of the Jeffersonville establishment. "All the city officials here are Roman Catholics, from street cleaner to judge," the Klan report darkly observed.[69] Frustrated by the refusal of the county sheriff to accept HTDA assistance in cracking down on vice near Terre Haute, Klan representatives also publicly lashed out at "the crowd of hangers-on at the jail and sheriff's office" that inhibited the rule of law, singling out for criticism "William McGuirk, prominent Knight of Columbus . . . Richard 'Little Dick' Werneke, also prominent Knight of Columbus," and "Denny Shay, the notorious, recently out of federal prison."[70] Another scalding report noted that the arrested owner of an illegal saloon in South Bend "donates $500 yearly to Notre Dame University, and leads all the west-end drives for the school's funds." Implying a network of Catholic lawlessness, the Ku Klux journalist added that "students of the school patronize his place, usually two and three deep before his bar after school sessions."[71] When the Protestant mayor of an Ohio town rebuked the Klan, hooded commentators likened the sentiments to those of "a Catholic politician" and noted that the area's leading critic of Ku Klux intervention was "a Catholic, and a rabid anti-Klansman."[72]

The alliance between organized vice and religious un-Americanism suggested by the Klan took overt political form in 1924, according to hooded analysis. Politics in one Indiana county "has simmered down to two issues, prohibition and the Klan," claimed the wary knights. "Bootleggers, gamblers and Roman Catholics have flocked to the [wet, anti-Klan] standard . . . and are striving to defeat the cause of Protestant Americanism."[73] Prohibition, the Invisible Empire, and American identity itself had become intertwined in the dry activism of the hooded knights. "It is peculiar, the kind of hard feeling the Klan stirs up," mused a West Virginia supporter of local Ku Klux raids. "The hard feeling seems to always come from the aliens and law breakers."[74]

The Invisible Empire's aggressive actions, while powerful in building local movements to enforce prohibition, nevertheless threatened to entangle mainstream dry forces in the bigotry, violence, and vigilantism associated with the Klan. The Klan's charge, for instance, that the "Jewish-Catholic controlled" New York legislature—which in 1923 repealed the state's prohibition enforcement act—had "swapped the constitution for a beer keg and virtually placed New York on record as seceding from the Union,"[75] undercut the educational work in wet communities by the Anti Saloon League and other dry advocates to reinvigorate support for national prohibition. Beyond the polarizing language of the Invisible Empire, the temptations and dangers inherent in following the Klan into the murky realms of informal, citizen-initiated law enforcement became apparent to the ASL in the confusing swirl of violence that engulfed southern Illinois by the mid-1920s.

The claims of dry reformers, most insistently voiced by the Anti-Saloon League, that prohibition would introduce an era of tranquility and progress was cruelly undercut in Williamson County, Illinois, from early 1924 to April 1926. Bloody combat between Klansmen led by Glenn Young and his crew of hired gunmen, bootleggers supported by immigrant mining communities hostile to prohibition, and corrupt, partisan lawmen savagely contradicted the reform hopes of prohibitionists. Twenty murders and anarchic conditions forced military intervention and occupation of the region. The violence, and the prominent role in it played by Young and his Klan sponsors, brought national condemnation of Illinois and the Invisible Empire.[76] Evans and the national Klan had celebrated Young's early exploits as a courageous moral stand against foreign and official outlaws, though the dry deputy's reckless destructiveness cooled this enthusiasm. After Young was gunned down, however, he was hailed in hooded encomiums as a martyr to the cause of lawfulness, Americanism, and prohibition.[77] Some Klan organizations felt compelled to distance themselves from such sentiments. "The Klan is not a law-enforcing body," insisted New York's king kleagle in the wake of the fatal shootout between Young and his wet assailants. "It does not and will not take the law into its own hands."[78] "Bloody Williamson" was a toxic misrepresentation of everything thoughtful drys had wished for prohibition.

Yet, alarmingly for mainstream prohibitionists, the Klan's violent missteps in southern Illinois had been accompanied by local Anti-Saloonists. Labor troubles and ethnic strife had long plagued the coal-mining towns of the region, and these tensions were exacerbated after the Eighteenth Amendment by inconsistent prohibition enforcement. In August 1921 the Illinois Anti-Saloon League participated in a series of raids led by the sheriff's office against illegal liquor sellers. Assisted by local Protestant ministers, the ASL encouraged the formation of voluntary law-and-order leagues that would pressure local government leaders to crack down on prohibition violations. Within a year, members of law-and-order leagues in Herrin, Marion, and other towns attended council meetings, fielded tickets in local elections, and expressed themselves to be "anxious and willing to volunteer as special police" in pursuit of bootleggers. In January 1923, unified by shared participation in the county Anti-Saloon League, the local associations coalesced into the Williamson County Law Enforcement League. Within months the Ku Klux Klan took over direction of the league and thereafter dominated the anti-liquor movement. At least two prominent figures associated with the county Anti-Saloon League, Baptist minister I. E. Lee and Sam Stearns, who headed Marion's law enforcement league and sat on the Williamson County Board of Supervisors, helped lead the Klan movement. Stearns, in fact, became exalted cyclops of the Marion klavern.[79]

As violence engulfed the region, the state Anti-Saloon League disengaged from the struggle. Yet partisans of the dry pressure group continued to express admiration for some of the fighting Klansmen. A Baptist editor attached to the league, for instance, commended John L. Whiteside, Stearns's successor as exalted cyclops and soon to be grand titan of all southern Illinois Klansmen,[80] as "a man who stands for the Anti-Saloon League work and for law and order." Despite Whiteside's recent arrest on murder charges following a deadly shootout that killed six men, this editor asked ASL superintendent F. Scott McBride to arrange for the Klansman's appointment as a U.S. marshal to further the "wonders [that] have been accomplished for law and order" in Williamson County.[81] Whiteside, it turned out, was not involved in the shooting and was soon released. McBride suitably cautioned the Illinois ASL superintendent to investigate the Whiteside endorsement "pretty carefully before you take any decisive step."[82]

Despite official discouragement, some local ASL supporters remained persistently attached to the Klan movement. Frustrations with the brazenness of prohibition violations, anger at the ineffectiveness of law enforcement and occasional official collusion with lawbreakers, and the attractiveness of direct, local action tempted many prohibitionists to join their hooded neighbors as dry vigilantes. While effective in some cases, cooperation with the Klan threatened to derail the discipline and independence of the principal advocacy group backing dry reform. It also bound up the dry movement with the Klan's restricted sense of American identity and its extensive portfolio of divisive commitments. In short, despite the Invisible Empire's genuine enthusiasm for prohibition enforcement, its actions threatened to disrupt and delegitimize the mainstream prohibition movement.

Infiltrating the Dry Mainstream

The Invisible Empire and its practice of grassroots prohibition enforcement posed an especially difficult problem for the Anti-Saloon League. Although cursed by many wets, the league reveled in its reputation as the disciplined organizational voice of the dry movement. From its 1893 founding in Ohio, the ASL developed a focused and effective public policy machine. A small, salaried body of officers and field agents, most of them Protestant ministers or attorneys, directed the anti-liquor sentiment of church people toward specific political ends. Through its state affiliates, the league prepared model legislation, drew up candidate lists, and focused attention on local referenda or bills in state legislatures aimed at maximizing the advance of dry territory. Similarly, the ASL orchestrated the lobbying campaign that resulted in the triumph of constitutional prohibition. As ruthless league pressure overcame the resistance of the Wilson administration to national prohibition, a journalist observed that "the average member of Congress is more afraid of the Anti-Saloon League than he is even of the President of the United States."[83] To a considerable degree, national prohibition was the singular achievement of the ASL.

League insiders attributed the organization's influence to its single-mindedness. However attractive other reforms or issues, from women's suffrage to moral hygiene, might be to its cause or constituency, the national ASL insisted that attacks on the liquor trade and enforcement of dry laws take precedence (though, in practice, state leagues sometimes endorsed anti-vice, sabbatarian, or even nativist initiatives).[84] After the *New York Times* reported in 1921 that Kansas ASL officials had participated in an anti-cigarette raid, William H. Anderson, New York's hard-charging league superintendent, wrote to the newspaper, "If the Anti-Saloon League in any jurisdiction is taking part in any fight against cigarettes or tobacco, or engaging in any activity except promoting enforcement of prohibition in harmony with the law . . . any such activity . . . is in absolute defiance of the constitution and policy of the league."[85] Prohibition alone also determined the ASL's political activities and alliances. Politicians who pledged to support the league's bills received its endorsement—even those who were personally wet, corrupt, or otherwise objectionable. Similarly, despite the overwhelming Protestant constituency of the league, the ASL officially welcomed support from dry Catholics, Jews, and nonbelievers.

The Invisible Empire's enthusiastic entry into prohibition enforcement, framed within its white Protestant notions of American identity, threatened to disrupt the ASL's effective methods and challenged its leadership of the dry movement. Shortly after the hooded governor of Colorado advocated a ban on sacramental wine, ASL leaders were contacted by "a very prominent Catholic friend of our cause [who was] deeply concerned over" the Klan's threat to the Mass.[86] League reports from the state downplayed the danger, but Catholic allies of the ASL could not take comfort from the Colorado league's intention in the next legislative session "to limit the amount of wines or liquors which may be purchased by a Rabbi or Priest for sacramental purposes."[87] The Klan's blunt connection of prohibition with anti-Catholicism, anti-Semitism, and hostility to immigrants could easily color the entire dry enterprise. Moreover, the tendency of Ku Klux vigilantes to intermingle raids on bootleggers, gamblers, and other moral offenders smudged the ASL's firm distinction between prohibition enforcement and all other issues.

The depth to which the Invisible Empire had penetrated the Anti-Saloon League's control of prohibition enforcement and the disunity it unleashed were revealed in the summer of 1924 when a league superintendent publicly attempted to combine the two movements. Dr. E. M. Lightfoot, a Baptist minister and salaried head of the South Carolina ASL, tried to recruit into the Klan an invited audience of about sixty men in a Bennettsville theater. Witnesses reported that the dry leader praised the work of the "silent forces" of the Invisible Empire in eliminating the sale of illegal liquor and related lawlessness in South Carolina. Lightfoot also endorsed the Klan's commitment to "restricted immigration, pure Americanism, racial purity, law enforcement and organization of the Protestants to offset the organization of the Catholics and Jews." Rather than generating agreement from the crowd of dry zealots he had selected for the meeting, Lightfoot's remarks provoked several "stirring" denunciations of the hooded order's bigotry and vigilante methods. One critic upbraided Lightfoot directly for connecting the Anti-Saloon League to the Klan. "I have for years been paying annually to the Anti-Saloon League," complained this "ashamed" fellow Baptist. "If you are going to spend your extra time organizing something to sow dissension I think I had better use that money for something else." Only about ten prospective Klansmen remained in the hall as the dissenters filed out.[88]

The national ASL, keen to dissociate its already-controversial public image from that of the far more problematic Klan, swiftly acted to discipline its state officers. Informed of Lightfoot's Klan activities by an official of the Federal Council of Churches, ASL general counsel Wayne Wheeler, the nation's most powerful prohibitionist, immediately directed league superintendent McBride to curb Lightfoot's "detrimental" moonlighting.[89] Within days the league's efficient communications network had reminded its workers that dry success hinged on adherence to the ASL's single focus on prohibition—"this one thing."[90] The league insisted that its officers "withhold our public activities from organizations over whose official acts we have no control."[91] Despite vigorous interest in prohibition enforcement demonstrated by klaverns in local communities across the nation, the ASL refused to compromise its single-issue priority, its autonomy of action, and its identity as the foremost moral and political exponent of the embattled prohibition reform.

Nevertheless, the league's disavowals did not dislodge the widespread perception among wets that the middle-class, professionally directed ASL worked in concert with hooded Klan vigilantes. In 1922 a representative of the Association Against the Prohibition Amendment commented that "in many parts of the country the Ku Klux Klan and the Anti-Saloon League were closely affiliated." To which Oscar Haywood, a national Klan lecturer, observed, "I think there is some truth in that," though he denied any "close alliance."[92] Within a few months of the South Carolina incident, the *Baltimore Evening Sun* charged that "if [the Invisible Empire] is not literally a part of the Anti-Saloon League, it is at least so close an ally as to be almost indistinguishable from it in many parts of the country."[93] The Klan press likewise quoted celebrated attorney and wet partisan Clarence Darrow's view that "the father and mother of the Ku Klux is the Anti-Saloon League. I would not say every Anti-Saloon Leaguer is a Ku Kluxer, but every Ku Kluxer is an Anti-Saloon Leaguer."[94] Rather than viewing Lightfoot's involvement with the Klan as an anomalous departure from league policy, many anti-prohibitionists asserted a fundamental affinity in outlook and policy between the hooded order, the ASL, and the dry cause.

Yet the Invisible Empire and the bureaucratic Anti-Saloon League were antagonists as much as they were dry partners. Welcome as the Klan's commitment to local prohibition enforcement may have been to some Anti-Saloon activists, the Invisible Empire remained a clear danger to the league, even a rival for the loyalty of dry Protestants. As early as 1922, ASL fieldworkers canvassing for subscriptions in Oklahoma encountered drys who "declined to support [the] League, having already given support to [the] KuKlux."[95] A league official in Nevada observed that the Klan was "strong as horse radish" in the state, hinting that hooded opinions might influence the direction of ASL efforts in that Western realm.[96] Indeed, within a year he, too, was denouncing "the Dago and Greek and Basks [*sic*] that . . . come here to violate our laws," and favorably mentioning the local Klan's preference for "deporting them half way to their native land and letting them walk or swim the balance of the way."[97]

Imperial Wizard Hiram Evans acknowledged in print the Invisible Empire's indebtedness to the ASL's political methodology, but he clearly believed that the Klan was the better representative of the Protestant values embodied in prohibition. "The Klan," he admitted in 1924, "functions along the same lines as the Anti-Saloon League . . . by persistently supporting men of certain types and beliefs" for public office.[98] Four years later Evans boasted, "Our influence is even greater than that of the Anti-Saloon League ever was. . . . We have recently completed a reorganization and revivification of the dry forces of the nation, following the decay that fell upon the Anti-Saloon League."[99] The hooded knights meant to supplant the ASL as the militant arm of Protestant prohibitionism.

Still, Lightfoot had not detected any inconsistency between his work for the ASL and his participation in the Klan until he was rebuked by rank-and-file drys and the league hierarchy. Some league officials were attracted to the hooded order's extralegal attempts to control bootlegging, an indication that the failure of state and national enforcement, as well as divisions within the ASL over enforcement policy, was causing frustration in dry ranks. Moreover, the South Carolina superintendent's willingness to frame his prohibitionist convictions within the intolerant worldview of the Klan and the vehement objections those positions sparked demonstrated the tenuous state of unity within the league during the difficult years of national prohibition. Potentially crippling disagreements among drys over the ethnic, religious, and cultural dimensions of prohibition made it all the more imperative that the league stick to its single-issue doctrine. Yet, as the South Carolina case revealed, the ASL remained ambivalent about the Klan. Although Lightfoot was reprimanded for his hooded affiliation, he remained South Carolina's superintendent. Nor was he alone. Sprinkled throughout the league's national and state apparatus were officials who maintained ties with the Invisible Empire. Indeed, Lightfoot's predecessor as South Carolina superintendent had promoted the Klan in the same town where Lightfoot held his ill-fated meeting.[100] Circumstances pushed the Klan and the ASL together as they struggled to make prohibition work. But as much as this pattern moved the Invisible Empire toward the mainstream of the dry movement, it also increased the perception that the Anti-Saloon League and the entire prohibition effort were out of step with the pluralistic realities of the New Era.

❖

Inconsistencies, divisions, and unresolved issues within the ASL aggravated the difficulties of enforcing the Eighteenth Amendment and propelled some league workers to join Klansmen in vigilante action. National prohibition had deepened a fundamental strategic disagreement within the league's leadership. Ernest H. Cherrington, director of the ASL's substantial publishing arm, advocated a patient education campaign to convert drinkers, especially recent immigrants, into prohibition supporters. He told a conference of New England league superintendents in 1925, "It is perfectly reasonable to say right here within these walls that we got Prohibition in the United States before the public sentiment of the United States was ready for Prohibition." Rather than pushing for additional coercive laws, let alone sanctioning vigilante enforcement, Cherrington proposed that the league help the public accept the dry initiative as a genuine reform.[101] Wayne Wheeler's faction, on the other hand, as part of its political emphasis, demanded strong law enforcement by public authorities to compel respect for prohibition.[102] Nativist attitudes that accompanied this viewpoint edged toward the Klan's positions. One state superintendent implored his colleagues not to "waste any sympathy on 'ignorant foreigners who don't understand our laws.' They knew enough to come here and certainly know enough to find the way back."[103] Rather than commit the league to one of these approaches, its divided leadership awkwardly tried to promote both of them.

Even by itself, law enforcement on the Wheeler model suffered from disabling shortcomings. The ASL hierarchy adamantly maintained that the league was not to act as a "detective agency."[104] In its early years, league superintendents had attempted to carry out private law enforcement, hiring investigators and pursuing individual violators, but they found the approach too costly, unevenly effective, and likely to produce friction with government authorities.[105] By the coming of national prohibition, and the Klan era, the league preferred the uniformity of government enforcement and saw its role as "an organization for the creation of public sentiment and for the direction of that public sentiment" onto public officials so as to maximize prohibition enforcement.[106] Thus in 1921, as Klan raiders first began to make their mark, rather than encouraging ASL followers to raid bootleggers, Wheeler's law enforcement program directed dry citizens to organize law enforcement conventions to encourage enforcement officers and prosecuting attorneys, to compile statistics, to "voice a dignified protest" when lawmen neglected their duties, and to support passage of tougher dry laws.[107] A bolder initiative to supply expert league attorneys to the states proved too expensive and was discontinued. In short, the league applied the same political methods that had produced national prohibition to the job of enforcement. Given the weakness of federal and state resources, this strategy carried no promise of success.

Rank-and-file drys quickly sized up the futility of old methods in meeting "this new crisis of law enforcement." An exasperated ASL supporter granted that the league had once "stir[red] up and marshall[ed] the Christian forces . . . in getting rid of the saloon . . . but if you mean to suggest that you are doing this kind of work now, allow me to suggest that you read the story of Rip Van Winkle."[108] Along with many others, he dropped his ASL subscription. Cherrington worriedly observed in 1924 that "the clutch is slipping" on prohibition sentiment.[109] Wheeler complained that same year that "few of the states have made even a gesture toward carrying out" his enforcement program. Frustrated drys had already turned to the Klan and vigilantism. "Other organizations," Wheeler admitted, "have stepped in in many places and have attempted to do enforcement work by wrong methods and have hurt rather than helped the cause."[110]

Pressured by grassroots drys outraged at evasions of the law, several state leagues began to undertake direct enforcement work along the same lines as the Invisible Empire. As early as 1921, Iowa's league superintendent personally made purchases of illegal liquor, obtained search warrants, and led police raiding parties against bootleggers and liquor-selling pharmacies.[111] New Jersey's ASL attorney reported to a 1924 league workers' conference that he and state league investigators worked directly with a special federal prohibition agent and a willing district attorney to obtain injunctions against bootleggers. Although this activism strayed from established league policy, the attorney maintained that "when the wheels are stuck and will not revolve, and folks are becoming discouraged and desperate, it may be very advisable to show the way, to cut new grooves, to get the officials initiated into doing their duty, to go out and get the evidence and place it, in concrete, affidavit form, in the hands of officials who otherwise would not—sometimes could not—get it."[112] The firewall between necessity and league doctrine had been breached. In some locales, arrangements with dry Klansmen, who were eager to "cut new grooves," became possible.

Thus in the spring of 1924 the Civic-Church League of Asbury Park welcomed the assistance of the Invisible Empire and the Anti-Saloon League in a bid to dry up the resort towns of coastal New Jersey.[113] The ASL furnished a detective to accompany a Civic-Church League member to a dinner for businessmen hosted by Asbury Park's mayor, which allegedly featured copious drinking of bootleg liquor and "an improper display" by five dancing women.[114] Klansmen and the pastors of the Civic-Church League met at a Methodist church and agreed to take the information to the public prosecutor. Two days later the assistant state superintendent of the ASL addressed another Civic-Church League meeting at the same church to coordinate a public anti-vice campaign. Grand Dragon Arthur Bell directed his hooded knights to guard the Civic-Church League witness of the infamous dinner from potential harm after he had been charged with perjury in his affidavit on the matter. Bell also acted as attorney for the reform group in the ensuing legal case. Although the grand jury dismissed the charges, Bell made it clear that "the Klan was [behind] the Civic-Church League and the Anti-Saloon League in the fight against the Mayor" and wide-open liquor violations in Monmouth County.[115]

The dangers inherent in dry partnerships with the Klan became evident in Indiana, where both the Anti-Saloon League and the Invisible Empire exercised political influence and attracted bitter opposition. The effective but brusque superintendent of the Indiana ASL, Edward S. Shumaker, was a relentless critic of prohibition violators and government officials who failed to strictly enforce the dry laws. In Indiana, thanks to the ASL's effective lobbying and hooded legislative support, these laws were more exacting than even the Volstead Act. Yet Shumaker tried to balance support for the Klan's effective assaults on lawbreakers with adherence to ASL cautions about avoiding bonds with the Invisible Empire. In 1924, Shumaker informed national ASL leaders that "the Klu [sic] Klux Klan . . . is doing many things which we would liked to have done, but we are not working with them in either an official or unofficial way."[116] As Shumaker's biographer observed, league loyalists realized that the Klan "was duplicating the League's ideals, mission, and political tactics." Hooded wire-pullers "not only perfected the [ASL's] tactic of political endorsement but also proved far superior at mobilizing voters behind approved candidates."[117] Still, many dry Indiana supporters of the ASL cheered the efforts of the Horse Thief Detectives and cooperated with prohibitionist Klansmen. In 1927, when Klan domination of the HTDA was well known and several instances of misbehavior by Ku Klux constables had stoked sentiment to shut down its operations, the league declared its admiration for the vigilantes. In a fairly short period, the official voice of the Indiana ASL noted, a handful of HTDA units had "made 26 raids, seized 5 stills, 16 barrels of mash, 199 quarts of white mule whisky, 260 cases of home brew, 77 quarts of whisky, 10 quarts of wine, 13 cases of beer, 13 cases of ale, two cases of champagne, one quart of grain alcohol, and 35 five-gallon packages of material for the manufacture of white mule whisky. . . . We believe that work of this fine character merits the commendation and not the censure of law abiding citizens."[118]

Journalists suggested more fundamental connections, linking the rise of the Indiana Klan to Shumaker's spadework in building the ASL as a pressure group. "Indianans," R. L. Duffus reported, "think that Shumaker and his league prepared the way for the Klan by drilling their followers to take orders and to apply the single test of wetness or dryness to candidates for political office."[119] Moreover, by politicizing Methodist and Baptist ministers, the ASL made it easier for the Indiana Klan to recruit clergymen, many of whom professed loyalty to both organizations.[120] Critics charged that the ASL and the Klan actively collaborated. "In raiding expeditions and other ventures, subdivisions of the two powers have frequently cooperated," claimed one disapproving reporter.[121] Other observers contended that league lobbyists and Klan legislators jointly produced Indiana's strict 1925 bone-dry law, though in reality ASL operatives drafted the bill and steered it to passage while hooded legislators merely supplied their votes.[122]

In 1928, Shumaker himself was uncomfortably identified with the Klan. Pat Emmons, the disaffected former exalted cyclops of St. Joseph County, testified that, at the behest of Indiana realm leaders, he had met with the ASL chief two years earlier on behalf of the senatorial aspirations of Arthur Robinson, a reputed Klansman and a personal friend of former Indiana grand dragon D. C. Stephenson. According to Emmons, Shumaker agreed that "the Anti-Saloon League, the Klan, and the [Protestant] church" should work together to elect Robinson.[123] Shumaker denied any knowing collusion with hooded interests, but his careful statements revealed the complicated relationship that prohibition enforcement had wrought between the Klan and the dry league. He stressed to skeptical reporters that the ASL maintained no "political" or "organic" links to the Invisible Empire, but in the same statement he endorsed the "splendid work" of the HTDA.[124] At the same time he acknowledged that the Indiana ASL newspaper had once profiled Emmons as a reformed bartender turned dry crusader.[125] And he did not challenge the Klan official's claim that in 1924 the league changed its endorsement for St. Joseph County sheriff after Emmons identified one of the candidates as a wet Catholic and the other as a dry Protestant.[126] Most significantly, Shumaker remarked that "Robinson was dry and always had been held in high esteem by the Anti-Saloon League and did not have to go through the Klan to get our support."[127] Thus joined by circumstances and shared dry priorities, Shumaker's supposed alliance with the hooded order was confirmed in public opinion by a conviction for contempt of court, brought on by his sharp criticism of Indiana judges. That seemed to parallel the spectacular downfall of Stephenson, convicted of murder and imprisoned one year earlier in 1926. A brief stay at the Indiana prison farm, in the exaggerated estimation of the *Nation*'s reporter, made Shumaker "a close publicity rival to that of his fellow Hoosier celebrity, ex–Grand Dragon D. C. Stephenson."[128]

Although the political interests of the Klan and the Indiana ASL often dovetailed, Shumaker's organization did maintain separation in membership, if not in public perception, from the Klan. Two important documents, a list of Indianapolis Klansmen published in the anti-Klan organ *Tolerance* and a 1925 manuscript roster of Indiana Klan officers, yield the name of only one officer of the Indiana ASL: George S. Henninger, a Methodist minister elected by his religious conference to the ASL board of trustees. Henninger was a vocal Klansman who supposedly screened out Catholic job applicants for the Klan administration of Indianapolis mayor John Duvall, but he did not exercise great influence in the state ASL.[129] Shumaker and other state league officials endorsed for league work a public prosecutor identified as a Klansman in the 1925 Klan roster.[130] Klansman Charles Orbison was also a former league official and state prohibition director.[131] But none of these ties indicate the degree of interaction between stealthy Klansmen and the lawyers and ministers of the Indiana league imagined by foes of both groups. Rather they are of a piece with the sporadic and situational connections that arose in prohibition work, such as the case in 1923 when George W. Titus, the leading Klansman in St. Joseph County, "repeatedly" gave the ASL "information upon stills and bootleggers."[132]

Nevertheless, the Klan's anti-liquor fight stirred up prejudices hidden within the omni-partisan coalition of the Anti-Saloon League. Just as the appeal of vigilantism brought some ASL drys into the orbit of the Klan, the ecumenism of official league doctrine sometimes slipped to reveal anti-Catholic sentiments similar to those of the Invisible Empire. Despite league rhetoric, only a handful of prominent Catholics were associated with the ASL. Patrick Callahan, the league's chief liaison to the Catholic community, often felt alone in a sea of evangelical Protestants. "We Congregationalists and Catholics are merely scenery at this Convention," a friend complained to him at the league's national meeting in 1927. "It is altogether a Methodist and Baptist movement."[133]

Callahan had to agree that the ASL gathering was "not comprehensive in religion." He contended that many of his co-religionists resisted prohibition for this very reason. "Most Catholics look upon [prohibition] not as political but as Protestantism," he confided to another dry Catholic, "or at least as

something that Protestant preachers and their churches are doing, and therefore they feel they must be against it."[134] Some within the ASL correspondingly held that Catholics could not be prohibitionists. A Protestant couple
from rural Illinois in 1925 threatened to stop sending money to the league
if Callahan were allowed to address the ASL's annual convention.[135] Thomas
Nicholson, a Methodist bishop and league stalwart, emphasized in 1925 that
the activities of the Klan required the ASL to remind its critics of the league's
commitment to "approaching Jews, Catholics, citizens of all classes and creeds
without any appeal of prejudice,"[136] but the ASL's deep Protestant roots and
its difficult relationship with wet Catholics instead offered further opportunities for interaction with dry Klansmen.

Harmful Crossovers

Mainstream prohibitionists in the Anti-Saloon League recognized the damage wrought by identification of dry policies with the divisive presence of the
Invisible Empire. But deficiencies in government enforcement, contradictions
in the ASL's enforcement positions, and demands for action from harried
grassroots drys pushed local branches of the league to support Klan-style
vigilantism and overlook Klan affiliations by some of its officials. The league
was jealous of its independence and reputation as the architect of national
prohibition, but its leadership—including the publicity-conscious Wheeler—
nevertheless tolerated the Klan membership of a very few major ASL figures.
The most prominent of these was Lycurgus Breckenridge Musgrove, a mil-
lionaire coal producer and philanthropist from Alabama who chaired the
ASL's executive committee during the campaign for national prohibition and
served on the league's national board of directors during the 1920s. A generous contributor to both the ASL and Evans's national Klan organization, between 1920 and 1926 Musgrove also conducted three political campaigns with
Klan support. Mixing endorsements of prohibition and labor with attacks on
the Catholic Church, he lost a close U.S. Senate race to Oscar Underwood
in 1920. In 1924 one of the most visible Klansmen in Alabama managed
Musgrove's battle with Underwood for presidential electors. Finally, in 1926,
Musgrove lost another Senate race to fellow prohibitionist Klansman Hugo
Black in a split Klan vote.[137]

Despite the high-profile airing of Musgrove's ties to both the hooded order
and the ASL, Wheeler was unruffled. In a conciliatory note to Musgrove after
the 1926 defeat, Wheeler matter-of-factly observed that "with the national
Klan going one way and the state Klan going the other the result was inevitable."[138] Musgrove's prestige and financial support may have muffled ASL

criticism of his Klan membership and political adventures; more important, Musgrove kept his league responsibilities separate from his Klan membership. He never seems to have mentioned the Invisible Empire or its aims when conducting league business. For the ASL, whose single-issue philosophy led it to support tainted political candidates, such as the corrupt Illinois senator Frank L. Smith, if they pledged to vote dry, Musgrove's devotion to prohibition when working in his official capacity was sufficient reason to ignore his identification with the hooded order.[139]

In a more modest example of this blinkered approach, national superintendent McBride responded to the demand of a Massachusetts minister that "the Catholic Church should be definitely and aggressively fought by the Anti Saloon League,"[140] with the suggestion that "it might be possible for you to give whatever aid you care to to that [anti-Catholic] fight as a wholly separate proposition from the Anti-Saloon League program and still support aggressively the Anti-Saloon League."[141] As Darrow had suggested, many rank-and-file knights also supported the ASL and were welcomed as long as they kept Klan concerns "wholly separate" from league activities.

An even greater test of the Anti-Saloon League's willingness to tolerate public displays of support for the Invisible Empire was provided by the colorful Georgia congressman William D. Upshaw. Upshaw was an entertaining and highly popular lecturer for the ASL as well as perhaps the most vocally adept defender of prohibition in Congress during his tenure from 1919 until 1927. He was also an outspoken friend of the Ku Klux Klan, though he was never proven to be a member of the hooded confederation. Upshaw was lavishly attentive to William J. Simmons when the founding imperial wizard appeared before a congressional committee in 1921. He contributed articles to the Georgia Klan publication *The Searchlight*, and concluded his affectionate correspondence with a Klan leader by using the ceremonial benediction supposedly known only to those familiar with Klankraft. Moreover, letters of Klan officials published in Georgia newspapers indicated that Upshaw worked as an agent for the Klan in Congress.[142] "If he was never a Klansman in fact," the historian Arnold Rice concluded, Upshaw "was always a Klansman in spirit."[143] Yet criticism of Upshaw from within the league appeared only when the Georgian's demand to be paid for making speeches for the ASL became public in 1926, thus compromising the dry federation's reform image.[144] Nevertheless, the ASL backed Upshaw that year in his unsuccessful reelection bid, even though his chief opponent was safely dry.[145] "We must not let them take away from us our leaders," McBride emphasized.[146] Upshaw had become a symbol of the Anti-Saloon League and its cause, and loyalty to both trumped his ties to the Klan and his embarrassing demands for money.

The national ASL leadership was more serious about discouraging its state workers from dalliances with the Klan since the dangers of poor discipline and dry vigilantism were concrete at the local level. Incidents involving ASL cooperation with hooded knights occurred nonetheless. In Wyoming the new league superintendent lost his position in 1926 when he strayed from league methods, "undertook to be elected head of the Ku Klux Klan of the state," and angled for high political office.[147] Two years earlier a stolen Klan membership list in Buffalo revealed that the popular western New York district ASL superintendent had been kluxed into the Invisible Empire.[148] In Milwaukee a maverick league official tried to recruit Klansmen into an abortive law enforcement agency he had created in the name of the ASL.[149] In 1927 the ASL superintendent of Alabama joined eminent Klansmen in defeating an anti-mask bill aimed at curbing Ku Klux vigilantism. He also encouraged public support for knights charged in a fatal flogging.[150] Unique was the ignominy that befell Georgia superintendent Charles O. Jones in 1925. When two of Jones's sons were arrested and convicted for prohibition violations while working as government dry agents, the fact that one of the sons had been personal assistant to former imperial wizard William Simmons gained national publicity.[151] League officials, at Jones's urging, wrote clemency requests for the two brothers to President Calvin Coolidge.[152] These episodes forged additional links in the popular imagination between the league and the Invisible Empire.

Yet even as they cracked down on unauthorized detective methods, top league officials seemed more forgiving of their subordinates who had made arrangements with the Klan. After his exposure as a Klansman, George Fowler, the Buffalo ASL official, was recommended by McBride to fellow league officers as a "high-class, aggressive young man" and was offered the Wisconsin league superintendency before he retired into the ministry.[153] Even Thomas Nicholson, a major anti-Klan figure in the ASL, inquired after Fowler's services.[154] The erring Milwaukee official, who had been a disruptive force with the Wisconsin league, was also offered another league job before he self-destructed and left prohibition work.[155] After a temporary Kansas league superintendent was unmasked as a hooded knight, McBride mused, "It would be better not to have a state superintendent who is a Klansman"—but the national superintendent still hoped to place the man in a less prominent ASL post. Only when it became clear that the Kansas Klansman had set himself against his erstwhile ASL colleagues did McBride blackball him.[156]

In other cases, when state officials took to heart league warnings to avoid direct ties with the Klan, top ASL officials appeared to be less vigilant than their junior associates. For instance, an alert league sympathizer in North Dakota warned McBride, who was intent on organizing the state, that a certain activist dry minister was "either a member [of the Klan] or so extremely friendly, that his appointment would at once raise the question whether the Anti-Saloon League is not being run by the Klan."[157] Yet when McBride instructed the new state superintendent to stamp out vigilantism, he failed to advise him to avoid the Klan-connected clergyman, even after the incoming superintendent specifically named the reputed Klansman, an old acquaintance, as a possible contact.[158]

On at least one other occasion, the league's leadership exhibited a puzzling silence on the divisive Klan question. After the cautionary circular letter of 1924 that followed the South Carolina Klan incident, West Virginia ASL superintendent O. M. Pullen ideally expressed fidelity to league methods. "Very many times I have been invited by good friends to join the Klan," Pullen recounted. "They have, also, asked me how they could give us the fullest cooperation in prohibition work. I have informed them that the Klan stand for certain things we do not, and that if their attitude on prohibition would come up to ours it would be necessary for them to put aside their hoods, work in the open, and, also, to enforce the law through the regularly constituted authorities."[159] Rather than commend Pullen for his clear articulation of league policy or even reprint the statement in league publications, as was often done with other noteworthy expressions of ASL aims, McBride ignored the letter. Inconsistent direction on how to handle Klan overtures allowed careless state ASL officials to stumble into crippling entanglements with Klansmen in the mid-1920s, sometimes hampering the dry work of the Invisible Empire and significantly damaging the standing of prohibition as a mainstream, respectable undertaking.

One such episode occurred in Kansas, where energetic, personable ASL superintendent Fred Crabbe promoted an ambitious law enforcement program similar to the one carried out in eastern regions of the state by Carl's hooded raiders. As with Carl's band of volunteers, Klansmen participated in the ASL campaign. An ASL district superintendent recalled meeting with "[s]ecret men who were gathering evidences in every way pos[s]ible and preparing for Raids."[160] The relationship soured when it came to light in September 1925 that Crabbe had pocketed locally donated funds earmarked for anti-liquor raids. Distressed Kansas ASL officials learned that "the Ku Klux Klan have a host of affidavits which they have been threatening to turn loose" if Crabbe did not resign.[161]

The Klan issue incapacitated the Kansas ASL even after Crabbe lost his post. John G. Schaibly, Crabbe's replacement, charged that the disgraced superintendent had funneled money to the state's attorney general and to a Kansas supreme court justice.[162] Both men were prominent Anti-Saloon League officials. Both also had participated in the state's legal effort to oust the Invisible Empire.[163] Schaibly, on the other hand, was a Klansman who in 1923 had broken up a Minneapolis church with his hooded activities. As the pastor of a Methodist congregation, he had invited a Klan speaker into the sanctuary, then "descended from the pulpit and lighted [a] cross himself" in solidarity with the Ku Klux movement.[164]

Suspecting that Schaibly sided with the Klan in its dispute with the Kansas ASL, defenders of the dry organization worked to expel the hooded superintendent. But the Klan membership of a state headquarters committeeman along with the hooded sympathies of the United Brethren ministers he represented complicated the effort to purge Klansmen from leading positions in the Kansas ASL. "As an organization [we] can neither be klan nor anti-klan," concluded a worried state ASL worker.[165] Eventually ASL officials forced out Schaibly, but they grumbled that their former colleague "would have [been] delighted to make a brand new lecture for the K.K.'s out of this wreckage of the League."[166] The aftermath of this jumbled affair interrupted the Klan's prohibition enforcement activities, hindered the effectiveness of the Kansas ASL for years, and suggested that prohibition could not be sustained as a public policy.[167]

A more public rift over the Klan in 1924 nearly destroyed the Texas Anti-Saloon League, advanced the collapse of the Texas Klan's unity, and compromised the prohibition regime in a bellwether Southwestern state. Central to the dispute were the volatile political ambitions of wet former governor James E. Ferguson, a polarizing figure who had been impeached in 1917 and barred thereafter from state office. In 1922, when the Klan issue had become paramount in state politics, Ferguson reinvented himself as an anti-Klan reformer and ran for the U.S. Senate.[168] The national ASL endorsed Ferguson's hooded opponent, Earle Mayfield, who became the first representative of the Invisible Empire elected to the Senate. Admitting it "peculiar that in this campaign we happen to be linked with the Klan behind Mayfield," Wayne Wheeler nevertheless pronounced the dry knight "a high-grade man."[169]

Two years later Ferguson returned in the proxy campaign of his wife, Miriam "Ma" Ferguson, for governor, and once again the Texas ASL superintendent Atticus Webb supported the dry Klan candidate, Felix Robertson, who, according to the *New York Times*, "made no effort to conceal his Klan affiliations."[170] At this point ASL national executive committeeman W. J. Milburn, a Texas resident, interjected himself into the campaign. Milburn charged that Webb was under the thumb of Klan leader Zeke Marvin, himself suspected of illegally selling liquor under the cover of medical prescriptions in his drugstore chain, and had surrendered the Texas ASL to the hooded empire.[171] Milburn accused Webb of holding a salaried position with the Texas Klan and inviting hooded representatives to attend the state ASL convention.

"Our duty is clear," Milburn declared. "There is no place in Texas for Lenins and Trotzkys and emperors and grand dragons and titans."[172] Webb retorted that Milburn had violated the ASL's neutrality policy by "doing everything on earth he can do to involve the Anti-Saloon League in Texas in the fight between the Klan and the anti-Klan."[173] Supporting Webb, the board of managers of the Texas league demanded that Milburn be expelled from the national ASL's executive committee.[174]

"The anti-Klan and Klan fight there had shot things pretty much to pieces," McBride concluded after an investigation. But, significantly, he determined that "Webb's endorsements [of dry Klansmen] were not far from the rules of the Anti-Saloon League . . . however, Milburn certainly has overstepped the proprieties" of his office.[175] The league hierarchy took no action, leaving a resentful Milburn on the executive committee, Webb presiding over the dispirited Texas league, the state Klan brawling its way to insignificance, and the nominally dry "Ma" Ferguson (along with her wet "secretary" husband) in the Texas governor's mansion.[176] Even as the ASL and the Klan fell apart in Texas, the willingness of the ASL to endorse known Klansmen solidified the popular impression of an alliance between the Anti-Saloon League and the Invisible Empire in an improper bid to support the sagging prohibition experiment.

The actions of William H. Anderson, the New York ASL's talented yet volatile superintendent, further reinforced the notion that the Klan and the league had joined in nativist advocacy of a fanatical version of prohibition. Anderson was abrasive and sensationalistic, but he had compiled an impressive record of dry legislative victories in the wet strongholds of Illinois, Maryland, and particularly New York. There his "meat-ax" methods had helped force the state into the prohibition column despite the considerable opposition of urban voters and New York City's Democratic Tammany organization.[177] Observers in the press considered Anderson to be "perhaps, the most outstanding figure in the group of men who removed the stigma of amateurishness from the prohibition movement."[178] Such celebrity made more newsworthy Anderson's decision in March 1920 to attack the Catholic Church as complicit with Tammany in defiance of prohibition. "Most of the officiary of the Roman Catholic Church in this state," he emphasized in a blunt clarification of his original remarks, "are in sympathy with the Tammany effort to destroy the prohibition victory."[179] He encouraged Protestants to rally against the alleged wet conspirators.[180]

By 1923, as Governor Al Smith's administration moved to revoke the state prohibition enforcement law and prosecutors charged the combative superintendent with financial misdeeds, Anderson intentionally introduced the Klan into the battle.[181] Although he denied belonging to the hooded order and rejected secrecy and lawlessness, Anderson "spoke in [the Klan's] defense in the friendliest manner conceivable," according to the *New York Times*, arguing that the Catholic-Tammany "politico-ecclesiastical combination" would drive embattled Protestants and prohibitionists into the Klan.[182] Shortly thereafter, Anderson was convicted of third-degree forgery and spent nine months in Sing Sing prison. His conviction deeply wounded the integrity of the league and significantly contributed to its decline as an effective political force.

Upon his release in 1925, Anderson quarreled with his successors in the New York league and openly worked to forge an alliance between Klansmen and ASL supporters. He founded an organization called the American Patriotic Prohibition Protestant Protective Alliance (soon shortened to American Protestant Alliance) and declared war on what he called "political Romanism."[183] Publishing in the Klan-allied Masonic journal *Fellowship Forum*, Anderson charged that ASL leaders "gladly accept financial, political, and moral support from members of the Ku Klux Klan. You are glad enough," he continued, "to have it nominate dry candidates for you to support. A very large proportion of those of your constituency who have not quit, gone to sleep, or become indifferent, are members or supporters of the Klan."[184] He implored ASL loyalists to affirm that organized wet Catholicism was "a common major enemy" of both drys and the Invisible Empire. He also contended, in print, "that the New York Anti-Saloon League is in touch with and cooperating with the Ku Klux Klan in New York in a legitimate and proper way."[185] Through the remainder of the prohibition decade, Anderson spoke against the presidential bids of Al Smith—the nation's leading wet Catholic politician—before Klan gatherings, wrote to a Catholic ASL worker that "the prohibition cause will not be saved in my judgment except through the influence and sentiment that the Ku Klux Klan represents," and encouraged his former ASL colleagues to support a nativist constitutional amendment reducing political representation for districts with large numbers of alien residents.[186]

For a time Anderson was shunned by the ASL, but more for his criticism of league leadership and his frank anti-Catholicism than for his remarks about the Klan. McBride assured concerned league supporters that Anderson had failed as "a team worker" and joked that the former superintendent's "new organization is an A.P.A. [a reference to the nativist American Protective Association of the 1890s] in earnest, with four P's in place of one!"[187] Others emphasized the league's traditional methods, especially in light of Al Smith's political ascendancy. "The Anti-Saloon League, by opposing wet candidates, has repeatedly defeated some contingent aligned with the wets," wrote a Tennessee league official. "If now, as some aver, the political part of the Roman Catholic Church has aligned itself with the wets in the hope of entrenching itself in power, the Anti-Saloon League . . . by defeating the wet combination will thereby defeat that contingent."[188] In 1928, ASL founder Howard Russell explained to Anderson's wife that "we have had, and now have, much aid from persons of the Roman Catholic faith, and I favor continued fellowship rather than antagonism by our League officers."[189]

Yet even in Anderson's case there was ambivalence in the ranks of the mainstream leader of prohibitionist sentiment. Anderson had been a strong critic of Wayne Wheeler, arguing in 1921 that "Mr. Wheeler jeopardizes [the ASL's] position in order to work quietly with the politicians."[190] Wheeler's dislike for Anderson influenced the latter's exile from the league. After Wheeler's sudden death in 1927, Anderson was again welcome at league meetings, where his admirers "almost mobbed the former outcast" and allowed him to speak in favor of his alien representation amendment.[191] As prohibition enforcement crumbled around the nation, the Klan, led by Evans, focused dry attention on Smith's 1928 presidential campaign, slurring his candidacy as a stalking horse for wet Roman rule.[192] Without invoking the Klan, James Cannon, the ASL's most powerful Southern Democrat, spearheaded Southern Protestant opposition to Smith with criticisms of Catholicism and the would-be "cocktail president" that approached Anderson's level of opprobrium.[193] "I have viewed with some concern Mr. Anderson in conference with various ones of our leaders at our conventions," one wealthy ASL figure noted cautiously in 1930. "Atmosphere is the most vital thing there is and I do not believe we can afford to have our cause touched with the atmosphere of anything Anti-Catholic."[194] Try as it might, mainstream prohibitionists could not alter the atmosphere of intolerance that linked the prohibition movement to the menace of the Klan.

The Invisible Empire was equally frustrated in its prohibition advocacy. Sometimes the Klan also suffered by making common cause with other organized drys, as in 1924 when Klans in Orange County, California, were nearly bankrupted by a joint law enforcement sweep with the ASL and civil authorities.[195] The ASL's hesitancy and inconsistency diminished the potential effectiveness of community enforcement as practiced by many klaverns.

But, ultimately, the Klan's hopes to enforce prohibition at the local level broke apart because they were unsupportable in a divided, pluralistic society. In some cases communities were too ethnically or religiously diverse to sustain Klan campaigns. In others, established authorities were hostile to extralegal pretensions in others. The destruction and occasional brutality of vigilante action, joined to the willingness of some hooded raiders to use the cover of dry enforcement to bully enemies of the Klan or punish dissident knights, further sapped popular tolerance of hooded constables.[196] As was illustrated in Colorado, Klan-supported politicians proved no more able to mount effective offensives against prohibition violations than had non-Protestant or "alien" public officials. Furthermore the persistent difficulty in enforcing controversial prohibition regulations blended into the web of internal disputes, scandals, and disappointments that by mid-decade immobilized the Klan movement.

Prohibition limped along for another eight years, but the Invisible Empire's presence as a vital force in the prohibition campaign faded midway into the 1920s. The *New Republic* declared in 1926 that "the Klan as a hooded order of night-riding moralists, interested mainly in local puritanical reforms, is passing."[197] Klansmen in the early 1920s had responded to popular and heart-felt concerns that the requirements of the law, even those as imperfect and strongly resented as were the demands of constitutional prohibition, meet with compliance. But their extralegal efforts on behalf of prohibition failed to draw the dry measure into the mainstream of acceptance. Instead, they furthered the isolation of prohibition as a radical, divisive, and ultimately untenable public policy error.

6

The Problem of Hooded Violence:
Moral Vigilantism, Enemies, and
Provocation

D URING THE BLOODY SUMMER OF 1925 IN MASSACHUSETTS, open-air meetings of Klansmen frequently degenerated into combat with angry opponents. After one such brawl, in which hidden Ku Kluxers fired buckshot into the ranks of their enemies before the usual exchange of stones and blows from clubs, several armed Klansmen were taken into custody by the local police. The next morning one of the hooded detainees was discovered to have supplemented the standard costume of the Invisible Empire with a steel helmet, which he was still wearing the day after the riot. Such headgear was now necessary, explained this veteran of anti-Klan attacks, since he had been struck over the head at previous Klan gatherings.[1]

Despite hooded objections and internal attempts to restrain lawlessness, violence appeared to be as much a part of the New Era's Klan movement as were the Invisible Empire's rituals, cloaked insignia, and native-born white Protestant chauvinism. Whatever hopes for reform, progress, and sociability Klansmen may have entertained when they entered the hooded order, the *New Republic* crisply observed in 1923, "[T]hese honorable and patriotic men ... are launching an engine of violence over which, in the nature of the case, they can have no control."[2] In this view, violence was the natural consequence of a "secret political society" engaged in cultural conflict. This was so even though violence was marginal to the experience of the vast majority of 1920s Klansmen.

Ku Klux enthusiasm in much of the nation focused on fraternalism, community formation, philanthropy, and the politics of white Protestantism in education, law enforcement, and governance. Klan-initiated violence was relatively rare outside the Southern and Southwestern realms, and even in the violent heartland of hooded moral regulation, the greatest waves of night riding and vigilantism had been curbed by the close of 1923. The ascendancy of Hiram Evans as imperial wizard late in 1922 ushered in a public drive for political influence and mainstream respectability for the Invisible Empire. Violent outbursts did not contribute to those goals. In an effort to discourage local vigilantism, many realms restricted the use of Klan robes and hoods outside the klavern.[3]

Irrespective of these efforts, the Klan movement could not shed its association with violence. For much of that stigma, the Invisible Empire itself was to blame. The founding myths of the second Klan linked the movement's origins to the most famous Southern lynching of the early twentieth century, that of the Northern-born Jewish businessman Leo Frank. Under dubious circumstances, Frank was convicted of the 1913 murder of Mary Phagan, a white Protestant working-class teenager employed in the Atlanta pencil factory he managed. In an atmosphere of intense pressure, Georgia's governor in 1915 commuted Frank's death sentence to life imprisonment. That decision elicited extraordinarily bitter protest from white, mostly Protestant Georgians, who also denounced what they considered to be the governor's high-handed reversal of the popular will demanding Frank's execution. Soon after, in an act applauded by local public opinion, a band of Marietta, Georgia, notables abducted Frank from prison and hanged him near Mary Phagan's childhood home.[4]

Despite claims to the contrary, historians have found no firm connections between the lynchers, who called themselves the Knights of Mary Phagan, and the revived Knights of the Ku Klux Klan that organized later the same year in Atlanta.[5] But the aggressively white Protestant "folk justice" that Georgians celebrated in the aftermath of the Frank lynching seemed congruent with the white Protestant nationalism espoused by William Simmons's Klan. The virulent anti-Semitism stoked by Tom Watson during the Frank trial also appeared in harmony with the Klan's later characterization of Jews as fundamentally alien and therefore dangerous to authentic American values. Watson himself became a warm admirer of the resurgent Klan. Unconnected in fact with the lynching of Leo Frank yet born in the same swirling emotional atmosphere of the World War I era that produced it, the 1920s Klan thus seemed to embody in organizational form the intolerance and vigilantism of Frank's killers as well as their devotion to an idealized social, cultural, and political order controlled by native white Protestant men.

Rather than distance the Invisible Empire from the sordid violence of the Frank lynching, early Klan publicists drew upon the notoriety of the affair to mobilize support for the growing organization. In 1922 a short article in the Georgia Klan's newspaper applauded a group of Atlanta residents who had taunted one member of Frank's defense team. As late as 1926, Georgia klaverns distributed a pamphlet linking the Frank case to the alien exploitation of "young Christian GIRLS" in Atlanta department stores. Ensuring that the reference was not too subtle for readers eleven years after the lynching, the circular specifically singled out for criticism a Jewish board member of one store. That "prominent highly educated Jew," the hooded constituency was informed, had used his financial resources "to defend the *notorious 'Leo Frank' for the dastardly outrage on the 'person of' and the murder of that sweet little innocent working 'girl' Mary Phagan*." The Klan's decision to align itself with popular support for the lynching bore fruit. According to one working-class observer, sensationalism surrounding the Frank case "caused the Ku-Klux to enlarge itself a whole lot around Atlanta."[6]

Georgia Klansmen embraced the legacy of vigilantism associated with the Frank lynching despite the fact that, at the time of the case, future knights disagreed over the proper punishment of the condemned man. Although many white Georgians who later joined the Klan demanded that Frank be executed with or without legal sanction, at least two prominent future Klansmen, one of whom became a kleagle, made public statements supporting clemency for Frank.[7]

In a similar fashion, even though the fledgling Oklahoma Klan did not participate in the Tulsa race riot of 1921, it profited from the wave of enthusiasm for Anglo-Saxon aggressiveness produced by the violence.[8] By accepting the tainted currency of white vigilante violence and the mass support it attracted, the Klan thereby collaborated in the construction of its own violent image. When the Invisible Empire later sought to downplay its violent reputation, Evans and other hooded officials discovered the difficulty of altering public perceptions.

The problem of violence in the Klan involved concrete examples of destructive vigilantism as well as unsavory associations. Violent episodes and appeals intersected the Klan movement in three distinct phases as the Invisible Empire rose and then rapidly declined between 1920 and 1925. During the explosive growth of the hooded order between 1920 and 1923, Ku Klux devotion to the task of community-level moral regulation engaged numerous knights in the rough correction of misbehaving neighbors. Drawing on traditions of coercive community action ranging from charivari to white-capping,* bands of Klansmen fanned out into the night to warn, intimidate,

---

*Charivari was a popular ceremonial device used to enforce community standards, often forcibly and even violently. White-capping, a more private form of collective violence, involved masked riders and was used to enforce political orthodoxy, settle economic disputes, or resist unwelcome change in the late nineteenth and early twentieth centuries, especially in the rural South.

or punish those who had deviated from the unwritten local codes of proper behavior.[9] In keeping with Southern and Southwestern patterns of heightened violence and greater recourse to informal enforcement of community standards, hooded moral regulation in those regions was more extensive and more violent than elsewhere within the Invisible Empire.

The second phase of Klan violence, strongest between 1923 and 1925, was more indirect and took place in areas where the Klan movement confronted numerous enemies, especially in the Midwest and Northeast. Bumptious assertiveness by Klansmen, usually involving Ku Klux parades or meetings in immigrant or Catholic settlements, provoked violent retaliation against the hooded interlopers. Posturing Klansmen often carried weapons to these confrontations but, just as frequently, absorbed most of the damage from the resulting combat. National Klan officers in Atlanta extolled the few hooded martyrs who perished in these clashes, manipulating the deaths to build solidarity and commitment among hesitant knights. The Klan riots of this period confirmed to most observers the fundamental association of the Invisible Empire with intentional disorder.

The third phase of violence associated with the Klan movement became more commonplace after 1925, as the Invisible Empire collapsed amid backbiting allegations of earlier brutality framed by a second wave of vigilante whipping that broke out in the deep South. As state investigations of the Klan multiplied, dissident factions broke off from the national organization, and hooded officials fought over the fragmentary remnants of Klan property and power, estranged Klansmen offered glimpses into the secret operations of the hooded order. Frequently these confessions included revelations, often highly exaggerated, of past Klan outrages that surpassed the violence of documented cases of hooded brutality. Moreover, former Klan officials revealed that representatives of the national Klan tried to reverse the decline of the secret order by promoting hatred and violent acts against Catholics, African Americans, and immigrants. National Klan lecturers hoped, unsuccessfully as it turned out, that aggressive strikes against the cultural enemies of white Protestant Americanism would restore enthusiasm for the hooded enterprise among the disaffected rank and file.

Even though some of the violent actions detailed in government hearings or newspaper interviews never took place, the testimony of former Klan officers was devastating to the hierarchy of the Invisible Empire. Lurid press accounts portrayed Evans and his Atlanta lieutenants promoting violence as a means to strengthen the faltering Klan movement, thus directly contradicting the imperial wizard's public commitment to eliminate violent misbehavior by hooded knights. Few 1920s Klansmen personally witnessed violent displays by their fellows, and fewer still acted brutally. But the violence associated with the Klan movement nevertheless helped destroy the influence of the Invisible Empire.

Imposing Morality

Much of the early enthusiasm that drove the Klan movement focused on the safeguarding of an idealized moral order that reflected native-born white Protestant values. Since in many communities Klansmen penetrated both public and private associations, the pursuit of moral order sometimes simultaneously followed legal, quasi-legal, and extralegal channels. In the enforcement of prohibition, for instance, police officers and sheriffs who were Klansmen had both the law and the power of their office with which to promote the dry vision. Other knights operated quasi-legally as constables against prohibition violators, while some carried only cultural commissions of their own invention to legitimize their vigilantism. A mixture of law and mainstream cultural sanctions also backed hooded policing of the color line. But because the Klan's understanding of white Americanism was more restrictive than that of the law or even of changing racial attitudes in the 1920s, Klansmen employed extralegal and sometimes violent means to secure white supremacy. Similarly, politics and stealth became Ku Klux weapons against Catholic inroads on Protestant cultural hegemony.

Secret, extralegal, intimidating, and occasionally violent acts by Klansmen marked each of these areas of cultural conflict. But the greatest concentration of nocturnal terrorism, organized brutality, and recourse to vigilante violence by the Klan movement was visited upon fellow white Protestants. Perhaps because it lay within the moral framework of expectation while falling outside the formal boundaries of the law, the Invisible Empire's concern with the faltering personal behavior of white Protestant community members was more likely to produce direct and sometimes severe intervention. An anti-Klan judge reported that hooded vigilantes stepped in to regulate misbehavior over which his office had no power: "the unfair but not criminal methods of slick crooks, the betrayals of women where more harm than good is done if the law is called in, the oppressions of money-lenders, the laziness of men who let their children starve."[10] When organized Protestantism was reluctant to confront local communicants, Klansmen plunged in. "They talked about morals in the churches," an exalted cyclops from Pennsylvania explained, "but if some young fellow got into trouble or some couple was about to get a divorce, the churches wouldn't mess in it. We acted." Assuming moral leadership in their communities, hooded regulators brashly penetrated the veil of family privacy to restore the collective moral equilibrium. "There were at least five couples in this community that were having domestic trouble which we helped straighten out," declared the Pennsylvania knight.[11] Parading Texas Klansmen, while also supporting prohibition and "Americanism," advertised their moral vigilantism with signs declaring "Wife beaters beware," "Crap shooters beware," and "Love thy neighbor as thyself, but leave his wife alone."[12]

As New Era Klansmen endured what they interpreted as alien assaults on white Protestant institutions, their intolerance for misbehavior by fellow white Protestants may also have reflected their fears for the durability of their own cultural domination. Whatever the cause, those who did not conform to the dictates of ideal family life were more likely to feel the sting of whips or the burning of hot tar applied by fearsome midnight assailants. Negligent parents, defiant children, and unfaithful spouses were common victims. In the violent Klan center of Macon, Georgia, for instance, irresponsible husbands and fathers were targets of the most notable incidents of hooded vigilantism in 1922 and 1923. Two of the victims were physicians, men whose status and visibility made their personal misbehavior more demoralizing to idealized community standards. A Klan detective informed the wife of the first victim of an extramarital excursion to Florida. Meanwhile, hooded teams administered two therapeutic beatings to the wandering husband. In the second case, a doctor who had abandoned his family in Boston and taken up residence with a local nurse was ordered out of Macon by a band of menacing Klansmen. Finally, Klansmen severely whipped a local man who had divorced his wife and conducted legal proceedings against his children. The vigilantes had consulted with the aggrieved former spouse before the attack and compelled the man's current companion to witness the beating.[13]

Contact between Klansmen and family members of those targeted by hooded violence was also evident in other Klan interventions. A California physician, doubly condemned for a crude sexual "frame-up" of his unknowing wife in a divorce suit and for "perform[ing] illegal operations on high school girls," was abducted by the exalted cyclops of the local Klan. In the presence of the offended wife and thirty knights, Klansmen stripped and brutally assaulted the wayward husband. Hanged until he passed out, the man was then revived and beaten with a thick rope and a loaded gun. The Klan leader later was sentenced to prison for the attack.[14] In a more private drama, Atlanta Klansmen entered a dispute between a father and his drunken, jobless, disrespectful adult son. Tension had escalated when the son beat up his father in a barroom. Secretly summoned by the older man without the knowledge of his wife, three carloads of Klansmen seized the defiant son, took him to a prepared site, and pounded him with a leather strap. The rough handling of the younger man, according to an observer familiar with the incident, "straightened that fellow out."[15]

In most of the above cases, Klansmen conferred with those who had been injured by cruel or irresponsible family members before launching their vigilante action. One of the most important elements of Ku Klux moral vigilantism, especially involving errant family members, was the cultural sanction given to extralegal Klan methods by the white Protestant community itself. Abundant evidence suggests that mistreated wives, worried parents, and the occasional desperate husband implored the knights of the Invisible Empire to intervene on their behalf against family members or intimates who had acted badly. Nancy MacLean reports that "an average of twenty letters *each week*" poured into the headquarters of Georgia's Klan "from women inviting the order to threaten or use violence against people whose conduct they disapproved of."[16] The grand dragon from another state told a journalist that his office received fifty such weekly appeals.[17] Similar requests for assistance appear in Klan sources throughout the South and Southwest, and north into Maryland, Pennsylvania, and even Wisconsin.

Although bigots or busybodies were responsible for some of the correspondence, most of those asking for intervention by the Klan were desperate family members who could not find a legal remedy for their situation. "I feel that I ought to have Justice," a Georgia woman informed the Klan. She was seeking to gain divorce and custody of her two children from an abusive (and Italian Catholic) husband. "If I can't have it from the Courts I know of no other one to go to except your organization."[18] Georgia klaverns received requests from both men and women for help in locating runaway spouses.[19] One Pennsylvania Klansman affirmed that "mothers and fathers would beg the Klan to instill the fear of God into wayward children who were otherwise unmanageable." The hooded official was struck by "the confidence these people had in the ability of the Klan to get things done. They placed a much higher estimate on the Klan in this respect than they did in the ordinary processes of the law."[20] The celebrated reform judge Ben Lindsey was told by several Denverites that if his court did not bring them satisfaction, "the matter would be taken up with the grand dragon."[21] Many white Protestants, at least for a short time in the early 1920s, seemed to accept the Klan as an informal agency capable of restoring moral stability to a society that had broken down in the public sphere.

Intervention by Klansmen into family affairs was moral regulation of a strictly private character, at least in a formal sense. Unlike the quasi-public actions of Klan constables enforcing prohibition laws, this more intimate level of community policing usually had no legal basis. Rather, beyond instances of simple revenge or malice, Klansmen and those who sought their help were motivated by a shared sense of behavioral norms that created an informal public interest in the resolution of family conflict. The desire to enforce an idealized

vision of native-born white Protestant family organization—featuring a pro-
vider husband/father, a sentimentalized but submissive wife and mother, and
obedient children—in a complex, increasingly diverse society lay behind much
of the moral vigilantism endorsed by the Klan and its supporters.

In that context, even hooded philanthropy could have a menacing undercurrent. A California widower received money from the secret order to
support his six children, but the aid came with a warning. "You are cautioned
not to part with any of your children without advice," the hooded benefac-
tors intoned, thus confirming their interest in supervising the struggling
household.[22] When fifty dollars donated by New Jersey Klansmen to help a
struggling mother disappeared, pistol-wielding knights accused her teenage
son of stealing the money and allegedly threatened him with knives and a
hangman's noose.[23]

Close attention to female sexuality confirmed a commitment to traditional
patriarchy that extended beyond the family unit to society at large.[24] Hooded
moral regulators guarded white, Protestant women from sexual exploitation but also sharply curtailed their sexual freedom. Thus Beaumont, Texas,
Klansmen in 1921 took it upon themselves to punish a doctor suspected of
performing abortions and a local man who had referred a woman to the
physician. The masked vigilantes were sufficiently confident of community
approval to take public credit for the whipping, claiming in a statement to
the local newspaper that "the eyes of the unknown had seen and observed
the wrong to be redressed."[25] Imperial Wizard Simmons revoked the charter
of the klavern for its breach of secrecy as much as for the violence. The Klan
movement in Beaumont, however, continued to prosper.

One of the notable features of the Invisible Empire's moral vigilantism
was the willingness of Klansmen to manhandle, strip, humiliate, and beat
white Protestant women whose sexual behavior violated paternalistic norms
or endangered the racial, ethnic, or religious integrity of Anglo-Saxon Protestant culture. Thus, in one of the iconic punishments of the Klan era, a
hooded Baptist minister in Alabama supervised the flogging of a married
couple whose wedding ceremony he had performed. Although both partners
had previously been divorced, Klansmen singled out the woman for moral
instruction. Carrying out the beating in the presence of her children, the
hooded minister of the Gospel handed the bleeding woman a few dollars,
some salve, and a sermonette on correct behavior. "Sister," he intoned, "you
were not punished in anger this evening; you were punished in a spirit of
kindness and correction, to set your feet aright and to show your children
how a good mother should go."[26]

Sustaining vigilante action of this type required a high level of community
consensus on the need for moral regulation and on the means to be employed

to punish wrongdoing and to restore correct behavior. In the absence of consensus, assertive actions by hooded vigilantes, to say nothing of violent depredations, were disruptive rather than restorative. News of the Alabama beating, part of a larger investigation of vigilante violence, raised public outcry and resulted in legal proceedings against the Klansmen involved. L. A. Nalls, the Baptist night-riding leader, left the state to avoid prosecution. Similarly, the captain of a notorious Oklahoma Klan's whipping squad came forward to renounce his participation in several brutal punishments, expressing particular regret for an instance in which hooded vigilantes castrated a man for incest with his daughter after a court had failed to convict him for the same offense.[27] Revelation of the work performed by Klan vigilantes plunged Oklahoma into a period of chaos and political instability. Clearly the effectiveness of the Klan's moral policing depended on community support and was highly sensitive to shifts in local opinion.

Most moral policing originated at the klavern level, but patterns of vigilantism and the extent of its organization within the structure of the Klan differed considerably. At one extreme, Wisconsin Klansmen rebuffed requests from outraged wives to punish abusive or misbehaving husbands.[28] In eastern Oregon the local klavern avoided direct confrontation with a father who failed to support his children and instead steered the case to public health authorities.[29] The Shock Committee of the Monticello, Arkansas, Klan acted as cautiously on moral issues as it did on prohibition enforcement. It forwarded the names of joyriding teens to their parents, composed "a strong friendly letter" to an irresponsible son, and advised the county prosecuting attorney that a local man had deserted his teenage wife. On the one occasion when Klan members ventured out to preach reform to an unmarried couple, a shotgun blast from the unwelcoming female partner sent the hooded knights back to the safety of the klavern.[30] On the other hand, Georgia's grand dragon directed individual klaverns to respond to specific pleas for assistance, in one case instructing a local Klan to search for a man who had abandoned his family almost a year earlier.[31]

Klaverns that demonstrated attentiveness to the same issue usually responded in ways that fit the local character of the Klan movement. Across the Invisible Empire, for instance, automobiles raised an alarm about the opportunities for illicit sexuality, especially among the younger set. "That darkened, curtained auto is the greatest evil of the age," a lecturer warned parents in Colorado Springs, some of whom joined the hooded order to find solutions. Yet vigilantism did not arise in southeastern Colorado. In nearby Pueblo the grand titan noted "27 automobiles parked at secluded spots along the highway," but the Klan-supported Law Enforcement League did not shoulder aside the police. Instead, it endorsed public cooperation between citizens and law enforcement bodies.[32] In Indiana, on the other hand, the semi-official status of the Horse Thief Detectives allowed Klansmen to patrol highways and roust couples in parked cars.[33] A Raleigh, North Carolina, pastor spoke on the topic "The Automobile, Women, and the Ku Klux Klan," and invited the Invisible Empire to employ instructive floggings against car-bound lovers. The local Klan reputedly helped force out a permissive police chief and conducted its own campaign against immorality.[34] In Denison, Texas, knights donned their hoods and robes and personally confronted the occupants of parked cars.[35]

Ku Klux officials usually blamed freelance vigilantes—either unauthorized Klansmen or impostors in hoods—for night-riding incidents. In one such case, a South Carolina man had sought the aid of the local klavern in a dispute with a neighbor. Rebuffed by the hooded group, the man organized "a little Klan of his own" to meet his needs. A counterfeit band of Klansmen sent a threatening note to the neighbor and, after failing to get satisfaction, fired twenty shotgun shells at him as he rode past in a buggy.[36] Most observers agreed that some vigilantes used the notoriety of the Ku Klux Klan to mask their unrelated actions. Klan officials, however, issued blanket denials of any involvement in vigilante violence. One enthusiastic California clergyman stated that "the bitterest enemies of the Klan have deliberately copied its costumes when carrying out nefarious plans, hoping to escape punishment and cast the blame on others." But with the characteristic overstatement that subverted defenses of the hooded order, he falsely averred that "all the celebrated cases in which the press convicted the Klan of atrocious crimes 'blew up' when evidence was demanded."[37]

Despite official disavowals, many klaverns had developed mechanisms to carry out effective moral intervention. The most common practice called for investigation of complaints and a graduated series of warnings before resorting to direct coercion. Maryland Klansmen, as we have seen, empowered a few knights to investigate charges of abuse lodged by a wife against her husband before confronting the man.[38] More formal arrangements existed in some large Southwestern klaverns, where violence was more commonplace. In Texas, letters and occasionally telephone calls warning the targets of Klan interest to reform their ways or to promptly leave town preceded violent hooded visitations.[39] Waco Klan officers managed a network of neighborhood spies to confirm specific reports of misbehavior. Many Southwestern and Southern Klans maintained standing vigilance committees that operated directly under the control of the exalted cyclops or the klavern's executive board, the Klokann. These bodies named erring community members, determined the method of intervention, and assigned Klansmen to carry out the prescribed action. The identities of the knights who performed the violent tasks of kidnapping, thrashing, and applying hot tar and feathers were kept confidential, even from fellow Klansmen. In some of the most violent klaverns, the whipping squads donned black masks and robes to emphasize their special status and duties.[40]

Still, enough publicity and judicial inquiry followed episodes of Klan vigilantism to reveal that the rough work of moral stewardship frequently involved locally prominent men. Police officers up to the rank of chief were implicated in hooded beatings, as were several clergymen. Amid the flare-up of Klan violence in Georgia in the twilight of the Klan movement, local figures of modest eminence joined in some of the most notable incidents. Among the squad that brutally whipped a woman and her son for poor behavior and infrequent church attendance were a well-known car dealer and the principal of a rural high school, who was also active in the Baptist Sunday school in addition to his role as an officer of the Invisible Empire.[41] Elsewhere several exalted cyclopes and even higher realm officials occasionally participated in attacks. Witnesses claimed that Hiram Evans, while exalted cyclops of the Dallas Klan, and Oklahoma grand dragon Clay Jewett personally directed especially vicious assaults.[42] Reckless, anonymous figures were responsible for many Klan depredations, but in the most combative pockets of the Invisible Empire the organized Klan movement itself was also culpable.

Evidence of considerable planning and resources attended not only violent excursions but also some hooded reform missions. Western Pennsylvania Klansmen carefully choreographed their interaction with a man who was not supporting his five children. First, the knights delivered a short-term supply of food to the destitute family. Next, a Klansman in street clothes announced an upcoming visit by a delegation of hooded knights. The robed Klansmen suggested that the reluctant job seeker inquire at a specific plant for work without revealing that a job had been arranged in advance. After working for a week, the man decided that he needed "to rest up a little." At this point a sterner delegation pressured him to get back to work and meet his family responsibilities.[43] After a Northeastern man shrugged off hooded advice to leave "a notoriously vicious woman," he immediately felt the sting of economic pressure orchestrated by the local Klan. In short order he lost his job, his rent increased, and merchants turned away his business.[44]

The Klan's influence also stretched across state lines. A committee from another Pennsylvania klavern pursued a wayward husband into another state and forced him to return home to support his family.[45] Cooperative intelligence across realms was also evident in cases of illicit sexuality. At the request of Florida Klan investigators probing one man's sexual misdeeds, Georgia knights looked into the background of a local woman he may have impregnated.[46]

Without question, Klansmen across the country monitored the moral climate in their communities. It is also clear that a smaller number of klaverns, sometimes encouraged by aggressive state organizations, actively intervened to influence the behavior of their neighbors, in some locations to the point of violence. Still, much of the celebrated Klan vigilantism of the early 1920s involved informal, ad hoc operations by individuals or small clusters of knights. After close study of the most violent section of the Invisible Empire, Charles Alexander concluded that "the preponderance of Klan vigilante acts featured a handful of Klansmen acting precipitately and without the sanction of local officers of the order."[47] In Georgia an epidemic of floggings at mid-decade aroused the state government against the Klan and forced the leadership of the realm to intervene. Georgia's grand dragon denounced the beating of an attorney by a gang of masked men, reportedly for prosecuting Klansmen in a fatal attack several months earlier, as "an unspeakable outrage" and offered a reward for the prosecution of the perpetrators. The violent crew "wore robes in imitation of Klan regalia," the hooded official protested, "but [they] were not in any sense Klansmen." Additional whippings by more easily identified Klansmen pushed the realm to support legislation making flogging a felony in Georgia.[48]

The violent potential of moral regulation not only damaged the public image of the Klan movement but also disturbed harmony within the klavern. Knights who were uncomfortable with the intrusive correction of other people's behavior complained that a small number of zealots and bullies used the Invisible Empire as a cover for their own violent desires. A forgettable reference during a meeting became an excuse for a few brutal types to climb into a car later and thrash "some poor old drunk." One Georgia Klansman questioned the moral integrity of knights who listened to the telephone conversations of others or abandoned their own families to creep about in the dark after a husband who was "out with other women."[49] Some unscrupulous Ku Kluxers distorted the supposed community purposes of hooded vigilantism and used Klan punishment squads as instruments of personal vengeance. After mauling a man who denied committing moral infractions, an Oklahoma Klansman learned that the victim owed a small debt to the chief officer of the klavern's vigilance committee.[50] "Out-kluxing the klan itself," Texans familiar with the hooded practice of sending warning letters appropriated the symbols of the Invisible Empire and mailed "informal warnings . . . to other individuals to satisfy personal grudges."[51] This kind of personalized violence and intimidation undercut the moral pretensions of hooded vigilantism.

Toleration for the violent adjustment of moral failings varied within the Invisible Empire. Coercion by Pennsylvania Klansmen in the family support cases noted above stopped short of actual violence. Adulterous knights in

La Grande, Oregon, were admonished in the privacy of the klavern, but no threats were made against them.[52] Grand Dragon Nathan Bedford Forrest III warned Georgia knights to avoid violent night riding, but his enthusiasm for moral correction enabled violence in the state to persist for years.[53] Although most California klaverns were quiet, knights in the hardscrabble Central Valley oil town of Taft took to the streets to beat and terrorize bawdy-house keepers, peddlers of illegal liquor or drugs, and those who represented "a menace to young girls and boys."[54] Southern Kansas Klansmen demonstrated a greater aptitude for violence than did their hooded brethren elsewhere in the state. In a town near the Oklahoma border that seethed with labor violence, knights tarred and feathered a misbehaving husband for "not living the right kind of life."[55]

Southwestern realms more openly practiced violence until the Evans regime curtailed physical punishment of errant citizens. In 1922 the imperial wizard's own Dallas Klan No. 66 reportedly had chastised some sixty-odd people at its own whipping ground in the Trinity River bottoms. Organized Klan whipping squads in Oklahoma and Louisiana punished a few hundred lawbreaking, unchaste, divorced, or irresponsible victims until the imperial edict to cease took hold. Beatings, floggings, and even shootings persisted in Alabama, South Carolina, and Georgia until the late 1920s.[56]

Greater Klan violence in the South and Southwest was partly a reflection of the violent character of the region. Murder statistics compiled by the insurance industry throughout the 1920s showed that Southern cities far outpaced the violent record of municipalities elsewhere, even those that suffered through the gang wars of the prohibition era. Among the Southern cities that consistently accounted for the top ten homicide rates, Memphis stood out with a murder rate seven times higher than the national average. In 1924 embarrassed municipal officials there refused to supply figures to the statistician conducting the annual study. Birmingham, Houston, Dallas, Jacksonville, Tampa, Nashville, and Little Rock all had murder rates that easily outstripped those of violent Northern centers such as Chicago.[57]

The pattern of Southern violence had been established well before the Klan's reemergence. "I am simply afraid to go out at night without [a gun]," one young worker reported from the Carolinas near the turn of the century. "They shoot about one hundred times every night." Respectable participants at a church picnic discussed the need "to have a pistol, a jack knife, and a pair of brass knucks . . . [as] proper accoutrements" for masculine life in Dixie.[58] Southern Ku Kluxers thus operated in a region that was already marked by unusually high levels of violence. A similar tradition of violence in southern Illinois contributed to the Klan liquor war in Williamson County, one of the only centers of sustained hooded violence north of the Ohio River.

Formal policing in the South also lagged behind much of the nation. Instead, a culture of collective, extralegal enforcement of community mores persisted. The swift recourse to brutality in the service of white supremacy was well known, but among whites the private resolution of personal injuries and criminal complaints was also notable. In an encounter that the historian Edward Akin likened to "an Appalachian feud," a party of armed Klansmen and their intended victim, a lumber camp worker fond of extramarital affairs, shot it out with each other. Although the lumber worker and one Klansman were killed, no legal consequences ensued.[59] In explaining the appeal of the Klan's vigilantism, one Southern governor invited observers "to imagine . . . what it would mean to live where it is practically impossible to enforce any law, where intimidation and abuse are customary, theft common, arson not unusual, and murder occasional—all unpunishable."[60] Indeed, the appeal of vigilantism was such that in the early stages of the revived Klan movement several groups not affiliated with the Invisible Empire imitated the methods of hooded moral regulation. Calling themselves the Black Vigilantes of the Night, African American night riders in Oklahoma abducted and whipped a black lawbreaker. A student group in Ada, Oklahoma, spirited an accused cheater to an isolated location and demanded that he adopt more upright conduct.[61]

This is not to argue that Southern sentiment universally welcomed violent justice performed by Klansmen or other disguised bodies. Several Southern newspaper editors were outspoken in their condemnation of night-riding Klansmen, especially during the 1926 resurgence of vigilantism. Julian Harris of the *Columbus Enquirer-Sun* won a Pulitzer Prize for his anti-Klan campaign and led a band of Georgia newspapers that confronted the violent and bigoted record of the Invisible Empire in the state. Local and state officeholders eventually moved against the hooded order, prosecuting knights for violent actions and demanding that the order unmask.[62] Oklahoma governor Jack Walton declared martial law in a misbegotten campaign to suppress the Klan and its violent self-professed moralism. But there was sufficient room in Southern culture to allow the expansion of Klan vigilantism, helping explain its greater prominence in that section of the country.

The Mark of Cain

Even in the South, there was an inherent risk when the Invisible Empire undertook to control private behavior. Once Klan officials or groups of knights assumed the right to act against community enemies, it was no longer clear whether the masked enforcers were operating at the request of injured petitioners or even in their interests. Between 1922 and 1923, several provocative assaults by Klan vigilantes on vulnerable-appearing women undercut rather than upheld mainstream standards of decorum and stirred resentment of the order. In the most publicized incident, about fifteen Texas knights, three of them improbably disguised as a clown or in women's clothes, burst into the household of an ailing woman in which small children played. The raiding party dragged the half-dressed woman out of her sickbed and at gunpoint forced her and the man who was visiting her into an automobile. Both of them were whipped. Crude oil was poured over the scourged man while the hair of the woman was roughly hacked off with a knife. Perhaps Klansmen thought that the woman, separated from her husband and in the company of another man, needed a stern reminder of her marital obligations. In reporting the incident, a Ku Klux editorialist slandered the victim as one of "the painted face girls of easy morals" who deserved punishment. But the estranged husband refused to follow the moral prompts of the vigilantes. He vilified "the murdering cowards" who abducted and beat his wife and spoke favorably of her character. The Goose Creek outrage resulted in fines for twenty-five knights and the end of an eighteen-month stretch of hooded vigilantism in the community.[63]

Protests had also met the violence inflicted by another band of Texas Klansmen two years earlier on a "delinquent but slow-witted young woman," abducted by the knights while she awaited legal proceedings on a bigamy charge. Ignoring the courts, the hooded moralists corrected the ethical lapse with hair clippers, a wet rope, hot tar, and feathers. This intemperate action raised objections not only because the Klansmen interfered with the formal system of justice but also because, in the course of the punishment, they stripped the offending young woman to the waist.[64] A group of North Carolina Klansmen, led by the chief of police, achieved similar notoriety by beating "two white women . . . on the naked flesh with a leather strap." One of the beaten women had supposedly mistreated her sick husband.[65] These and other episodes in which women were stripped and humiliated by hooded defenders of correct behavior left it unclear, especially to prim moralists, which party had committed the greater moral infraction.

As Klan vigilantes moved beyond the family circle to direct attention onto the sexual practices of single adults, the personal habits of gamblers or idlers, and the sharp economic methods of local businessmen, their violent outbursts appeared to be even more self-indulgent and materially motivated. Unable to separate the interests of the Invisible Empire from the welfare of the community, masked Klansmen lashed out at identifiable enemies who were often community leaders rather than deviants. Business rivals of fellow knights, critics of the hooded fraternity, and disaffected Klansmen who chafed under the misrule of corrupt or autocratic Klan officials became the targets of

Ku Klux coercion or violent attacks. When a Texas sheriff interrupted a 1921 Klan parade near Waco, furious knights struck back. In the ensuing melee, two gunshots felled the sheriff, and another member of his posse, an assistant football coach at Baylor University, received a fatal stab wound. Even though several other bystanders were hurt, participating Klansmen showed little remorse and blamed the lawmen for interfering with the hooded procession.[66]

Public critics or political opponents of the Klan were sometimes visited with violent retribution. The Catholic mayor horsewhipped by Kansas Klansmen was beaten not only for his heterodox religion but also because he had refused to allow the Ku Kluxers to gather in a hall he owned. In 1923 a Georgia merchant who led resistance to the hooded order in his county had his store burned down.[67] Masked attackers who opposed the hiring of a Yankee city manager in Columbus, Georgia, manhandled the official and bombed the mayor's back porch. Several journalists and attorneys who worked against the Klan were threatened or assaulted.[68] A Basque immigrant who had denounced the Klan was beaten by a masked knight in the only violent act perpetrated by the Monticello, Arkansas, Klan.[69]

Not even the ties of Klankraft could protect rebellious knights from internal persecution or, in some cases, brutal retaliation. As the Klan movement around Philadelphia disintegrated in 1926, the imperious field representative of the national Invisible Empire, Paul Winter, applied the instruments of intimidation against his hooded critics. Winter responded to challenges within the order by subverting the business interests of dissident Klansmen and organizing a Super-Secret Society of black-robed thugs to attack and terrorize fellow knights.[70] In Buffalo, hooded pursuit of a police spy who had infiltrated the Klan played out in a spectacular burst of violence that was out of character with the dominant pattern of the Invisible Empire in the region. The undercover agent and a national Klan investigator shot each other to death in a shocking exchange that also wounded Buffalo's kleagle and another knight, triggering the rapid collapse of Ku Klux activism in western New York.[71]

❖

The moral presumptions of the Klan, its willingness to move outside the law and to employ violence against suspected malefactors, and its tendency to strike out against vocal critics of the hooded order all came together disastrously in the dreary flat country of northern Louisiana in the late summer of 1922. As was often the case in local manifestations of the Klan movement, Ku Klux–related conflicts in Morehouse Parish followed the established channels of area rivalries and disputes. Bastrop, a small commercial town with a pulp mill and the strict Protestant folkways conducive to the Invisible Empire, was the stronghold of the Morehouse Klan. The nearby settlement of Mer Rouge, a political rival of Bastrop and the target of hooded anti-vice raids, was also the locus of anti-Klan sentiment in the region. After an escalating series of incidents, featuring threats and the display of handguns on both sides, masked Klansmen seized five well-known Mer Rouge men from a convoy of automobiles. Three of the men, two of them exhibiting the marks of a brutal whipping, later turned up, but the other two, including the most brazen opponent of the Bastrop Klan, disappeared after being observed in the custody of a black-hooded punishment squad. Searchers later fished two horribly mutilated bodies out of a local lake, identified only by clothing and jewelry as the missing men.[72]

Local tensions and the extralegal might of the Klan were so great that the state government stepped in to investigate the matter. A round of public hearings in January 1923 could not make a conclusive case against the accused exalted cyclops, J. K. Skipworth, and Dr. B. M. McKoin, the most prominent Mer Rouge knight, and the murders went unsolved. But the investigation revealed to an intensely interested national audience the Klan's poisonous influence in Morehouse Parish. One former knight testified that "after [the Klan's] advent, friends became enemies; it separated the people and brought about disorders." "Old Skip," the elderly Confederate veteran who directed the Bastrop klavern, exercised dangerous authority and evidently took pleasure in tormenting his personal enemies. Louisiana's attorney general asserted that under Skipworth's supervision, "the flogging of citizens, their deportation and banishment, and other kindred offenses were but mere pastimes, and of such frequent occurrence that they were accepted as commonplace things, the protest against which was itself sufficient ground for deportation."[73] On the night of the incident, Skipworth had ordered an interruption of telephone service between Bastrop and Mer Rouge, after which the lines were cut. Later reports suggested that the bodies of the murdered men had been crushed on the wheels of logging carts.[74] The investigation also confirmed that the Klan had enveloped and rendered powerless the local network of governance and law enforcement. The sheriff and district attorney were reputed to be members of Skipworth's klavern. Journalists reported that three-quarters of the grand jury members considering the evidence in the case were themselves Klansmen.[75] Here was the reputed invisible government of the hooded empire at its worst.

The sinister influence of the Klan's secret hold on government and its disturbing capacity for violence of an especially raw nature prompted national outrage. Unlike "sporadic" outbreaks of labor violence, the *New York Times* explained as the Mer Rouge episode unfolded, the hooded order posed a more dangerous threat "as a brooding, continual conspiracy against the reign of law."[76] Reports that national Klan attorneys and investigators aided the Mer Rouge culprits in evading justice worsened the image of the hooded band.[77] Internally, Klan officials informed knights in other realms, such as an Oregon klavern, that "the Louisiana affair was just a political issue," a "bluff" magnified by the desperate enemies of the Invisible Empire.[78]

The Klan press also treated the Mer Rouge investigation as a "frameup." The Midwest's most influential Ku Klux newspaper dismissed the proceeding as a "Judicial Burlesque" perpetrated by "liquor anarchists" and the political allies of the Knights of Columbus. As the inquiry ended, the *Fiery Cross* doubted that anyone had been murdered and declared that the hooded order "stands spotless and white in the searchlight of public opinion."[79] But the reality of the matter was that the national Klan movement, including its more peaceable realms, had been badly tarnished by the Southwestern violence. "The country has not forgotten the lesson of Mer Rouge," exclaimed a magazine article about the New York Klan.[80]

As the public hearings in the Mer Rouge case began, the ill-fated administration of Oklahoma governor John C. "Jack" Walton also commenced its course toward a showdown with the state Klan. Walton, a Democrat backed by the Farmer-Labor Reconstruction League, had hopes for extensive reforms on behalf of working-class people, but his administration soon bogged down in financial difficulties, compromising alliances, and the destructive consequences of Walton's impulsive decision-making. The governor's posture toward the politically powerful and violent Invisible Empire in Oklahoma was at first mixed. On the one hand, "Our Jack" had secretly acted to become an "at-large" member of the Klan. Yet as governor he had ordered an inquiry into a Klan whipping. By August 1923, however, Walton had made the politically motivated decision to do battle with the Oklahoma Klan. The governor declared martial law in the hooded stronghold of Tulsa, suspended habeas corpus, convened a military court to take testimony in cases of Klan violence and misconduct, banned hooded parades throughout the state, and demanded that the exalted cyclops of the Muskogee Klan resign forthwith. Walton eventually placed the entire state under martial law, stationed National Guard machine guns in front of public buildings, and launched additional military investigations of Klan violence.[81]

As at Mer Rouge, the Klan superficially fended off the government investigation in Oklahoma. Walton's rash actions, many observers within and outside Oklahoma agreed, raised the volatile governor above the hooded vigilantes as a threat to order. He tried to censor newspapers, used troops to block a hostile grand jury from meeting, turned away the state legislature from a special session, and attempted to stop an election intended to give the legislature the power to meet over his objection. He misperceived the willingness of Oklahomans to surrender their civil liberties in order to disrupt the Invisible Empire.[82] "Why not supersede the civil authorities with the military whenever Tom, Dick or Harry blacks the eyes of Bill, Sam or Walt?" asked one hostile newspaper.[83] The Oklahoma legislature, its strong Klan component temporarily united with other lawmakers, impeached the volatile governor and removed him from office in November 1923. Boisterous Oklahoma Klansmen traveling to the giant Klan celebration at the Texas State Fair decorated their train with a sign boasting, "Did we impeach Walton? Hell yes!"[84] In 1924, membership in the Oklahoma Klan crested at nearly one hundred thousand.

Walton may have been defeated, but the revelations of his military courts further solidified the image of unrestrained Klan violence in the Southwest. A parade of witnesses gave details on Klan whippings—120 such incidents in Tulsa County alone.[85] Thirty-one accused participants in punishment squads confessed their membership in the Invisible Empire.[86] Four of them were convicted and sentenced to prison, though only a single Klansman—a Broken Arrow constable who had beaten a married woman for "improper relations"—actually served time.[87] Moreover, the national Klan leadership was forced to confront the issue of violence. "Floggers need not attempt to shield themselves behind the power of the Klan," Evans announced. "The Klan has no room for such men."[88]

Across the Southwest, efforts to rein in the freewheeling vigilantism of the Klan now appeared. Exasperated by the participation of police officers and public officials in Klan beatings, the Dallas County Citizens League organized in April 1922 to break the link between the Invisible Empire and public service.[89] The following year Texas Rangers and a few determined prosecutors built successful cases against a handful of night-riding Ku Kluxers.[90] In post-Walton Oklahoma, several hooded legislators supported a "milk and water" anti-Klan bill that barred wearing masks in public. Even though the requirement for Klan officers to register with the state was struck from the bill, the law was nonetheless notable as the first state ban on Ku Klux disguises.[91] In 1924 a collection of anti-Klan groups rose to contest the expansion of the Oklahoma Klan. Within two years, its membership had plummeted to fewer than eighteen thousand.[92]

The culminating episode of the first violent phase of the Klan, the shocking murders at Mer Rouge, fastened a permanent public impression of violence on the Invisible Empire. Together with the Oklahoma Klan war and the public campaign in Texas to curtail night riding, the Louisiana murders made it clear that violence, isolated though it was to specific sections of the Invisible Empire, was undermining the national Klan movement. This prompted the imperial leadership under Evans to forcibly downplay direct moral policing and redeploy hooded energy into political channels. The central role of the Klan hierarchy in reducing violence had been noted by a Texas newspaper, which remarked on "the suspiciously sudden cessation of floggings."[93] But even though such maneuvers reduced the number of violent incidents, they did not eradicate the close association between the Ku Klux Klan and violent disorder.

Provoking Violence in the North

As the Klan's officers acted to eradicate hooded vigilantism in the Southern and Southwestern realms, a second blast of violence shook the Klan movement. Unlike the initial outbreak of night riding, this did not involve the midnight correction of white Protestant behavior. Rather, the occasional spasms of violence that accompanied the expansion of the hooded order into the North in 1923 and continued into 1925 were large-scale and public affairs, often involving hundreds, even thousands, of brawling participants. They also developed out of the disruptive and highly politicized issues of ethnicity, religion, and prohibition enforcement that fueled the growth of the Invisible Empire in the Midwest and mid-Atlantic states. Although the backdrop to the violence was the intrusion of hooded regulators into the homes, schools, and habits of immigrants and Catholics, the clashes themselves took place at Klan marches, mass initiations, and other displays of hooded power in mixed neighborhoods and other contested sites. In these riotous incidents, Klansmen often armed themselves and provoked confrontation by their unwanted gatherings in immigrant and Catholic districts, but organized and enraged opponents of the Invisible Empire inflicted most of the gunshot wounds, broken bones, and bloodied heads on outnumbered knights.

With the characteristic twist that confounded hooded efforts to fit into the mainstream of the New Era, the violent episodes in Northern realms stemmed from the overhaul of the Klan initiated by Hiram Evans to rid the Invisible Empire of its association with night-riding brutality. After pushing the inattentive Colonel Simmons aside in 1922, the new imperial wizard increased the national organization's supervision of local Klans, introduced a drive for new members and greater revenue, and diverted the moral energy of Klansmen from private vigilantism to public political activism. Under the Evans regime, fewer knights had the opportunity to slip out and torment their misbehaving neighbors. On the other hand, in the Northern realms large Klan ceremonies intended to attract members and the commitment to institutionalize Protestant standards through political means invited conflict with the numerous cultural and political enemies of the Invisible Empire.

The new patterns of violence played out most prominently in western Pennsylvania. Evans himself was present in late August 1923 as thousands of knights from nearby states prepared to follow a mass meeting with a march through the grimy industrial town of Carnegie on the outskirts of Pittsburgh. Despite the obviously hostile intentions of Catholics in Carnegie and the refusal by the community's mayor to issue a permit for the march, Evans urged the Pennsylvania Klan leadership to carry on with the parade. Townspeople maneuvered cars to block the path of the oncoming knights and manhandled several marching Klansmen; then, inevitably it seemed, gunfire echoed across the assembly, killing one hooded marcher, Thomas Abbott. Evans appeared to embrace the outbreak of violence since it apparently confirmed the threat to American institutions posed by lawless immigrants and priest-shackled Catholics.[94] "Klansman Abbott was killed because he exercised his constitutionally guaranteed right of peaceable assembly, free speech and free movement over the highways of our country," Evans announced. "We are determined that . . . our great land shall be made safe for native born Americans."[95] In a more private remark, Evans allegedly estimated that Abbott's murder would bring twenty-five thousand additional knights into the Invisible Empire.[96] Breakaway Klansmen later testified that Pennsylvania grand dragon Sam Rich encouraged additional riots "similar to the one in Carnegie" as a way to "bring up [membership in] the Klan."[97]

Whatever Klan leaders may have uttered, the Invisible Empire did not shrink from the consequences of violence at Carnegie. The Klan press celebrated the martyred Abbott, and Evans appealed for "Thomas Abbott nights" at klaverns to raise money and mobilize the hooded armies for further confrontations.[98] Meanwhile Pennsylvania knights challenged their antagonists by marching into a second town. Only a few ragged volleys of gunfire resulted, which a hooded organizer characterized as "a disappointment."[99] Pressing on in early 1924, a third march led to the desired outcome in Lilly, Pennsylvania. Anti-Klan rowdies turned a firehose on the hooded marchers, shooting and brawling ensued, and, in a confused exchange of gunfire, the lives of three local men were sacrificed in the interests of provocation.[100] Since three women who had cheered on the marching Ku Kluxers were beaten by the anti-Klan mob in Lilly, and a jailed Klansman died of pneumonia while in custody after the riot, the Invisible Empire acquired a fresh set of victims on which to build native white Protestant outrage.[101] Even though many ordinary Klansmen feared these dangerous encounters, knights began to make a show of arming themselves ("sometimes for advertising purposes," the same Klan witness later admitted) and exchanging militaristic banter before mass rallies.[102]

Other episodes of mass violence broke out around the time of the Carnegie confrontation and fed the Klan's demand for a resurgence of native-born

American political control of a dangerously pluralistic nation. Nearly two weeks before the Carnegie riot, one hundred Klansmen meeting near Steubenville, Ohio, were assaulted by some three thousand enraged onlookers. Blackjacks and pistols seriously hurt several participants.[103] Eastern Ohio knights called for protection from the governor and the resignation of Steubenville's mayor and police chief for allowing the city to become "a dump hole of moral pollution and degeneracy."[104] Five days after Carnegie, an outdoor naturalization ceremony in New Castle, Delaware, was disrupted by one thousand attackers shouting, according to Klan sources, "Hurrah for the Irish."[105] Amid gunfire and fighting that injured fifty people, escaping knights drove their cars into the anti-Klan crowd. As the fleeing caravan motored through an African American hamlet, local residents added a barrage of stones. The savaged Ku Kluxers urged prosecution of the rioters.[106] Abused Klansmen in New Jersey, whose meetings had been violently interrupted by angry mobs, sent a petition to state officials demanding protection of their right to assemble.[107] One animated Klan supporter dubiously asserted that "Klansmen suffer from violence and usurped authority but never use them." The Invisible Empire, he intoned, "always meets savagery and bigotry with forbearance."[108]

Despite the assurances of loyal Klansmen, the context of recent disorder did not suggest hooded restraint. In the aftermath of the Mer Rouge revelations and the Southwestern atrocities, as the Oklahoma standoff unfolded and the war in the southern Illinois coalfields worsened, and amid evidence of a widening ethnic and religious conflict in Northern communities, the Invisible Empire's claim that it was now the victim of unwarranted violence rather than its perpetrator was met with skepticism. The American Civil Liberties Union agreed with Evans that the Klan's rights had been violated at Carnegie but questioned "the sincerity and genuineness of your sudden concern for free speech" in the light of numerous hooded outrages against labor organizers and Catholics.[109] Although troubled by mob violence against Klan demonstrations, press reaction to anti-Klan rioting usually suggested hooded culpability for its provocative displays. "No local chapter of the Klan can blind itself to its risk and responsibility when it marches through the streets of a city," one typical critique emphasized. "In challenging law and order for the protection of others, it discards law and order for the maintenance of its own rights."[110]

Instead of appearing as a secondary and regionally restricted element of the Klan movement, many observers by this time understood violence to be an essential component of Klan strategy and behavior. The judge in the trials stemming from the Lilly riot specified that "wearing robes and hoods by members of the Ku Klux Klan constituted a challenge to attack."[111] Edward Clarke, the deposed agent of the Simmons regime, stressed in 1924 testimony that hooded knights courted violence at the direction of Atlanta Klan headquarters. Evans had instilled military discipline and central direction in the Invisible Empire, he argued, and so "high officials of the Klan were entirely cognizant of the violence and cruelties carried out by members of the order."[112] The *New York Times* editorialized that the battering of hooded knights in Steubenville was a case of the secret order being "compelled to take a dose of its own medicine." The Klan felt free to attack others, the newspaper pointed out, "but when the Klansmen are set upon by a larger mob, then there are piteous whines and a hasty rush for the protection of the law which the Klan supersedes so long as it has the upper hand."[113] "Whenever the Klan appears," a New Mexico newspaper concluded, "sooner or later there is riot and violence and murder."[114]

In fact, as earlier chapters have shown, many klaverns resisted appeals to violence, and some powerful realms, such as Indiana, were generally devoid of violent episodes. Nevertheless, the continuation of Klan provocations and anti-Klan rioting through the middle of the decade deepened the impression of endemic hooded violence. The themes that underlay Klan riots in the North—prohibition, ethnic and religious tension, and politics—coalesced again in northeastern Ohio in 1924. Prohibition enforcement pitted knights against the drinking and bootlegging immigrant enclaves in the industrial centers near Youngstown. Hooded attempts to purge Catholic influence from the public schools further sharpened conflict. In a projection of power intended to influence the upcoming state election, Klansmen proposed to march into the heart of Niles, Ohio, where the bitterly anti-Klan Knights of the Flaming Circle resided. The buildup to the November march featured several preliminary clashes in which partisans from both sides were shot, stabbed, or beaten. Dynamite blasts rocked the homes of the police chief and the Klan-supported mayor of Niles.[115]

In the end, the Klan march never took place. Armed and angry anti-Klan crowds blocked the roads, pulled surprised knights from their cars, and fired volleys of gunfire at others. Klansmen ran the blockade, and some discharged their own weapons. About a dozen people were seriously hurt before the sheriff disbanded the unofficial Klan constables sworn in by the mayor to protect the march and the state sent in the National Guard. Several Klansmen had to leave the area, don their Guard uniforms, and return to keep the peace they had earlier disturbed.[116]

The violence in Niles broke up the local Klan movement. Clyde Osborne, Ohio's new grand dragon, had hoped the march would reinvigorate the faltering local klaverns, beset by factionalism and the publication of stolen Klan membership lists. To emphasize the appeal of the Invisible Empire as a law-abiding body and to contrast its disciplined comportment with that of its disorderly, bootlegging, alien adversaries, Osborne had ordered the hooded rank and file to disarm and march unmasked. In the aftermath of the melee, the grand dragon appeared powerless to control his knights. The vice-attacking mayor was blamed for fomenting disorder by deputizing Klansmen and then absenting himself from the area as confrontation loomed. And the Knights of the Flaming Circle proved their ability to defend their turf against hooded invaders. Crestfallen and intimidated, many area knights quietly put away their hoods and robes.

The stout and sometimes life-threatening resistance with which anti-Klan mobs met hooded demonstrations diminished the enthusiasm of Midwestern knights for continued confrontation. During the Niles riot a trainload of Klan reinforcements realistically assessed the situation and, without alighting, returned to its point of origin.[117] Days after the violence in Ohio, rail cars filled with armed knights rolled into northwest Indiana. Imperial Wizard Evans blustered to local Klan leaders that he himself was willing to "lead [a] parade right out on the campus of Notre Dame . . . and if some of those priests come out it will be up to us to hit him [*sic*] in the nose."[118] This seeming eagerness to challenge the Catholic bastion of Notre Dame University, however, contrasted with the more cautious behavior of hooded Midwesterners. The preceding May, surprised Klansmen gathering for a similar rally quickly retreated as Notre Dame students tore the robes off outnumbered Ku Kluxers and pelted them with potatoes, bottles, and rocks.[119] Evans then canceled an October South Bend rally meant to influence the coming election, citing violent threats against Klansmen, and rescheduled the event to take place after the vote.[120] The swagger of the Klan representatives failed to conceal the obvious hooded retreat in the face of menacing opposition. The now-meaningless parade attracted no violence and little interest.

The final large-scale outbreaks of anti-Klan rioting took place in Massachusetts in the warm months of 1924 and 1925. Absent from the state was the hooded bravado that had set off violent retribution in Pennsylvania and Ohio. The Klan movement had been met with scorn in the cradle of the American Revolution. In January 1923 the lower house of the Massachusetts legislature unanimously approved a resolution condemning the Invisible Empire as "dangerous to American rights."[121] Even private meetings of the hooded order were imperiled by Boston Mayor Curley's ban on Ku Klux assemblies, a level of repression that stirred reluctant protest from the American Civil Liberties Union. Unable to display their power by marching near immigrant neighborhoods, Massachusetts knights instead were assaulted as they attempted to hold outdoor rallies in several locations outside Worcester in the central part of the state.[122]

The initiative and the bulk of the violent behavior in the 1924 encounters were clearly with the determined enemies of the Klan in Massachusetts. In several cases Klan meetings required police protection. Tracing the location of Klan gatherings, hostile crowds surrounded the rallying knights, trapped them inside their protective circle of automobiles, then beat the hapless Ku Kluxers as they sought to escape.[123] The pattern repeated itself in 1925 with Klansmen on the receiving end of punches, bricks, stones, clubs, and bullets.[124]

Such was the violent reputation of the hooded order that the Klan still took most of the public blame for the violence. After the first major clash, police confiscated weapons from Klansmen arriving for a subsequent open-air rally. As the battles escalated in 1925, Klansmen were more likely to carry weapons and fight back against the anti-Klan mobs. Press accounts of these encounters emphasized Klan armaments and brutality, such as the attack on a police officer by an alleged knight wielding "a piece of steel cable," even while reporting that the hooded participants were more likely to end up bruised and bloodied.[125] After several violent episodes in August 1925, the state Law and Order League asked the governor to ban further Klan meetings "on the ground that they incite to riot."[126] The Invisible Empire's participation in violence once more had undermined its claims to represent community values and good order.

Despite the taste for rioting displayed by a few New England knights, most Klansmen in the region were deterred by violence rather than attracted to the hooded order as a symbol of Americanism under assault. Anti-Klan violence brutally confirmed the reality of the ethnic and religious pluralism of the New Era, making the Klan's demand for a restricted American identity appear as impossible as it was inflammatory. Even without hooded night riders usurping the prerogatives of the police and the courts, the Northern Klan movement's incitement to violence through provocative display, intolerant sentiments, and aggressive political thrusts further confirmed the Invisible Empire's association with disorder and lawlessness. The actual record of violence linked to the Klan thus was more important than the absence of violent activity from the hooded experience of most 1920s Klansmen in confirming the unwelcome place of the Klan movement in New Era society. Hooded testimony from the margins of the Invisible Empire clarified the dispiriting impact of violence on the more cautious rank and file of the Klan movement. "We talked only about 'true Americanism'—never said or did anything against anybody," recalled a Utah knight. "But the newspapers were full of stories about disturbances down South and other places, so I quit because I didn't want people to think I was a racist or bigot."[127] Both by acting violently, even for a limited period in a geographically restricted region, and by attracting violence against itself, the Klan movement severely tested the commitment of its own members and alienated the American mainstream in the postwar years.

Tarring the Robes

The violent accompaniment to the Klan's sagging fortunes after 1925 did further damage to its mainstream aspirations. The nasty resurgence of whipping in the Deep South in 1926 and 1927 prompted another wave of criticism that battered the struggling Invisible Empire. Violent floggings in Alabama forced the state's attorney general to renounce his membership in the Klan and prosecute Ku Klux whipping squads.[128] Press exposés portrayed some of the Alabama moral regulators as misfits and sadists: the former village drunkard now an unforgiving moral zealot, a well-known rake incongruously punishing the sexual misbehavior of others, and a trafficker in illegal whiskey cruelly appraising the uprightness of his neighbors.[129] Georgia state officials felt compelled to suppress a new rash of Klan floggings in their state as well.[130] Persistent Klan vigilantism in one Florida county forced the governor to threaten martial law against Ku Klux outlaws.[131] As the imperial staff of the Invisible Empire desperately sought to revive the Klan movement, these additional outbreaks of violence smothered any hope for renewed vitality.

Not only did the leadership of the Klan fail to stamp out eruptions of violence after 1925, testimony of disaffected Klansmen suggested that agents of the national Klan, following the lead of Evans himself, were deeply implicated in the hooded order's violent career. In 1928 a series of lawsuits between dissident knights and Atlanta loyalists were joined by attempts in several states to disband the Klan. Together these proceedings directed an unforgiving light on the inner workings of the Invisible Empire. The testimony in these inquiries revealed unseemly power struggles among the Klan elite that made a mockery of the claims of brotherly Klannishness.

But the estranged Klansmen involved in the cases also leveled charges of heretofore undisclosed violent acts of unsurpassed brutality. A dissident knight from Texas testified that several men were burned to death in solemn ceremonies carried out before hundreds of assembled Klansmen. These tortures were among the punishments allegedly ordered by informal Klan courts over which, the claim went, Evans sometimes personally presided.[132] Ousted imperial wizard William Simmons suggested that Evans tried to arrange his murder as the two men battled for control of the Invisible Empire.[133] D. C. Stephenson, the disgraced former grand dragon of Indiana, charged a year earlier that a black-clad gang of Ohio knights loyal to Evans had opened fire on a group of Italians in 1923, fatally wounding two of them. Stephenson recalled that Evans did not deny the incident but instead had joked that the gunmen should have been more accurate.[134] Others stepped forward to claim that they had been instructed to kill by their hooded superiors.[135] Pennsylvania knights reported that the realm's grand dragon ordered the kidnapping of a small girl from her grandparents, who never recovered the child.[136]

None of these remarkable allegations were proven true, but other testimony revealed a cynical manipulation of violence by state and national Klan leaders, much of it at the expense of rank-and-file knights. An Ohio Klansman admitted that Ku Kluxers in Dayton "bombed their own meetings to increase membership."[137] Simmons alleged that after a Klansman nearly died in anti-Klan rioting in Perth Amboy, New Jersey, Evans observed, "If the Klan can make it look as if we are being persecuted, it will help increase our membership."[138] The judge in a Pennsylvania inquiry concluded that Evans's provocative actions before the Carnegie riot made the imperial wizard "directly responsible for the riot and bloodshed which ensued."[139] In another proceeding an alienated Indiana Klan officer recounted that speakers sent from Atlanta unsuccessfully urged local Klansmen to display more of the violent "Southern spirit" of the Klan to reverse the order's decline.[140]

Uttered amid the wreckage of the once-prosperous Klan movement, these charges did not materially contribute to the decline of the already shattered dynamism of the Invisible Empire. The most dramatic allegations of violence made by disaffected knights were probably untrue. Others may have been exaggerated. But the testimony was sufficient to confirm that Evans and his lieutenants had played with fire in their attempts to build and sustain the Klan enterprise. Too often Klan officials tolerated violence in their pursuit of native white Protestant cultural hegemony or incited violence against the order to ignite white Protestant militancy. Those decisions undercut Evans's desire to extend the Klan's mainstream influence through political engagement. Moreover, disputes over violence worsened the antagonism between local klaverns and Atlanta-based officials seeking tighter control over the movement, a struggle that carried over into the Klan's political machinations. In both its violent manifestations and its political ambitions, the Klan organization pushed beyond the grassroots support that had made the Invisible Empire a social movement of national consequence.

7

The Search for Political Influence and the Collapse of the Klan Movement

IN THE SUMMER HEAT OF WASHINGTON IN 1925, the Invisible Empire arranged a massive public demonstration of its power and unity. Carried by some fifty chartered trains and countless automobiles, by August 8 tens of thousands of hooded loyalists had crowded into the nation's capital. For about three and a half hours, a stream of unmasked white-robed marchers, estimated by police to number between thirty-five thousand and forty-five thousand, paraded down Pennsylvania Avenue, transforming the muggy thoroughfare into what one observer reported "looked like a gigantic snow bank." Klan bands and drill teams entertained the onlookers packed "four and five deep" along the parade route while banners, flags, and flecks of red, yellow, and olive drab–colored hats and robes stood out amid the overwhelming flood of white regalia. At the head of the procession, dramatically costumed in a purple Klan robe, Imperial Wizard Hiram Evans savored the applause of the crowd. Although a thunderstorm scattered the Klansmen after the parade, the day had been a triumph of Ku Klux spectacle. "Sight Astonishes Capital," the *New York Times* headlined its report.[1]

Impressive as display, the Washington march nonetheless could not conceal the faltering influence and organizational disarray of the Invisible Empire. Broken by scandal and political setbacks, the enormous Texas and Indiana realms sent disappointingly small delegations to the event. The huge contingent from Pennsylvania, the largest in the parade, masked the internal division and resentment toward national Klan representatives that would shortly rip asunder that state's Klan. Akron's klavern sent one thousand delegates to the march, along with a women's glee club that attracted special attention. But the significant expenditures entailed in such ceremony, including the maintenance of a paramilitary drill squad and the proposed construction of a large auditorium, split apart the Akron Klan movement within a year.[2] Hooded secrecy surrounding the event prevented Washington authorities from having sufficient water or medical facilities available for overheated and exhausted knights, many of whom required refreshment from the canteens of U.S. Marines stationed at the endpoint of the march.

In 1925 the political clout of the Invisible Empire suggested by the march was as gossamer as the movement's pretensions of solidarity. Evans, whose political ambitions for the hooded order had led him to move imperial headquarters to the nation's capital that year, hoped that the involvement in local civic affairs that had spurred the rapid expansion of the Klan movement at the beginning of the decade could be steered toward state and national political influence. In numerous communities aroused Klansmen had asserted important control over school policy and teacher appointments, prohibition and morals enforcement, and public works. Encouraged by the Klan hierarchy to vote as a bloc in obedience to secret Ku Klux endorsements, state Klans had elected fellow knights and sympathizers to office across the country. Journalists emphasized the "invisible government" exercised by the hooded order over state legislatures and governors in Texas, Oklahoma, Colorado, Oregon, and Indiana. With the election of hooded senators in Texas and Colorado, Ku Klux influence crept into Washington.

But by the close of the 1925 legislative session, the bright promise of mainstream political influence suggested by the Invisible Empire's political thrusts in 1922 and 1923 turned to disappointment. Unlike the Ku Klux activists who shook up local communities by seizing control of school boards, law enforcement, and town councils, hooded legislators did not transform state government into nodes of native-born white Protestant cultural assertiveness. Even in states considered Klan strongholds, legislatures failed to pass significant packages of Klan-approved laws. Instead, Klansmen in politics proved inept as legislators and executives, even if eager to dole out patronage to hooded associates and indulge in fraternal power struggles.

For a few years the Invisible Empire excelled at political pressure, during which time most New Era politicians resisted forthright debate on the hooded order. But the Klan was a divisive, irritating presence in politics, hampering party discipline and constructive governance. It did not prove to be the foundation of a winning political coalition with a realistic chance of enacting a legislative agenda. After meager performances from the Klan politicians elected in 1922, Ku Klux political influence peaked in 1924 with the election of hooded state governments in Indiana and Colorado. Nationally the Invisible Empire's ability to stave off a proposal to denounce the hooded order by name at the Democratic national convention in New York City suggested the political strength of the Klan movement. But the noteworthy failures of hooded lawmakers in the Indiana and Colorado realms and the destructive aftermath of the convention fight derailed the Klan's bid for lasting political legitimacy. Exposed as a problem for political parties and a poor vehicle for legislative accomplishment, Klan political influence plummeted in 1925, matching the drop off in membership that accompanied spectacular scandals besetting Klan officials in Indiana, Colorado, and other hooded power bases. The public spotlight fell on the foibles and misbehavior of Klan leaders, demoralizing schisms between local and national Klan factions, and the manifold weaknesses of the Klan movement. Thus the *New York Times* accurately diagnosed the quixotic purpose of the 1925 extravaganza as a "two-fold object of impressing the Government . . . and counteracting the reported tendency toward disintegration" in the once-imposing secret order.[3] Like much of Ku Klux ceremony, the Klan's attempt to assert national political power was by then an earnest and theatrical exercise of flamboyant but essentially empty gestures.

The Texture of Hooded Politics

Contradictions that were ultimately fatal to the Klan movement complicated the hooded order's activism in politics and public policy. The secrecy and fraternal nature of the organization, which strongly appealed to many rank-and-file Klansmen, aligned awkwardly with the need for public advocacy that accompanied involvement in statecraft. Some knights had difficulty separating the fraternal aspects of their identity from the political activism and deal making demanded by Klan officers. These Klansmen preferred to use their votes solely in support of fellow knights rather than to elect sympathetic outsiders who had secretly pledged to cooperate with Klan leaders while in office. Pat Emmons, the exalted cyclops of a northern Indiana klavern, reported that knights from his region "believed at all times in going down the line back of any man, regardless of his politics, if he was a real klansman and could match [membership] cards." Emmons and his fellows bitterly resented attempts from Imperial Wizard Evans and his Indiana lieutenants to have U.S. Senator James Watson "crammed down on our throats" without proof that Watson, a strong ally of the hooded order, had been naturalized into the Invisible Empire.[4] Policymaking by Klansmen in high office sometimes resembled the business relationships of Klannishness more than it did actual governance. Clarence Morley, the Ku Klux governor of Colorado, expended more energy trying to appoint fellow Klansmen to government posts than he did in pursuing substantive legislation. Hooded mayors, school board officers, and police chiefs oftentimes seemed to view their official responsibilities as fulfilled once they had dismissed Catholics and Jews from offices under their control and filled the empty positions with reliable Klansmen.

Stubborn attachment to the fraternal understanding of Klan politics often reflected quarrels over the nature of the movement between grassroots knights and the organization's hierarchy. Emmons had "heated arguments" with his grand dragon, an Evans loyalist, who pushed the alienated Hoosier knight to accept that "this organization is not a Lodge, not a club . . . [and] not a benevolent organization," but rather "an army of Protestant Americans . . . built to get political control."[5] Confusion over the purpose of the Klan movement was exacerbated by Evans himself, who blandly maintained that the Invisible Empire was "not in politics" even as he sought to impose greater organizational discipline in pursuit of political influence.[6]

However much political involvement inflamed divisions among Klansmen, the goals of the Klan movement of the 1920s necessitated it. Just as the Invisible Empire mobilized silently to control moral behavior and public institutions, so too did it direct its secret membership to influence public policy. In the pluralistic New Era, the intersection between politics, private behavior, and contested American institutions required hooded political action if the Klan's vision of Americanism were to prevail. Klan leaders assembled an intricate underground political machine to mobilize hooded voters but avoided the public manifestations of a political movement. The imperial wizard's Cheshire Cat–like disavowal of political engagement was intended to remove any suspicion that the Invisible Empire would launch a third party to challenge the political establishment. Aware of the short life and limited accomplishments of the People's Party, the Progressive Party, and other rebellious movements that had broken away from the dominant party arrangement, Klan leaders determined to work within the architecture of the two-party system.

Evans was open in acknowledging that the Invisible Empire's program of immigration restriction, public school support, prohibition enforcement, and defense of native-born white Protestant values and cultural dominance "must result in political action and can be carried out in no other way."[7] But in keeping with the Invisible Empire's preference for secret actions and hidden influence, Evans determined to play the public game of politics in the shadows. He would influence officeholders and politicians to act in the interests of the Klan while the organization cultivated its image of mysterious authority. Cloaked strategists worked both sides of the party divide, though the Klan usually established stronger relationships with the dominant party in a region—Democrats in the South and often Republicans in the Midwest and along the Pacific Coast. In some realms, political alliances compelled hooded officials to ignore their own partisan identities. Republican grand dragons managed the mostly Democratic Klan politics of Oklahoma and Arkansas while for a time a Democratic grand dragon solidified the hold of the Invisible Empire over Indiana's Republican establishment. This approach combined the nonpartisan pressure-group tactics of such lobbies as the Anti-Saloon League with the danger and uncertainty that was associated with Ku Klux vigilantism. "All [the Klan's] organized unity, all its ability to strike suddenly and in the dark, all its secret information and its terrorism, are even more effective [in politics] than in ordinary life," observed the reporter Stanley Frost, since politicians were easily intimidated by shows of force.[8]

The ideal of efficient Ku Klux political mobilization was best exemplified by the "military machine" developed by D. C. Stephenson, the Midwest's primary hooded organizer and the preening grand dragon of the powerful Indiana realm. Stephenson had risen from obscure origins in Texas. Searching for an outlet to express his pent-up ambitions, as a young man he bounced from job to job in a string of Southwestern and Midwestern towns: organizing for socialist politicians in Oklahoma, doing newspaper and printing work in Oklahoma and Iowa, pursuing a stint of soldiering at the end of World War I, and finally gaining experience as a traveling salesman and coal dealer in Ohio and Indiana. Along the way he romanced and then abandoned several women. Then Stephenson found his identity in the Klan. His oratory, honed by a lifetime of political rallies and sales patter, had a magnetic appeal to Midwestern knights. His well-fed face and stout figure suggested prosperity and vitality. His blue eyes commanded attention and respect. Stephenson covered up his past and began life anew as the "Old Man," the charismatic icon of the Indiana Klan. He was just over thirty years old.

Stephenson was indifferent to the moral agenda of the Klan movement, showing no personal loyalty to the codes of sexual restraint and prohibition compliance that motivated the activism of many grassroots knights. Moreover, public policy interested him only in so far as it could be manipulated to increase his leverage over public officials or provide him with concrete financial rewards. Yet the vain, personally undisciplined Stephenson possessed a rare talent for the intricacies of political organization and hidden electoral influence. Under his supervision, the Indiana Klan burrowed into the vitals of the state's electoral system and established a network of political communication and mobilization that commanded respect from politicians and officeholders, and outlasted the brief tenure of the flamboyant grand dragon.[9]

At Stephenson's insistence, each klavern in Indiana maintained a political committee that investigated all candidates for local and county office. In addition to party affiliation, these committees determined the ethnic background, religion, and fraternal associations of aspirants for office and their family members, including the schools attended by candidates' children. They also drew up thumbnail sketches of each candidate, recording representative political positions of interest to the Invisible Empire, such as prohibition, the World Court, and, most consistently, the candidate's stated outlook on the Ku Klux Klan. Data on state and national candidates were passed up to state officials.[10] Slates of local, county, state, and national candidates were then drawn up and distributed to Klan members. These Ku Klux "information bulletins" noted the candidates who were favorable toward the Klan, those who were opposed, and those who took a neutral position.[11] The hooded rank and file were made to understand by realm officials that silence regarding the Invisible Empire in such a profile indicated "that candidate is a Klansman."[12]

The better organized realms, including Indiana, also developed procedures for selecting a single Klan candidate from a pool of hooded rivals. If two or more Indiana Klansmen were on the ticket for the same office, a confidential discussion on the floor of the klavern settled on the knight who would receive the united support of his hooded brethren.[13] Klaverns in Mahoning County, Ohio, also held internal elections to choose between contending Klansmen.[14] Arkansas and Texas klaverns conducted "elimination primaries" in advance of official elections. These secret Klan canvasses, in which rank-and-file Ku Kluxers cast ballots by mail or in special gatherings, concentrated the strength of hooded voters behind a single office seeker in the primary or general election.[15] Usually Klansmen who were defeated in the Invisible Empire's internal vote dropped out of the race and endorsed the collective choice of area knights. On some occasions, hooded strategists allowed several reputed Klansmen to populate a ticket so as to misdirect anti-Klan activists from the authentic hooded candidate. In the 1922 Texas senatorial campaign that raised the first Klansman into the U.S. Senate, Evans, at the time the national Klan's second in command, permitted one primary contender to go public with his Klan affiliation while the Ku Klux hierarchy quietly shifted hooded support to the eventual winner, Earle B. Mayfield, who concealed his Klan ties.[16]

Once candidates had been screened, the "military machine" organized the vote. Hooded officials at the county, township, precinct, and block levels monitored support for Klan-backed candidates and helped direct the vote.[17] The grand dragon urged local Klan officers "to diplomatically get such information [from the secret bulletins] to Protestant people in your County."[18] Klansmen distributed slates of favored candidates in Protestant neighborhoods, in most cases immediately before election day. Unlike the Klan's internal documents, these lists did not discuss candidates' attitudes toward the Klan nor mention the Invisible Empire, since a public association with the hooded order would backfire against many vote seekers. Instead, the compact slates listed those candidates who were Catholics, Protestants, or members of Protestant fraternal orders, allowing "100% American" chauvinists to select the culturally correct ticket. One such handbill reminded voters that the township trustee "employs all township school teachers." Another slate, labeled "Protestant School Ticket," identified the five levers on the voting machine (along with the names of the Klan-backed candidates) that would guarantee "better school conditions."[19] Indiana knights were adept at delivering such lists, tightly bound by clothespins, onto the porches of voters by election day.

Klansmen elsewhere imitated the Indiana model of hooded mobilization. In some Pennsylvania communities well disposed toward the Invisible Empire, Klansmen prepared cards listing the names of favorable candidates for public distribution. Labeled "the People's Choice," these slates appeared without attribution in mailboxes on election mornings.[20] Colorado Klansmen blanketed neighborhoods during a 1924 primary election with "pink tickets" identifying the religious allegiances of candidates and denoting Protestants who were nevertheless "unsatisfactory because of Roman Catholic Affiliations and Friendships."[21] In a close approximation of the Indiana system, Colorado grand dragon John Galen Locke organized a political chain of command from the county level down to individual neighborhoods in which more than six Klansmen resided. He rooted the standards of secrecy and discipline of the system in "those of the United States army, where the command of a superior officer is never questioned."[22] Dallas knights maintained an extensive system that made use of poll-tax lists to keep tabs on hooded voters. These knights were taxed one dollar each for election expenses and directed to boost the Klan's favored candidates in their precincts. Klan No. 66 operated its own campaign headquarters until the completion of the Democratic primary elections—which in Texas determined the ultimate winners—then let the party organization take over.[23] Hooded poll watchers stood vigil in Arkansas and in some Maryland communities, just as they did in Indiana.[24]

Even when political issues were confined to matters of local school administration and small-town governance, Klansmen employed the essential elements of hooded political mobilization. Dormant after its activities on behalf of Oregon's mandatory public school attendance bill some seven months earlier, the electioneering machine of the La Grande, Oregon, klavern sprang into motion in June 1923 behind the school board candidacies of two local knights. The hooded assembly appointed a committee to design "separate tickets [to] be printed for our candidates, giving the reason why they should be elected and these [to] be placed under every door in town on Sunday, June 17." All Klansmen residing in the election district also received election notices, which they were instructed to return to the klavern secretary after they voted. Turnout for the school board election was half again higher than that of recent school elections, and both hooded candidates won their races.[25] In Wisconsin, where Klan political influence rarely extended beyond local affairs, a hooded organizational network nonetheless operated. Following the selection of candidates in the klavern, each knight was expected to extol the virtues of the Klan-backed office seeker to ten non-Klansmen. This "decade" technique expanded hooded influence in local elections, usually without even mentioning the Invisible Empire.[26]

The short-term effectiveness of Klan political techniques in Anaheim, California, where a handful of policemen performed their duties in hoods and robes during a period of Klan domination, was underscored by the measures adopted by anti-Klan forces to expunge Ku Klux influence over city hall. After regaining control of the city council from the Klan in 1925, the political foes of the Invisible Empire made it illegal to disseminate "handbills and flyers in public places." Suppressing the Klan voting slates that mysteriously surfaced just before elections was only the first step in denying political influence to the Invisible Empire in this Orange County municipality. The Anaheim council also gave itself the power to prevent private associations "detrimental to the public" from recruiting new members within city limits. The hidden ranks and underground communications network of the Invisible Empire were so effective that some political opponents of the Klan declined to compete with them.[27]

The capabilities of Ku Klux electoral organization were illustrated in the 1924 campaign in St. Joseph County, Indiana, which contained a large immigrant population hostile to the hooded order. At the direction of state Klan officials, county Klansmen had organized a special body of one hundred knights, split evenly between Republicans and Democrats. This cloaked intelligence force forwarded information on local political conditions to the hierarchy and agitated in the interest of Klan-backed candidates. The local Klan also slipped hooded spies onto the staff of each of the county's three major newspapers. These agents, including the son of one anti-Klan editor, gave advance notice of upcoming editorials and endorsements, allowing the Klan to prepare responses to adverse stories, including consumer boycotts or takeover bids for the papers that quieted some of the anti-Klan reporting.

In preparation for the election, Klan leaders offered local Protestant ministers honorary membership in the Invisible Empire and even "a little money" for pro-Klan speaking engagements, so as to maximize the platform for electioneering. Having gained access to churches, Klan operatives placed their political slates inside Protestant Sunday school newspapers the weekend before the vote. On election eve Klansmen fanned out to leave a special copy of the *Fiery Cross* on the porch of each known Protestant voter. Ku Klux officials boasted that they distributed fifty thousand Klan slates overnight in South Bend. On election day a hooded nerve center serviced by a bank of telephones directed a fleet of two hundred automobiles to ferry Protestant voters to the polls while a band of female hooded volunteers stood at the ready to watch the children of "100%" women while they voted. With a solid yet secret hooded vote, the Klan's slate was elected to office.[28] Performances such as this justified journalistic descriptions of the Klan political machine as a cloaked "super-Tammany" that was active across the breadth of the Invisible Empire.[29]

Rarely did the political machinations of the Klan operate so smoothly, even in Indiana. As with other matters in the Invisible Empire, engagement and coordination in political matters varied within realms and among individual klaverns. State officials frequently complained that klavern leaders ignored political work and failed to provide timely information about candidates.[30] Exalted cyclopes in Georgia sometimes neglected to read political bulletins from realm headquarters to their knights. "A large number of . . . your Klan have failed to register and are therefore not able to vote in your election," Georgia's exasperated grand dragon grumbled to one klavern leader in 1926.[31] In their only organized strike for political power, Michigan Klansmen failed to settle on a single hooded candidate in the 1924 Republican gubernatorial primary. The two Klansmen on the ballot split the vote of the Invisible Empire and were both defeated.[32]

Elsewhere disappointed Ku Klux office seekers occasionally refused to abide by the judgment of their fellows to support rival Klansmen and continued their candidacies in close races. Such a circumstance divided the Klan vote in the 1924 Arkansas Democratic gubernatorial race, thus effectively ending the Invisible Empire's pretensions to statewide political influence. The Arkansas campaign illustrated other difficulties that by 1924 disrupted hooded political discipline. Democratic Klansmen resented the intrusion of Republican grand dragon James A. Comer, a top Evans lieutenant, into the affairs of their party. Disapproval of Comer's high-handed manner in selecting the official hooded aspirant for the Democratic gubernatorial nomination resulted in significant defections by unhappy knights and defeat for Comer's hooded favorite. One Klan rebel reported that "Judge Martineau was the anti-Klan candidate. Yet, he got lots of Klan votes. . . . [I] voted for Martineau; because I liked him *personally*."[33]

Disputes within the Invisible Empire even hurt the formidable Indiana Klan machine. At least one Hoosier exalted cyclops temporarily withheld detailed local information from realm headquarters, fearing that Stephenson would bypass grassroots Klan sentiment and throw the concentrated hooded vote in unanticipated directions.[34] Once the Old Man, weakened by a destructive rivalry with Imperial Wizard Evans, began to lose his hold over the Indiana Klan, slate making became even more centralized in the hands of realm officials appointed by the national headquarters.[35] This change put the Klan's political organization out of touch with local conditions and prompted resistance from grassroots Klansmen. A caustic tug of war resulted between klavern officials committed to community activism and realm officers beholden to Evans.

Exalted Cyclops Pat Emmons complained that all the funds of the St. Joseph klavern were burned up in political work with little benefit to the rank-and-file Klansmen and to the detriment of local fraternalism and ceremony.[36] W. Lee Smith, the Indiana realm's chief of staff and later grand dragon, angrily demanded loyalty and political cooperation from Emmons while threatening to suspend the charter of the recalcitrant South Bend local.[37] At the height of the dispute, Emmons barred the grand dragon and his political exhortations, "by man power" if necessary, from the floor of his klavern. Political skullduggery had destroyed the spirit of the Klan, the onetime evangelist charged. His knights "felt that they had been sold a nice suit of clothes [by the leaders of the Invisible Empire] and [instead] had been delivered a suit of overalls."[38] Alienated from the Invisible Empire, Emmons halted payments to state and national Klan headquarters and reconfigured his klavern as the Valley Tabernacle Association, an independent club for native-born white Protestant men "which was not to be a political organization in any sense of the word." Some eight hundred former St. Joseph Klansmen followed Emmons into the breakaway group.[39]

In neighboring Ohio, Grand Dragon Clyde Osborne, a committed GOP activist, began to take similar liberties in dictating electoral choices for Buckeye Klansmen. In 1924 a political unknown, Klansman Joseph Sieber, challenged a prominent anti-Klan candidate for the Republican gubernatorial nomination. Even though Sieber's home Klan, the massive Akron klavern, did not make its endorsement of Sieber binding on the hooded membership, Osborne organized Klan support behind the hooded dark horse. Sieber made a strong showing, but he lost to anti-Klan former governor Harry Davis in the primary election. Sieber then announced a willingness to continue as an independent candidate, a successful tactic used by the Klan to elect candidates in states dominated by one party. Osborne, however, denounced the beaten Klansman as "Ubiquitous Joe" and commanded the hooded rank and file to switch their support to the incumbent Democratic governor, who was considered neutral on the Klan.[40] This directive required Ku Klux voters to split the ticket, since the Invisible Empire also endorsed Republican Calvin Coolidge for president. Temporary success rewarded the 1924 exercise in political gymnastics as both Coolidge and Democratic Ohio governor "Vic" Donahey remained in office.[41] Donahey, however, vetoed the Klan's 1925

"Bible bill," requiring daily Bible readings in public schools, which had been the Invisible Empire's principal legislative achievement. In 1926, Klan voters received a green ticket once again instructing loyal knights to vote for Sieber. The slate was purportedly the work of the Ohio Good Government League. Osborne, however, served as the secretary for the phantom league; he and his lieutenants had crafted the endorsements.[42] Broken by infighting in the state's largest klavern and dissatisfied with the hairpin turns required by hooded politics, Ohio Klansmen ignored Osborne's directive. The Akron Klan refused to issue an endorsement for the election, and Sieber stumbled to defeat, winning only two Ohio counties.[43]

Evans himself redirected the Invisible Empire's political attention to Washington, nursing national political ambitions for his talented political troubleshooter, attorney William Zumbrunn, a sophisticated insider capable of wielding hidden influence for the Klan in the august chambers of Congress. The imperial wizard emphasized to a hooded skeptic that "what the Klan must do is to not spend their time just on the local program, but on the national program." Soon, Evans supposedly confided, "we can control the United States Senate" and perhaps "get a man who is favorable in . . . for President of the United States."[44] Surrendering to visions of Klan senators, congressional delegations, and possibly even a hooded president, Evans allowed the national Klan to drift dangerously away from the grassroots political concerns that remained the anchor of hooded political power in the 1920s. In turn, some local Klans withdrew from political activism. Others recognized insuperable barriers to hooded political influence. In urban communities with substantial Catholic and immigrant populations, some Klansmen did not even attempt to pursue Ku Klux politics beyond the neighbourhood level. A Pittsburgh exalted cyclops counseled a fellow knight "who was running for office to make his contribution to the Catholic Church" and conceal his ties to the Klan.[45]

Hooded political engagement clearly heightened the tension between, on the one hand, the local autonomy and community initiative that had first energized the Klan movement as a civic force and, on the other, the imperatives of centralized control that were formalized in Klan doctrine. In public, Evans insisted that the voting information distributed by hooded officials was merely advisory and that ordinary Klansmen were "free to act upon it as they see fit," without coercion from the Klan hierarchy.[46] Yet in a speech to grand dragons, the imperial wizard had identified "the idea of co-ordination" as a central strength of the organization that allowed the Invisible Empire to "function . . . almost entirely as a unit."[47] Klan officials celebrated the highly organized communications network that could, according to Stanley Frost, mobilize "the entire membership . . . in less than two hours."[48] The reporter estimated that "in nearly ninety per cent of the cases . . . the Klan apparently has cast a practically solid vote," which, as in Indiana, sparked additional support from white Protestants outside the hooded order.[49] In tight campaigns, realm leaders interrupted regular klavern business and turned meetings into political rallies. Colorado Klan officials threatened that knights faced suspension from hooded concord if they failed to register to vote.[50]

Political coordination made for effective electoral influence, but many rank-and-file knights acted like the cogs in the political wheel that the system made them out to be. Frost found many Klansmen to be "docile and dependent," waiting for "the word" to come down from headquarters determining for whom they should cast ballots.[51] Such knights did not resemble the alert defenders of pure Americanism extolled in the mythology of the Invisible Empire. Political convictions, aside from a universal reaction against Catholics and "aliens," could not be deeply rooted in such a system of arranged voting. Indeed, dissident Klansmen observed that the spirit and function of Klan fraternalism were betrayed as the movement turned to politics. As the order gathered in new members to strengthen the political clout of the Invisible Empire, klaverns became too crowded for effective fellowship or secret rituals.[52] Frost speculated that noticeable shortcomings of the Klan in 1924—"the acceptance of riffraff members, the carelessness about collecting dues and even initiation fees, the tolerance of grafters and self-seeking leaders in minor places"—stemmed from the leadership's absorption in political affairs.[53] Some local Klansmen, appealing to the original purposes of the secret order, struck back against the national organization's close supervision of hooded voting. Emmons and other Indiana klavern leaders encouraged their knights to ignore the headquarters voting guides and support Democrats and Republicans of their choice if actual Klansmen were not candidates for office.[54]

❖

Despite the corrosive problems associated with the hooded entry into politics, an ineluctable logic drove the Klan into electoral activism. The Klan movement arose partly to remedy the political system's failure to safeguard "American" practices, values, and laws in a dangerously pluralistic republic. "The Klan teaches that the rights of American citizenship should be exercised in the fullest degree by all loyal Americans so that foreign and un-American influences shall not control the destinies and sap the loyalty of this nation," a Texas great titan reminded an audience of Ku Klux officers in 1923.[55] Prohibition enforcement was one practical example of a cultural contest that required political involvement to reinforce the rule of law and native white Protestant moral control. "We are working here to assist in law enforcement," related an El Paso Klansman. "That's why we got into politics."[56] Others detected similar stakes in the battle over public schools. Klan leaders expanded these local insights into a uniform civic commitment that was sustainable only through political action. Since vigilant public institutions sympathetic to the Invisible Empire were vitally important to the continued supremacy of native-born white Protestant values, argued the Texas great titan, "the Klan in every city stands adamantly for good government."[57] Klansmen had a solemn obligation not just to vote but to cast ballots informed by hooded principles and, at times, specifically directed by their Ku Klux superiors.

The hooded resolve to act politically arose from grassroots conditions as much as from instructions issued by the Klan hierarchy. Unresponsive public authorities and elite indifference to the infrastructure that nurtured democracy had propelled Klansmen into local political activism. In the Colorado community of Cañon City, Klansmen organized against "an old political group" that "owned all the real estate and the business houses and controlled the two banks." Under the misrule of the "gang," recalled a hooded knight, "our schools were no good . . . our streets were dirt, our sidewalks wooden. . . . There were no lights in any of the public schools. We members of the Klan decided that we wanted to make a change in that, which we did."[58] Klaverns across the country acted in similar ways as the second Klan emerged as a major phenomenon in the early 1920s.

Given the centrality of political action in the formation of the second Klan, the project of electing fellow knights to office and seizing the levers of power to fight off the challenge of ethnic and religious pluralism was a natural outgrowth of the grassroots Klan movement. Yet the bid for mainstream political influence championed by Evans nevertheless compromised the community basis of the Klan movement and imposed the interests of the national Klan organization over the diverse constituent parts of the Invisible Empire. Beyond the sacrifice of grassroots energy that followed from a state and national political emphasis, the stakes of the imperial wizard's political gamble were high. "The really vital strength, the true hope or menace, of the Ku Klux Klan lies in politics," Frost declared in early 1924.[59] The momentum of the movement would be lost without the full-scale jump into political activity.

Ku Klux political engagement was necessary to sustain the Klan enterprise, but political setbacks were likely to tear the hooded movement apart. Frost reported in 1924 that Klan officials believed "they will have difficulty even holding the organization together without a [political] victory, and that it is absolutely necessary if they are to keep on growing." The hooded power brokers also knew, he continued, "how fast their mushroom growth will crumble under any adversity."[60] By steering Klansmen—often reluctantly— into political action, Evans and his associates created significant expectations from the rank and file. A social movement premised on the need to fortify

American institutions against destabilizing challenges demanded results from its political ventures that went beyond electing candidates. As Evans argued at the Klan's 1924 Imperial Klonvocation, true Americanism "means allowing Americans [meaning native-born white Protestants, not tainted 'Cosmopolitans'] to determine what, as a nation, they wish to do, and then to do it."[61] Concrete policy achievements that institutionalized Ku Klux values needed to accumulate if the hooded entry into politics were to be justified. As Frost indicated, the Klan in politics "is playing for results alone, while the ordinary political party must play chiefly for office."[62]

As was the case with nativism, anti-Catholicism, and even moral vigilantism, political mobilization undermined the Klan movement even as it attracted members and raised the profile of the Invisible Empire. Just as it was more difficult to control state legislatures and congressional delegations than it had been to pack school boards and sheriffs' offices with like-minded neighbors, the Klan hierarchy discovered that it was even harder to develop workable legislation that would significantly alter public policy. The hooded empire had the ability to place friends in office, but its political network was ill suited to the task of lawmaking. Klan politicians and officeholders discovered that, in the oft-repeated words of hooded rhetoricians, putting "none but Americans on guard" in public office was inadequate as a means to advance the concerns of rank-and-file knights.[63] Such a strategy also highlighted the degree to which Klan politics involved a deliberate effort to empower the national coterie of hooded officers, most obviously Imperial Wizard Evans himself, the master draftsman of the project to assert Klan authority in public life. While the political strength of the Invisible Empire was genuine and influential in electoral terms, it was also fragile and easily disrupted. The early political successes of the movement masked that weakness. Ironically, the surreptitious and mysterious qualities of the Klan movement that were the basis of its political power also concealed, for a short while, the Invisible Empire's fatal political shortcomings.

Hollow Victories

The Klan movement burst into American politics in 1922 with an immediate impact that startled observers outside the hooded brotherhood. In its early Southwestern hotbed, the Invisible Empire filled sheriff's offices, judgeships, and municipal positions with Klansmen or open sympathizers with the cloaked order. The victory in Dallas County was so thorough that Texas knights took to the streets in a spontaneous victory march that mocked the beaten anti-Klan candidates and pilloried newspapers that were critical of the Ku Klux movement.[64] More noteworthy to national observers were the hooded gains in state capitals and Congress. Chief executives considered friendly to the Invisible Empire governed in Texas and Arkansas, where the governor's secretary was a prominent knight. Texas Klansmen boasted that they enjoyed a majority in both houses of the state legislature. No major opposition to the hooded order was evident in the Arkansas legislature, unlike in other Southwestern states. Arkansas legislators acknowledged the power of the Klan, and critics of the Ku Kluxers kept their own counsel.[65] Although Jack Walton defeated the Klan favorite for governor in Oklahoma, political reporters asserted that "the masked crowd has a clear majority in the lower house and is strong enough in the upper to make its influence count when necessary."[66] Despite fallout from the power struggle between Simmons and Evans, Georgia Klansmen helped defeat a governor who had suggested that the Klan unmask, replacing him with a more compliant chief executive.[67]

Special notice was paid in 1922 to the sudden rise to political power of the Invisible Empire in Oregon, symbolized by the surprising triumph of Democrat Walter Pierce over Republican incumbent Ben Olcott in a state with "a confirmed Republican habit." Olcott was an outspoken enemy of the Klan. After vigilante incidents in southern Oregon in 1921, he issued a proclamation ordering "that unlawfully disguised men be kept from the streets," and he vigorously advanced the prosecution of Klansmen suspected of vigilante violence. Yet in 1922, Pierce, "a perennial and oft-defeated aspirant for gubernatorial honors, was swept into office by the largest majority ever accorded a Governor of the State." Klansmen intended not to empower Oregon Democrats but to punish Olcott and to reward Pierce for his advocacy of mandatory public schooling. The journalist Waldo Roberts emphasized that "the Klan controls the State House of Representatives, controls by a small majority the State Senate, and the plums are going out, not to Democrats, but in the main to those Pierce supporters of both parties who are either members of the Klan or not actually opposed to it."[68] In actuality the Klan had firm control of less than one-quarter of the Oregon Senate, and a hooded monopoly on patronage was uncertain—but in the immediate aftermath of the election, Invisible power seemed unassailable.[69]

In 1922 the Klan also made its mark on national offices. Analysts estimated that some seventy-five congressional representatives "owe[d] their election in large part to the support of the masked organization."[70] The election of Texas Klansman Earle Mayfield to the U.S. Senate, however, was the Klan's signal political victory that year. Evans played an important role in the campaign, plotting strategy, browbeating Mayfield's hooded rivals into supporting roles in the electoral drama, and, most likely, funneling Klan money into the race to overcome legal challenges to Mayfield's bid. When opponents contested

Mayfield's right to the Senate seat, charging undue Klan influence and excessive campaign expenditures, Evans stage-managed the defense. Zumbrunn earned his spurs as a savvy political counsel for the Klan as Mayfield's attorney in the inquiry, but the investigation unearthed evidence of Klan violence and a thirst for power by Evans that hurt both the Klan and its imperial wizard. Ultimately, even as he publicly repudiated his membership in the Invisible Empire, Mayfield took his place as a hooded senator. The Senate seat came at a cost to Evans and offered uncertain benefits, but he was willing to pay the price to gain a foothold in the nation's most powerful political institution.[71]

Despite the success of Klan-backed candidates in 1922, evidence that the Invisible Empire was more adept at targeting enemies than at producing Klan-favored legislation quickly accumulated. The "religious issue," as the press called it, seemed central to Klan votes in some races. The unexpected defeats of two popular Jewish officeholders, a congressman in Indiana and an esteemed Texas state senator favored to win a congressional seat, were attributed to negative Klan votes. In the case of Indiana's Milton Kraus, an effective three-term representative, Klan voters threw their support to a non-Klansman who had not sought the support of the Invisible Empire. A Catholic running for Indiana state treasurer and a Hoosier Supreme Court clerk married to a Catholic also were targeted by Klan voters on religious grounds, and defeated. Hooded ballots also harried critics of the Klan from office, even when, unlike the cases of the gubernatorial elections in Oregon and Georgia, the alternative candidates made no pledges to the Invisible Empire.[72] Indiana Klansmen knifed popular Republican senator Albert Beveridge for his criticism of the secret order, though it meant crossing party lines to elect Democrat Samuel Ralston, who had made only the mildest of overtures to the Ku Kluxers.[73] Democratic Klan voters turned on powerful Missouri senator James Reed, one of Capitol Hill's most searing disparagers of the Invisible Empire, and instead flocked to the support of his GOP opponent, another Klan enemy. Reed survived the challenge, but Klan defections cost him more than fifteen thousand votes.[74]

The political victories of 1922 did not result in a surge of Klan-influenced legislation. Oregon's public school law, the primary legal milestone of the Klan movement, was achieved through the initiative process, not legislative enactment. It was therefore more closely tied to the demonstrated power of hooded electoral mobilization than to legislative coordination. Moreover, the Oregon law failed to survive the scrutiny of the courts and never took effect. Only one clear Ku Klux bill, a ban on religious garb in public schools—meant to expel a handful of nuns from public teaching posts—became law in Oregon. Legislators killed ill-considered Klan proposals to eliminate Catholic prison chaplains, dry up the supply of sacramental wine, and strike Columbus

Day from the list of recognized holidays.[75] Texas Klansmen preferred to work through sheriffs, judges, and local authorities while the hooded lawmakers in Austin remained quiescent. By 1924 the counterwave against the Klan and the election of Ma Ferguson stilled any hopes of a Texas legislative package from the Invisible Empire.

Klansmen in state office proved to be more interested in defensive maneuvers that protected the Invisible Empire than in bold policy initiatives to "Americanize" public life. Klan lawmakers and their allies prepared countermeasures to frustrate the substantial anti-Klan movements that had arisen in most states. Fifteen state assemblies in 1923 introduced anti-Klan bills that, if enacted, would have compelled state Klan organizations to unmask or to open their membership lists to public scrutiny. Hooded influence blocked most of the bills and amended others to the point that Klan authorities found them tolerable.[76] The Klan contingent in the Oklahoma legislature was powerful enough to defeat Governor Walton's war on the hooded order and to help impeach him, but it did not enact a string of laws reflecting the social convictions of Oklahoma Klansmen. Oregon knights managed to install their favorite, the aptly named Kaspar K. Kubli, as lower house speaker, but the legislative majority continued to brush aside hooded bills.[77]

The pattern continued in 1924 as powerful Klan movements in Indiana and Colorado achieved electoral success followed by legislative inaction. Stephenson's Indiana machine gained traction by 1923 and filled city and state offices with Klan sympathizers in 1924. But this bellwether Klan political operation was better fitted for patronage than policy. Since Klansmen formed a minority in the state Democratic Party (controlling at most one-quarter of the delegates in the Democratic state convention) and Democratic boss Thomas Taggart kept the party organization formally anti-Klan, the Invisible Empire infiltrated the state GOP.[78] The progress of this effort became clear in 1923 when Lawrence Lyons, the Republican state chairman, revealed that he had joined the hooded order six weeks earlier but now felt compelled to renounce his Klan connections.[79] One defection did not matter so much, however, when so many Republican officeholders and hopefuls had contracted alliances with the Klan. Stephenson's methods bound his political confederates to appoint Klansmen to office and to protect the interests of the Invisible Empire in exchange for hooded votes and money. The Old Man insisted that key Republican hopefuls sign secret agreements to seal alliances, which he kept in a central archive, his storied "black boxes," to guarantee results. The alleged pact with Indianapolis mayor (and Klansman) John Duvall, in which Duvall promised Stephenson power over city appointments, and a copy of a $2,500 check made out to Governor Ed Jackson later became key artifacts of the Klan's hold over Republican elected officials.[80] The Indiana Klan dominated the 1924 state GOP convention and swept to power in that year's election as Klan-backed candidates filled the legislature.

Stephenson's organization had promised Indiana Klansmen that it would enact a hooded legislative agenda, called the "Americanization and Education" program, composed of a series of proposals to strengthen public schools and eradicate Catholic influence over public education. But the package of bills expected by the Hoosier rank and file fell victim in January 1925 to internal Klan politics and to Stephenson's greed. Although the charismatic grand dragon had helped Evans turn Imperial Wizard William Simmons out of power in 1922, Stephenson disliked the "southerners" who controlled the Klan's Atlanta headquarters. For his part, Evans felt that Stephenson was too ambitious and independent. After Evans backed out of Stephenson's scheme to take over Indiana's Valparaiso University, the furious grand dragon unloaded on the Klan hierarchy. Evans and his Southern compatriots, Stephenson told his followers, "donated $100,000 to erecting a monument to the . . . rebels who tried to destroy America, yet they refused to give a single dollar for Valparaiso University to help educate the patriots of the North who saved the nation to posterity, unsullied from the contamination of Southern traitors."[81] Evans replaced Stephenson as grand dragon with Walter Bossert, then in the spring of 1924 banished the volatile Old Man from the Klan. Yet, amazingly, Stephenson was allowed to direct the 1924 election campaign in Indiana as the Klan tried to paper over the disabling schism in pursuit of political power.

The Hoosier Klan's 1924 political victories took place under the unsteady authority of two competing grand dragons. As the legislature convened in 1925, Stephenson had broken irrevocably from Evans and led a rival Indiana Klan. The hooded contingent in the legislature was divided between Stephenson loyalists and those who held firm with Evans and Bossert. Stephenson ruled the senate while Evans's followers controlled the lower house. The ten-point Klan legislative program was dashed to pieces by the self-destructive infighting of a divided Klan.[82] Stephenson commanded his senate followers to kill several education bills to frustrate Bossert and Evans. In other cases he sacrificed Klan bills in favor of deals on insurance regulation and highway policy that would bring money to his commercial coal interests.[83] In the end, only a single measure from the Klan program—an inoffensive requirement that Indiana students study the Constitution—was enacted into law. Hooded legislators voted for the Indiana Anti-Saloon League's strict state prohibition law, but the Klan machinery had not initiated the proposal. The mighty influence projected by the Klan's electoral machinery dissolved in the pettiness and disorder of hooded legislative bickering.

Ineptitude and an obsession with office, rather than internal division, undermined the Colorado Klan's political success in 1924. The hooded political thrust was orchestrated by Grand Dragon John Galen Locke, who despite his many eccentricities attracted the devotion of Colorado's hooded rank and file. A devotee of homeopathic medicine and celibacy, Locke maintained a private hospital to which was attached the basement headquarters of the Colorado Klan. Locke's sanctuary featured an armory, picture gallery, and ceremonial chair for the grand dragon, near which lolled his Great Dane and dalmatian dogs before the watchful eyes of hooded bodyguards. The grand dragon himself did not cut a dashing figure. Locke was short and fat, sported an old-fashioned Van Dyke beard, and possessed an unusually high-pitched voice, the result of an ill-fated intervention into a knife-wielding brawl. But this "Buddha with a goatee" nevertheless had the organizational skills and personal charisma to inspire the rangy Klansmen of Colorado to follow his lead.[84]

During the buildup to the election, Grand Dragon Locke made brusque use of power but also moved with swift discipline to prepare for the statewide vote. Hooded votes had elected a Klan mayor, Democrat Benjamin Stapleton, in 1923 in Denver, but the cautious Stapleton offset his Klan backers with appeals to a wider constituency. Locke, a personal friend of the mayor, nevertheless harassed him, issuing demands that Stapleton appear at Klan meetings, denouncing his occasional appointments of Jews and Catholics to municipal office, and threatening to launch a recall petition unless the mayor augmented his appointments of Klan judges with a hooded police chief. Stapleton complied by naming Klansman William Candlish chief of police. "Doc Locke" responded with a qualified endorsement. "We have decided to support you again," the grand dragon announced on behalf of the Denver klavern. "We will elect you. But if you ever go back on us again, God help you!"[85] But the Candlish appointment had also energized anti-Klan forces in Denver. Led by District Attorney Philip Van Cise, whose agents had infiltrated Klan meetings, and reform judge Ben Lindsey, in 1924 the anti-Klan movement sought to recall Stapleton and warn of the Invisible Empire's impending takeover of state politics.[86] Klan bullies shouted down Van Cise and Lindsey. "A jeering, howling mob of [Klan] hoodlums" overwhelmed the district attorney at one public meeting. Klan partisans hissed Lindsey and turned out the lights at another attempted anti-Klan rally.[87]

Even as he coerced Stapleton and silenced respected public officials, Locke quietly engineered the hooded order's takeover of the Colorado Republican Party. Klansmen packed the GOP state convention to ensure the selection of Klan-backed candidates. The grand dragon secured undated letters of resignation from the candidates, which he kept on file to guarantee hooded control over them. He also arranged an alliance with wealthy Republican senator Lawrence Phipps, a non-Klansman who funded the hooded campaign chest in exchange for secret Klan votes.[88] Two other true Klansmen were designated for office: Rice Means to fill a short-term vacancy in the Senate, and Clarence Morley, a sycophantic admirer of Locke, for governor. Because Colorado's primary law allowed Democrats to vote in the Republican election, Locke directed Democratic Klansmen to concentrate their votes on Republican candidates.[89] Stapleton, Phipps, Means, Morley, and a host of hooded state legislators swept into office in November 1924. "The Klan leaders voted their membership almost as the Kaiser handled the Prussian army," observed one beaten candidate.[90]

The mastery of the Invisible Empire's political campaign quickly unraveled in the state legislature in 1925. Although Morley favored a statewide ban on sacramental wine and the construction of a state female reformatory to compete with Catholic rehabilitation homes (neither measure became law), the hooded governor's chief goal was to revise Colorado's public bureaucracy so as to pack state institutions with fellow knights. As soon as he was sworn in, the new governor appointed his patron Locke to an honorary colonelcy in the Colorado National Guard and hunted for open positions he could fill with eager Klansmen. With a bow to improved efficiency and smaller government, Morley presented thirty-seven bills to shut down or reconfigure state boards and agencies ranging from the State Tax Commission, the Board of Corrections, and the Board of Nursing Examiners to the Colorado Fish and Game Department. Minimal government, however, was not Morley's aim. The governor possessed almost no authority to fire officeholders from existing boards, but if entirely new administrative structures were created, he could staff the offices with loyal Klansmen and sympathizers.[91]

Klan-controlled legislators were lined up behind the measures. When Representative Martha Long, a member of Locke's female Klan organization, hesitated to abolish the Board of Nursing Examiners, hooded discipline cracked down on her. She had requested permission from Governor Morley to vote her conscience on the matter, but she was directed by the Klan's house whip to consult the grand dragon instead. Long refused to see Locke and voted to retain the nursing board. Her Klan card was pulled, and the bills she thereafter proposed were confined to committee. "Klan leaders are determined to control or wreck the party," she protested.[92]

But the Invisible Empire did not have control of the party in the statehouse. Even though a lopsided Republican majority dominated both houses of the legislature, the Republican delegation was split between Klansmen and anti-Klan or independent representatives. The handful of Klan Democrats did not outweigh the combined power of nonhooded Republicans and Democrats. The senate was a particular bottleneck for Klan legislation. Because of senatorial holdovers and anti-Klan sentiments among some Republicans, only twelve Republican votes out of a 21–14 GOP majority were in Morley's pocket. The governor and Klan legislators needed the help of non-Klan law-makers to pass the bills. Klan-arranged party caucuses failed to break down the opposition. To mollify party holdouts, Klan Republicans named key in-dependent Republicans to critical committee posts. Eventually five anti-Klan senators occupied the all-important Calendar Committee, which controlled the release of bills for consideration. The blundering hooded leadership had unwittingly handed its enemies total control over the Klan's legislative pack-age. Throttled by the Calendar Committee, only three of Morley's reorgani-zation bills reached the senate floor. The only one to become law abolished the outdated and patronage-free Board of Horseshoe Examiners. Two other mild bills supported by the Invisible Empire—one mandating display of the national flag in public schools and the other making the operation of a liquor still a felony—entered the Colorado legal code in 1925. It was a feeble out-come after the great Klan triumph of 1924.[93]

Morley and his hooded legislative allies further sullied the political reputa-tion of the Klan with clumsy retaliation against their more nimble legislative foes. The governor, in a fit of powerlessness, vetoed salary appropriations for several boards and tried to hold up funding for the University of Colorado. When he could, Morley appointed several exalted cyclopes and other high-profile knights to vacant positions, but legal challenges and delays ensured that only a few of these ever assumed their offices. Unable to do much else, the humbled governor appointed Grand Dragon Locke to the state Board of Medical Examiners, a move that gave some credibility to the marginal profes-sional status of Doc Locke, an unconventional physician who had been kept out of the principal state medical associations. Capable of assembling a fear-some electoral machine, the Colorado Klan had performed dismally in office, essentially ending further hopes of effective policymaking.[94]

The collapse of the Klan's legislative programs in Colorado and Indiana presaged the disintegration of hooded unity in what had been political strong-holds of the Invisible Empire. In 1925 dramatic scandals destroyed the careers of both John Galen Locke and D. C. Stephenson. As the legislature convened in January, outgoing Denver district attorney Van Cise jailed the eccentric grand dragon on charges of kidnapping and conspiracy. Locke had foolishly used his own medical office and threats of castration to browbeat a teenage knight into a forced marriage. Locke managed to get out of jail, but he was soon back behind bars as the result of feuding within the Invisible Empire. Rice Means, the short-term Klan senator elected in 1924, believed that Locke had not adequately supported him in the race and used his new office to strike at the grand dragon. He initiated a tax investigation of Locke, which revealed that the grand dragon had failed to file income tax returns from 1913 to 1924.

Locke was jailed for ten days, fined fifteen hundred dollars, and ordered to pay nearly fifteen thousand dollars in back taxes. The charges created a crisis of confidence among Colorado Klansmen and set off a free-for-all in the state realm. Means and Stapleton led an effort to drive Locke from power and asked Imperial Wizard Evans to step in. Evans, who disliked Locke's freelancing and his recent flair for negative publicity, demanded that the Colorado grand dragon resign. Locke's supporters, in turn, banished Means, Stapleton, and several other members of the rebel group. Under continued pressure from Evans, the disaffected Colorado Klan chieftain cut ties with the national Ku Klux Klan and led about five thousand hooded followers into a rival organization called the Minute Men of America. As the leaders of the Invisible Empire wrestled for power, the Colorado Klan movement fell apart. A scattering of about one thousand Klansmen remained to survey the shattered remnants of a movement that had aspired to control the state just a year earlier. The poor performance of Klansmen in office, from police officers and prohibition constables to the feckless members of the 1925 legislature, had doomed Colorado's Invisible Empire even before Locke's precipitous fall.[95]

Greater spectacle attended the Klan's collapse in Indiana because of Stephenson's notoriety, the severity of his crime, and the Klan's recognized political influence in the state. The ease with which Stephenson had discarded the Klan's anti-Catholic public education program in the legislative session of 1925 indicated his loose commitment to the priorities of the hooded rank and file. The Old Man's excessive taste for liquor and brutal sexuality also contrasted dramatically with the Invisible Empire's stated devotion to enforcing prohibition and upholding community moral standards. On several occasions and in locales ranging from hotel rooms to a car parked along the roadside, a drunken Stephenson had attempted violent sexual assaults on women or was observed by officers of the law in compromising sexual circumstances. Once more, in March 1925, as the Klan's legislative program unraveled, the embattled grand dragon assaulted a young office worker on an overnight train to Chicago. The woman, Madge Oberholtzer, fled the train, took bichloride of mercury tablets, lingered in agony for a month, and died. She survived long enough to give statements detailing Stephenson's sudden, mauling attack on her. The erstwhile grand dragon was charged with murder as prosecutors argued that infections from the vicious bites Stephenson had inflicted in the railcar encounter killed Oberholtzer, not the poison she took after the attack. Stephenson was convicted of second-degree murder and sentenced to prison.[96]

As he toppled from power, the disgraced Old Man pulled the Indiana Klan and its political toadies down with him. Stephenson's defenders claimed that Evans and his henchmen had framed the Indiana Klan leader, pointing out that Evans had used compromising photographs to blackmail other Klan rivals. During the dispute with the imperial wizard, Stephenson's yacht had blown up under mysterious circumstances, and unknown parties torched his empty house the night following Madge Oberholtzer's funeral. Unproven claims later surfaced that agents dispatched by Evans threatened other witnesses in the case, one of whom was found murdered.[97]

Whatever the circumstances that led to his conviction, neither the national Klan nor Stephenson's many friends in government made a move to secure a pardon for the onetime personification of the law in Indiana. Stephenson therefore opened the contents of his black boxes to the press, revealing his contract with Indianapolis mayor Duvall, a string of checks that supported the election of Governor Ed Jackson, and information that linked Jackson and other state GOP officials with the attempted bribery of another former governor.[98] Governor Jackson became a pariah while several others named in Stephenson's records served time behind bars, but the biggest loser in the tawdry episode was the Indiana Klan. Already reeling from the legislative disappointment of 1925, it broke apart amid the disheartening revelations of the Stephenson inquiry. Evans prompted an additional hooded secession in Indiana when he replaced Grand Dragon Walter Bossert, his handpicked alternative to Stephenson, after Bossert refused to align the remnants of the Indiana Klan behind Senator James Watson's reelection in 1926.[99]

By 1925 other centers of Klan political power also burned out. Factionalism, charges of prohibition violations against Grand Dragon Zeke Marvin, and a strong reaction against revelations of earlier Klan violence opened up political opportunities for an anti-Klan coalition in Texas. Klansmen there proved unable to mobilize against the political challenge of the impeached former governor Jim Ferguson, who sought a return to power against his hooded enemies through his wife, Miriam "Ma" Ferguson's surrogate 1924 gubernatorial campaign. The bonnet beat the hood in the Democratic primaries, as defeated candidates in the first round rallied to support Ma Ferguson in the runoff election against Klan candidate Felix Robertson.[100] "I am for Mrs. Ferguson," asserted one of the first-round losers, "because her election means the defeat of [a] secret political organization. . . . When the issue of free government is at stake, every other question dwindles."[101] The Fergusons surged to victory as the Texas Democratic convention turned against the hooded order and an improbable Klan-Republican alliance failed to stop the Democratic nominee.[102] Driven from the legislature and faced with a hostile state administration, the Invisible Empire's political influence in Texas shriveled. One of the beaten Klan candidates washed his hands of Evans and the hooded political enterprise. "I can better serve myself, my family, my church and my Government out of the Klan than in it," he observed. "The Klan has ceased to be a fraternal order and has become a political machine controlled by the heads of the Klan."[103]

Restive Klansmen also acted against the political opportunism of their leaders in Oklahoma and, as we have seen, in Arkansas. In 1924, Oklahoma Klansmen again battled Jack Walton as the former governor ran for the U.S. Senate. Determined to halt Walton's bid at the Democratic primary, most of the state's Klansmen seemed to favor fellow knight E. B. Howard. But at the last moment Grand Dragon Clay Jewett, a Republican, endorsed another Democratic candidate. Amid confusion, Walton won the Democratic primary. Angry Democrats within the Klan charged that the grand dragon had arranged for Walton's nomination so that the Klan and other anti-Waltonites would turn to the Republican nominee, W. B. Pine, to keep Walton out of the Senate. Pine, with Klan support, did win the election.[104] But many hooded Oklahoma Democrats had had enough of Klan politics and their Republican grand dragon. One klavern leader, a newspaper publisher, complained that under Jewett the Klan had "degenerate[ed] . . . into a political machine with a Republican engineer at the throttle" who aimed "to discredit, disrupt and demoralize the Democratic party in the state."[105] After 1924 the unity of the Oklahoma Klan crumbled, and the Invisible Empire lost its political punch. In Arkansas, Democratic knights rebelled against their Republican grand dragon during the 1924 election itself, refusing to vote as a bloc in support of their leader's chosen candidate.

Hooded political influence seemed to be at a standstill. In Oregon the Klan's enthusiasm for Governor Pierce cooled amid legislative deadlock and patronage disappointments. In 1923 hooded conspirators initiated a failed recall campaign against Pierce. Dissatisfaction with the imperious leadership of Grand Dragon Fred Gifford, whose close ties to Portland utility companies also sparked controversy, further eroded the hooded order's political potency.[106] One klavern, citing interference from Gifford, broke away from the Oregon Klan in 1923, and others withheld dues in the hopes of driving out the embattled grand dragon.[107] After Gifford attempted to boss the rank and file in the 1924 senatorial election, leading to the defeat of popular hooded candidates, comity and political influence disappeared from the Oregon Klan. Gifford left the hooded order in an atmosphere of recrimination in 1925, and the Klan's influence receded to the backwaters of Oregon society.[108]

Elsewhere across the Invisible Empire, large ethnic or Catholic communities, hostile party organizations, or the popularity of noted anti-Klan statesmen inhibited the extension of hooded influence in public affairs. The Alabama Klan was powerful in Birmingham and culturally assertive across the state, but vigorous opposition to the hooded order by the state's most distinguished politician, Democratic senator and 1924 presidential hopeful Oscar

W. Underwood, delayed the Invisible Empire's effective political power until 1926. Underwood retired that year and was replaced in the Senate by Klansman Hugo Black, whose later career on the Supreme Court belied his early hooded affiliation.[109] Evidence from Maine that a friendly governor and alert electioneering might signal the emergence of an outpost of Ku Klux power in the Northeast also flickered temporarily from 1924 to 1926.[110] But by then the opportunity for national political prominence represented by the debate over the Invisible Empire at the Democratic national convention of 1924 had passed.

Klankraft in Congress and Party Councils

Grand in its aspirations for political influence in Washington, the achievements of the Invisible Empire in Congress and in the national councils of the major political parties were modest. As at the state level, the primary actions of hooded lobbyists and lawmakers in Washington were defensive in nature. Evans poured substantial resources into the defense of Mayfield's Senate seat, but the Texas Klansman did little to promote the interests of the Invisible Empire after he secured his place in the upper house. William Upshaw, the voluble Georgia congressman who was widely recognized for his enthusiastic advocacy of prohibition and the Invisible Empire, acted chiefly to protect the Klan from assault rather than promote hooded legislative initiatives. In 1921 he shielded Imperial Wizard Simmons from the hostile questions of House investigators, and at the end of his congressional career in 1926 he rebuked President Calvin Coolidge and his spokesman, C. Bascom Slemp, for sidestepping pointed questions on the Invisible Empire during the 1924 elections. Upshaw, a Democrat, noted the Republican president's willingness to offer praise to a Catholic gathering while maintaining a careful silence on the Klan.[111] Despite Upshaw's partisan tweaking of Coolidge's studied equivocation, the main achievement of the Klan in Washington at the high point of its influence was to sidetrack denunciation of the Invisible Empire by prominent political leaders, not to assert Ku Klux authority and power.

Although the Klan promoted several specific legislative issues before Congress in the mid-1920s, it had little noticeable impact on the final disposition of those questions. Congressional debate over the creation of a federal Department of Education, long sought by Evans, was not principally driven by Klan lobbyists. The National Education Association and the Southern Jurisdiction of Scottish Rite Masons were more directly involved in the intricacies of policy discussions with lawmakers. Hooded interest in the matter failed to dislodge the Department of Education bills from committee in 1924 and

1926.[112] Indeed, Senator Lawrence Phipps, the Colorado Republican who had traded money for Klan votes in 1924, sponsored an alternative bill in the 1926 session that helped derail interest in a stronger federal presence in education.[113] Rather than advancing education reform, the Invisible Empire's presence in the centralized schools coalition brought into question the integrity of the professional educators who crafted the federal Education Department bills, and the reform remained stalled in Congress throughout the New Era.

The Klan also had difficulty transferring its strong grassroots influence over prohibition to national decision-making. Passionate though many knights were on the need for prohibition enforcement, the major influences over federal laws during the period remained the wet lobbies and the Anti-Saloon League. The Klan's support of prohibition enforcement was well known, but its impact on specific national legislation was minimal. An effective national prohibition policy was never enacted.

Even the legislative victories celebrated by the Klan involved only minor input by the Invisible Empire. The curtailment of free immigration exemplified by the 1924 National Origins Act, which established strict national quotas from European states and restricted the number of immigrants allowed into the United States, exemplifies the pattern. In 1923, Evans had dismissed "proportionate immigration law" as an indecisive half-measure. "We admit that undesirable immigration is poison," he stressed to a gathering of Klan officers, "and they propose to give us one-half glass today and one-half glass next month."[114] Other hooded officials called for a decade-long suspension of immigration and a ban on non-English-language publications in the United States.[115] Yet the Klan mustered its legions to support Representative Albert Johnson's bill because the measure sharply restricted immigration from Eastern and Southern Europe and thereby reduced the flow of Jews and Catholics into the United States.[116] Klan publications followed the course of the bill through Congress and, as the measure came to a vote, urged Klansmen to inundate their elected officials in Washington with entreaties to support immigration restriction. "Every Klan newspaper in this country should aid in this fight," the imperial wizard's official journal demanded. "Specific and adequate warning should be issued through every agency the Klan has."[117] Klan petitions "deluged members from the South," demanding passage of the National Origins bill.[118]

Despite thorny features that discriminated against Eastern and Southern Europeans and risked a diplomatic break with Japan over the exclusion of its citizens, the final version of the National Origins bill surged to victory. Yet, as the historian John Higham concluded, "Klan backing made no material difference" in the outcome.[119] The postwar atmosphere that had inspired the growth of the Klan had also produced a powerful mainstream sentiment wary of open borders. By 1924 a broad coalition ranging from the American Federation of Labor to the Daughters of the American Revolution (and including such stalwart foes of the Ku Kluxers as Alabama's Oscar Underwood) stood behind immigration restriction. The passage of literacy requirements for immigration in 1917 and Johnson's first immigration quota bill in 1921 predated the political mobilization of the Klan movement. Immigration restriction did not require hooded leadership.[120]

The Klan's role in the lobbying effort was seldom acknowledged by supporters of restriction. Instead, opponents of the bill highlighted hooded approval of the measure as a way of delegitimizing restrictionist sentiment. Thus, in the aftermath of a near fistfight with a supporter of the bill on the floor of the House, Massachusetts congressman James A. Gallivan identified an undemocratic alliance of the Klan and the kaiser on the side of curbing immigration. The German idea of the "superman" that was "sponsored in this country by the Ku Klux Klan seems to have found an expression in this proposed legislation," he warned.[121] Although Evans claimed the legislative victory as the product of the Klan's influence, the hooded order's endorsement probably hurt the bill's chances for passage as much as it contributed to its success.

The Invisible Empire also sought to block American entry into the Permanent Court of International Justice, commonly called the World Court. Such a step, Klan analysts argued, would subject American democracy to the flawed, Catholic-influenced legal traditions of the Old World. The mainstream press reprinted breathless headlines from Klan sources contending that the proposed international judicial body was a "'back door' into the League of Nations, where America's interests would be outvoted ten to one." In the hooded order's nativist scenario, cosmopolitan plotters could then override American immigration restrictions. The "Vatican would use [the] World Court as [a] tool for Romanizing America," the Klan press howled, "and [would] force Papist aliens into [the] country."[122]

The coalition opposing the World Court was somewhat diverse, including such prominent enemies of the Invisible Empire as Missouri senator James Reed, but some Senate foes of the body felt that the Klan's "nation-wide organization might help arouse the people" against internationalist intrigue. Nevertheless, by 1925, the hooded order had become a dubious ally in a legislative fight. Reporters considered the Klan's participation in the anti–World Court coalition a potential "boomerang." "Disgust over the methods of this secret organization is so wide-spread in Congress," reported the *New York Times*, "that any alliance between it and World Court opponents is likely to bring to the President's [pro-court] side a number of Senators whose attitude toward his recommendation [of membership] is uncertain."[123]

In the end, the impact of the Klan's lobby on the World Court debate was negligible. Although Evans's loyalists enjoined Klansmen to pressure their senators to vote against accepting the court, in January 1926 solons apparently shrugged off hooded influence to vote with the majority in favor of the court.[124] Neither of Colorado's Klan-supported Republican senators rejected the World Court, though Klansman Rice Means voted with the opposition on a delaying tactic. But for the final vote the hooded senator preferred to take direction from Coolidge's White House and endorsed the court. Fellow knight Earle Mayfield of Texas followed the same course, ignoring the determined opposition of Evans and the national Klan. Despite a direct appeal from Ohio grand dragon Clyde Osborne, the state's two Republican senators also voted to join the court.[125] One of them, Frank Willis, reputedly had been elected with Klan votes because of his dry convictions.[126] Apparently only the four Klan-controlled senators from Indiana and Oklahoma followed the directives of the Invisible Empire to vote against the court.[127]

Ordinary Klansmen seemingly echoed the indifference shown by the Klan's Senate allies. A 1924 analysis of hooded voters indicated that rank-and-file knights from New Jersey and Pennsylvania showed little interest in the World Court question. More than sixty of those questioned expressed no preference on joining the court. Those who did take a side were split between supporters and opponents of the international body.[128] Presiding over a divided and reduced membership, and ignored by elected officials, the Klan hierarchy asserted only limited influence over an issue which it defined as central to the beliefs of the Invisible Empire. The World Court proposal passed through Congress but then was vetoed by Coolidge in 1926 after he reconsidered the implications of American international commitments. Once again, the Klan's impact on its favored legislation was mostly negative.

❖

Blunted as an effective legislative force, the Invisible Empire's hopes for lasting political power depended on its ability to influence elections and to extract promises of favorable treatment from candidates. Yet by 1924, at the height of its electoral success, the secret order revealed itself to be a divisive and therefore unwelcome presence in national party politics. Although the Ku Klux hierarchy celebrated the national party conventions of that year as confirmations of hooded power, at that point the failure of Imperial Wizard Evans's program for mainstream political influence became clear.

At the Republican convention the Klan's lack of discipline and cohesion was displayed in a minor episode. Aware of hooded affiliations in pockets of the national GOP, the party attempted to emulate the famous taciturnity of its leader, President Calvin Coolidge, and say nothing substantial about the Klan. An attempt by a minority of anti-Klan Republicans to include a condemnation of the Invisible Empire in the party plank was squelched in favor of a softer statement upholding constitutional principles of civil and religious liberty. But the hooded bull got loose in the china shop and did some damage. A sixty-man Klan delegation had taken up residence near the convention to safeguard the interests of the hooded order. One of them, Milton Elrod, the editor of Indiana's Klan newspaper, released a statement demanding that the Republicans select the Hoosier Klan's favorite son, Senator James Watson, as vice president on the Coolidge ticket or risk the wrath of disappointed knights.[129]

This foolish movement from the shadows of backroom influence—the hooded order's favored political domain—to the glare of a public endorsement led to clumsy backtracking and recrimination within the Klan establishment. Watson, never a serious candidate for the nomination but now clearly out of the question, was stricken by the public embrace from the supposedly secret order.[130] In private he wailed, "My God, they have ruined me," while in public he denied affiliation with the Klan and rejected its offer of support.[131] Evans stepped in and countermanded Elrod's press release, declaring that the imperial wizard alone spoke for the Klan, and he had authorized no endorsement. Press accounts, however, indicated that the Watson endorsement was the result of a conference between Evans and Klan lieutenants, and that the imperial wizard had checked and approved Elrod's statement.[132] It was a maladroit performance for an organization purported to operate with stealthy efficiency.

At the Democratic convention in New York City, the Klan was at the center of a more fundamental and disabling controversy. Riven between the largely dry, Protestant, old-stock constituency of its rural Southern and Western wing, on the one hand, and the wet, immigrant, Catholic, urban flavor of its Northeastern and Midwestern elements on the other, in 1924 the Democrats confronted critical questions about their basic identity and policies. The prospect of a debate over the Klan threatened to turn the deep divisions of the party into open wounds. Southern Democrats, even many in the anti-Klan movement, feared that a blunt condemnation of the hooded order would drive several Democratic states in the South and Midwest to the Republicans. On the other hand, Northeastern delegates and anti-Klan firebrands like Underwood demanded a forthright condemnation of the Invisible Empire as a necessary step to "save the party and spell victory in November."[133]

The major presidential hopefuls reflected the quandary. William G. McAdoo had ties to the West, the South, and the Wilson administration. He did not support the Invisible Empire, but he was aware that Klansmen favored his candidacy. McAdoo correspondingly took care to avoid explicit criticisms of the secret order. The other major contender was the garrulous Governor Al Smith of New York, a charismatic wet, Catholic embodiment of American pluralism who stood in direct refutation of the Klan's beliefs. Even without the nearby presence of Evans and Klan lobbyists, the convention in Madison Square Garden could not have avoided confronting the reality of the Invisible Empire. Tension among the delegates was so strong that, according to Stanley Frost, many of them went about the floor and convention hotels with firearms in their pockets.[134]

The Democrats proceeded to tear their party apart as they fought over the Klan. Hoping to contain the explosiveness of the Klan question, the platform committee defeated a passionate minority demand to denounce the hooded order by name. Instead, it "condemn[ed] any effort to arouse racial or religious dissension" without mentioning the Klan, the most notable exponent of those qualities in the New Era.[135] But the dispute spilled onto the floor of the convention, sparking at least one fistfight, producing dramatic and contentious language from delegates and speakers, prompting jeers from the galleries packed with Smith's admirers, and stirring the police to take up positions between warring delegations. William Jennings Bryan, three-time Democratic presidential candidate and elder statesman of the party, pleaded with his fellow Democrats to accept the majority plank. "Three words were more to [the anti-Klan Democrats] than the welfare of a party in a great campaign," complained the Great Commoner.[136]

Yet not even a party figure as revered as Bryan could dull the frank contempt many Democrats felt for sidestepping the Klan issue. One speaker dismissed the vague majority language as "an obvious, stuttering, stammering and falling failure." "You cannot kill a snake by taking it in your arms and kissing it to death, and you cannot smother the Ku Klux Klan by love and affection," advised an anti-Klan Tennessee delegate.[137] In an atmosphere of near chaos marked by the rigorous use of the unit-vote rule and the application of relentless pressure on anti-Klan holdouts, the convention approved the cautious language of the majority report, but only by a single vote out of nearly eleven hundred cast (a margin later expanded to four votes). The division on the Klan plank accurately reflected the convention's shattered unity. The divided Democrats could not agree on either McAdoo or Smith, and after 103 ballots the exhausted delegates nominated the noted attorney John W. Davis for president.[138]

Evans portrayed the disarray of the Democrats as a triumph for the Invisible Empire. In the midst of the enemy's country, before a hostile, baying gallery, the Klan had defeated furious attempts to condemn it by name. Yet it was at best a strange victory to be censured, if not explicitly named, by formal statements from both political parties. Reporters noted that hooded lobbyists were "surprised" at the widespread hostility to the Klan on display among angry Democrats.[139] One Klan delegate admitted leaving the convention "in a very bitter frame of mind."[140] During the convention debates, not even the opponents of the anti-Klan statements offered strong support to the Invisible Empire. The gentlest remarks granted the patriotism, Christian fervor, and good intentions of Klansmen but dismissed the actions of the hooded fraternity as "mistaken," "misguided," or "wrong." Bryan predicated his unwillingness to name the Klan on the belief that the hooded body "is nearly dead and . . . will soon pass away."[141]

Whatever sense of accomplishment the Invisible Empire drew from staving off outright denunciation at the party conventions quickly dissipated in the general election and its disappointing aftermath. Shortly after the convention, Democratic nominee John W. Davis offered an explicit condemnation of the Ku Kluxers, stating that hooded intolerance "does violence to the spirit of American institutions and must be condemned by all those who believe, as I do, in American ideals."[142] The plain remarks elicited enthusiasm at Davis rallies, so the candidate maintained his criticism of the Invisible Empire throughout the 1924 campaign.[143] Charles W. Dawes, the GOP vice-presidential candidate, also commented on the shortcomings of the Invisible Empire, though he professed to understand the desire for upright law enforcement that motivated many grassroots knights.[144]

Thereafter the Atlanta hierarchy appeared friendlier to Coolidge and the Republicans. But after the incumbent's landslide victory, the hooded order was denied the Mexican ambassadorship for Zumbrunn (intended to ward off the Vatican's interference with the secular Mexican government) that Evans expected as recompense for the Klan's contribution to Coolidge's victory.[145] Moreover, as Frost observed, the Klan "was forced out into the open" and "seen by the whole Nation in the act of reaching for control of the Government" in the 1924 campaign, yet had only barely avoided defeat at Madison Square Garden.[146] Exposed as an enemy of party cohesion and revealed to be less formidable than expected as a voting bloc, the Klan's ability to influence politics began to fade.

The scandals and legislative disappointments of 1925 further undermined the Klan as a political force. The senators elected in the hooded campaigns of 1922 and 1924 lost their reelection bids, served out their terms, and returned home. Early in 1926 a *New York Times* headline declared "The Klan's Invisible Empire Is Fading" as it recounted the retreat of the hooded tide in state after state. The entire slate of Klan-backed candidates in the 1926 Georgia Democratic primary suffered defeat, though the hooded order retained vigor in some of the state's municipalities.[147] Pockets of Klan political influence held on in the South after 1926, but hooded Democrats could not prevent the nomination of Al Smith as the Democratic standard-bearer for president in 1928. Earlier that year, in response to another upsurge in night riding, Evans renounced the use of masks in Klan ritual and regalia. Once again, but this time in a more realistic vein, the embattled imperial wizard declared that "the order has no political ambitions for itself or for its members."[148]

Powerful as an expression of grassroots sentiment in community politics, the Klan movement had weakened noticeably on the national stage. Disconnected from the energy of fraternal local knights, the Invisible Empire suffered from the inconsistencies and weaknesses of its flawed leaders. Its skill at political mobilization could not overcome its amateurishness and disorganization at the helm of government. As its onetime adherents cast off their hoods and abandoned the shell of an organization that the Klan had become after 1925, the full consequences of Evans's campaign to centralize the Invisible Empire played out. For a turbulent half-decade, as the United States struggled with its pluralistic destiny, the Klan had come together in defense of a more unitary, restrictive understanding of American identity. It offered to some fraternalists a celebration of native-born white Protestant community. In some locales it became the vehicle for local reforms. But in the end, the Klan movement exposed the changing nature of American identity more than it determined the content of Americanism in the New Era. It was an obstacle more than an answer, a protest more than a prognosis. The failure of the hooded assembly to influence government substantially at the state and national levels was the most concrete sign of that fundamental limitation.

8

Echoes

A MID THE COLLAPSE OF HOODED POLITICAL FORTUNES IN 1925, a solitary example of the disillusionment and cynicism that marked the destruction of the Klan phenomenon as a popular mass movement of the 1920s quietly unfolded along a southeastern Texas roadside. After a klavern meeting, perhaps one beset by the factionalism, financial pressures, or air of defeat that pervaded Texas Klans by that point, a homeward-bound knight stopped by the side of the pavement and burned his hood and robe.[1] In the middle years of the 1920s, estimates of Klan membership dropped from the millions to a few hundred thousand. Some robust centers of hooded activism nearly vanished altogether.

Yet echoes of the mighty Klan movement of the postwar New Era reverberated through the remainder of the 1920s and beyond. Imperial Wizard Hiram Evans maintained the exoskeleton of the national Klan, even if the vital interior that powered the hooded order had withered. As Stanley Frost observed in 1928, "Evans is the whole of the Klan to-day."[2] He orchestrated a second Washington parade in 1926, though it drew only half as many knights as the monster rally a year earlier. Acknowledging the loss of members suffered by the Invisible Empire, Evans nevertheless asserted that a smaller, more dedicated body of knights could still muster political strength. Through Klan publications, the imperial wizard demonstrated a heightened interest in prohibition enforcement and maintained his zealous attack on "alienism." Both topics were tied to the Klan's final political battle—the attempt to keep Al Smith from the presidency in 1928.

The Smith nomination of 1928 demonstrated the reality of American pluralism as well as its contested nature, a conflict that extended well beyond the diminished ranks of the Klan. Resolute against a repeat of the divisions that marked the 1924 convention, Democrats agreed early on the nomination of the wet New Yorker. Smith renounced the mildly supportive party plank on prohibition enforcement and declared for modification of prohibition. The Klan railed against Smith's wet cosmopolitanism and his Catholicism and attempted to influence a movement of Southern Democrats to support Republican Herbert Hoover. In the end, as part of a national landslide, Hoover defeated Smith in five Southern states and in the Southwestern states of Texas and Oklahoma that had earlier been dominated by the Invisible Empire. The historian Allan Lichtman contends that the cultural division between Catholics and Protestants was a powerful force in the final outcome, but that the Klan was nevertheless incidental to the result. A broader unease with Smith's wet assertiveness, his connection to New York machine politics, his embodiment of immigrant Americanism, and his Catholicism, along with prosperity and Republican incumbency, cut into support for the Democratic nominee. The hooded order aired these issues, but from an extremist and badly compromised position.[3]

Mainstream Southern politicians and prohibitionists, most vocally Bishop James Cannon, led the partial Democratic defection from Smith. Evans himself noted early in 1928 that "Southern politicians, like most others, have almost entirely abandoned any hope of using the Klan *as a political organization.*"[4] Even a handful of prominent former Southwestern Klan figures stayed true to their Democratic faith and supported Smith. Most of the anti-Smith Democrats, many of whom had fought the hooded order, downplayed the Klan's participation in the campaign. Smith supporters, on the other hand, emphasized the Klan's opposition, knowing the negative connotations carried by associations with the faltering hooded body. In the end, despite the disruption of the Democratic "solid South," the region in which the Klan movement held its last toehold gave more support to Smith than the rest of the nation, providing the New York governor with six of the eight states in his column. The 1928 election marked the last substantial echo of Ku Klux political intrigue.[5]

As the political enterprise that came to dominate the Klan movement at mid-decade faded, other echoes of controversies that had damaged hooded unity continued to sound. A wave of beatings in Alabama and attempts to close down inquiries into hooded violence persisted into 1928 and reminded observers of the entrenched lawlessness that clung to the fabric of the Invisible Empire.[6] In 1936 the murder of a Michigan man at the hands of the Black Legion, a violent band of former Klansmen, further tarnished the reputation of the real Klan.[7] Four years later a Georgia victim of a Klan beating died after hooded vigilantes left him exposed to the elements overnight.[8] Even as the Invisible Empire shrank to the margins of American consciousness, it could not twist free of violent episodes that stimulated greater official hostility.

So too did the taint of scandal and fraud pursue several notable Klansmen after their departure from the Invisible Empire. Clarence Morley, the Ku Klux governor of Colorado, in the mid-1930s was convicted of mail fraud in connection with his stock brokerage business and sentenced to five years' imprisonment in Leavenworth federal penitentiary. His mentor, John Galen Locke, faced additional charges of tax evasion in 1928, which, though resolved in his favor, added to his unhappy legacy.[9] The persistent fraternalist, Pat Emmons of Indiana, was indicted by Canadian officials for embezzlement while trying to build a Klan-like body in Saskatchewan.[10] Evans himself was embroiled in lawsuits and fined fifteen thousand dollars in 1937 for shady dealings concerning government contracts. He gave up his hold on the Invisible Empire two years later.[11] Each of these episodes served as a soft reminder of the internal corruption that had contributed to the breakup of the Klan movement in the 1920s.

The fragmentation of the Klan into separate shards of native-born white Protestant identity constituted another echo of the 1920s movement. Hooded factionalism, rivalries, and Evans's drive to centralize and politicize the Klan movement ignited an evanescent burst of alternative patriotic organizations populated by disaffected knights. The Minute Men of America, the Allied Protestant Americans, the Improved Order of Klansmen, the Independent Klan of America, and other groups tried to reassemble the energy and force of the original Klan movement, but they quickly dissipated. The unified Klan of the early 1920s could not hold together against internal dissent and the force of American pluralism. The fate of its successor organizations reflected the increasing exclusion from the national mainstream of the restricted vision of American identity promoted by the massive Klan phenomenon of the New Era.

Ultimately, as the Klan splintered in the 1940s into a collection of rival associations, only the regalia and the reputation of the 1920s Klan remained. The revived Klan movement of the civil rights era represented a resentful, outlaw resistance against the shifting American mainstream of cultural and civic values, even if it intersected for a time with broader Southern patterns of white supremacist convictions, hostility to labor unions, and anti-Communist superpatriotism. Insignificant in number, prone to violence, and embittered against a social and political order they detest, Klansmen today are scattered across the disaffected landscape of the far right. Their white supremacist doctrine is opposed by established government policy and runs against the grain of American cultural assertions. With only a few thousand members in several Klan organizations, late twentieth-century Klansmen had no realistic hope of mainstream acceptance or political influence. There is a distant, distorted echo of the 1920s Klan movement in the blunt racism and white supremacist bluster of modern Klansmen, but the context of the 1920s movement was significantly different. In its wide, if short-lived, appeal, its power at the local and state level, and its embattled proximity to a changing American mainstream, the phenomenon of the New Era Klan movement remains historically distinctive.

Afterword

Historians and the Klan

T HE CONTRADICTIONS OF THE KLAN MOVEMENT—its mixture of the common-place and the extreme, its civic expression and violent outbreaks, the depth of its appeal and its rapid, spectacular dissolution—have made the 1920s Ku Klux Klan a particularly difficult puzzle for historians.[1] Beyond the inherent interpretive problems in evaluating a complicated social movement, the secrecy and disingenuousness of the self-styled Invisible Empire created an imbalance in the documentary record of the second Klan. Klansmen (usually) hid their identity in public behind masks and were instructed to deny their membership in the order when questioned about it.[2] Membership lists were kept strictly confidential, and individual klaverns closely guarded their minute books. Enemies of the Klan periodically stole and published Klan membership lists to undermine the hooded order (indeed, the Chicago-based journal *Tolerance* devoted itself to revealing the identities of secret Ku Kluxers), but, while helpful in recovering portions of the Klan's vital statistics, these sources were usually incomplete and frequently inaccurate. For instance, *Tolerance* mistakenly listed William Wrigley Jr., the sportsman and chewing gum magnate, as a Klansman and printed numerous corrections of similar errors concerning lesser known individuals.[3]

On the other hand, the leaders and official representatives of the hooded order, Imperial Wizard Hiram Evans in particular, freely identified themselves, gave interviews, wrote articles in the popular press about the Klan's beliefs and political positions, and directed at least a portion of their official duties to the public sphere. The Klan also published its own magazines and newspapers, such as the official journal from Atlanta, the *Kourier,* or Indiana's *Fiery Cross.*

Some of these publications, especially newspapers, provided glimpses of local concerns and conditions in the grassroots of Klandom, but the heavy hand of grand dragons or the imperial hierarchy was usually evident. An overrepresentation of elite sources on the Klan movement was therefore available to contemporary observers. Key facts such as membership figures relied on Klan statements, usually inflated, or fairly broad estimates by informed outsiders. Insights into the inner workings of Klandom came from investigative journalists, revelations by estranged Klansmen, testimony obtained in the course of efforts undertaken by several states to revoke Klan charters, government hearings, or legal documents and depositions produced by the many lawsuits and occasional criminal proceedings that punctuated the active history of the 1920s Klan. Taken together, these records were rich and revelatory but not comprehensive. They also highlighted national Klan concerns over local issues, the perspectives of leaders over the perception of ordinary knights, and the impact of Klan misdeeds over routine behavior.

Although much of the journalistic coverage of the Klan in the 1920s was discerning, the absence of local records led the first serious studies of the second Klan to miss some essential features of the movement. Beginning with John M. Mecklin's 1924 analysis, *The Ku Klux Klan: A Study of the American Mind*, and carrying into the 1960s, scholars and popular writers depicted the Klan movement as an irrational rebuke of modernity by undereducated, economically marginal bigots, religious zealots, and dupes willing to be manipulated by the Klan's cynical, mendacious leaders. It was, in this view, a movement of country parsons and small-town malcontents who were out of step with the dynamism of twentieth-century urban America. As Mecklin put it, even though the Klan drew on common themes and prejudices rooted in the historical experience of the United States, the hooded order was "a refuge for mediocre men, if not weaklings," attracted from the "more or less ignorant and unthinking middle class" of back-roads America. These followers supposedly found in the elaborate ceremonies and simplistic crusades of the Invisible Empire relief from "the drabness of village and small town life" and the "monotonous and unimaginative round" of their daily existence.[4] Emphasis was also placed on the Klan's Southern roots and its violent repression of African Americans, Jews, and Catholics, often in contrast to more tolerant, urbane sentiments expressed by the Klan's critics. Rather than explaining the Klan as a product of 1920s America, assembled from its current fears and aspirations, the initial historical portrait of the second Klan characterized the Invisible Empire as an anachronistic holdover from the nineteenth century, at odds with its own society.

An inescapable ideological context after World War II also framed historical considerations of the Klan. In the wake of the wreckage produced by nationalistic, racially charged mass movements of the 1930s and 1940s, and the repressive atmosphere of McCarthyism in the early Cold War, American scholars regarded popular movements from the Klan to the late nineteenth-century populist rebellion with suspicion as pathways to intolerance, anti-intellectualism, and even dictatorship. After all, Evans himself described the Klan as representing "a movement of the plain people, very weak in the matter of culture, intellectual support, and trained leadership."[5] Some journalists in the 1920s argued that the Klan was a prototype for American fascism, a claim later taken up by the historians Robert Moats Miller and, most recently, Nancy MacLean.[6] Others who had witnessed in the early 1950s the disturbing, seemingly credulous, popular support for Joseph McCarthy's reckless charges of disloyalty against unoffending Americans found it reasonable to conclude that "relatively unprosperous and uncultivated" folk had been seduced by the Klan's insistence that alien values imperiled Protestant cultural and political ascendancy in the 1920s.[7] The perspective from a later social movement, the campaign for civil rights, also influenced impressions of the second Klan. In many Southern states, civil rights activism was met by yet another incarnation of the Ku Klux Klan, which functioned as the terroristic wing of the massive resistance to desegregation and voting rights that erupted among white Southerners. The shadow of that crudely violent and racist Klan revival further distorted considerations of the 1920s Klan phenomenon. Influenced by the evidence of intolerance, racism, and violence that marred the public record of the 1920s Klan, hampered by the absence of thorough membership records, and reflecting the low regard for mass movements among intellectuals, a generation of scholars concluded that the second Klan was a violence-prone fringe movement populated by outcasts and losers on the margins of the white Protestant population of the New Era.

By the 1960s, however, historians began to challenge some of the central assumptions about the 1920s Klan. By refocusing attention from the national Klan hierarchy to the particular locations where the hooded order flourished, historians developed a keener appreciation of the context, variety, and depth of the Klan movement. The small-town and village base of the Ku Klux enthusiasm was effectively refuted by Kenneth Jackson's *The Ku Klux Klan in the City*. Jackson documented the centrality of the urban Klan in the 1920s. Not only did about half the membership of the Invisible Empire reside in cities, but the concentration of Klansmen in some cities (up to fifty thousand in Chicago, thirty-eight thousand in Indianapolis, thirty-five thousand in Detroit and in greater Philadelphia, twenty-three thousand in Denver, and twenty-two thousand in Portland, Oregon), along with the location of realm headquarters in urban centers, made the urban-based Klan especially influential. Moreover, Jackson argued that many Klansmen resided in transitional

urban neighborhoods, where they came into conflict with aspiring immigrants, black migrants, Catholics, and Jews moving into those contested areas.
Whereas the village-based interpretation of the Klan emphasized the abstract,
essentially ideological, clash between small-town Klansmen and minority
groups they rarely encountered, the daily friction between urban Klansmen
and their "alien" neighbors situated the Klan more concretely in the contested
cultural landscape of the 1920s.[8] Historians became more careful to point out,
as Robert Moats Miller exemplifies, that the Klan "tapped rather than created
Negrophobia and anti-Catholicism, so it did not so much inspire as reflect a
pervasive Anglo-Saxon racism."[9] The Klan movement also came into focus
as a more diverse phenomenon, encompassing both urban and small-town
experiences.

Regional studies of the Klan also demonstrated greater complexity and
variation on the matter of the hooded order's violence. Charles Alexander in
The Ku Klux Klan in the Southwest examined the first great hotbed of Klan
expansion in the 1920s, the states of Louisiana, Texas, Oklahoma, and Arkansas, from which the first alarms concerning the violent character of the
second Klan emerged. Alexander chronicled ample evidence of vigilantism
and brutality on the part of Southwestern Klansmen, but he found most of
it not to be directed in any sustained pattern against blacks, Catholics, Jews,
or immigrants. Rather, it was aimed at fellow white Protestants. Violations of
anti-vice laws (mainly bootlegging, gambling, and prostitution) and transgressions against traditional moral standards (adultery, abdication of family
responsibilities, defiance of parents, and sexual attachments across racial or
ethnic lines) prompted intimidating visits from masked Klansmen, painful
and humiliating punishment, and demands for reformed behavior or immediate departure from the community. Alexander's research underlined the
significance of the moral crisis perceived by Klansmen and the varied uses of
violence in the Klan's quest for white Protestant hegemony.[10] In contrast to
the Southwestern experience, Norman Weaver's pioneering 1954 analysis of
the Midwestern realms of Indiana, Ohio, Wisconsin, and Michigan found no
significant record of violence or physical intimidation in one of the Invisible
Empire's principal strongholds.[11]

Historians also had begun assembling evidence that brought into question
the prevailing assumptions about rank-and-file Klansmen. The increasing
availability in archives of state and local Klan membership information and a
few klavern minute-books, though geographically scattered and incomplete,
allowed scholars to move beyond conjecture and compile statistical analyses
of Klan membership.[12] In keeping with the growing interpretive emphasis on
the second Klan's representative rather than marginal status in 1920s society,
scholars found Klansmen to fit the overall demographic, occupational, and

religious patterns of their communities, especially among white Protestants. In most locales, few members from the highest or lowest economic strata joined the Klan. The most thorough recent study concluded that Ku Kluxers were "less likely to hold unskilled jobs and more likely to be in service jobs or [to be] professionals" than were non-Klansmen. Moreover, the study found that hooded knights were slightly better educated than their typical fellow citizens and more likely to be married. By most accepted economic and social measurements, Klansmen were better characterized by their stability than by marginal status.[13]

Historians' reevaluation of the 1920s Ku Klux Klan was also influenced by the emergence of social history as a major disciplinary force in the 1970s. Moving beyond the traditional narratives and sources that featured elite decision-makers, social history investigated the viewpoints and agency of ordinary people. It sought out sources—tax records, church files, rosters of voluntary associations, and court documents—and used quantitative methods that allowed the reconstruction of "history from the bottom up," with an emphasis on local conditions and everyday experience.[14] The characteristic form of social history investigation was the community study, an intensive analysis of associational networks, economic relationships, governance, belief systems, behavioral patterns, and forces of conflict and comity that made up the structure of life at the grassroots level. These were the sorts of documents and approaches that a new generation of historians of the Klan movement would use to get inside the Invisible Empire. Significantly, the social history perspective also approached popular movements with respect and sought to understand the beliefs and behavior of ordinary Americans in their own terms before subjecting them to critical analysis. In contrast to the 1950s historians who distrusted popular social movements as illiberal and repressive, the academic atmosphere has more recently been open to careful consideration of the Klan movement as an expression of popular belief, despite its racial exclusivity and intolerant worldview.

New sources and a new approach to historical scholarship produced in the 1980s and 1990s a series of focused studies on individual Klan communities that have very nearly turned the traditional interpretation of the 1920s Klan on its head. Close examinations of grassroots Klan activism in Anaheim, California; El Paso, Texas; Buffalo, New York; small communities in Oregon and northeastern Ohio; and, most important, the bellwether Klan states of Colorado and Indiana, concluded that the popular Klan of the 1920s, while diverse, was more of a civic exponent of white Protestant social values than a repressive hate group.[15] The most outspoken advocate of this "populist" interpretation of the Klan, Leonard Moore, fittingly titled his thorough examination of the Indiana Klan *Citizen Klansmen*. Acknowledging the sordid behavior and intolerant rhetoric of the Klan hierarchy, Moore emphasized the civic activism of Hoosier knights. Spurning violence and largely ignoring Indiana's small minority population, the Invisible Empire, according to Moore, "became a kind of interest group for average white Protestants who believed that their values should be dominant in their community." Up to one-third of white native-born Protestant men in Indiana joined the hooded order, representing all Protestant liturgical traditions, including German Lutherans, other than the nonpolitical fundamentalist sects.[16]

Elsewhere the new Klan community studies revealed some evidence of violence and intolerance, but, for the most part, local Klansmen were engaged in civic campaigns to enforce prohibition, improve public schools, demand better performance from elected officials, and even repair local infrastructure against the resistance of business elites and entrenched political rings. These Klansmen resembled their white Protestant neighbors, except for the hooded knights' greater engagement in civic organizations, community-building, elections, and public life in general. The second Klan became, according to Moore, "a means through which average citizens could resist elite political domination and attempt to make local and even state governments more responsive to popular interests."[17] As befitted populists, local Klansmen were often embroiled in policy conflicts with powerful local interests. "Do you know that you have been at the mercy of a political ring for nearly a quarter of a century?" Colorado knights informed their Fremont County neighbors in 1924. "Do you know that the leaders of the Independent Party [then challenging the Klan insurgency] have been that ring? They have had their hands on the public money all that period, have had court procedures in their hands and have managed the affairs of county and city alike. Politically, they have owned Fremont County, body and soul."[18] In Salt Lake City the small Klan movement criticized the political dominance of Mormon religious authorities.[19] Borrowing the language of the 1890s populists, some Klansmen referred to themselves as the "plain people" battling for the values held by most ordinary Americans.[20] The restrictive racial and religious identification of the Klan made its white Protestant nationalism an exclusive form of populism, but Moore argued that the grassroots Klan phenomenon was still more of a mainstream movement in 1920s America than it was a product of fringe beliefs and violent extremism.

While accepting portions of the populist interpretation, other historians have criticized key elements of it. Many historians of the Southern realms, for example, continue to insist on the centrality of violence and racism in the 1920s Klan. Violence was an accepted and "pervasive part of Klan activity in Alabama," concluded Glenn Feldman, even as an essential feature of moral regulation.[21] Moreover, "the revival of the KKK in Alabama coincided with a dramatic increase in mob violence, especially violence directed at the published enemies of the Klan—blacks, Catholics, Jews, immigrants, and the offenders of a variety of moral and community sensibilities."[22] So extensive was Klan violence in Alabama that its brutal image undermined the often progressive initiatives of the Invisible Empire and disrupted the hooded order's political challenge against the state's dominant planters and industrialists. Basing her conclusions on a close investigation of an Athens, Georgia, klavern, Nancy MacLean argues that Southern Klansmen developed a more sinister brand of mass mobilization: reactionary populism. Determined to uphold their racial, class, and gender privileges, Klansmen mounted a popular movement to reassert control over independent women and refractory African Americans; to protect white small property holders and middling merchants from chain stores, banks, and other forms of concentrated capital; and to choke off dangerous class consciousness on the part of workers. As the representatives of white Protestant hegemony, Klansmen acted violently, according to MacLean, "because they believed they had a *right* to use" violence. Patriarchal, racist reaction and not reform, in her view, motivated the Klan movement and therefore made the hooded order the closest American analogue to fascism rather than a popular democratic movement such as the People's Party of the 1890s.[23]

Most of the populist Klan historians fault MacLean for extrapolating beyond the limits of her evidence. They also emphasize that the largest and most dynamic area of Klandom lay outside the violent South, thus diminishing the significance of her findings for the overall Klan movement of the 1920s. Yet even if MacLean is vulnerable to the specific complaints of her fellow historians, it remains true that the breadth, sophistication, and analytical boldness of *Behind the Mask of Chivalry* make her study the best-known and most influential single book on the 1920s Klan. Thus the historical debate on the New Era Ku Klux movement is stuck in an unresolved minor key. MacLean's sweeping interpretation is contested by most specialists in the field while remaining influential in the wider scholarly community.[24] On the other hand, the populist community studies have cast doubt on the salience of bigotry and violence in the Klan movement at the grassroots level—but have not adequately incorporated the undeniable presence of violence, racist beliefs, and anti-Catholic activism into a balanced appraisal of the Klan phenomenon.

The latest examination of the 1920s Klan, Rory McVeigh's *The Rise of the Ku Klux Klan*, reflects the concerns with social movement mobilization, theoretical development, and national patterns that have characterized most sociological investigations of the hooded order.[25] Such inquiries have their place in the scholarly search for meaning. Historical understanding, however, requires attention to specificity, acknowledgment of the peculiar uniqueness of historical context, the willingness to accept contradictions, and the patience to discern patterns in a myriad of local variations. The New Era Klan movement was a complex and fragile undertaking, distinctive in its local manifestations yet subject to the influence of national figures and distant events. Klansmen were often average members of their communities, but their membership in the Invisible Empire just as often provoked fierce controversy. Ultimately most Americans in the 1920s found the Klan incompatible with order, civility, and improvement in a pluralistic democracy. For some, deep regret accompanied the discovery. The task of the historian is to examine the context and circumstances that led different groups of people to that realization.

Notes

Preface

1. David J. Goldberg, *Discontented America: The United States in the 1920s* (Baltimore: Johns Hopkins University Press, 1999).

2. David A. Horowitz, "The Normality of Extremism: The Ku Klux Klan Revisited," *Society* 35 (September-October 1998), 71, 77.

Chapter 1: The Klan in 1920s Society

1. All information regarding the Mt. Ranier Klan activities is drawn from the records of the Knights of the Ku Klux Klan, Klan No. 51, Mt. Rainier, Maryland, Special Collections, University of Maryland Libraries.

2. Series I, Klan No. 51 Records, minutes of March 23, 1925.

3. Series I, Klan No. 51 Records, minutes of March 13, 1924.

4. Series I, Klan No. 51 Records, minutes of January 22, 1925 (see also September 11, 1924).

5. Series I, Klan No. 51 Records, minutes of April 10, 1924.

6. Series I, Klan No. 51 Records, minutes of September 13, 1923

7. Series I, Klan No. 51 Records, minutes of October 9, 1924.

8. Series I, Klan No. 51 Records, minutes of November 8, 1923.

9. Series I, Klan No. 51 Records, minutes of December 23, 1924.

10. Series I, Klan No. 51 Records, minutes of January 22, 1925.

11. Series I, Klan No. 51 Records, minutes of August 11, 1923.

12. Series I, Klan No. 51 Records, minutes of January 8, 1924.

13. Series I, Klan No. 51 Records, minutes of February 26, 1925.

14. William Allen White, *The Autobiography of William Allen White* (New York: Macmillan, 1946), 631.

15. Thomas R. Pegram, "Kluxing the Eighteenth Amendment: The Anti-Saloon League, the Ku Klux Klan, and the Fate of Prohibition in the 1920s," in Wendy Gamber, Michael Grossberg, and Hendrik Hartog, eds, *American Public Life and the Historical Imagination* (Notre Dame, Ind.: University of Notre Dame Press, 2003), 244–49.

16. Donald Holley, "A Look behind the Masks: The 1920s Ku Klux Klan in Monticello, Arkansas," *Arkansas Historical Quarterly* 60 (Summer 2001), 136–37.

17. Kathleen Blee, *Women of the Klan: Racism and Gender in the 1920s* (Berkeley: University of California Press, 1991), 168–71.

18. "Dr. Evans, Imperial Wizard, Defines Klan Principles and Outlines Klan Activities," *Imperial Night-Hawk* 1 (January 13, 1924), 2.

19. Allen W. Trelease, *White Terror: The Ku Klux Klan Conspiracy and Southern Reconstruction* (New York: Harper and Row, 1971), 383–418. Historians disagree on the connections between the various incarnations of the Invisible Empire. Popular studies like Wyn Craig Wade's *The Fiery Cross* (New York: Oxford University Press, 1987) present an essential continuity of white supremacist purpose and violent method over a century of Klan activism. The standard scholarly survey—David M. Chalmers, *Hooded Americanism: The History of the Ku Klux Klan*, 3rd ed. (Durham, N.C.: Duke University Press, 1981)—is more careful about the distinctive features of the Klan during Reconstruction, the 1920s, and thereafter, but nevertheless sees the hooded order as "part of an enduring tradition" (7) that merits comprehensive analysis across the decades. In contrast, more recent studies of the 1920s Klan, especially at the grassroots level, acknowledge symbolic links to the Reconstruction Klan but strongly emphasize the distinctive character of the 1920s mass movement and downplay comparisons with the splinter Klan revivals of later decades. In an analysis of the original Klan's use of costumes and carnivalesque theatricality, Elaine Frantz Parsons makes a welcome argument for the distinctive cultural context of the Reconstruction Klan's terrorist methodology. "The Reconstruction-era Ku Klux Klan," she writes, "was intimately intertwined with, and completely dependent on, contemporary popular cultural forms and institutions" (Elaine Frantz Parsons, "Midnight Rangers: Costume and Performance in the Reconstruction-Era Ku Klux Klan," *Journal of American History* 92 [December 2005], 811).

20. John Higham, *Strangers in the Land: Patterns of American Nativism, 1860–1925*, 2nd ed. (New York: Atheneum, 1970), 265–99.

21. William G. Shepherd, "How I Put Over the Klan," *Collier's* 82 (July 14, 1928), 6–7, 32; Chalmers, *Hooded Americanism*, 28–31.

22. David M. Kennedy, *Over Here: The First World War and American Society* (New York: Oxford University Press, 1980), 81.

23. Glenn Feldman, *Politics, Society, and the Klan in Alabama, 1915–1949* (Tuscaloosa: University of Alabama Press, 1999), 22–23.

24. Kenneth T. Jackson, *The Ku Klux Klan in the City, 1915–1930* (New York: Oxford University Press, 1967), 7–8.

25. Robert L. Duffus, "Salesmen of Hate: The Ku Klux Klan," *World's Work* 46 (May 1923), 34–36.

26. Jackson, *Klan in the City*, 70, 81, 118–19, 199–200; Larry R. Gerlach, *Blazing Crosses in Zion: The Ku Klux Klan in Utah* (Logan: Utah State University Press, 1982), 117; MacLean, *Behind the Mask of Chivalry: The Making of the Second Ku Klux Klan* (New York: Oxford University Press, 1994), 13; Pegram, "Kluxing the Eighteenth Amendment," 244.

27. Robert Moats Miller, "A Note on the Relationship between the Protestant Churches and the Revived Ku Klux Klan," *Journal of Southern History* 22 (August 1956), 355–68.

28. MacLean, *Behind the Mask*, 8.

29. Chalmers, *Hooded Americanism*, 254.

30. Charles P. Sweeney, "The Great Bigotry Merger," *The Nation* 115 (July 15, 1922), 10; Glenn Michael Zuber, "'Onward Christian Klansmen!' War, Religious Conflict, and the Rise of the Second Ku Klux Klan, 1912–1928" (PhD dissertation, Indiana University, 2004), 33–35, 51.

31. Leonard J. Moore, *Citizen Klansmen: The Ku Klux Klan in Indiana, 1921–1928* (Chapel Hill: University of North Carolina Press, 1991), 70–75. (The pattern may be true for the South as well, but the data are less clear. See MacLean, *Behind the Mask*, 8, 202n8.)

32. Robert Alan Goldberg, *Hooded Empire: The Ku Klux Klan in Colorado* (Urbana: University of Illinois Press, 1981), 7.

33. Zuber, "'Onward Christian Klansmen!'," 79–83.

34. "Texas Klansman Outlines Principles upon Which the Knights of the Ku Klux Klan Is Founded," *Imperial Night-Hawk* 1 (April 4, 1923), 7.

35. Ward Greene, "Notes for a History of the Klan," *American Mercury* 5 (June 1925), 241–42. Many of the *New York World* articles were based on the research reproduced in Henry P. Fry, *The Modern Ku Klux Klan* (Boston: Small, Maynard, 1922; reprinted Honolulu: University Press of the Pacific, 2003).

36. "Wizard in Vigorous Defense of Ku Klux," *New York Times* (hereafter *NYT*), October 13, 1921, 1.

37. "Wizard Collapses Defending Ku Klux," *NYT*, October 14, 1921, 1.

38. "Congress Inquiry in Ku Klux Is Off," *NYT*, October 18, 1921, 6.

39. Chalmers, *Hooded Americanism*, 38.

40. Kallen quoted in Christopher Capozzola, *Uncle Sam Wants You: World War I and the Making of the Modern American Citizen* (New York: Oxford University Press, 2008), 212.

41. See Goldberg, *Discontented America.*

42. "Klan Joins Fight on World Court," *NYT*, November 7, 1925, 1.

43. "World Court Vote Faces Long Delay," *NYT*, January 22, 1926, 1.

44. Higham, *Strangers in the Land*, 198–200.

45. Kallen quoted in Morton Keller, *Regulating a New Society: Public Policy and Social Change in America, 1900–1933* (Cambridge, Mass.: Harvard University Press, 1994), 226.

46. W. E. B. DuBois, "The Shape of Fear," *North American Review* 223 (June 1926), 293.

47. Hiram W. Evans, "The Klan's Fight for Americanism," *North American Review* 223 (March 1926), 45

48. Sweeney, "Great Bigotry Merger," 9.

49. Quoted in Zuber, "'Onward Christian Klansmen!'," 231.

50. "*K. K. K.*," *Outlook* 136 (January 9, 1924), 51.

51. Frank Bohn, "The Ku Klux Klan Interpreted," *American Journal of Sociology* 30 (January 1925), 405–7.

52. Stanley Frost, "When the Klan Rules: The Giant in the White Hood," *Outlook* 135 (December 19, 1923), 675.

53. See Stanley Coben, *Rebellion against Victorianism: The Impetus for Cultural Change in 1920s America* (New York: Oxford University Press, 1991), 136–58.

54. Lynn Dumenil, "'The Insatiable Maw of Bureaucracy': Antistatism and Education Reform in the 1920s," *Journal of American History* 77 (September 1990), 518.

55. Jon Gjerde, *The Minds of the West: Ethnocultural Evolution in the Rural Middle West, 1830–1917* (Chapel Hill: University of North Carolina Press, 1997), 276.

56. Thomas R. Pegram, "Hoodwinked: The Anti-Saloon League and the Ku Klux Klan in 1920s Prohibition Enforcement," *Journal of the Gilded Age and Progressive Era* 7 (January 2008), 95–97.

57. MacLean, *Behind the Mask*, 31.

58. Michael A. Lerner, *Dry Manhattan: Prohibition in New York City* (Cambridge, Mass.: Harvard University Press, 2007), 172–81.

59. MacLean, *Behind the Mask*, 111–16.

60. Blee, *Women of the Klan*, 49–55.

61. Dorothy Schwieder, "A Farmer and the Ku Klux Klan in Northwest Iowa," *Annals of Iowa* 61 (Summer 2002), 317.

62. Jackson, *Klan in the City*, 10. Some sources estimate that Clarke and Tyler employed as many as eleven hundred kleagles (Charles C. Alexander, *The Ku Klux Klan in the Southwest* [Lexington: University of Kentucky Press, 1965], 7; see also William G. Shepherd, "Ku Klux Koin," *Collier's* 82 [July 21, 1928], 39).

63. Duffus, "Salesmen of Hate," 34–36, quotation on 34.

64. Roland G. Fryer Jr. and Steven D. Levitt, "Hatred and Profits: Getting under the Hood of the Ku Klux Klan," National Bureau of Economic Research Working Paper No. W13417, September 1, 2007, 11, 33, 4.

65. *State of Indiana vs. the Knights of the Ku Klux Klan*, deposition of Hugh F. Emmons, February 20, 1928, 25, microfilm transcript, Indiana Historical Society (hereafter referred to as "Emmons desposition").

66. Goldberg, *Hooded Empire*, 11.

67. Chalmers, *Hooded Americanism*, 100–104; Duffus, "Salesmen of Hate," 37–38; "Deposed Goblins Say Klan Is Broken," *NYT*, December 3, 1921, 7; "Simmons Defies Klan 'Muckrakers,'" *NYT*, December 8, 1921, 9; "Klan Makes Simmons Emperor for Life," *NYT*, November 29, 1922, 2.

68. Duffus, "Salesmen of Hate," 32.

69. Stanley Frost, "When the Klan Rules: The Giant Clears for Action," *Outlook* 135 (December 26, 1923), 716.

70. "Klan Editor Kills Simmons's Counsel in Atlanta Office," *NYT*, November 6, 1923, 1.

71. "Klan Ousts Clarke from Official Post," *NYT*, March 7, 1923, 1; "Emperor Simmons Gains Control of Klan by Court Action Which Ties Up All Funds," *NYT*, April 4, 1923, 1; "Commission Rule Ordered for Klan," *NYT*, April 8, 1923, 22; "Klan Funds Tied Up by an Injunction," *NYT*, June 1, 1923, 14; "Orders Klan Secrets Kept," *NYT*, June 23, 1923, 13; "Accuse Klan Chiefs of Irregularities," *NYT*, October 30, 1923, 22; "Ku Klux Klan Ousts Simmons and Clarke," *NYT*, January 12, 1924, 1; "Says Simmons Sold His Rights in Klan," *NYT*, February 13, 1924, 5.

72. Schwieder, "A Farmer and the Klan in Northwest Iowa," 306.

73. Goldberg, *Hooded Empire*, 98–99. See chapter 6 for specific episodes of violence.

74. Norman Fredric Weaver, "The Knights of the Ku Klux Klan in Wisconsin, Indiana, Ohio and Michigan" (PhD dissertation, University of Wisconsin, 1954), 212–21; Stanley Frost, "The Klan Shows Its Hand in Indiana," *Outlook* 137 (June 4, 1924), 190; Emmons deposition, 25, 45–46.

75. See chapter 7 for a detailed discussion of politics and the Klan.

76. Robert A. Hohner, *Prohibition and Politics: The Life of Bishop James Cannon, Jr.* (Columbia: University of South Carolina Press, 1999), 227.

77. Charles C. Alexander, "Kleagles and Cash: The Ku Klux Klan as a Business Organization, 1915–1930," *Business History Review* 39 (Autumn 1965), 365 (other historians estimate forty-five thousand members [Wade, *Fiery Cross*, 253] and "close to a hundred thousand" [Chalmers, *Hooded Americanism*, 305]).

78. Jackson, *Klan in the City*, 253–54.

Chapter 2: Building a White Protestant Community

1. Knights of the Ku Klux Klan to Dear Sir, November 25, 1924, Roll 12, Ernest Hurst Cherrington Series, Microfilm Edition of the Temperance and Prohibition Papers, Ohio Historical Society.

2. Fry, *Modern Ku Klux Klan*, 13–15.

3. Emmons deposition, 371–85, quotations on 376–77, 378–79, 385.

4. Lynn Dumenil, *Freemasonry and American Culture, 1880–1930* (Princeton, N.J.: Princeton University Press, 1984), 125.

5. Evans quoted in Zuber, "'Onward Christian Klansmen!'," 188–89.

6. Shepherd, "How I Put Over the Klan," 32.

7. Ku Klux Klan Form P-217 50M 7-29-21, Series IV, Box 1, Folder 9; The Ku Klux Klan Tillamook, Oregon Chapter No. 8, 1922–1929, Bx 46, Division of Special Collections and University Archives, University of Oregon.

8. Petition of John Edward Rogers, April 1, 1926, Tillamook Klan.

9. Fry, *Modern Ku Klux Klan*, 68–70, quotation on 70.

10. Blee, *Women of the Klan*, 167.

11. Goldberg, *Hooded Empire*, 13.

12. Christopher N. Cocoltchos, "The Ku Klux Klan in Anaheim, California," in Shawn Lay, ed., *The Invisible Empire in the West: Toward a New Historical Appraisal of the Ku Klux Klan of the 1920s* (Urbana: University of Illinois Press, 1992), 107.

13. "Klan Aids Negro Church," *NYT*, June 17, 1924, 33.

14. "Klan in Texas State House," *NYT*, April 28, 1923, 21.

15. "Klan Pays Negro Church Debt," *NYT*, November 29, 1924, 15.

16. "Negroes and Klansmen March in Church Parade," *NYT*, September 27, 1925, 1.

17. Mark N. Morris, "Saving Society through Politics: The Ku Klux Klan in Dallas, Texas, in the 1920s" (PhD dissertation, University of North Texas, 1997), 61.

18. William D. Jenkins, *Steel Valley Klan: The Ku Klux Klan in Ohio's Mahoning Valley* (Kent, Ohio: Kent State University Press, 1990), 87.

19. Moore, *Citizen Klansmen*, 38–39.

20. *Senatorial Campaign Expenditures: Hearings before a Special Committee Investigating Expenditures in Senatorial Primary and General Elections. United States Senate, Sixty-Ninth Congress* (Washington, D.C.: U.S. Government Printing Office, 1926), 2054

21. Ibid., 2055.

22. David A. Horowitz, ed., *Inside the Klavern: The Secret History of a Ku Klux Klan of the 1920s* (Carbondale: Southern Illinois University Press, 1999), 69–70, quotation on 70.

23. See Emerson H. Loucks, *The Ku Klux Klan in Pennsylvania: A Study in Nativism* (Harrisburg, Pa.: Telegraph Press, 1936), 82, for Klan policies on late dues and taxes.

24. *Senatorial Campaign Expenditures*, 2060; Emmons deposition, 14.

25. Moore, *Citizen Klansmen*, 46.

26. Jackson, *Klan in the City*, 237.

27. *Senatorial Campaign Expenditures*, 2028–29.

28. Blee, *Women of the Klan*, 165.

29. Kathleen M. Blee, "Evidence, Empathy, and Ethics: Lessons from Oral Histories of the Klan," *Journal of American History* 80 (September 1993), 601.

30. Lynn Dumenil, *The Modern Temper: American Culture and Society in the 1920s* (New York: Hill and Wang, 1995), 238.

31. Loucks, *Klan in Pennsylvania*, 58.

32. "Bargersville Gets a Thrill," *Fiery Cross*, February 16, 1923, 5.

33. Leroy Percy, "The Modern Ku Klux Klan," *Atlantic Monthly* 130 (July 1922), 126.

34. Goldberg, *Hooded Empire*, 59–60.

35. Holley, "A Look behind the Masks," 131.

36. "Huge Ceremonial Doubles Citizenship of Klan at Clanton, Alabama," *Imperial Night-Hawk* 2 (May 14, 1924), 8.

37. Charles Rambow, "Ku Klux Klan in the 1920s: A Concentration on the Black Hills," *South Dakota History* (Winter 1973), 76.

38. Blee, *Women of the Klan*, 169.

39. Chalmers, *Hooded Americanism*, 219.

40. Robert L. Duffus, "Ancestry and End of the Ku Klux Klan," *World's Work* 46 (September 1923), 528.

41. Morris, "Saving Society through Politics," 133.

42. Loucks, *Klan in Pennsylvania*, 88.

43. Goldberg, *Hooded Empire*, 27

44. Ibid., 97.

45. Blee, *Women of the Klan*, 165, 169.

46. Tom Rice, "Protecting Protestantism: The Ku Klux Klan vs. the Motion Picture Industry," *Film History* 20 (2008), 367–80.

47. "Catholic Propaganda Clutches Movies," *Imperial Night-Hawk* 1 (October 10, 1923), 4; "Movies Broadcasting Foreign Propaganda," *Imperial Night-Hawk* 2 (June 25, 1924), 2; for an example of a South Carolina boycott of *The Pilgrim*, see "Klan Komment," *Imperial Night-Hawk* 1 (May 9, 1923), 3.

48. Rice, "Protecting Protestantism," 370; "'Bella Donna'—Bah!" *Fiery Cross*, April 27, 1923, 4.

49. "Constructive Law Enforcement—Sheet Three," in *A Suggested Course of Study in the Fundamentals of Klankraft* (Atlanta: Knights of the Ku Klux Klan, 1925), Defendant's Exhibit No. 1, Emmons deposition.

50. Tom Rice, "'The True Story of the Ku Klux Klan': Defining the Klan through Film," *Journal of American Studies* 42 (2008), 471–88, quotation on 476.

51. Eckard V. Toy, "Robe and Gown: The Ku Klux Klan in Eugene, Oregon, during the 1920s," in Lay, *Invisible Empire in the West*, 153.

52. "The Story of 'The Toll of Justice,'" promotional pamphlet, author's collection.

53. "Wilbert Pictures Company Presents Mildred Melrose in a Mighty Drama of the Underworld," promotional poster, author's collection.

54. *Colonel Mayfield's Weekly* quoted in Casey Edward Greene, "Apostles of Hate: The Ku Klux Klan in and near Houston, Texas, 1920-1982" (MA thesis, University of Houston, Clear Lake, 1995), 27.

55. See M. William Lutholtz, *Grand Dragon: D. C. Stephenson and the Ku Klux Klan in Indiana* (West Lafayette, Ind.: Purdue University Press, 1991), 83–93, for a restrained account.

56. Blee, *Women of the Klan*, 135–36, quotation on 136.

57. Moore, *Citizen Klansmen*, 99.

58. Grand Dragon, Realm of Indiana to All Exalted Cyclops, Other Officers and Members of the Invisible Empire Realm of Indiana, June 13, 1924, Plaintiff Exhibit 30, Emmons deposition.

59. "Only 5,000 of Klan Invade Fort Wayne," *NYT*, November 11, 1923, 18.

60. Goldberg, *Hooded Empire*, 97.

61. "Thousand Rally to the Klan in Texas," *Imperial Night-Hawk* 1 (October 31, 1923), 6; Morris, "Saving Society through Politics," 134–35; and Rosalind Benjet, "The Ku Klux Klan and the Jewish Community of Dallas, 1921–1923," *Southern Jewish History* 6 (2003), 158.

62. Photograph reproduced in "Welcome to Kolorado, Klan Kountry," *Colorado Springs Independent*, May 22, 2003 (online edition).

63. Moore, *Citizen Klansmen*, 97.

64. Morris, "Saving Society through Politics," 134.

65. Blee, *Women of the Klan*, 165.

66. "Saturday, August 20, 1927, Field Day and Baseball Game, Benefit of Jr. O.U.A.M. Orphans' Home and Klan Haven Home, American League Park," pamphlet,

Records of the Knights of the Ku Klux Klan, Klan No. 51; Loucks, *Klan in Pennsylvania*, 93. For more on Klan baseball teams, which even played all-black and Jewish nines, see "Indiana Klans Have Baseball Teams," *Imperial Night-Hawk* 1 (April 4, 1923), 3; Brian Carroll, "Beating the Klan: Baseball Coverage in Wichita before Integration, 1920–1930," *Baseball Research Journal* 37 (Winter 2008–2009), 51–61; and "Ku Klux Klan Faces Hebrews Labor Day," *Washington Post*, September 1, 1926.

67. Moore, *Citizen Klansmen*, 95.

68. Duffus, "Ancestry and End of the Ku Klux Klan," 528.

69. "75,000 Klansmen Gather in Dallas to Impress Nation," *NYT*, October 21, 1923, 1, 3.

70. "Flames Burn a Fiery Cross," *Fiery Cross*, March 23, 1923, 8.

71. William Clayton Wilkinson Jr., "Memories of the Ku Klux Klan in One Indiana Town," *Indiana Magazine of History* 102 (December 2006), 345–46, quotations on 346.

72. Moore, *Citizen Klansmen*, 47–52.

73. Shawn Lay, *Hooded Knights on the Niagara: The Ku Klux Klan in Buffalo, New York* (New York: New York University Press, 1995), 106–7.

74. Loucks, *Klan in Pennsylvania*, 87.

75. Gerlach, *Blazing Crosses in Zion*, 93, 107–8, quotation on 77.

76. Horowitz, *Inside the Klavern*, 62.

77. Yvonne Brown, "Tolerance and Bigotry in Southwest Louisiana: The Ku Klux Klan, 1921–23," *Louisiana History* 47 (Spring 2006), 158.

78. Gerlach, *Blazing Crosses in Zion*, 76.

79. "Pittsburgh Church Puts Klansmen Out," *NYT*, April 2, 1923, 1.

80. Feldman, *Klan in Alabama*, 61–62.

81. Horowitz, *Inside the Klavern*, 7–8, 13, 19, 107.

82. Chalmers, *Hooded Americanism*, 143; Richard E. Jones, "The Politics of the Ku Klux Klan in Kansas during the 1920s" (MA thesis, Emporia State University, 2007), 9, 11–13.

83. Goldberg, *Hooded Empire*, 80.

84. MacLean, *Behind the Mask*, 69–72, 182.

85. Brooks R. Blevins, "The Strike and the Still: Anti-Radical Violence and the Ku Klux Klan in the Ozarks," *Arkansas Historical Quarterly* 52 (Winter 1993), 412–19, quotation on 414.

86. Minutes of September 13, 1923, Mt. Rainier Klan No. 51.

87. Minutes of April 20, 1924, Mt. Rainier Klan No. 51.

88. Loucks, *Klan in Pennsylvania*, 92; Chalmers, *Hooded Americanism*, 239–40.

89. "Contributions Bring Abbott Trust Fund to Total of $10,637.98," *Imperial Night-Hawk* 1 (November 7, 1923), 7.

90. Cocoltchos, "Klan in Anaheim," 108–9.

91. Horowitz, *Inside the Klavern*, 27, 36, 39, 54, 58, 79, 88.

92. Clement Charlton Moseley, "The Political Influence of the Ku Klux Klan in Georgia, 1915–1925," *Georgia Historical Quarterly* 57 (1973), 247; Emmons deposition, 142.

93. Chalmers, *Hooded Americanism*, 117.

94. Horowitz, *Inside the Klavern*, 56.

95. Ibid., 44.

96. Greene, "Apostles of Hate," 37.

97. Loucks, *Klan in Pennsylvania*, 89.

98. Moore, *Citizen Klansmen*, 104.

99. "Okmulgee Klansmen Give Worthy Widow $2,000 Bungalow," *Imperial Night-Hawk* 1 (September 19, 1923), 5.

100. Suzanne H. Schrems, "The Ultimate Patriots? Oklahoma Women of the Ku Klux Klan," *Chronicles of Oklahoma* 79 (Summer 2001), 195–96.

101. "Junior Pig Club," "Klan Komment," *Imperial Night-Hawk* 2 (January 23, 1924), 5.

102. Emmons deposition, 173.

103. Edward P. Akin, "The Ku Klux Klan in Georgia: Social Change and Conflict, 1915–1930" (PhD dissertation, UCLA, 1994), 640.

104. "Klan Plays Part of Good Samaritan to Modern Magdalene," *Fiery Cross*, February 23, 1923, 1.

105. Horowitz, *Inside the Klavern*, 42–43, quotation on 42.

106. Ibid., 37–38, quotation on 38.

107. Loucks, *Klan in Pennsylvania*, 91.

108. Shawn Lay, *War, Revolution, and the Ku Klux Klan: A Study of Intolerance in a Border City* (El Paso, Tex.: Texas Western Press, 1985), 76, 109.

109. Greene, "Apostles of Hate," 37.

110. "Jefferson City Klan Aids Boy Scouts," *Imperial Night-Hawk* 1 (September 12, 1923), 4.

111. Roger K. Hux, "The Ku Klux Klan in Macon, 1919–1925," *Georgia Historical Quarterly* 62 (Summer 1978), 158.

112. "Charleston Klansmen Put Over 'Y' Drive," *Imperial Night-Hawk* 1 (April 25, 1923), 4.

113. Alexander, *Klan in the Southwest*, 92.

114. Goldberg, *Hooded Empire*, 16.

115. Ibid., 155.

116. Horowitz, *Inside the Klavern*, 82, 83, 98.

117. "Salvation Army Hut Built by Klansmen," *Imperial Night-Hawk* 1 (August 15, 1923), 4.

118. Blee, *Women of the Klan*, 134.

119. Greene, "Apostles of Hate," 38.

120. Hux, "Klan in Macon," 158.

121. Lay, *War, Revolution, and the Klan*, 109.

122. Ibid., 76, 111.

123. Greene, "Apostles of Hate," 37–38.

124. A Great Titan of the Realm of Texas, "The Klan as a Civic Asset," *Papers Read at the Meeting of Grand Dragons, Knights of the Ku Klux Klan at their First Annual Meeting Held at Asheville, North Carolina, July 1923* (reprint ed., New York: Arno, 1977), 69.

125. "Sordid Story of Girls' Shame Causes Klan at Shreveport to Plan Protestant Refuge," *Imperial Night-Hawk* 1 (May 9, 1923), 2.

126. "Kansas Klansmen to Build Big Hospital," *Imperial Night-Hawk* 1 (June 27, 1923), 4; "Will Break Ground for $125,000 Hospital to be Erected by Klansmen at El Dorado, Ark.," *Imperial Night-Hawk* 1 (June 27, 1923), 8.

127. Moore, *Citizen Klansmen*, 105; Allen Safianow, "'Konklave in Kokomo' Revisited," *The Historian* 50 (May 1988), 333n12, 344–45; and Blee, *Women of the Klan*, 136, 143–44.

128. Moore, *Citizen Klansmen*, 105–6, quotations on 105.

129. Safianow, "'Konklave' Revisited," 344.

130. "Dallas Klan Completes $75,000 Protestant Home for Orphan Children," *Imperial Night-Hawk* 1 (June 6, 1923), 8; Morris, "Saving Society through Politics," 60–61, 135, 143–44; Blee, *Women of the Klan*, 143.

131. Loucks, *Klan in Pennsylvania*, 93.

132. Loucks, *Klan in Pennsylvania*, 154–61; Blee, *Women of the Klan*, 62–63.

133. Charles Postel, *The Populist Vision* (New York: Oxford University Press, 2007), 3–33.

134. Alexander, "Kleagles and Cash," 354–55.

135. Horowitz, *Inside the Klavern*, 84, 86.

136. Loucks, *Klan in Pennsylvania*, 94–95, quotation on 94

137. Emmons deposition, 273–81, quotation on 281.

138. Ibid., 282–83.

139. Grand Dragon, Realm of Indiana to All Organizations in the Realm of Indiana, November 20, 1923, Plaintiff Exhibit 31, Emmons deposition.

140. Grand Dragon, Realm of Indiana to All Exalted Cyclops, Kligrapps, Other Officers and Members of the Invisible Empire Realm of Indiana, January 15, 1924, Plaintiff Exhibit 32, Emmons deposition.

141. Grand Dragon, Realm of Indiana to All Exalted Cyclops, Kligrapps, Other Officers and Members of the Invisible Empire Realm of Indiana, June 13, 1924, Plaintiff Exhibit 30, Emmons deposition.

142. Samuel Taylor Moore, "Consequences of the Klan: Results of the Hoosier Experiment in Invisible Monarchical Government," *Independent* 113 (December 20, 1924), 534.

143. Horowitz, *Inside the Klavern*, 65, 66, 95.

144. Dumenil, *Modern Temper*, 312.

Chapter 3: Defining Americanism

1. Stanley Frost, "When the Klan Rules: Invoking the Whirlwind," *Outlook* 136 (January 16, 1924), 100.

2. Hiram Wesley Evans, "The Klan: Defender of Americanism," *Forum* 74 (December 1925), 814.

3. Dr. H. W. Evans, "Our Mission of Protestant Solidarity," *Kourier Magazine* 2 (July 1926), 4.

4. Evans, "Defender of Americanism," 806. Evans repeated these assertions as part of his standard public overview of Klan beliefs. For a nearly identical recitation of the case against pluralism, see Evans, "Fight for Americanism," 40–43.

5. Dr. H. W. Evans, "Our Constant War against Alienism," *Kourier Magazine* 2 (May 1926), 5.

6. Frost, "Invoking the Whirlwind," 102.

7. A National Lecturer, "The Klan: Protestantism's Ally," *Kourier Magazine* 1 (August 1925), 12.

8. Keller, *Regulating a New Society*, 5.

9. Evans, "Fight for Americanism," 53.

10. James Weldon Johnson, Secretary, National Association for the Advancement of Colored People to Editor of *The Forum*, Forum 75 (February 1926), 307.

11. Fry, *Modern Ku Klux Klan*, 94.

12. Evans, "Defender of Americanism," 803.

13. Evans, "Fight for Americanism," 52.

14. "75,000 Klansmen Gather in Dallas to Impress Nation," 3.

15. Evans, "Defender of Americanism," 804.

16. An Exalted Cyclops, "Principles and Purposes of the Knights of the Ku Klux Klan," *Papers Read at the Meeting of Grand Dragons, 1923*, 129.

17. Evans, "Fight for Americanism," 52.

18. Quoted in MacLean, *Behind the Mask*, 132.

19. Evans, "Fight for Americanism," 52.

20. Evans, "Fight for Americanism," 53.

21. Matthew Frye Jacobson, *Whiteness of a Different Color: European Immigrants and the Alchemy of Race* (Cambridge, Mass.: Harvard University Press, 1998), 227.

22. See Brown, "Tolerance and Bigotry in Southwest Louisiana," 162.

23. Dr. H. W. Evans, "The Attitude of the Knights of the Ku Klux Klan toward the Jew," *Papers Read at the Meeting of Grand Dragons, 1923*, 121–22.

24. Jacobson, *Whiteness*, 57.

25. Gerlach, *Blazing Crosses in Zion*, 78–79.

26. Jacobson, *Whiteness*, 78–83, 96–97.

27. Jonathan Peter Spiro, *Defending the Master Race: Conservation, Eugenics, and the Legacy of Madison Grant* (Burlington: University of Vermont Press, 2009), 161–66; M. Gidley, "Notes on F. Scott Fitzgerald and the Passing of the Great Race," *Journal of American Studies* 7 (August 1973), 172n4 (*Gatsby*, 173); Matthew Pratt Guterl, *The Color of Race in America, 1900–1949* (Cambridge, Mass.: Harvard University Press, 2001) (Harding, 54; Garvey and DuBois, 142).

28. Evans, "Fight for Americanism," 36.

29. Guterl, *Color of Race*, 32–37.

30. Evans, "Fight for Americanism," 43.

31. John Higham, *Strangers in the Land*, 282.

32. Evans, "Attitude toward the Jew," 122.

33. Evans, "Defender of Americanism," 812.

34. Evans, "Fight for Americanism," 60.

35. Madison Grant, *The Passing of the Great Race* (New York: Charles Scribner's Sons, 1916), 16.

36. Jacobson, *Whiteness*, 91.

37. Ibid., 96–97.

38. Guterl, *Color of Race*, 98. Although he denied it, Stoddard was reputed to be one of the founding officers of the Massachusetts Klan and was publicly labeled "the most prominent member" of Boston's klavern (*Boston Sunday Advertiser*, January 7, 1923, 1; reference provided by Professor Mark P. Richard).

39. Fry, *Modern Ku Klux Klan*, 104–5.

40. "Methodist Bishop Defends the Negro," *NYT*, March 4, 1926, 11.

41. Evans, "Fight for Americanism," 53.

42. Dr. H. W. Evans, "Where Do We Go from Here," *Papers Read at the Meeting of Grand Dragons, 1923*, 12–13, quotation on 11.

43. "75,000 Klansmen Gather in Dallas," *NYT*, October 25, 1923, 3.

44. Evans, "Attitude toward the Jew," *Papers Read at the Meeting of Grand Dragons, 1923*, 121.

45. MacLean, *Behind the Mask*, 145–46.

46. Evans, "Fight for Americanism," 45.

47. Ibid., 40.

48. H. W. Evans, "The Catholic Question as Viewed by the Ku Klux Klan," *Current History* 26 (July 1927), 563.

49. Thomas J. Shelley, "'What the Hell Is an Encyclical?' Governor Alfred E. Smith, Charles C. Marshall, Esq., and Father Francis P. Duffy," *U.S. Catholic Historian* 15 (Spring 1997), 99.

50. Evans, "Catholic Question," 568.

51. Horowitz, *Inside the Klavern*, 148; Lay, *Hooded Knights on the Niagara*, 76.

52. Lay, *Hooded Knights on the Niagara*, 47.

53. Ibid., 43.

54. Emmons deposition, 38, 129–34, 265–69, quotation on 329.

55. Ibid., 330.

56. Benjet, "The Klan and the Jewish Community of Dallas," 139, 140.

57. "75,000 Klansmen Gather in Dallas," 1, 3.

58. "Why They Join the Klan," *New Republic* (November 21, 1923), 321.

59. Jackson, *Klan in the City*, 201.

60. Grand Dragon of South Carolina, "The Regulation of Immigration," *Papers Read at the Meeting of Grand Dragons, 1923*, 72.

61. Alexander, *Klan in the Southwest*, 24.

62. Ruben Donato, *Mexicans and Hispanos in Colorado Schools and Communities, 1920–1960* (Albany: State University of New York Press, 2007), 49–53.

63. "Mexican Immigrants Flock over Border," *Imperial Night-Hawk* 1 (May 30, 1923), 4.

64. "Imperial Wizard Outlines Attitude of the Klan toward Unrestricted Immigration," *Imperial Night-Hawk* 1 (April 25, 1923), 6.

65. Shawn Lay, *War, Revolution, and the Klan*, 159.

66. Gary Michael Roldan, "Activities of the Ku Klux Klan in Kern and Los Angeles Counties, California, during the 1920s" (MA thesis, California State University, Fresno, 1996), 24–25; Christopher N. Cocoltchos, "The Invisible Government and the Viable Community: The Ku Klux Klan in Orange County, California, during the 1920s" (PhD dissertation, UCLA, 1979), 235, 238–40 (for a different assessment of the southern California Klan's disposition toward Mexican migrants, drawn from 1930s evidence, see Carlos M. Larralde and Richard Griswold del Castillo, "San Diego's Ku Klux Klan, 1920–1980," *San Diego History* 46 [Spring/Summer 2000], 68–89).

67. MacLean, *Behind the Mask*, 49; Feldman, *Klan in Alabama*, 56–57.

68. Alexander, *Klan in the Southwest*, 26.

69. Scott Ellsworth, *Death in a Promised Land: The Tulsa Race Riot of 1921* (Baton Rouge: Louisiana State University Press, 1982), 65–66, 71.

70. William M. Tuttle Jr., *Race Riot: Chicago in the Red Summer of 1919* (New York: Atheneum, 1970), 257.

71. W. Fitzhugh Brundage, *Lynching in the New South: Georgia and Virginia, 1880–1930* (Urbana: University of Illinois Press, 1993), 19–23.

72. Akin, "Klan in Georgia," 624–27.

73. Elizabeth Robeson, "An 'Ominous Defiance': The Lowman Lynchings of 1926," in Winfred B. Moore Jr. and Orville Vernon Burton, eds., *Toward the Meeting of the Waters: Currents in the Civil Rights Movement of South Carolina during the Twentieth Century* (Columbia: University of South Carolina Press, 2008), 65–92.

74. Quoted in Akin, "Klan in Georgia," 630.

75 A Great Titan, Realm of Texas, "The Officers of a Klan and Their Responsibility to Law Enforcement," *Papers Read at the Meeting of Grand Dragons, 1923*, 56–57.

76. Akin, "Klan in Georgia," 631.

77. Norman Fredric Weaver, "The Knights of the Ku Klux Klan in Wisconsin, Indiana, Ohio and Michigan" (PhD dissertation, University of Wisconsin, 1954), 285–87.

78. Jackson, *Klan in the City*, 140.

79. For a full discussion of the case, see Kevin Boyle, *Arc of Justice: A Saga of Race, Civil Rights, and Murder in the Jazz Age* (New York: Henry Holt, 2004).

80. Moore, *Citizen Klansmen*, 144.

81. Emma Lou Thornbrough, "Segregation in Indiana during the Klan Era of the 1920's," *Mississippi Valley Historical Review* 47 (March 1961), 599–601.

82. "The Klan's Attitude toward the Negro," *Imperial Night-Hawk* 2 (July 23, 1924), 2.

83. MacLean, *Behind the Mask*, 127.

84. Goldberg, *Hooded Empire*, 25–26.

85. Chalmers, *Hooded Americanism*, 32–33, quotation on 33.

86. Sweeney, "Great Bigotry Merger," 9.

87. Sweeney, "Great Bigotry Merger," 10; Chalmers, *Hooded Americanism*, 33.

88. Stanley Frost, "When the Klan Rules: The Crusade of the Fiery Cross," *Outlook* 136 (January 9, 1924), 66.

89. Arnold S. Rice, *The Ku Klux Klan in American Politics* (Washington, D.C.: Public Affairs Press, 1962), 47.

90. Chalmers, *Hooded Americanism*, 226.

91. Michael Newton, *The Invisible Empire: The Ku Klux Klan in Florida* (Gainesville: University Press of Florida, 2001), 49–56.

92. Alexander, *Klan in the Southwest*, 66.

93. For pre-Klan examples of warning out or proscriptions on black residency in Southwestern towns, see Ray Stannard Baker, *Following the Color Line: American Negro Citizenship in the Progressive Era* (New York: Doubleday, 1908), 71–72, and Alfred L. Brophy, *Reconstructing the Dreamland: The Tulsa Riot of 1921* (New York: Oxford University Press, 2002), 123–24nn24–28.

94. Akin, "Klan in Georgia," 619–23.

95. Chalmers, *Hooded Americanism*, 41.

96. Quincy Roland Lehr, "Terror, Reform, and Repression: Oklahoma Politics in the Early 1920s" (PhD dissertation, Columbia University, 2006), 182.

97. Ibid., 172.

98. Judith Stein, *The World of Marcus Garvey: Race and Class in Modern Society* (Baton Rouge: Louisiana State University Press, 1986), 158.

99. Morris, "Saving Society through Politics," 232.

100. "Robed Riders Lead Public Klan Parade," *NYT*, June 3, 1923, S8.

101. Lecturer, "Protestantism's Ally," *Kourier* 1 (August 1925), 10.

102. Frost, "Crusade of the Fiery Cross," 66.

103. Bohn, "Klan Interpreted," 388.

104. Edward T. Devine, "The Klan in Texas," *Survey* 48 (April 1, 1922), 10.

105. Peggy Pascoe, *What Comes Naturally: Miscegenation Law and the Making of Race in America* (New York: Oxford University Press, 2009), 168, 180–82; "The Blood of White America Must Be Kept Pure and Uncontaminated," *Imperial Night-Hawk* 1 (August 15, 1923), 6.

106. "Killing and Terror Laid to Klan Chiefs in Pittsburgh Trial," *NYT*, April 10, 1928, 1, 16, quotation on 1.

107. Loucks, *Klan in Pennsylvania*, 180; "Killing and Terror," 16.

108. Goldberg, *Hooded Empire*, 17.

109. Robert L. Duffus, "The Ku Klux Klan in the Middle West," *World's Work* 46 (August 1923), 370.

110. Loucks, *Klan in Pennsylvania*, 40.

111. Weaver, "Klan in Wisconsin, Indiana, Ohio, and Michigan," 115.

112. Alexander, *Klan in the Southwest*, 52.

113. *Senator from Texas: Hearings before a Subcommittee of the Committee on Privileges and Elections, United States Senate, Sixty-Eighth Congress* (Washington, D.C.: U.S. Government Printing Office, 1925), 113; Morris, "Saving Society through Politics," 127.

114. Casey Edward Greene, "Apostles of Hate," 34–35 (see *Senator from Texas*, 118, for a revealing but slightly garbled account of this incident).

115. Greene, "Apostles of Hate," 36–37, quotation on 37.

116. "Evansville Klansmen to Aid Vice Clean-up," *Fiery Cross*, October 10, 1924, 1.

117. Quoted in Ellsworth, *Death in a Promised Land*, 99–100.

118. "Bootlegging Said to Be on Decrease," *Fiery Cross*, November 30, 1923, 9.

119. Waldo Roberts, "The Ku-Kluxing of Oregon," *Outlook* 133 (March 14, 1923), 490.

120. Edward T. Devine, "More about the Klan," *Survey* 48 (April 8, 1922), 42.

121. Lehr, "Terror, Reform, and Repression," 171.

122. Devine, "More about the Klan," 42.

123. Alexander, *Klan in the Southwest*, 41.

124. Ibid., 64.

125. Newton, *Invisible Empire*, 58.

126. Feldman, *Klan in Alabama*, 97.

127. Loucks, *Klan in Pennsylvania*, 40.

128. Michael M. Jessup, "Consorting with Blood and Violence: The Decline of the Oklahoma Ku Klux Klan," *Chronicles of Oklahoma* 78 (Fall 2000), 300.

129. Alexander, *Klan in the Southwest*, 41.

130. "White Caps Strike Terror over South," *NYT*, July 19, 1921, 17.

131. Feldman, *Klan in Alabama*, 98.

132. Akin, "Klan in Georgia," 637.

133. Alexander, *Klan in the Southwest*, 52.

134. Akin, "Klan in Georgia," 661.

135. Evans, "Our Mission of Protestant Solidarity," 4.

136. Lowell Mellett, "Klan and Church," *Atlantic Monthly* 132 (November 1923), 588.

137. Schwieder, "A Farmer and the Klan in Northwest Iowa," 299–304.

138. Robert L. Duffus, "How the Ku Klux Klan Sells Hate," *World's Work* 46 (June 1923), 180.

139. Evans, "Fight for Americanism," 45.

140. Morris, "Saving Society through Politics," 261–62.

141. "Negroes Form Klan," *NYT*, March 22, 1924, 12; Thornbrough, "Segregation in Indiana," 612; and Blee, *Women of the Klan*, 169.

142. Weaver, "Knights of the Klan in Wisconsin, Indiana, Ohio and Michigan," 74–75.

143. Table BG 334: "Church and Congregation Membership by Denomination, 1790–1995," *Historical Statistics of the United States* (Millennial Edition Online, Cambridge University Press, 2009).

144. Martin J. Scott, S.J., "Catholics and the Ku Klux Klan," *North American Review* 223 (June 1926), 272.

145. Evans, "Fight for Americanism," 46.

146. Scott, "Catholics and the Klux Klan," 274.

147. Patrick H. Callahan to Daniel Bride, April 12, 1929, Roll 19, Ernest Hurst Cherrington Series, Microfilm Edition of the Temperance and Prohibition Papers, Ohio Historical Society.

148. "Sparks from the Fiery Cross," *Fiery Cross*, June 20, 1924, 4.

149. Evans, "Fight for Americanism," 46–47.

150. *The Barbarism of Slavery: Speech of Hon. Charles Sumner, on the Bill for the Admission of Kansas as a Free State, in the United States Senate, June 4, 1860* (New York: The Young Men's Republican Union, 1863), 38.

151. Higham, *Strangers in the Land*, 179–81; C. Vann Woodward, *Tom Watson: Agrarian Rebel* (New York: Macmillan, 1938; reprint ed., New York: Oxford University Press, 1963), 419–21 (for one klavern's interest in the *Rail Splitter*, see Horowitz, *Inside the Klavern*, 130).

152. Blee, *Women of the Klan*, 89–91 (see also the Klan account of a Catholic attempt to disrupt an appearance by Jackson in "Call the Cops!" *Fiery Cross*, March 16, 1923, 2).

153. Horowitz, *Inside the Klavern*, 125.

154. Goldberg, *Hooded Empire*, 31 (a third former nun was popular among eastern Oregon Klansmen; see Horowitz, *Inside the Klavern*, 20, 21, 23, 76).

155. "Romans Ordered to Vote for Al Smith and Walsh," *Fiery Cross*, April 4, 1924, 8.

156. Higham, *Strangers in the Land*, 57.

157. Robert D. Johnston, *The Radical Middle Class: Populist Democracy and the Question of Capitalism in Progressive Era Portland, Oregon* (Princeton, N.J.: Princeton University Press, 2003), 222, 228, 231.

158. Pegram, "Hoodwinked," 112–13.

159. "Masons and the Klan," *NYT*, September 2, 1923, XX10.

160. Quoted in Morris, "Saving Society through Politics," 255.

161. Zuber, "'Onward Christian Klansmen!'," 238–39.

162. Quoted in Chalmers, *Hooded Americanism*, 123.

163. Fry, *Modern Ku Klux Klan*, 109.

164. Loucks, *Klan in Pennsylvania*, 106.

165. Morris, "Saving Society through Politics," 254.

166. Lay, *Hooded Knights on the Niagara*, 77; Goldberg, *Hooded Empire*, 8.

167. Stanley Frost, "When the Klan Rules: The Business of 'Kluxing,'" *Outlook* 136 (January 23, 1924), 146.

168. Morris, "Saving Society through Politics," 255; Mellett, "Klan and Church," 588; Loucks, *Klan in Pennsylvania*, 106; William Alexander Percy, *Lanterns on the Levee: Recollections of a Planter's Son* (New York: Knopf, 1941), 232.

169. Devine, "More about the Klan," 42.

170. Frost, "Invoking the Whirlwind," 101.

171. Mellett, "Klan and Church," 591.

172. Michael D. Jacobs, "Catholic Response to the Ku Klux Klan in the Midwest, 1921–8" (PhD dissertation, Marquette University, 2001), 317.

173. Christopher J. Kaufmann, *Faith and Fraternalism: The History of the Knights of Columbus* (revised ed., New York: Simon and Schuster, 1992), 276–301.

174. "K. of C. Names Tobin Supreme Director," *NYT*, August 7, 1924, 17.

175. Goldberg, *Hooded Empire*, 8.

176. Morris, "Saving Society through Politics," 258.

177. Bohn, "Klan Interpreted," 388.

178. Frost, "Invoking the Whirlwind," 101.

179. Fry, *Modern Ku Klux Klan*, 110–13.

180. "Plans a Movement for Nation's Youth," *NYT*, December 30, 1923, 3.

181. Chalmers, *Hooded Americanism*, 138.

182. "Reports on Spurious Oath," *NYT*, June 30, 1929, N2.

183. "Minister Indicted in Fake K. of C. Oath," *NYT*, December 1, 1928, 4.

184. Horowitz, *Inside the Klavern*, 88.

185. Goldberg, *Hooded Empire*, 120.

186. "Fiery Cross near K. of C.," *NYT*, August 25, 1924, 2.

187. Devine, "More about the Klan," 42.

188. Chalmers, *Hooded Americanism*, 149–50.

189. John Moffatt Mecklin, *The Ku Klux Klan: A Study of the American Mind* (New York: Harcourt, Brace, 1924), 205.

190. Gerlach, *Blazing Crosses in Zion*, 109.

191. Horowitz, *Inside the Klavern*, 17.

192. Ibid., 61–62.

193. Jacobs, "Catholic Response to the Klan," 311.

194. Gerlach, *Blazing Crosses in Zion*, 91–92, quotation on 91.

195. Patrick G. O'Brien, "'I Want Everyone to Know the Shame of the State': Henry J. Allen Confronts the Ku Klux Klan, 1921–1923," *Kansas History* 2 (Summer 1996), 106.

196. Goldberg, *Hooded Empire*, 31–32.

197. Jacobs, "Catholic Response to the Klan," 325, 326n383; "Catholic Church Set Afire," *NYT*, April 15, 1928, 29.

198. Lay, *Hooded Knights on the Niagara*, 77.

199. Emmons deposition, 133–38, quotation on 133, quotation on 136–37.

200. "Says Duvall Asked $3,000 for City Job," *NYT*, September 17, 1927, 3.

201. Shawn Lay, "Imperial Outpost on the Border: El Paso's Frontier Klan No. 100," in Lay, *Invisible Empire in the West*, 85.

202. Goldberg, *Hooded Empire*, 155.

203. Jacobs, "Catholic Response to the Klan," 301.

204. Goldberg, *Hooded Empire*, 31.

205. "Who's Who," *Fiery Cross*, May 11, 1923, 1.

206. Blee, *Women of the Klan*, 148.

207. Ibid., 150.

208. Moore, "Consequences of the Klan," 534–35.

209. Jackson, *Klan in the City*, 219.

210. Blee, *Women of the Klan*, 149.

211. Chalmers, *Hooded Americanism*, 180; Jacobs, "Catholic Response to the Klan," 288.

212. Jacobs, "Catholic Response to the Klan," 288.

213. Blee, *Women of the Klan*, 150.

214. Goldberg, *Hooded Empire*, 130–31.

215. Jacobs, "Catholic Response to the Klan," 294–95.

216. Ibid., 290 (for a rare instance of Catholics boycotting a Southern Klansman, see "Boycott and Abuse Roanoke Klansman," *Imperial Night-Hawk* 1 [May 23, 1923], 4).

217. Jacobs, "Catholic Response to the Klan," 296–97; "Arrest Seventy-Five Klansmen at Funeral," *NYT*, July 7, 1923, 4; "Hearing Set for 72 Klansmen," *NYT*, July 8, 1923.

218. Jacobs, "Catholic Response to the Klan," 70, 134.

219. Ibid., 300.

220. "Memorial Service Marred by 'K.K.K.'" *NYT*, May 31, 1924, 2; "Seized Klan Wreath Ordered Replaced," *NYT*, May 31, 1923, 1, 10.

221. "Klan Makes Issue in Maine Politics," *NYT*, September 10, 1923, 19.

222. Jacobs, "Catholic Response to the Klan," 309–55, *passim*.

223. Mark Paul Richard, "'This Is Not a Catholic Nation': The Ku Klux Klan Confronts Franco-Americans in Maine," *New England Quarterly* 82 (June 2009), 293.

224. Schwieder, "A Farmer and the Ku Klux Klan in Northwest Iowa," 303 (for additional reports of armed Klansmen, see Loucks, *Klan in Pennsylvania*, 57).

225. Jacobs, "Catholic Response to the Klan," 326–27, 319.

226. Jacobs, "Catholic Response to the Klan," 347–51; Schwieder, "A Farmer and the Klan in Northwest Iowa," 301–2; Jenkins, *Steel Valley Klan*, 122; and David J. Goldberg, "Unmasking the Ku Klux Klan: The Northern Movement against the KKK, 1920–1925," *Journal of American Ethnic History* 15 (Summer 1996), 43.

227. Chalmers, *Hooded Americanism*, 238.

228. "Indiana Protestants Outraged by Infuriated College Students," *Imperial Night-Hawk* 2 (June 4, 1924), 2; Todd Tucker, *Notre Dame vs. The Klan: How the Fighting Irish Defeated the Ku Klux Klan* (Chicago: Loyola Press, 2004), 145–78.

229. Chalmers, *Hooded Americanism*, 272–73; "Fifty Hurt in Two Bay State Klan Battles; in One 500 Foes Clash with 200 Knights," *NYT*, July 30, 1924, 1; "Mob of 800 in Worcester Beats Klansmen and Wrecks Cars after Order's Big Meeting," *NYT*, October 19, 1924, 1; "Score Are Hurt in Bay State Klan Riot: Three Arrested after Siege in Farmhouse," *NYT*, August 3, 1925, 1; "1,000 in Bay State Engage in Klan Row," *NYT*, August 13, 1925, 21; "Hundreds in Klan Riot," *NYT*, September 19, 1925, 9.

230. Loucks, *Klan in Pennsylvania*, 166.

231. Ibid., 188.

232. Embrey B. Howson, "The Ku Klux Klan in Ohio after World War I" (MA thesis, Ohio State University, 1951), 70.

233. "North Carolina Klan Splits with Dr. Evans," *NYT*, February 23, 1927, 18.

234. Jenkins, *Steel Valley Klan*, 160–61.

235. Lay, *War, Revolution, and the Klan*, 88, 139.

236. "K. of C. Take Charge of Ku Klux Rally," *NYT*, April 15, 1923, 54; "Knights of Columbus Shake Faith in Klan," *NYT*, April 16, 1923, 18.

237. Arthur E. Walker to P. H. Callahan, December 16, 1929, Roll 19, Cherrington Series, Temperance and Prohibition Papers.

238. Lay, *Hooded Knights on the Niagara*, 77–78.

239. Jacobs, "Catholic Response to the Klan," 375.

240. Richard, "'This Is Not a Catholic Nation,'" 302.

241. Jacobs, "Catholic Response to the Klan," 359.

242. Ibid., 370.

243. Lynn Dumenil, "The Tribal Twenties: 'Assimilated' Catholics' Response to Anti-Catholicism in the 1920s," *Journal of American Ethnic History*, 11 (Fall 1991), 25, 27–29, 32; Jacobs, "Catholic Response to the Klan," 360–61.

244. "500 Rout Speaker at Klan Meeting," *NYT*, June 5, 1923, 4.

245. Jacobs, "Catholic Response to the Klan," 362.

246. Goldberg, "Unmasking the Ku Klux Klan," 40.

247. See, for instance, "The Ku Klux Klan," *North American Review* 223 (June 1926), 268–309.

248. O'Brien, "I Want Everyone to Know," 107–10.

249. See "Ku Klux and Crime," *New Republic* (January 17, 1923), 189; Leroy Percy, "The Modern Ku Klux Klan," *Atlantic Monthly* 130 (July 1922), 128.

250. Walter Johnson, ed., *Selected Letters of William Allen White, 1899–1943* (New York: Henry Holt, 1947), 220.

251. An Exalted Cyclops, "Principles and Purposes of the Knights of the Ku Klux Klan," *Papers Read at the Meeting of Grand Dragons, 1923*, 126.

Chapter 4: Learning Americanism

1. "Will Furnish Float," *Imperial Night-Hawk* 2 (July 2, 1924), 3.

2. "The Little Red Schoolhouse Is One of the Most Sacred of American Institutions," *Imperial Night-Hawk* 1 (August 27, 1923), 3.

3. Dr. H. W. Evans, *The Public School Problem in America* (Atlanta?: K.K.K., n.d. [1924]), 6, 19.

4. Blee, *Women of the Klan*, 157–62; Grand Dragon of Oregon, "Responsibility of Klankraft to the American Boy," *Papers Read at the Meeting of Grand Dragons, 1923*, 84–89.

5. "Education, the Most Valuable Thing in World, Must Not Be Cheapened," *Imperial Night-Hawk* 1 (May 23, 1923), 2.

6. Evans, *Public School Problem*, 5.

7. A Great Titan of the Realm of Georgia, "Endorsement of Policies," *Papers Read at the Meeting of Grand Dragons, 1923*, 17.

8. Evans, "Where Do We Go from Here?" 11.

9. Evans, *Public School Problem*, 12.

10. "Public Schools Should Be Carefully Guarded against Un-American Influences," *Imperial Night-Hawk* 1 (May 30, 1923), 2.

11. Evans, *Public School Problem*, 10, 12 (italics in original).

12. Horowitz, *Inside the Klavern*, 63.

13. Ibid., 62.

14. Jones, "Klan in Kansas," 30.

15. "Ku Klux Protest Honor to Late Dean," *NYT*, June 22, 1922, 36.

16. "Vote 314 X Yes and Have Free Public Schools," campaign flyer, Box 2, Series VI, The Ku Klux Klan, Tillamook, Oregon Chapter No. 8, Bx 46, division of Special Collections and University Archives, University of Oregon.

17. Evans, *Public School Problem*, 14.

18. Evans quoted in JoEllen McNergney Vinyard, *For Faith and Fortune: The Education of Catholic Immigrants in Detroit, 1805–1925* (Urbana: University of Illinois Press, 1998), 238.

19. W. C. Wright, "The Relation of the Protestant Church to Citizenship," *Imperial Night-Hawk* 2 (May 7, 1924), 2–3; "American Government and Civilization Dependent on Protestant Anglo-Saxons," *Imperial Night-Hawk* 1 (March 12, 1924), 6.

20. "Little Red Schoolhouse," 3.

21. Evans, *Public School Problem*, 4.

22. David B. Tyack, *The One Best System: A History of American Urban Education* (Cambridge, Mass.: Harvard University Press, 1974), 127.

23. "Program Concerning Public School Problem Outlined by Imperial Wizard," *Imperial Night-Hawk* 1 (February 14, 1924), 7 (these figures differ from those reported in Evans's *Public School Problem*, the pamphlet version of this address, but they match the percentage listed in Kennedy, *Over Here*, 188).

24. Alexander J. Inglis quoted in Evans, *Public School Problem*, 7.

25. "What Schoolmen Recommend," *NYT*, March 15, 1923, 18.

26. Hal S. Barron, *Mixed Harvest: The Second Great Transformation in the Rural North, 1870–1930* (Chapel Hill: University of North Carolina Press, 1997), 71, 73, quotation on 71.

27. William A. Link, *The Paradox of Southern Progressivism, 1880–1930* (Chapel Hill: University of North Carolina Press, 1992), 276.

28. Ibid., 269–73.

29. Evans, *Public School Problem*, 5.

30. Loucks, *Klan in Pennsylvania*, 137–38.

31. "What Shall We Do to Be Saved?" *Imperial Night-Hawk* 1 (November 21, 1923), 2.

32. William F. Russell, "Who Shall Mold the Mind of America?" *School and Society* 22 (August 15, 1925), 187.

33. "What Shall We Do to Be Saved?" 3.

34. "Making Teaching Efficient and Patriotic," *Outlook* 122 (May 21, 1919), 100.

35. David Tyack, Thomas James, and Aaron Benavot, *Law and the Shaping of Public Education, 1785–1954* (Madison: University of Wisconsin Press, 1987), 169–76. (Statistics in preceding paragraphs also come from this source.)

36. Keller, *Regulating a New Society*, 58.

37. "American Citizens Must Awake to Needs of Public Schools," *Imperial Night-Hawk* 1 (May 9, 1923), 5.

38. "Education, Must Not Be Cheapened," 2.

39. Schwieder, "A Farmer and the Klan in Northwest Iowa," 308.

40. Moore, *Citizen Klansmen*, 147–49; "The 'Minority Faction,'" *Fiery Cross*, September 21, 1923, 4.

41. Goldberg, *Hooded Empire*, 124.

42. Loucks, *Klan in Pennsylvania*, 139.

43. Jackson, *Klan in the City*, 121.

44. "Klan Komment," *Imperial Night-Hawk* 1 (September 26, 1923), 5.

45. "Klan Gives $4,000 to School Fund," *Imperial Night-Hawk* 1 (September 26, 1923), 7.

46. Cocoltchos, "Invisible Government and Viable Community," 346–47, quotation on 347.

47. Lay, *War, Revolution, and the Klan*, 92–103, 111–12 ("stairs," "Bolsheviks," 93; "political machine," "common people," 98).

48. "Education Must Not Be Cheapened," 2.

49. "American Citizens Must Awake to Needs of Public Schools," *Imperial Night-Hawk* 1 (May 9, 1923), 5.

50. "Sterling-Reed Educational Bill Awaits Committee Action," *Imperial Night-Hawk* 2 (May 14, 1924), 2.

51. "Eleven States Have No Law against Employment of School Children," *Imperial Night-Hawk* 2 (May 28, 1924), 2.

52. Quoted in Keller, *Regulating a New Society*, 209.

53. Feldman, *Klan in Alabama*, 28; "Klan Komment," *Imperial Night-Hawk* 1 (June 27, 1923), 5; and "Klan as a Civic Asset," 66–67.

54. Akin, "Klan in Georgia," 456–59 ("Strayer-Engelhardt," "3.5 million," quotation on 456), 443–46 ("cozy relationship"), 429–30 ("ineffective superintendent"), 461–62 ("free textbooks," quotation on 461).

55. Akin, "Klan in Georgia," 425–33, 463–66.

56. John Lee Maples, "The Akron, Ohio Ku Klux Klan, 1921–1928" (MA thesis, University of Akron, 1974), 50–68.

57. Chalmers, *Hooded Americanism*, 227.

58. Moore, *Citizen Klansmen*, 149.

59. Lay, *War, Revolution, and the Klan*, 112–13, 185n30.

60. Feldman, *Klan in Alabama*, 57.

61. Loucks, *Klan in Pennsylvania*, 139.

62. Lay, *Hooded Knights on the Niagara*, 155–56n37.

63. "Reasons Why Bible Reading Should Be Practiced in the Public School," *Imperial Night-Hawk* 2 (September 10, 1924), 2.

64. "Second Imperial Klonvokation Held at Kansas City, September, 23–25," *Imperial Night-Hawk* 2 (October 8, 1924), 8.

65. "American Government and Civilization Dependent on Protestant Anglo-Saxons," 2–3, 6–7, quotation on 7.

66. Evans, *Public School Problem*, 20–21 (italics in original).

67. Akin, "Klan in Georgia," 448.

68. Akin, "Klan in Georgia," 448; MacLean, *Behind the Mask*, 113.

69. Evans, "Defender of Americanism," 813.

70. "Man Was Never a Jelly Fish, Declares Writer in Attack on Evolution Theory," *Imperial Night-Hawk* 1 (May 16, 1923), 2.

71. Cocoltchos, "Invisible Government and Viable Community," 446.

72. Ray Ginger, *Six Days or Forever? Tennessee v. John Thomas Scopes* (New York: Oxford University Press, 1974; original ed., Boston: Beacon Press, 1958), 12; Keller, *Regulating a New Society*, 63. Ohio Grand Dragon Clyde Osborne, in a recital of Klan Christian doctrine, stated that the hooded order "does not deny the possibility of organic evolution" (Howson, "Klan in Ohio," 88).

73. "Teacher, a Negress, Gets Special Class," *NYT*, September 8, 1923, 13.

74. Jenkins, *Steel Valley Klan*, 153–54, 112–13, quotation on 153; for similar charges that Catholic teachers in Worcester, Massachusetts, "attempt[ed] to instill Catholic teachings into the public school work," see "Another Town Voices Protest against Influence in Schools," *Fiery Cross*, March 23, 1923, 3.

75. Jenkins, *Steel Valley Klan*, 110.

76. Loucks, *Klan in Pennsylvania*, 140–42.

77. Akin, "Klan in Georgia," 470–71.

78. "Thirteen Crosses Burned in Jersey," *NYT*, November 26, 1923, 14.

79. Frank M. Cates, "The Ku Klux Klan in Indiana Politics, 1920–1925" (PhD dissertation, Indiana University, 1971), 86; "Hoosiers Aroused over History Book Selection," *Fiery Cross*, April 27, 1923, 10.

80. The Fiery Cross Pub Co Per Paul B. Brewer to All Hydras, Titans, Furies, Exalted Cyclops, Terrors and Faithful Klansmen, Realm of Indiana, December 23, 1924, Plaintiff Exhibit 45, Emmons deposition.

81. Philip N. Racine, "The Ku Klux Klan, Anti-Catholicism, and Atlanta's Board of Education, 1916–1927," *Georgia Historical Quarterly* 57 (Spring 1973), 70–73, quotation on 73.

82. Dumenil, "The Tribal Twenties," 40–43.

83. Jonathan Zimmerman, "'Each "Race" Could Have Its Heroes Sung': Ethnicity and the History Wars in the 1920s," *Journal of American History* 87 (June 2000), 92–111 ("none but Americans," 108; "*Wake up!,*" 99–100; "Boastful," 109).

84. Toy, "Robe and Gown," 170–74.

85. Goldberg, *Hooded Empire*, 90, quotation on 92.

86. "Forrest Tells Aims of Ku Klux College," *NYT*, September 12, 1921, 12.

87. "Life Lines," *Life* 82 (September 13, 1923), 13; James K. McGuinness, "The Season Ahead," *Life* 82 (November 15, 1923), 14; L. H. R., "Grain and Chaff in the Week's Grist of News," *NYT*, October 25, 1925, XX2.

88. *The Ku-Klux Klan: Hearings before the Committee on Rules, House of Representatives, Sixty-Seventh Congress, First Session* (Washington, D.C.: U.S. Government Printing Office, 1921), 107–10; "Forrest Tells Aims"; "Ku Klux to Build 'Hall of Invisibles,'" *NYT*, September 19, 1921, 16.

89. *Ku-Klux Klan Hearings*, 109.

90. Ibid., 110.

91. "Forrest Tells Aims."

92. Bohn, "Klan Interpreted," 395.

93. "Shearith Israel Renovates . . . 'All Southern' Lanier University," *Morningside/ Lenox Park Association Newsletter* (June 1981).

94. "Klan to Perpetuate Valpo," *Fiery Cross*, August 24, 1923, 1, 7; "A Klan University," *NYT*, July 28, 1923, 6; "Ku Klux Won't Buy Valparaiso School," *NYT*, September 6, 1923, 19; Chalmers, *Hooded Americanism*, 168–69; and Lutholtz, *Grand Dragon*, 76–77.

95. Tyack, James, and Benavot, *Law and the Shaping of Public Education*, 164.

96. "Knights of Ku Klux Klan Inaugurates National Program of Education," *Imperial Night-Hawk* 1 (March 19, 1924), 3.

97. Grand Dragon, Realm of Colorado (John Galen Locke), "A Klansman's Obligation as a Patriot to His God, His Country, His Home, and His Fellowmen," *Papers Read at the Meeting of Grand Dragons, 1923*, 61.

98. Tyack, James, and Benavot, *Law and the Shaping of Public Education*, 165.

99. Racine, "Klan, Anti-Catholicism, and Atlanta's Board of Education," 64–66; Zuber, "'Onward Christian Klansmen!'," 348.

100. Newell G. Bringhurst, "The Ku Klux Klan in a Central California Community: Tulare County during the 1920s and 1930s," *Southern California Quarterly* 82 (Winter 2000), 378.

101. "Reasons Why Bible Reading Should Be Practiced in the Public School," 3.

102. "Hayes Asks Schools to Teach Religion," *NYT*, January 22, 1923, 15; "Three Faiths Unite to Teach Religion to School Children," *NYT*, February 18, 1924, 1; "Wants All Pupils Taught Religion," *NYT*, January 21, 1925, 19; "All Creeds Urge Religion for Youth," *NYT*, February 2, 1925, 19; Zuber, "'Onward Christian Klansmen!'," 337, 344–49, quotations on 346.

103. Moore, *Citizen Klansmen*, 180.

104. Jenkins, *Steel Valley Klan*, 130.

105. "Reasons Why Bible Reading Should Be Practiced in the Public School," 3.

106. "Explains Klan Invitation," *NYT*, May 25, 1923, 19.

107. Zuber, "'Onward Christian Klansmen!'," 316–17.

108. "Put Bible in School," *Imperial Night-Hawk* 1 (November 7, 1923), 8.

109. Richard, "'This Is Not a Catholic Nation,'" 291.

110. Weaver, "Klan in Wisconsin, Indiana, Ohio, and Michigan," 236–37; "Ohio Governor Vetoes School Bible Bill," *NYT*, May 1, 1925, 3.

111. Moore, *Citizen Klansmen*, 179–81; Chalmers, *Hooded Americanism*, 248; see also "Will Test Delaware Law for Bible Reading in Schools," *NYT*, June 1, 1925, 17.

112. Brisbane quoted in Douglas J. Slawson, *The Department of Education Battle, 1918–1932* (Notre Dame, Ind.: University of Notre Dame Press, 2005), 115.

113. Richard, "'This Is Not a Catholic Nation,'" 293–95.

114. Weaver, "Klan in Wisconsin, Indiana, Ohio, and Michigan," 165; Horowitz, *Inside the Klavern*, 62–63.

115. "Klan's Influence in the Schools," *NYT*, November 16, 1923, 16.

116. Slawson, *Department of Education Battle*, 138.

117. Howson, "Klan in Ohio," 75; Lawrence J. Saalfeld, *Forces of Prejudice in Oregon, 1920–1925* (Portland, Ore.: Archdiocesan Historical Commission, 1984), 39, 63; and Weaver, "Klan in Wisconsin, Indiana, Ohio, and Michigan," 166.

118. Maples, "Akron, Ohio Klan," 62.

119. Vinyard, *For Faith and Fortune*, 106.

120. "Religious Tests Barred in Jersey," *NYT*, April 26, 1924, 15.

121. Cates, "Klan in Indiana Politics," 166.

122. Racine, "Klan, Anti-Catholicism, and Atlanta's Board of Education," 68–69.

123. Slawson, *Department of Education Battle*, 108–9.

124. "Vote 314 X Yes and Have Free Public Schools" ("no religious question," "Power houses"); "All for the Public School and the Public School for All," Ancient and Accepted Scottish Rite School Committee ("only sure foundation"), 1922 pamphlets, Box 2, Series VI, Tillamook, Oregon, Ku Klux Klan papers.

125. Vinyard, *For Faith and Fortune*, 222–38.

126. "The Oregon School Law," *NYT*, August 5, 1923, E4.

127. Horowitz, *Inside the Klavern*, 21–24, 37, quotation on 76.

128. John A. Jeffrey, "Public Schools of Vital Importance," *Imperial Night-Hawk* 1 (October 10, 1923), 5.

129. Slawson, *Department of Education Battle*, 108, 114, 135.

130. Vinyard, *For Faith and Fortune*, 238.

131. Alexander, *Klan in the Southwest*, 112.

132. Vinyard, *For Faith and Fortune*, 238–40.

133. Jacobs, "Catholic Response to the Klan," 233.

134. "Compulsory Laws for School Scored," *NYT*, May 6, 1925, 22.

135. Vinyard, *For Faith and Fortune*, 240.

136. "Court Invalidates Oregon School Law," *NYT*, April 1, 1924, 1.

137. Keller, *Regulating a New Society*, 53 ("Prussian"); Dumenil, "Insatiable Maw of Bureaucracy," 499–524, Slawson, *Department of Education Battle*; "Defends Federal Education Measure," *NYT*, March 13, 1922, 7 ("our flag"); "Opposes Education Bill," *NYT*, February 16, 1923, 12.

138. "Defends Federal Education Measure."

139. "Fears Federal Rule in Education Bill," *NYT*, December 12, 1924, 20.

140. Jeffrey, "Public Schools," 5; "Sterling-Reed Education Bill Awaits Committee Action," *Imperial Night-Hawk* 2 (May 14, 1924), 2–3.

141. "The Towner-Sterling Bill Will Be Revived; Klansmen Should Work for Its Passage," *Imperial Night-Hawk* 2 (June 6, 1923), 2; *A Suggested Course of Study in the Fundamentals of Klankraft* (Atlanta: Knights of the Ku Klux Klan, 1925), n.p., Defendant's Exhibit No. 1, 531, Emmons deposition.

142. "Towner-Sterling Bill Will Be Revived," 2.

143. *Fundamentals of Klankraft*, labeled 531.

Chapter 5: Dry Americanism

1. From "Local Officers of the Ku Klux Klan in Indiana, 1925," 22–23, typescript, Indiana Historical Society, Indianapolis.

2. "Men and Women Are Held in Booze Raid," *Fiery Cross*, July 13, 1923, 11 (William Worster was the injured knight).

3. "Klansmen Lend Aid in Booze Clean-Up," *Fiery Cross*, August 29, 1924, 6.

4. "Praises Klan Help in Enforcing Laws," *Fiery Cross*, October 10, 1924, 6.

5. "Klansmen Protect Chruch Threatened by Lawless Gang," *Fiery Cross*, February 22, 1924, 2.

6. "The Rise and Fall of the K. K. K." *New Republic* 53 (November 30, 1927), 34.

7. Moore, *Citizen Klansmen*, 191.

8. Thomas R. Pegram, *Battling Demon Rum: The Struggle for a Dry America, 1800–1933* (Chicago: Ivan R. Dee, 1998), 148–59.

9. National Commission on Law Observance and Enforcement, *Enforcement of the National Prohibition Laws*, vol. 5 (Washington, D.C.: U.S. Government Printing Office, 1931), 503.

10. Ibid., vol. 2, 197.

11. Charles Merz, *The Dry Decade* (New York: Doubleday, 1931), 201–6.

12. E. P. Alldredge to Boyd Doty, June 30, 1924, Roll 2, Francis Scott McBride Series, Microfilm Edition of the Temperance and Prohibition Papers, Ohio Historical Society.

13. Pegram, *Battling Demon Rum*, 115.

14. Lerner, *Dry Manhattan*, 124–25, quotations on 124.

15. "Stills and Mash Are Taken in Ohio Raids," *Fiery Cross*, December 14, 1923, 3.

16. Patrick H. Callahan to Camden R. McAtee, May 31, 1929, Roll 19, Ernest Hurst Cherrington Series, Microfilm Edition of the Temperance and Prohibition Papers, Ohio Historical Society.

17. Callahan to C. E. Silcox, April 26–29, 1929, and Callahan to Mrs. Anna Marden DeYo, May 23, 1929 (quotation), both Roll 19, Cherrington Series.

18. Richard L. Watson, ed., *Bishop Cannon's Own Story: Life As I Have Seen It by James Cannon, Jr.* (Durham, N.C.: Duke University Press, 1955), 327.

19. Hohner, *Prohibition and Politics*, 231.

20. Ibid., 227.

21. Ibid., 188.

22. Lerner, *Dry Manhattan*, 200–204.

23. Marni Davis, "'On the Side of Liquor': American Jews and the Politics of Alcohol, 1870–1936" (PhD dissertation, Emory University, 2006), 205–28, quotation on 228.

24. "Foreign Influences," *Fiery Cross*, July 25, 1924, 4.

25. Dr. H. W. Evans, "Our Alien Crime-Plague and Its Cure," *Kourier Magazine* 2 (March 1926), 1–7 ("influx," 1, "Arizona," 5); Dr. H. W. Evans, "Laxity toward Law Enforcement Must Stop," *Kourier* 2 (June 1926), 1–9 ("existence" 1, "folly" 4, "create public sentiment" 7).

26. Lutholtz, *Grand Dragon*, 36–39, 98–100.

27. *State of Indiana vs. the Knights of the Ku Klux Klan*, Emmons deposition, February 20, 1928, 395–96 ("a lot of whiskey"); Alexander, *Klan in the Southwest*, 195.

28. Goldberg, *Hooded Empire*, 7, 19–22, 32, 152, 121–22, 65–66, 94–95.

29. Roger K. Hux, "The Ku Klux Klan and Collective Violence in Horry County, South Carolina, 1922–1925," *South Carolina Historical Magazine* 85 (July 1984), 214, 216.

30. Emmons deposition, 164.

31. Mika Smith, "Hooded Crusaders: The Ku Klux Klan in the Panhandle and South Plains, 1921–1925" (MA thesis, Texas Tech University, 2008), 53.

32. Goldberg, *Hooded Empire*, 102.

33. Morris, "Saving Society through Politics," 53; Duffus, "How the Klan Sells Hate," quotation on 183.

34. Maples, "Akron, Ohio Klan," 42.

35. Ibid., 43.

36. Holley, "A Look behind the Masks," 145.

37. Horowitz, *Inside the Klavern*, 62 ("Smith Bros."), 28 ("King of Bootleggers"), 48–49, 88, 92–94, 131, 133–35, 136.

38. Alexander, *Klan in the Southwest*, 31.

39. *The Ku-Klux Klan: Hearings before the Committee on Rules, House of Representatives, Sixty-Seventh Congress, First Session* (Washington, D.C.: U.S. Government Printing Office, 1921), 6.

40. Alexander, *Klan in the Southwest*, 50–51, 76–77; "Masked Vigilantes Kill 1 in Arkansas," *NYT*, November 30, 1922, 14; "2,000 Flee from Raiders," *NYT*, December 1, 1922, 6.

41. Chalmers, *Hooded Americanism*, 119–20; Walter D. Kamphoefner, "The Handwriting on the Wall: The Klan, Language Issues and Prohibition in the German Settlements of Eastern Texas," *Southwestern Historical Quarterly* 112 (July 2008), 60, 62–63.

42. Alexander, *Klan in the Southwest*, 69.

43. Ibid., 77.

44. Holley, "A Look behind the Masks," 145.

45. Chalmers, *Hooded Americanism*, 152.

46. Lay, *Hooded Knights on the Niagara*, 73–74.

47. Jones, "Klan in Kansas," 27–28.

48. Nicola Criscione interview, O.H. 311, May 8, 1984, Youngstown State University Oral History Program, Ku Klux Klan Project, 6–8.

49. "Ft. Wayne Klan Hits Vice," *Fiery Cross*, July 20, 1923, 1, 3, quotations on 1.

50. "Gary Very Sick City," *Fiery Cross*, April 6, 1923, 5.

51. "Lima Decrees End of Bootleggers," *Fiery Cross*, April 27, 1923, 6.

52. "Klan Breaks Back of Bootlegging Ring," *Fiery Cross*, August 8, 1924, 5.

53. "Indianapolis Law Enforcement Campaign Opens," *Fiery Cross*, April 6, 1923, 7.

54. Emmons deposition, 227–50.

55. "Roman Ryan Wars on Horse Thief Sleuths," *Fiery Cross*, October 17, 1924, 1 (for additional evidence of Klan purchases of illegal liquor, see "Ft. Wayne Klan Hits Vice," 1).

56. Maples, "Akron, Ohio Klan," 42.

57. "Sparks from the Fiery Cross," *Fiery Cross*, March 21, 1924, 4.

58. "Our Higher Idea," *Fiery Cross*, December 14, 1923, 4.

59. "The Officers of a Klan and Their Responsibility to Law Enforcement," in *Papers Read at the Meeting of Grand Dragons, 1923*, 56, 58.

60. "Message of National Importance Is Issued by South Carolina Official," *Imperial Night-Hawk* 1 (July 11, 1923), 7.

61. Masatomo Ayabe, "The Ku Klux Klan Movement in Williamson County, Illinois, 1923–1926" (PhD dissertation, University of Illinois, 2005), 28.

62. "Klan Demands Dry Raids," *NYT*, September 26, 1922, 6.

63. "Dry Raid Starts Row," *NYT*, December 22, 1924, 32.

64. "Bootleggers Put in Jail at Muskegon," *Fiery Cross*, December 28, 1923, 8.

65. "Klan Raids in Birmingham," *NYT*, January 5, 1926, 15; Feldman, *Klan in Alabama*, 44–45.

66. Maples, "Akron, Ohio Klan," 42.

67. Jason S. Lantzer, *"Prohibition Is Here to Stay": The Reverend Edward S. Shumaker and the Dry Cause in America* (Notre Dame, Ind.: University of Notre Dame Press, 2009), 120, 240n27.

68. "Now Is Not This Just Too Terrible," *Fiery Cross*, July 20, 1923, 8; "H.T.D.A. Wins Legal Battle," *Fiery Cross*, October 14, 1924, 1; "Roman Ryan Wars on Horse Thief Sleuths," 1.

69. "Williamson County Tactics Displayed at Jeffersonville," *Fiery Cross*, March 28, 1924, 6.

70. "Armstrong Weak in Citing His Record as Sheriff of Vigo," *Fiery Cross*, April 4, 1924, 1, 5, quotation on 5.

71. "Long Wait Brings Beer Action," *Fiery Cross*, April 6, 1923, 5.

72. "Mayor Cornwell on Record against a Cleanup at London," *Fiery Cross*, February 29, 1924, 1, 5, quotation on 5.

73. "Wet Leaders Join against the Klan," *Fiery Cross,* October 31, 1924, 5.

74. "Foreigner Attacks Klansmen After 'Ad' Makes Appearance," *Fiery Cross*, August 15, 1924, 1, 5.

75. "Booze Guzzling Favored by New York Assembly," *Imperial Night-Hawk* 1 (May 16, 1923), 7.

76. "'Bloody Williamson,'" *NYT*, January 27, 1925, 12.

77. Ayabe, "Klan Movement in Williamson County," 333–34.

78. "State Head Defends Klan," *NYT*, February 2, 1925, 2.

79. Ayabe, "Klan Movement in Williamson County," 88–132, quotation on 94.

80. For Whiteside's Klan affiliation, see Ayabe, "Klan Movement in Williamson County," 276n51.

81. W. P. Throgmorton to McBride, November 15, 1924, Roll 8, McBride Series; "Troops Keep Peace after Herrin Fight," *NYT*, September 1, 1924, 3.

82. McBride to Frank L. Ebbert, November 20, 1924, Roll 2, McBride Series.

83. Peter H. Odegard, *Pressure Politics: The Story of the Anti-Saloon League* (New York: Columbia University Press, 1928), 128.

84. Jack S. Blocker Jr., *Retreat from Reform: The Prohibition Movement in the United States, 1890–1913* (Westport, Conn.: Greenwood Press, 1976), 219.

85. William H. Anderson to editor, *NYT*, September 23, 1921, 11.

86. F. Scott McBride to Rev. A. J. Finch, April 11, 1925, Roll 3, McBride Series; Goldberg, *Hooded Empire*, 85.

87. Finch to McBride, April 14, 1925, Roll 3, McBride Series.

88. "Klan Organization Meeting Stirs Debate in Marlboro," *The State* (Columbia, South Carolina), July 7, 1924, 6, clipping enclosed in Boyd Doty to McBride, July 28, 1924, Roll 2, McBride Series.

89. Wayne Wheeler to McBride, July 12, 1924, McBride to Wheeler, July 21, 1924, Roll 3, McBride Series.

90. "Form Letter Sent to All State Superintendents," July 21, 1924, Roll 3, McBride Series.

91. E. J. Moore to E. M. Lightfoot, July 22, 1924, Roll 5, McBride Series.

92. "Pastor Says Klan Plans World Drive," *NYT*, November 27, 1922, 1.

93. "Look Out, John," *Baltimore Evening Sun*, August 28, 1924, clipping, Roll 9, McBride Series.

94. "Darrow Says He Opposes Prohibition," *Fiery Cross*, November 7, 1924, 2.

95. Minutes of Anti-Saloon League Speakers and Field Secretaries Conference, July 26–27, 1922, 5, Executive Committee File, Roll 87, Cherrington Series.

96. E. F. Jones to McBride, November 19, 1924, Roll 4, McBride Series.

97. E. F. Jones to Boyd D. Doty, February 9, 1925, Roll 2, McBride Series.

98. Frost, "Crusade of the Fiery Cross," 66.

99. Hiram Wesley Evans, "The Ballots behind the Ku Klux Klan," *World's Work* 55 (January 1928), 246–47.

100. "Klan Organization Meeting Stirs Debate in Marlboro," *The State*, July 7, 1924, 6.

101. "Report of the New England Workers Conference of the Anti-Saloon League Held in Christian Endeavor Bldg., Clark Memorial Hall, Boston, Mass., February 16, 1925," 8, Roll 7, McBride Series.

102. K. Austin Kerr, *Organized for Prohibition: A New History of the Anti-Saloon League* (New Haven, Conn.: Yale University Press, 1985), 213–41.

103. "Superintendents and Workers Conference of the Anti-Saloon League of America, Held at the Raleigh Hotel, Washington, D.C., January 9, 1924," 9, Roll 87, Cherrington Series.

104. F. Scott McBride, "Report to the Biennial Meeting of the Board of Directors of the Anti-Saloon League of America," 1925, Roll 14, McBride Series.

105. Ann-Marie Szymanski, "Dry Compulsions: Prohibition and the Creation of State-Level Enforcement Agencies," *Journal of Policy History* 11 (Spring 1999), 115–46; see the report of Louis Wien Detective Agency, July 10, 1918, in Edward S. Shumaker Papers, Roy O. West Library, DePauw University.

106. McBride, "Report to the Board of Directors," 1925, Roll 14, McBride Series.

107. Wayne B. Wheeler, "The League's Program for Law Enforcement and the Need of Further Legislation," in *Proceedings of the Twentieth National Convention of the Anti-Saloon League of America* (Washington, D.C.: ASLA, 1921), 113–18, quotation on 114.

108. E. P. Alldredge to Boyd Doty, June 30, 1924, Roll 2, McBride Series.

109. "Report of Ernest H. Cherrington to the Executive Committee of the Anti-Saloon League of America, Washington, D.C., November 25, 1924," Roll 84, Cherrington Series.

110. Wayne B. Wheeler, "Report of the Legal and Legislative Department of the Anti-Saloon League of America, Quarter Ending November 25, 1924," Roll 84, Cherrington Series.

111. "Anti-Saloon League Stirs Up the Animals," newspaper clipping, January 1922, Roll 13, Cherrington Series.

112. G. Roneland Munroe, "Compelling Law Enforcement in Face of Official Opposition," January 9, 1924, 4–7, quotation on 7, Roll 87, Cherrington Series.

113. "Grand Jury to Sift Asbury Park 'Orgy,'" *NYT*, April 8, 1924, 21; "Tell of Deal Beach Dinner," *NYT*, April 18, 1924, 2; "Hetrick Exonerated on Dinner Charge," *NYT*, May 2, 1924, 9; Chalmers, *Hooded Americanism*, 243–48.

114. "Asbury Park Mayor Accused in Pulpits," *NYT*, April 7, 1924, 1.

115. "Affidavit Backs Asbury Charges," *NYT*, April 9, 1924, 23.

116. Edward S. Shumaker to F. Scott McBride, July 25, 1924, Roll 8, McBride Series.

117. Lantzer, *"Prohibition Is Here to Stay,"* 124–25.

118. "Horse Thief Detective Associations," *American Issue* (Indiana Edition) 22 (April 30, 1927), 1.

119. R. L. Duffus, "A Political Volcano Seethes in Indiana," *NYT*, October 2, 1927, XXI.

120. Deborah B. Markisohn, "Ministers of the Klan: Indianapolis Clergy Involvement with the 1920s Ku Klux Klan" (MA thesis, Indiana University, 1992), 40–57.

121. Louis Francis Budenz, "Indiana's Anti-Saloon League Goes to Jail," *Nation* 125 (August 24, 1927), 178.

122. Transcript of Taped Interviews with Harold Feightner, 1972, 33–34, manuscript section, Indiana State Library; Moore, *Citizen Klansmen*, 181; Lantzer, *"Prohibition Is Here to Stay,"* 127.

123. Emmons deposition, 64, quotation on 77–78.

124. "Shumaker Denies Dry and Klan Link," *Indianapolis Times*, February 21, 1928, 1; "Shumaker in Statement," *Indianapolis News*, February 22, 1928, 13.

125. "A Reformed Saloonkeeper and Gambler," *American Issue* (Indiana Edition) 9 (December 22, 1914), 8.

126. Emmons deposition, 88–93.

127. "Doesn't Recall Pact," *Indianapolis Star*, February 21, 1928, 8.

128. Budenz, "Indiana's Anti-Saloon League," 177.

129. "Exposure of 12,208 Ku Klux in Marion County, Indiana," *Tolerance*, June 6, 1923, 2, microfilm, Indiana Historical Society; "Local Officers of the Ku Klux Klan in Indiana 1925," 25, typescript (SC 2419), Indiana Historical Society; Zuber, "'Onward Christian Klansmen!',", 280.

130. Edward S. Shumaker to McBride, July 3, 1926, Roll 14, McBride Series; "Local Officers," 21.

131. "First Indianapolis List," *Tolerance*, April 1, 1923, 16.

132. "South Bend Paper Is Discredited," *Fiery Cross*, February 26, 1923, 4.

133. Patrick H. Callahan to Mrs. Carlton M. Sherwood, January 9, 1928, Roll 19, Cherrington Series.

134. Callahan to Dr. Denis A. McCarthy, marked February 21–March 4, 1929, Roll 119, Cherrington Series.

135. Mr. and Mrs. William W. Daw to *American Issue*, n.d. (probably October 1925), Roll 11, McBride Series.

136. Thomas Nicholson to Doctor McBride, November 27, 1925, Roll 7, McBride Series.

137. Feldman, *Klan in Alabama*, 64–66, 82–83; J. Wayne Flint, "Organized Labor, Reform, and Alabama Politics, 1920," *Alabama Review* 23 (July 1970), 166–71; "L. B.

(Breck) Musgrove Dies," *Birmingham News*, July 4, 1931, 1, clipping, Roll 91, Cherrington Series.

138. Wayne B. Wheeler to L. B. Musgrove, September 1926, Roll 15, McBride Series.

139. Boyd Doty to McBride, December 2, 1926, Roll 11, McBride Series; Wayne B. Wheeler, "Report of the Legal and Legislative Department, Anti-Saloon League of America, Quarter Ending November 16, 1926," 8, Roll 84, Cherrington Series.

140. E. Wayne Stahl to McBride, n.d. (August 1926), Roll 14, McBride Series.

141. McBride to Stahl, August 11, 1926, Roll 14, McBride Series.

142. Moseley, "Klan in Georgia," 246–47, 253; Thomas R. Pegram, "Prohibition," in Julian E. Zelizer, ed., *The American Congress: The Building of Democracy* (Boston: Houghton Mifflin, 2004), 424–25.

143. Rice, *Klan in American Politics*, 59.

144. Odegard, *Pressure Politics*, 205n50.

145. "Wheeler Gives New Data," *NYT*, July 3, 1926, 1–2.

146. McBride to Charles O. Jones, July 19, 1926, Roll 13, McBride Series.

147. William L. Wade to McBride, September 17, 1926, Roll 15, McBride Series.

148. Lay, *Hooded Knights on the Niagara*, 68–69.

149. "Hutton Maps New Vice War," *Milwaukee Sentinel*, August 7, 1925, clipping, Roll 6, McBride Series.

150. Feldman, *Klan in Alabama*, 138–30, 153.

151. "Dry Leader's Sons Held in Liquor Deal," *NYT*, April 19, 1925, 9; "Neufield Jones Gets Two Years in Atlanta," *NYT*, September 26, 1925, 5.

152. Charles O. Jones to McBride, May 20, 1926; McBride to Jones, May 26, 1926, Roll 13, McBride Series. As a paid Klan agent, Neufield Jones also undermined the New York operations of the Anti-Klan American Unity League in 1922 (Jacobs, "Catholic Response to the Klan," 107–8, 108n116).

153. McBride to George B. Safford, October 2, 1925, Roll 8, McBride Series; McBride to Rev. George A. Fowler, December 31, 1925, Roll 3, McBride Series.

154. Thomas Nicholson to McBride, September 12, 1925, Roll 7, McBride Series.

155. McBride to David L. McBride, June 16, 1925, Roll 6, McBride Series.

156. McBride to Julius Smith, October 21, 1925, Roll 8, McBride Series; McBride to Brother Superintendents, March 25, 1926, Roll 11, McBride Series.

157. Charles A. Pollack to McBride, November 23, 1925, Roll 7, McBride Series.

158. McBride to Thomas W. Gales, February 8, 1926, Roll 12, McBride Series; Gales to McBride, December 12, 1925, Roll 3, McBride Series.

159. O. M. Pullen to McBride, July 25, 1924, Roll 7, McBride Series.

160. Samuel G. Jones to McBride, January 27, 1926, Roll 13, McBride Series.

161. Julius Smith to McBride, September 6, 1925, Roll 8, McBride Series; see also Samuel G. Jones to McBride, February 10, 1926, and McBride to Jones, February 15, 1926, Roll 13, McBride Series.

162. W. G. Clugston, "The Anti-Saloon League's Lost Virtue," *Nation* 122 (February 24, 1926), 203–5; "Strange News from Kansas," *NYT*, February 26, 1926, 20; "Griffith and Hopkins Accused," *Kansas City Post*, December 10, 1925, clipping, Roll 5, McBride Series.

163. "Report of Francis Scott McBride, General Superintendent, to the Executive Committee of the Anti-Saloon League of America at Washington, D.C., March 10, 1926," 5–8, Roll 84, Cherrington Series; Richard J. Hopkins to Howard H. Russell, December 15, 1925, Roll 89, Cherrington Series; "Kansas High Court Outlaws the Klan," *NYT*, January 11, 1925, 16.

164. "Church Lighted by Fiery Cross at Minneapolis," *Fiery Cross*, May 11, 1923, 1.

165. Julius Smith to McBride, September 16, 1925, Roll 8, McBride Series.

166. J. A. McClellan to McBride, December 25, 1925, Roll 5, McBride Series.

167. Robert Smith Bader, *Prohibition in Kansas* (Lawrence: University Press of Kansas), 209–11.

168. Lewis L. Gould, *Progressives and Prohibitionists: Texas Democrats in the Wilson Era* (Austin: University of Texas Press, 1973), 215–21.

169. "'Drys' and Ku Klux Combine in Texas," *NYT*, August 5, 1922, 6.

170. "Both Sides Predict Victory in Texas," *NYT*, August 22, 1924, 3.

171. W. J. Milburn to McBride, May 8, 1924, Roll 6, McBride Series.

172. "Cites Evidence of Klan's Activities," *Dallas Morning News*, August 21, 1924; clipping in Atticus Webb to McBride, September 1, 1924, Roll 9, McBride Series.

173. Webb to McBride, August 21, 1924, Roll 9, McBride Series.

174. Webb to the Executive Committee, Anti-Saloon League of America, n.d., marked September–October 1924, Roll 9, McBride Series.

175. McBride to Wayne Wheeler, September 18, 1924, Roll 6, McBride Series.

176. "Report to the Executive Committee of the Anti-Saloon League of America by Francis Scott McBride, General Superintendent. Given at Washington, D.C., November 25, 1924," 4, Roll 84, Cherrington Series; "Woman Governor or Klan: A Texas Choice," *NYT*, August 3, 1924, XX3; "The Fergusons Stand Back to the Wall," *NYT*, December 6, 1925, XX3.

177. Odegard, *Pressure Politics*, 228

178. "Not a Case against Prohibition," *Outlook* 136 (February 13, 1924), 252.

179. "Anderson in New Attack," *NYT*, March 10, 1920, 17.

180. William H. Anderson, *To the Pastors of New York State Who Intend to See the Prohibition Fight Through*, Anti-Saloon League of New York pamphlet, March 17, 1920, Roll 76, Cherrington Series.

181. William H. Anderson to Charles S. Whitman, September 5 and November 8, 1923, William H. Anderson Papers, Special Collections, University of Chicago Library.

182. "Anderson Talks on Ku Klux Klan," *NYT*, September 9, 1923, E1; "Says Tammany 'Wets' Make Klan Members," *NYT*, October 1, 1923, 9.

183. William H. Anderson, *American Protestant Alliance: A Comprehensive Introductory Working Outline of Its Philosophy, Principles, Purpose, Policy and Program* (New York, 1926), 36–37.

184. Anderson, *They Cannot Dodge These Facts*, October 31, 1925, 1, American Protestant Alliance pamphlet (reprinted from *Fellowship Forum*), Roll 1, McBride Series.

185. *A Letter to The Dry Protestant Pastors of New York State from William H. Anderson*, June 7, 1926, American Protestant Alliance pamphlet, 5, Roll 76, Cherrington Series.

186. "Fist Fights Mark Klan Celebration," *NYT*, August 21, 1927, 24; Anderson to Colonel Patrick H. Callahan, November 23, 1927, Roll 76, Cherrington Series; Anderson to Ernest H. Cherrington, July 24, 1930, Roll 16, Cherrington Series.

187. McBride to R. H. Scott, July 15, 1924, Roll 8, McBride Series; McBride to Edwin Rawden, n.d., marked June–July 1925, Roll 7, McBride Series.

188. Andrew B. Wood to Senator Thad H. Caraway, August 7, 1926, Roll 15, McBride Series.

189. Howard H. Russell to Mrs. William H. Anderson, April 16, 1928, Anderson Papers.

190. Anderson to Purley A. Baker, February 17, 1921, Roll 76, Cherrington Series.

191. "W. H. Anderson Welcomed," *Baltimore Sun*, December 7, 1927, 1.

192. "Al Smith Discards Mask," *Kourier Magazine* 4 (June 1928), 1–4.

193. Hohner, *Prohibition and Politics*, 218.

194. Delcevare King to Cherrington, July 19, 1930, Roll 89, Cherrington Series.

195. Cocoltchos, "Invisible Empire and Search for the Orderly Community," 114–15.

196. Emmons deposition, 240–46.

197. "The Klan Sheds Its Hood," *New Republic* 45 (February 10, 1926), 311.

Chapter 6: The Problem of Hooded Violence

1. "16 Klansmen Held for Bay State Riot," *NYT*, August 12, 1925, 23.

2. "Ku Klux and Crime," *New Republic* 33 (January 17, 1923), 190.

3. Stanley Frost, "When the Klan Rules: The Giant Clears for Action," *Outlook* 135 (December 26, 1923), 718.

4. Leonard Dinnerstein, *The Leo Frank Case* (New York: Columbia University Press, 1968). For a provocative analysis of the gender and sexual ideologies that underlay the class and religious dimensions of the case, see Nancy MacLean, "The Leo Frank Case Reconsidered: Gender and Sexual Politics in the Making of Reactionary Populism," *Journal of American History* 78 (December 1991), 917–48.

5. MacLean, *Behind the Mask*, 12 (for an example of a "claim to the contrary," see Wade, *Fiery Cross*, 144).

6. Akin, "Klan in Georgia," 174–85, quotations on 184–85, 177.

7. Ibid., 176–77n6.

8. Alexander, *Klan in the Southwest*, 44.

9. Bertram Wyatt-Brown, *Southern Honor: Ethics and Behavior in the Old South* (New York: Oxford University Press, 1982), 440–41; William F. Holmes, "Whitecapping: Agrarian Violence in Mississippi," *Journal of Southern History* 35 (May 1969), 165–85; Barton C. Shaw, *The Wool-Hat Boys: Georgia's Populist Party* (Baton Rouge: Louisiana State University Press, 1984), 119.

10. Stanley Frost, "When the Klan Rules: The Lure of the White Masks," *Outlook* 136 (January 30, 1924), 184.

11. Loucks, *Klan in Pennsylvania*, 39.

12. Alexander, *Klan in the Southwest*, 42.

13. Hux, "Klan in Macon," 157; "Klansmen Kidnap Bright and Mrs. Pace; Beat Man Senseless," *NYT*, April 5, 1923, 1.

14. Roldan, "Klan in Kern and Los Angeles Counties," 60, 68.

15. Akin, "Klan in Georgia," 663–66, quotation on 666.

16. MacLean, *Behind the Mask*, 121.

17. Frost, "Lure of the White Masks," 184.

18. MacLean, *Behind the Mask*, 122.

19. Akin, "Klan in Georgia," 651.

20. Loucks, *Klan in Pennsylvania*, 44.

21. Ben B. Lindsey, "My Fight with the Ku Klux Klan," *Survey* 54 (June 1, 1925), 274.

22. Roldan, "Klan in Kern and Los Angeles Counties," 63–64.

23. "Klan Threatens Boy with Rope and Knife," *NYT*, May 10, 1923, 1, 8.

24. See MacLean, *Behind the Mask*, 114–16.

25. "Another Is Tarred by Mysterious Band," *NYT*, July 24, 1921, 15; Fry, *Modern Ku Klux Klan*, 186; Alexander, *Klan in the Southwest*, 42 (quotation).

26. William G. Shepherd, "The Whip Hand," *Collier's* 81 (January 7, 1928), 8–9, quotation on 8.

27. Jessup, "Consorting with Blood and Violence," 311.

28. Weaver, "Klan in Wisconsin, Indiana, Ohio and Michigan," 115n42.

29. Horowitz, *Inside the Klavern*, 37–38.

30. Holley, "A Look behind the Masks," 146.

31. Akin, "Klan in Georgia," 647, 651, 660.

32. Goldberg, *Hooded Empire*, 54 ("curtained auto"), 65 ("27 automobiles").

33. Emmons deposition, 235–36; "Indianapolis Law Enforcement Campaign Opens," *Fiery Cross*, April 6, 1923, 7.

34. Chalmers, *Hooded Americanism*, 94.

35. Alexander, *Klan in the Southwest*, 76.

36. Hux, "Klan and Collective Violence in Horry County," 214–15, quotation on 215.

37. Bruce Brown, "The Conflict of the Ages," *Imperial Night-Hawk* 2 (July 16, 1924), 3.

38. Minutes of January 22, 1925, Series I, Records of the Knights of the Ku Klux Klan, Klan No. 51, Mt. Rainier, Maryland.

39. Max Bentley, "The Ku Klux Klan in Texas," *McClure's Magazine* 57 (May 1924), 17; Morris, "Saving Society through Politics," 126.

40. Alexander, *Klan in the Southwest*, 59–61.

41. "Woman Charges Klan Whipped Her and Son," *NYT*, June 15, 1927, 9; Akin, "Klan in Georgia," 688–89; Chalmers, *Hooded Americanism*, 76.

42. Alexander, *Klan in the Southwest*, 66, 80.

43. Loucks, *Klan in Pennsylvania*, 42–43.

44. Stanley Frost, "When the Klan Rules: The Specter's Heavy Hand," *Outlook* 136 (February 13, 1924), 261.

45. Loucks, *Klan in Pennsylvania*, 42.

46. Akin, "Klan in Georgia," 647.

47. Alexander, *Klan in the Southwest*, 59.

48. "Georgia Opens War on Masked Mobs," *NYT*, December 29, 1926, 2 (quotations); Akin, "Klan in Georgia," 686–89, 694.

49. Akin, "Klan in Georgia," 668.

50. Jessup, "Consorting with Blood and Violence," 311.

51. Bentley, "Klan in Texas," 17.

52. Horowitz, *Inside the Klavern*, 90.

53. Akin, "Klan in Georgia," 660–61.

54. Roldan, "Klan in Kern and Los Angeles Counties," 60–63, quotation on 62.

55. O'Brien, "I Want Everyone to Know," 194n19.

56. Morris, "Saving Society through Politics," 128–29.

57. "1,910 Murders Done in 28 Cities in 1921," *NYT*, December 7, 1922, 21; "1,877 Murdered in 28 Cities in 1922, *NYT*, June 14, 1923, 9; "10,000 Murdered in America in 1923," *NYT*, May 8, 1924, 31; "New York's Homicides Jump to 387 in a Year," *NYT*, May 21, 1925, 1; "Memphis Statistics," *NYT*, May 31, 1925, XX12; "Murders in 1925 Made High Record," *NYT*, April 1, 1926, 10; "Drop in Homicide Rate in 1926 Seen Despite Wave of Crime," *NYT*, January 2, 1927, E1; "Murder Death Rate Shows Drop Here," *NYT*, June 2, 1927, 28; "Finds Murder Rate Doubled since 1900," *NYT*, March 14, 1929, 11.

58. Edward L. Ayers, *The Promise of the New South* (New York: Oxford University Press, 1991), 155.

59. Akin, "Klan in Georgia," 681–82.

60. Frost, "Lure of the White Masks," 184.

61. Lehr, "Terror, Reform, and Repression," 183.

62. Thomas Boyd, "Defying the Klan," *Forum* 76 (July 1926), 48–56; Chalmers, *Hooded Americanism*, 74–75.

63. Bentley, "Klan in Texas," 19–20 ("murdering cowards," 20); Greene, "Apostles of Hate," 42–45 ("painted face," 43).

64. "White Caps Strike Terror over South," *NYT*, July 19, 1921, 17; Bentley, "Klan in Texas," 17–18; Fry, *Modern Ku Klux Klan*, 189; Chalmers, *Hooded Americanism*, 41.

65. "Police Chief Charged with Whipping Women," *NYT*, April 26, 1923, 8.

66. "Posse Fights Klan in Lorena, Texas, Streets," *NYT*, October 2, 1921, 1; "Grand Jury to Act on Ku Klux Clash," *NYT*, October 3, 1921, 1; "6 Judges, 2 Cities Warn Klan in Texas," *NYT*, October 5, 1921, 15.

67. Akin, "Klan in Georgia," 675–76.

68. Ibid., 656–57.

69. Holley, "A Look behind the Masks," 143.

70. Loucks, *Klan in Pennsylvania*, 170–73.

71. Lay, *Hooded Knights on the Niagara*, 130–33.

72. Leonard Lanson Cline, "In Darkest Louisiana," *Nation* 116 (March 14, 1923), 292–93; Duffus, "How Klan Sells Hate," 174–75; "Ex-Klansman Links Mer Rouge Murders with Ku Klux Band," *NYT*, January 10, 1923, 1, 5; Alexander, *Klan in the Southwest*, 68–75.

73. Duffus, "How Klan Sells Hate," 174, 177.

74. "Says Klan Checked Mer Rouge Inquiry," *NYT*, October 31, 1923, 19.

75. Cline, "Darkest Louisiana," 292–93.

76. "The Ku Klux Mischief," *NYT*, November 23, 1922, 20.

77. "Says Klan Checked Mer Rouge Inquiry."

78. Horowitz, *Inside the Klavern*, 59; see also "Klan Head Assails Mer Rouge Hearing," *NYT*, January 27, 1923, 15.

79. "Klan Leader Claims Bastrop Probe Frameup," *Fiery Cross*, March 30, 1923, 3; "The Parker-Coco Judicial Burlesque," *Fiery Cross*, February 2, 1923, 1; "The Mer Rouge Case," *Fiery Cross*, February 2, 1923, 7 ("liquor anarchists"); "Now Isn't This Nice of Mr. Coco?" *Fiery Cross*, March 2, 1923, 6 ("Knights of Columbus"); "Klan Denied Privilege of Producing 'Murdered' Man in the Living Flesh," *Fiery Cross*, March 23, 1923, 1, 3 ("spotless").

80. "Law for Others—Not for the Ku Klux Klan!" *Outlook* 134 (June 6, 1923), 109.

81. H. J. Haskell, "Martial Law in Oklahoma," *Outlook* 135 (September 26, 1923), 133; Aldrich Blake, "Oklahoma's Klan-Fighting Governor," *Nation* 117 (October 3, 1923), 353; Stanley Frost, "Behind the White Hoods: The Regeneration of Oklahoma," *Outlook* 135 (November 21, 1923), 492–95; Alexander, *Klan in the Southwest*, 135–54. For a thorough analysis of the Walton administration, see Lehr, "Terror, Reform, and Repression," 229–80.

82. "The Remedy for Lawlessness Is Law," *Outlook* 135 (October 3, 1923), 172; "The People Still Rule," *Outlook* 135 (October 17, 1923), 253.

83. Lehr, "Terror, Reform, and Repression," 259.

84. Alexander, *Klan in the Southwest*, 153.

85. "Bares Terrorism of Tulsa Floggers," *NYT*, September 7, 1923, 17; Alexander, *Klan in the Southwest*, 151.

86. Alexander, *Klan in the Southwest*, 67.

87. "Constable Sent to Jail," *NYT*, August 28, 1923, 4.

88. "The Klan's Attitude toward Whipping," *Imperial Night-Hawk* 1 (September 12, 1923), 4

89. Morris, "Saving Society through Politics," 94–96.

90. Alexander, *Klan in the Southwest*, 81; Chalmers, *Hooded Americanism*, 45.

91. Alexander, *Klan in the Southwes*, 157 (quotation); Lehr, "Terror, Reform, and Repression," 290–92, 295.

92. Jessup, "Consorting with Blood and Violence," 297.

93. Morris, "Saving Society through Politics," 132.

94. "Klansman Is Slain, Many Are Injured, in Riot at Carnegie," *NYT*, August 26, 1923, 1, 13; "Klan Members Mass on Carnegie Hill," *NYT*, August 27, 1923, 1–2; Loucks, *Klan in Pennsylvania*, 50–54.

95. "Klan Members Mass," 2.

96. Loucks, *Klan in Pennsylvania*, 54.

97. "Killing and Terror Laid to Klan Chiefs in Pittsburgh Trial," *NYT*, April 10, 1928, 16.

98. "Abbott Trust Fund Growing Steadily; Now Amounts to $12,487.35," *Imperial Night-Hawk* 1 (November 23, 1923), 5; "Klankraft Spreads over Pennsylvania," *Fiery Cross*, September 21, 1923, 5.

99. Loucks, *Klan in Pennsylvania*, 56.

100. "25 Klansmen Face Trial for Murder for Lilly Killings," *NYT*, April 7, 1924, 1, 4; "Klansmen Freed of Slaying at Lilly," *NYT*, June 15, 1924, 17; Loucks, *Klan in Pennsylvania*, 55–57.

101. "Klan Dragon Pleads Self-Defense," *NYT*, April 7, 1924, 4.

102. Loucks, *Klan in Pennsylvania*, 57–58; "Burnings at Stake at Behest of Evans Told at Klan Trial," *NYT*, April 11, 1928, 14 (quotation).

103. "Klansmen Rush to Ohio Riot Scene," *NYT*, August 17, 1923, 1; "Klansmen Are Struck Down in Mob Riots," *Fiery Cross*, August 24, 1923, 1, 8.

104. "Steubenville Klan Asks State Guard," *NYT*, August 19, 1923, 2; "Klansmen Rush to Ohio," 2 ("dump hole").

105. "Klansmen Are Shot; No Arrests Made," *Imperial Night-Hawk* 1 (September 19, 1923), 5 ("hurrah for Irish"); "Five Shot in Riot at Klan Initiation," *NYT*, September 1, 1923), 5.

106. "Investigation of Anti-Klan Riots Now Under Way," *Fiery Cross*, September 14, 1923, 7.

107. "Klansmen Protest 'Invasion of Mobs,'" *NYT*, June 17, 1923, 3; "Alien Riots in Perth Amboy near Rebellion as Foreign Born Reign," *Fiery Cross*, September 7, 1923, 1, 8.

108. Brown, "Conflict of the Ages," 3.

109. "Offers to Defend Klan," *NYT*, September 10, 1923, 19.

110. "The Klan as the Victim of Mob Violence," *Literary Digest* 78 (September 8, 1923), 12–13, quotation on 12.

111. "31 Are Found Guilty in Lilly Klan Fight," *NYT*, June 13, 1924, 21.

112. "Klan Issue Rises and Is Bothering Both Big Parties," *NYT*, May 14, 1924, 1.

113. "Taking Its Own Prescription," *NYT*, August 18, 1923, 8.

114. "Klan Issue Rises."

115. "Ohio City in Terror, Fearing Klan Clash," *NYT*, November 1, 1924, 17; "Klan and Foes Riot, Wound 12 in Niles, O.; Troops Hold Town," *NYT*, November 2, 1924, 1; "The Riot at Niles," *Outlook* 138 (November 12, 1924), 396; Jenkins, *Steel Valley Klan*, 117–51.

116. Weaver, "Klan in Wisconsin, Indiana, Ohio and Michigan," 263–64.

117. Jenkins, *Steel Valley Klan*, 137.

118. Emmons deposition, 218–19 (quotation), 220–22.

119. "Indiana Protestants Outraged by Infuriated College Students," *Imperial Night-Hawk* 2 (June 4, 1924), 2.

120. Emmons deposition, 203–18, 418–19.

121. "Massachusetts House Condemns Klan," *NYT*, January 17, 1923, 8.

122. "Upholds Klan Meeting," *NYT*, October 22, 1923, 25.

123. "More Arrests Made in Klan Rioting," *NYT*, August 2, 1924, 10; "Mob of 800 in Worcester Beats Klansmen and Wrecks Cars after Order's Big Meeting," *NYT*, October 19, 1924, 1.

124. "Held for Klan Riots," *NYT*, June 21, 1925, 15; "1,000 in Bay State Engage in Klan Row," *NYT*, August 13, 1925, 21; "Hundreds in Klan Riot," *NYT*, September 19, 1925, 9.

125. "1,000 in Bay State Engage in Klan Row"; see also "16 Klansmen Held for Bay State Riot," *NYT*, August 12, 1925, 23.

126. *NYT*, August 13, 1925, 21 (quotation); "There She Is, But Where Is She At?" *NYT*, August 14, 1925, 12.

127. Gerlach, *Blazing Crosses in Zion*, 153.

128. "Alabama's Floggers," *Literary Digest* 95 (October 29, 1927), 11–12; Feldman, *Klan in Alabama*, 92–115.

129. William G. Shepherd, "The Whip Wins," *Collier's* 81 (January 14, 1928), 32.

130. Akin, "Klan in Georgia," 689.

131. Chalmers, *Hooded Americanism*, 228.

132. "Burnings at Stake at Behest of Evans Told at Klan Trial," *NYT*, April 11, 1928, 1, 14.

133. "Marked for Death, Says Klan Founder," *NYT*, April 5, 1928, 29.

134. Testimony quoted in Lutholtz, *Grand Dragon*, 77.

135. "Burnings at Stake at Behest of Evans," 1, 14.

136. "Killing and Terror Laid to Klan Chiefs in Pittsburgh Trial," *NYT*, April 10, 1928, 16.

137. "Burnings at Stake at Behest of Evans," 14.

138. "A Judicial Spanking for the Klan," *Literary Digest* 97 (April 28, 1928), 9.

139. "Judge Throws Klan Out of His Court," *NYT*, April 14, 1928, 8.

140. Emmons deposition, 38.

Chapter 7: The Search for Political Influence and the Collapse of the Klan Movement

1. "Sight Astonishes Capital," *NYT*, August 9, 1925, 1.

2. Maples, "Akron, Ohio Klan" 97, 101–9.

3. "Sight Astonishes Capital."

4. U.S. Senate, Sixty-Ninth Congress, *Senatorial Campaign Expenditures: Hearings before a Special Committee Investigating Expenditures in Senatorial Primary and General Elections* (Washington, D.C.: U.S. Government Printing Office, 1926), 2028–29 ("down the line," 2028), 2045 ("crammed").

5. Emmons deposition, 354–56.

6. Stanley Frost, "When the Klan Rules: The Plan to Capture Washington," *Outlook* 136 (February 27, 1924), 350 ("not in politics"); "Dr. Evans, Imperial Wizard, Defines Klan Principles and Outlines Klan Activities," *Imperial Night-Hawk* 1 (January 23, 1924), 2.

7. Frost, "Plan to Capture Washington," 350.

8. Stanley Frost, "The Giant Begins to Rule Us," *Outlook* 136 (February 20, 1924), 309.

9. Lutholtz, *Grand Dragon*, 8–15; *Senatorial Campaign Expenditures*, 2135.

10. Weaver, "Klan in Wisconsin, Indiana, Ohio and Michigan," 200–204; Emmons deposition, 96–98.

11. Walter F. Bossert to All Great Titans, Exalted Cyclops and Unit Officials, October 17, 1924, Plaintiff Exhibit 7, Emmons deposition.

12. Walter F. Bossert to All Grand Officers, Great Titans and Exalted Cyclops, October 18, 1924, Plaintiff Exhibit 8, Emmons deposition.

13. Weaver, "Klan in Wisconsin, Indiana, Ohio and Michigan," 211.

14. Howson, "Klan in Ohio," 66.

15. Alexander, *Klan in the Southwest*, 114.

16. U.S. Senate, Sixty-Seventh Congress, *Senator from Texas: Hearings before a Subcommittee of the Committee on Privileges and Elections* (Washington, D.C.: U.S. Government Printing Office, 1925), 54–55; Alexander, *Klan in the Southwest*, 122–23.

17. Bossert to All Great Titans, Exalted Cyclops and Unit Officials, October 17, 1924.

18. Bossert to All Grand Officers, Great Titans and Exalted Cyclops, October 18, 1924.

19. Weaver, "Klan in Wisconsin, Indiana, Ohio and Michigan," 212–14 ("township school teachers," "Protestant School Ticket," facing 219).

20. Loucks, *Klan in Pennsylvania*, 102.

21. Goldberg, *Hooded Empire*, 76.

22. Ibid., 68–69, quotation on 69.

23. Morris, "Saving Society through Politics," 149–51.

24. Minutes of September 13, 1923, Klan No. 51, Mt. Rainier, Maryland; Alexander, *Klan in the Southwest*, 114.

25. Horowitz, *Inside the Klavern*, 109–10, quotation on 109.

26. Weaver, "Klan in Wisconsin, Indiana, Ohio and Michigan," 118.

27. Cocoltchos, "Invisible Empire and Search for the Orderly Community," 116.

28. Emmons deposition ("one hundred," 191–92; "newspapers," 110–23; "Protestant ministers," 194–96, quotation on 196; "Sunday school," 99; "porch," 171–72; "fifty thousand," 156; "cars," 187–88; "female hooded volunteers," 168–69; "elected," 191).

29. Duffus, "Klan in the Middle West," 363.

30. Weaver, "Klan in Wisconsin, Indiana, Ohio and Michigan," 202, 217.

31. Akin, "Klan in Georgia," 546–47, quotation on 546.

32. Weaver, "Klan in Wisconsin, Indiana, Ohio and Michigan," 277–78.

33. Alexander, *Klan in the Southwest*, 186–90, quotation on 190.

34. Weaver, "Klan in Wisconsin, Indiana, Ohio and Michigan," 217.

35. Ibid., 203n18.

36. Emmons deposition, 172–78, 24–28.

37. W. Lee Smith to Pat Emmons, August 6, 1926, Plaintiff Exhibit 4, Emmons deposition.

38. Emmons deposition, 60–61 ("man power" on 61), 326 ("overalls").

39. *Senatorial Campaign Expenditures*, 2026, quotation on 2029.

40. Maples, "Akron, Ohio Klan," 37–38, quotation on 38; Weaver, "Klan in Wisconsin, Indiana, Ohio and Michigan," 235–37; Alexander, *Klan in the Southwest*, 113.

41. Howson, "Klan in Ohio," 69–70.

42. Ibid., 67.

43. Maples, "Akron, Ohio Klan," 100.

44. Emmons deposition, 148.

45. Loucks, *Klan in Pennsylvania*, 102.

46. Frost, "Giant Begins to Rule Us," 309.

47. Evans, "Where Do We Go from Here?," 8.

48. Frost, "Giant Begins to Rule Us," 311.

49. Ibid., 310.

50. Goldberg, *Hooded Empire*, 75.

51. Frost, "Giant Begins to Rule Us," 309.

52. Weaver, "Klan in Wisconsin, Indiana, Ohio and Michigan," 131; Howson, "Klan in Ohio," 52.

53. Frost, "Giant Begins to Rule Us," 308.

54. *Senatorial Campaign Expenditures*, 2041.

55. "Klan as a Civic Asset," 67.

56. Shawn Lay, "Imperial Outpost on the Border: El Paso's Frontier Klan No. 100," in Lay, *Invisible Empire in the West*, 84.

57. "Klan as a Civic Asset," 67.

58. Goldberg, *Hooded Empire*, 120–21.

59. Frost, "Giant Begins to Rule Us," 308.

60. Ibid., 308.

61. H. W. Evans, "The Klan of Tomorrow," *Imperial Night-Hawk* 2 (October 15, 1924), 7.

62. Frost, "Plan to Capture Washington," 350.

63. See, for instance, Goldberg, *Hooded Empire*, 70, and Weaver, "Klan in Wisconsin, Indiana, Ohio and Michigan," 121.

64. Morris, "Saving Society through Politics," 155–56; "Shadow of Ku Klux Klan Grows Larger in Congress and Nation," *NYT*, December 10, 1922, 116.

65. "Klan Dominating 3 Southwest States," *NYT*, November 1, 1923, 1, 3.

66. "Klan Shadow Falls on Nation's Politics," *NYT*, November 18, 1923, XX3.

67. Moseley, "Klan in Georgia," 36–38; Chalmers, *Hooded Americanism*, 71–72.

68. Roberts, "Ku-Kluxing of Oregon," 490; State of Oregon, Executive Department, Proclamation, May 13, 1922, Mss 308, Ben W. Olcott, Papers Concerning the Ku Klux Klan, Oregon Historical Society Research Library ("unlawfully disguised men").

69. Saalfeld, *Forces of Prejudice in Oregon*, 37–38.

70. "Shadow of Ku Klux Klan Grows Larger in Congress and Nation," 116.

71. Alexander, *Klan in the Southwest*, 125–27; "Says Klan Spent $25,000 in Texas," *NYT*, May 21, 1924, 2.

72. "Shadow of Ku Klux Klan Grows Larger in Congress and Nation," 116.

73. Cates, "Klan in Indiana Politics," 71–72.

74. "Shadow of Ku Klux Klan Grows Larger in Congress and Nation," 116.

75. Chalmers, *Hooded Americanism*, 89; Roberts, "Ku-Kluxing of Oregon," 491; Saalfeld, *Forces of Prejudice in Oregon*, 38–39.

76. Cates, "Klan in Indiana Politics," 77.

77. Saalfeld, *Forces of Prejudice in Oregon*, 38–39.

78. Cates, "Klan in Indiana Politics," 128–29.

79. Ibid., 80–81.

80. *Senatorial Campaign Expenditures*, 2293; for Duvall's denial of a pact with Stephenson, see 2296–97.

81. Cates, "Klan in Indiana Politics," 106.

82. Cates, "Klan in Indiana Politics," 161; Moore, *Citizen Klansmen*, 179–81.

83. Cates, "Klan in Indiana Politics," 166–68; Lutholtz, *Grand Dragon*, 170–74.

84. Goldberg, *Hooded Empire*, 15–16, quotation on 15.

85. Goldberg, *Hooded Empire*, 29–33, quotation on 32; Robert T. Laugen, "The Promise and Defeat of the Progressive Public: Reform Politics in Colorado, 1902–1929" (PhD dissertation, University of Colorado, 2005), 316–17.

86. Laugen, "Progressive Public," 318.

87. Ibid., 319

88. Ibid., 317, 320.

89. Goldberg, *Hooded Empire*, 76–77; Laugen, "Progressive Public," 319–20.

90. Goldberg, *Hooded Empire*, 77.

91. Goldberg, *Hooded Empire*, 85–86, 88; Laugen, "Progressive Public," 328–29.

92. Laugen, "Progressive Public," 337–38, quotation on 338.

93. Goldberg, *Hooded Empire*, 87–91.

94. Ibid., 92, 94.

95. Ibid., 98–99, 104–8.

96. Lutholtz, *Grand Dragon*, 96–102, 183–301.

97. Moseley, "Klan in Georgia," 95; Lutholtz, *Grand Dragon*, 148–49, 204–5, 315–24.

98. Duffus, "Political Volcano," XX1, XX11.

99. *Senatorial Campaign Expenditures*, 2082–85, 2090; Chalmers, *Hooded Americanism*, 173.

100. Alexander, *Klan in the Southwest*, 192–99.

101. "Klan's Hold Slipping in the Southwest," *NYT*, August 17, 1924, XX4.

102. Alexander, *Klan in the Southwest*, 196–99.

103. "Klan's Hold Slipping in Southwest," XX4.

104. "Klan's Hold Slipping in Southwest," XX4; Alexander, *Klan in the Southwest*, 200–205.

105. Alexander, *Klan in the Southwest*, 206.

106. Chalmers, *Hooded Americanism*, 89–91; Horowitz, *Inside the Klavern*, 144–45; Saalfeld, *Forces of Prejudice in Oregon*, 56–60.

107. Horowitz, *Inside the Klavern*, 55.

108. Toy, "Robe and Gown," 175–76.

109. Feldman, *Klan in Alabama*, 70–71, 81–86, 121.

110. Chalmers, *Hooded Americanism*, 276–78; "The Klan at Bay," *Current Opinion* 77 (October 1, 1924), 420.

111. "The 'Invisible Empire' in the Spotlight," *Current Opinion* 71 (November 1921), 562; "House Wets Attack Fund for Dry Army," *NYT*, June 27, 1926, 20.

112. Slawson, *Department of Education Battle*, 120–22. For Klan dissatisfaction with the NEA's handling of education reform bills, see *Imperial Night-Hawk* 1 (June 6, 1923), 7.

113. Slawson, *Department of Education Battle*, 168.

114. Evans, "Where Do We Go from Here?," 12.

115. "Poorly Restricted Immigration Is One of the Greatest Perils Confronting America," *Imperial Night-Hawk* 1 (August 29, 1923), 2.

116. "Dr. Evans, Imperial Wizard, Defines Klan Principles and Outlines Klan Activities," *Imperial Night-Hawk* 1 (January 23, 1924), 2.

117. "Every Influence Needed on Side of Restrictive Immigration Bill," *Imperial Night-Hawk* 1 (March 15, 1924), 8.

118. "Immigration Bill Taken Up in House," *NYT*, April 6, 1924, 10.

119. Higham, *Strangers in the Land*, 321.

120. Dumenil, *Modern Temper*, 206–7; "Applaud Alien Bill in D.A.R. Convention," *NYT*, April 19, 1924, 2; "Senate Reaffirms Ban on the Japanese by Formal Vote, 71–4," *NYT*, April 17, 1924, 5 (Underwood).

121. "Immigration Bill Starts Fist Fight," *NYT*, April 9, 1924), 25; see also "Speakers Attack Alien Quota Bill," *NYT*, March 3, 1924, 12.

122. "Klan Joins Fight on World Court," *NYT*, November 7, 1925, 1.

123. Ibid., 2.

124. "Senate Votes to Join World Court, 76 to 17," *NYT*, January 28, 1926, 1.

125. "All Reservations of Court's Friends Win in the Senate," *NYT*, January 27, 1926, 1.

126. "Reverses of Klan Surprise Capital," *NYT*, September 16, 1926, 3.

127. Chalmers, *Hooded Americanism*, 285.

128. "Pink Ballots for the Ku Klux Klan," *Outlook* 137 (June 25, 1924), 308–9.

129. On Watson and the Klan, see "Klan Issue Rises and Is Bothering Both Big Parties," *NYT*, May 14, 1924, 1.

130. "Vice Presidency in Doubt," *NYT*, June 10, 1924, 1.

131. Chalmers, *Hooded Americanism*, 202.

132. "Klan Out for Watson; Senator Disavows It," *NYT*, June 10, 1924, 3.

133. "Menace of Ku Klux Worries the South," *NYT*, June 27, 1924, 5.

134. Stanley Frost, "The Klan's ½ of 1 Per Cent Victory," *Outlook* 137 (July 9, 1924), 385.

135. "Text of Platform as Presented to the Democratic National Convention," *NYT*, June 29, 1924, 4.

136. "Text of the Klan Debate," *NYT*, June 29, 1924, 1.

137. "Text of Klan Debate," 6, 7.

138. Richard V. Oulahan, "Tense Feeling on Ku Klux," *NYT*, June 29, 1924, 7; "Georgia Beats Klan Plank," *NYT*, June 29, 1924, 5.

139. "Predict Klan Row Will Injure Party," *NYT*, June 29, 1924, 6.

140. Ibid., 7.

141. "Text of Klan Debate," 6.

142. "Davis Denounces Ku Klux Klan by Name," *NYT*, August 23, 1924, 1.

143. Chalmers, *Hooded Americanism*, 214.

144. "General 'Opposed to' Klan," *NYT*, August 24, 1924, 2.

145. *Senatorial Campaign Expenditures*, 2046; Chalmers, *Hooded Americanism*, 284.

146. Frost, "½ of 1 Per Cent," 387.

147. "Invisible Empire Is Fading," *NYT*, February 21, 1926, XX1; Rice, *Klan in American Politics*, 63–64.

148. "Klan Doffs Mask and Changes Name," *NYT*, February 23, 1928, 1.

Chapter 8: Echoes

1. Alexander, *Klan in the Southwest*, 252.

2. Stanley Frost, "The Masked Politics of the Klan and How the Candidacy of Smith May Be Affected," *World's Work* 55 (February 1928), 405.

3. Allan J. Lichtman, *Prejudice and the Old Politics: The Presidential Election of 1928* (Chapel Hill: University of North Carolina Press, 1979), 40–76.

4. Hiram Wesley Evans, "The Ballots behind the Ku Klux Klan," *World's Work* 55 (January 1928), 248.

5. Alexander, *Klan in the Southwest*, 238–49.

6. William G. Shepherd, "The Whip Wins," *Collier's* 81 (January 14, 1928), 30, 320–23.

7. Chalmers, *Hooded Americanism*, 308–10.

8. Akin, "Klan in Georgia," 694.

9. Goldberg, *Hooded Empire*, 210–11n47 (Morley), 112 (Locke).

10. "P. Emmons Relates His Experiences as Canadian Organizer," *Rochester* (Indiana) *News Sentinel*, February 15, 1928, reproduced in Wendell C. and John B. Tombaugh, *Fulton County Indiana Handbook, D-E* (Rochester, Ind.: Tombaugh House, 2001), 163–64.

11. Chalmers, *Hooded Americanism*, 317.

Afterword: Historians and the Klan

1. For important reviews of Klan historiography, see Leonard J. Moore, "Historical Interpretations of the 1920s Klan: The Traditional View and Recent Revisions," in Shawn Lay, *Invisible Empire in the West*, 17–38, and Lay, *Hooded Knights on the Niagara*, 177–91.

2. Duffus, "Klan in the Middle West," *World's Work* 46 (August 1923), 367–68; Shepherd, "Ku Klux Koin," 9.

3. Jacobs, "Catholic Response to the Klan," 79–81.

4. Mecklin, *Ku Klux Klan*, 103–5, 109 ("mediocre men").

5. Evans, "Fight for Americanism," *North American Review* 223 (March 1926), 49.

6. Arthur Corning White, "An American Fascismo," *Forum* 72 (November 1924), 636–42; "Our Own Secret Fascisti," *Nation* 115 (November 15, 1922), 514; Bohn, "Klan Interpreted," 397; Robert Moats Miller, "The Ku Klux Klan," in John Braeman, Robert H. Bremner, and David Brody, eds., *Change and Continuity in Twentieth-Century America: The 1920s* (Columbus: Ohio State University Press, 1968), 228, 238; MacLean, *Behind the Mask*, 179–84.

7. Richard Hofstadter, *The Age of Reform: From Bryan to FDR* (New York: Vintage, 1955), 293.

8. Jackson, *Klan in the City*, 235–45.

9. Miller, "Ku Klux Klan," 227.

10. Alexander, *Klan in the Southwest*, 21–81.

11. Weaver, "Klan in Wisconsin, Indiana, Ohio and Michigan," 42, 298–99.

12. See, for example, the La Grande, Oregon, Klan minutes in Horowitz, *Inside the Klavern*, and the Monticello, Arkansas, records used in Holley, "A Look behind the Masks," 131–50.

13. Fryer and Levitt, "Hatred and Profits," 17–19 (there were fewer professionals among Pennsylvania Klansmen).

14. Peter Novick, *That Noble Dream: The "Objectivity Question" and the American Historical Profession* (New York: Cambridge University Press, 1988), 442.

15. Cocoltchos, "Invisible Government and the Viable Community"; Lay, *War, Revolution, and the Klan*; Lay, *Hooded Knights on the Niagara*; Horowitz, *Inside the Klavern*; Jenkins, *Steel Valley Klan*; Goldberg, *Hooded Empire*.

16. Moore, *Citizen Klansmen*, 188, 7, 52.

17. Moore, "Historical Interpretations of the 1920s Klan," 34.

18. Goldberg, *Hooded Empire*, 127.

19. Gerlach, *Blazing Crosses in Zion*, 37–38.

20. Evans, "Fight for Americanism," 33–43. A recent influential study of 1890s populism, which, like the Klan community studies, emphasizes the modern character of the movement, also presents the agrarian radicals as active in "spreading the principle of racial distance" that reinforced the place of Anglo-Saxons at the apex of early twentieth-century American society; therefore the populists, in this view, took "part in shaping the racial order" that Klansmen defended (Charles Postel, *The Populist Vision* [New York: Oxford University Press, 2007], 176).

21. Feldman, *Klan in Alabama*, 89.

22. Ibid., 72.

23. MacLean, *Behind the Mask*, 158.

24. Shawn Lay, "Hooded Populism," *Reviews in American History* 22 (December 1994), 672–73; Leonard J. Moore, review of *Behind the Mask of Chivalry*, *Journal of American History* 82 (June 1995), 321.

25. Rory McVeigh, *The Rise of the Ku Klux Klan* (Minneapolis: University of Minnesota Press, 2009).

Index

Abbott, Thomas, 177

African Americans, 52, 57, 58, 69, 102, 170; and American color line, 22, 50, 59, 60–61, 63, 224; anti-Klan actions, 81, 87, 178; comments on Klan, 11, 49, 67; economic pressure against, 62–63; outside Klan's definition of American identity, 48, 59; and pluralism, 87, 124; and prohibition, 124, 125; Protestantism, 48, 70; strikebreakers, 34; and vice, 66–67; violence against, 12, 59–61, 62, 65–67, 160

Akin, Edward, 38, 101, 170

Alexander, Charles C., x, 58, 168, 224

Allen, Henry J., 87

Allied Protestant Americans, 219

American Civil Liberties Union, 178, 180

American Federation of Labor, 117, 211

American Legion, 10, 30, 39, 96, 106; Houston controversy over Klan donations, 40

American Protective Association (APA), 72, 89, 113, 154

American Protective League, 7

American Unity League, 81, 87, 136, 258n152

Anderson, William H., 74, 140, 155; anti-Catholicism of, 153–55; and Klan, 154

anti-Catholicism, xi, xii, 224; in American Protestant culture, 8, 9, 12, 49, 72–76, 78, 87; ex-nuns, 74; and Knights of Columbus, 76–77; and prohibition, 124, 125, 147, 149, 153–55. See also education

Anti-Saloon League (ASL), 21, 74, 123, 128, 139, 189, 202, 210; and Catholics, 140, 147–48; and Klan, 140–55; in Williamson county war, 137–39

APA. See American Protective Association

Arkansas: politics in, 189, 193, 199; strike, 35; vice in, 130–31, 165. See also Monticello, Arkansas, Klan

Association Against the Prohibition Amendment, 141

baseball, 31–32

Baylor University, 172

A Note on the Author

Thomas R. Pegram is professor of history at Loyola University Maryland. Born in Hammond, Indiana, he grew up in the Midwest and California, then studied at Santa Clara University and Brandeis University, where he received a PhD in American history. He has also taught at the Ohio State University. He is also the author of *Battling Demon Rum: The Struggle for a Dry America, 1800–1933* and *Partisans and Progressives: Private Interest and Public Policy in Illinois, 1870–1922*. He lives with his family in Baltimore County, Maryland.